Understanding and Social Inquiry

EDITED BY

Fred R. Dallmayr

and

Thomas A. McCarthy

UNIVERSITY OF NOTRE DAME PRESS

NOTRE DAME   LONDON

Copyright © 1977 by
University of Notre Dame Press
Notre Dame, Indiana 46556

Library of Congress Cataloging in Publication Data
Main entry under title:

Understanding and social inquiry.

Includes bibliographies and index.
CONTENTS: Introduction: The crisis of understanding.—Max Weber on
Verstehen: Weber, M. Objectivity in social science and social policy. Weber,
M. Basic sociological terms. Parsons, T. Value-freedom and objectivity.
Habermas, J. Discussion.—The positivist reception: Abel, T. The operation
called *Verstehen*. Rudner, R. On the objectivity of social science. Taylor, C.
Interpretation and the sciences of man. [etc.]
1. Sociology—Methodology—Addresses, essays, lectures. 2. Know-
ledge, Sociology of—Addresses, essays, lectures. I. Dallmayr, Fred R.,
1928– II. McCarthy, Thomas A.
HM24.U53   301′.01′8   76–22404
ISBN 0–268–01912–6
ISBN 0–268–01913–4 pbk.

Manufactured in the United States of America

Preface

THE PRESENT VOLUME IS A PRODUCT OF THE COLLABORATION BETWEEN A philosopher and a social scientist, more specifically, a political scientist. The initial impulse for the endeavor stemmed from practical and pedagogical considerations. In teaching courses on the philosophy and methodology of the social sciences, we were handicapped by the lack of a suitable compendium of materials dealing with the problematic of *Verstehen*, or interpretive understanding. The relatively few available texts and collections did not reflect the full range and diversity of the intellectual currents pertinent to the theme.

The selection of materials was guided by this pedagogical concern. Rather than propounding a particular doctrine, we have tried to acquaint the reader with the complexity of the issues involved in the interpretive dimension of social inquiry. The materials were arranged with a view to stimulating discussion through the presentation of contrasting positions. This dialectical intention is evident in the volume as a whole—in that the Weberian tradition is contrasted with logical empiricism, which is in turn contrasted with the theory of "language games," phenomenology and hermeneutics—as well as in the individual sections, where the respective position is not only presented and defended but exposed to critical queries and counterarguments.

Fred Dallmayr wishes to express his gratitude to Donald R. Wagner for his diligent and thoughtful assistance in collecting relevant bibliography and also in tracing the broad perimeters of the theme. Thomas McCarthy wishes to thank the Alexander von Humboldt Foundation for a fellowship, which enabled him to complete his share of the work on this volume. Both editors appreciate the permissions granted by the publishers to reprint materials for which they hold the copyrights. The original source is indicated at the beginning of each selection.

F.R.D.
T.A.McC.

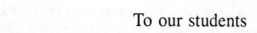

To our students

Contents

PART THREE

The Wittgensteinian Reformulation

PART FOUR

Phenomenology and Ethnomethodology

PART FIVE

Hermeneutics and Critical Theory

Introduction:
The Crisis of Understanding

CUSTOMARILY THE TERM "UNDERSTANDING" IS USED TO DENOTE A TYPE OF inquiry germane to the humanities and some of the social sciences, in contradistinction to the method of empirical "explanation" indigenous to the natural sciences. Yet, despite the importance of methodological considerations, the significance of "understanding" does not properly come into view in a simple confrontation of the "two cultures" conceived as academic disciplines or research strategies. The contours of the issue emerge only against the background of far-reaching, secular developments in our age: the so-called knowledge explosion or the triumph of scientific and technological rationality. Contemporary science and technology afford the human mind access to the remotest and most recondite reaches of the natural universe—to the inner workings of molecules and the physical and chemical conditions of "outer space." While man's empirical knowledge in our century has expanded at an exponential rate, however, his sense of purpose or direction seems to have atrophied; although more knowledgeable about the world than any of his forebears, man today is more ignorant or at a loss as to what he and his accumulated knowledge are *all about*. Confronted with a rationally functioning but ultimately silent universe, he asks the question: what is the point? Viewed in this context contemporary methodological issues reveal their salience and underlying agony: the concern with "understanding" as a type of inquiry results from a crisis of human understanding.

That methodological reorientation should derive from broad intellectual predicaments is not an entirely novel occurrence. Throughout history, whenever existing conceptions of the world became dubious or lost their plausibility, new avenues of inquiry were typically cleared to facilitate man's continued quest for knowledge and self-knowledge. At its inception, modern natural science itself was the result of a crisis of understanding—more specifically, of a growing rupture between man and nature (or a certain metaphysical-theological conception of nature). When man was no longer able to view himself as an integral part of creation and when the divine "book of nature," the "*biblia naturae*," was no longer intelligible to him as a direct key to the workings of the

1

universe, he began to investigate nature as a set of empirical processes in accordance with strict logical-mathematical canons (*more geometrico*) and later in accordance with the method of experimental replication.[1] The collapse of the medieval cosmos, however, laid the foundation not only for a new treatment of nature, but also for new efforts of human self-understanding. When God was no longer immediately perceived in his creation, it became imperative both for theologians and believers in general to place increasing emphasis on God's special revelation, his "word" as contained in the Bible—a revelation that was accessible to man alone among all creatures due to his capacity for language. This trend led to comprehensive endeavors at biblical exegesis or scriptural "hermeneutics," during the Reformation and post-Reformation period. Simultaneously with this attentiveness to Scripture, man began to discover (or rediscover) himself in his own works. This initiative took the form of a revival of antiquity and of a renewed reading of classical texts, which had previously either been ignored or been known only in theological disguise. Thus, the Renaissance inaugurated the development of philological and cultural interpretation.[2]

At the beginning, the two seedlings of early modernity—science and interpretive understanding—were able to coexist more or less peaceably and without mutual recriminations; but harmony soon gave way to antagonism. During the Enlightenment, logical calculation and empirical analysis began to gain ascendancy over and challenge the intrinsic value of cultural traditions; the attack was continued on a more pragmatic level by utilitarianism with its emphasis on measurable personal gain. An initial response to this challenge can be found in the writings of Giambattista Vico, whose thesis *verum et factum convertuntur* suggested that history and culture were more readily intelligible than nature since man was (at least in a loose sense) their author and thus could recapture himself in records of the past. Vico's lead was continued, in a speculative vein, by the idealist and romanticist movements with their stress on internal or spiritual experience; romanticism in particular presented the entire world of culture (if not of nature) as an emanation of human sensitivity and ingenuity, especially of the creative endeavors of leading individuals. Restricted from the outset to small philosophical or literary circles, however, these movements vanished with the rise of the industrial era committed to efficient production. By that time, utilitarianism had found a major ally in positivism—a doctrine centering on the proposition that only empirical and scientifically useful knowledge deserves the title "knowledge" at all and that all competing types of cognition or inquiry belong to more primitive stages of civilization. Couched at first as a vague formula, positivism began to implement its program in the later part of the nineteenth century, with the result that all disciplines were soon faced with the alternative of either embracing scientific method or facing extinction.

This situation—the claim of empirical science to absolute supremacy—constitutes the immediate background for the intellectual "crisis" of our age and for the intense ferment in the republic of letters accompanying this crisis. The following pages intend to give a condensed synopsis of the major battles and skirmishes resulting from the positivist offensive in our century. One point that should emerge clearly from this account is that successive encounters have affected not only the arsenal of weapons but also the respective self-image of the contestants in the sense that both science and interpretive understanding are today involved in a process of serious self-scrutiny and reevaluation.

The story of the contemporary crisis of understanding opens, in this volume, with one of the leading pioneers, or "founders," of present-day sociology, Max Weber.[3] Weber's lifetime witnessed some of the first impressive advances of positivism on the road to hegemony and also some of the first comprehensive and methodologically scrupulous efforts to block and checkmate this assault. Although highly inventive and innovative in his sociological investigations, Weber's philosophical outlook and also his attitude toward "understanding" were heavily indebted to prominent intellectual currents of his time, especially to Dilthey's historical inquiry and to neo-Kantianism; brief comments on these sources of inspiration may serve to place his approach into relief. Wilhelm Dilthey is known as the architect of the so-called *Geisteswissenschaften*—a philosophical and methodological bulwark designed to stem the tide of positivist science. His arguments were directed primarily against British spokesmen of positivist empiricism, such as John Stuart Mill, but one should note some subterranean ties that link him to his opponents. While an advocate of empiricist methodology for purposes of sociological inquiry, Mill as a political theorist was also a great defender of liberal individualism; whatever his other preferences, Dilthey shared at least Mill's latter premise, although individualism in his view referred not so much to the ownership of possessions as to the capability of designing cultural artifacts. In elaborating his cultural and historical methodology, Dilthey drew heavily on the teachings of Schleiermacher (a distinguished philosopher and theologian of the romanticist period) and also on the writings of the German "Historical School" (a scholarly offshoot of the same era). Both Schleiermacher and nineteenth-century German historians were strongly committed to the notion of "individuality" construed as a microcosm or as the focal point of a given historical and cultural context.[4]

Dilthey's outlook was molded not only by the legacy of individualism but also, at least in his early writings, by what has been called "psychologism." The choice of the term *Geisteswissenschaften* ("mental sciences") was itself an indication that the distinctive feature of the proposed approach was its focus on internal, psychic experience as contrasted to the occurrences of external nature. The basic task of the *Geisteswissenschaften*, which, in Dilthey's view, included history, the humanities, and even part of the social sciences, was to examine manifestations of human creativity and intentionality with the goal of recapturing in past documents and cultural records the original spirit that animated their authors. According to Dilthey, this type of inquiry was bound to produce more reliable and more intelligible results than any other cognitive endeavor, since, in his words, "only what mind has produced, mind can fully understand." The occurrences of the natural or physical world, on the other hand, were relatively opaque and could be rendered accessible only by means of the abstract explanatory constructs of natural science disclosing lawlike uniformities and causal connections: "Nature we explain; psychic life we understand [*verstehen*]."

Obviously, in its reliance on internal experience, Dilthey's approach could serve as barrier to positivist hegemony only as long as "mind" and "psyche" were themselves immune from scientific explanation; one of the chief developments during his life, however, was precisely the transformation of psychology into an empirical discipline. On this score his strategy thus needed to be corrected—and was corrected by, among others, a group of neo-Kantian thinkers led by Heinrich Rickert, who otherwise were wholly in sympathy with his antipositivist stance. In Rickert's writings the remedy resided in a recourse to the Kantian distinction between facts and (transtemporal) norms; this distinction, he argued, was crucial not only for combatting "psychologism" but also for finding an ordering principle in history. Only through their relationship to normative values could historical events acquire cultural significance; Dilthey's approach for this reason was recast by Rickert under the label of "cultural sciences" (*Kulturwissenschaften*).[5]

The bifurcation of natural and cultural sciences became a cornerstone of Weberian sociology, although one should keep in mind that his methodological views underwent subtle modifications over the years. His early essay on " 'Objectivity' in Social Science and Social Policy" (published in 1904) faithfully reflected Rickert's teachings. Sociology was presented by Weber as one of the cultural sciences, and the latter were defined as "those disciplines which analyze the phenomena of life in terms of their cultural significance." The significance of cultural events was said to derive from a "value-orientation" toward these events, since "empirical reality becomes 'culture' to us because and insofar as we relate it to value ideas." The examination of social phenomena in terms of cultural meaning, Weber added, was "entirely different from the analysis of reality in terms of laws and general concepts"—although the focus on causal and logical relationships performed an important "preliminary task."

Similar notions can still be found in Weber's monumental study entitled *Economy and Society* (published posthumously in 1921), but the gap between cultural understanding and causal analysis was narrowed, and sociology was treated more clearly as a general or systematic science. The study defined sociology as "a science which attempts the interpretive understanding of social action" where the term "action" covered "all human behavior when and insofar as the acting individual attaches a subjective meaning to it," while "social" implied that the action "takes account of the behavior of others and is thereby oriented in its course." Meaningful action was segregated in the study from merely externally induced or "reactive behavior" unrelated to an "intended purpose"; but Weber cautioned that the dividing line could not "be sharply drawn empirically." Moreover, despite the elaboration of a variety of sociologically relevant activities, *Economy and Society* placed central emphasis on "instrumental-rational" action—a type in which the end is basically given and the means-ends relationship can be treated as a precise, quasi-causal relationship. Regarding the notion of action, one should add that it referred only to "the behavior of one or more *individual* human beings"—a carry-over of Dilthey's (and Rickert's) individualism. Social aggregates or groupings, in Weber's view, could never constitute genuine units of analysis: "For the subjective interpretation of action in sociological work these collectivities must be treated as *solely* the resultants and modes of organization of the particular acts of individual persons, since these alone can be treated as agents in a course of subjectively understandable action."[6]

Weber's impact on social science and social theory has been profound and complex. By and large, positivist social scientists have tended to be apprehensive about his notion of interpretive understanding, while many critics of positivism have been attracted to his work precisely because of this feature. Actually, however, reactions on both sides of the fence have been more variegated. Despite his endorsement in some nonpositivist circles, resolute defenders of "cultural" inquiry have found his legacy too deeply imbued with systematic and empiricist leanings to provide an adequate rallying point for their cause.

Attitudes in the other camp also have tended to differ. Some champions of a scientific sociology concluded that Weber's work was sufficiently close to their own aspirations to serve as a precedent or springboard for "rigorous" inquiry, given certain corrections or amendments. According to Talcott Parsons, the leading proponent of this view, the major correction needed was the introduction of a general or systematic perspective. While strongly approving the pivotal role assigned to social action, Parsons argued that to permit scientific analysis, human behavior needed to be seen as part of an overarching network or a "social system." Once it was recognized that social systems pursued certain necessary goals—especially the goal of system maintenance and adaptation—individual social actions could be scientifically explained in terms of their instrumental relationship to such goals as their "final cause," that is, in terms of their "functional" or "dysfunctional" contribution to system stability.[7] As students of Weber were quick to point out, Parsonian sociology involved an excessive pruning or streamlining of Weberian teachings; above all, the central category of interpretive understanding was rendered virtually obsolete by the stipulation of a preordained teleology.

On the whole, Parson's reformulation remained an isolated venture in Weberian scholarship; the bulk of his sympathizers were too apprehensive of "cultural" exegesis to follow his lead. The dominant posture adopted by positivists and especially by logical empiricists was to treat Weber indeed as a herald of social research but as one who never caught sight of the promised land. For methodological purposes, Weber's legacy in this view constituted not an alternative but at best a preamble to scientific inquiry. Interpretive understanding in particular—to the extent that it was not completely exorcised—was viewed not as an integral ingredient but as a prefix or embroidery in the anteroom of research, useful for generating "heuristic" insights and for aiding in the formulation of hypotheses. As Otto Neurath, one of the early logical empiricists, once formulated the issue: while helpful for increasing the serendipity or alacrity of the scientist, understanding was as little a part of his actual empirical work as a cup of coffee consumed in the course of his investigations. This "cup-of-coffee" theory of understanding was quickly picked up by other members of the logical-empiricist movement and became a standard weapon in its intellectual arsenal. Typically, the term "understanding" in this context tended to be identified with psychological empathy or with the reenactment or "reproduction" of mental and emotive processes. As one may note, the logical-empiricist reception virtually reversed the order of priorities sketched in Weber's early writings, where causal or scientific explanation was presented as a "preliminary task" or heuristic prelude to sociological inquiry. More importantly, the identification of understanding with psychological empathy ignored the neo-Kantian restatement and entirely bypassed the controversy over "psychologism." As one observer has noted: "The mistake of both the orthodox critics and certain advocates of *Verstehen* is their common acceptance of the idea that the meaningfulness of social action is elucidated by getting inside people's heads by setting into operation a mental process called 'understanding.' "[8]

Battles sometimes continue to be fought when the original motives have vanished or been seriously modified. While the empiricist offensive against Weber's legacy was still in full swing, developments were already afoot that were destined to recast the underlying issues in completely new terms. These developments occurred in two very different settings and involved very divergent lines of argument: the one arose in the ambiance of positivism within the largely Anglo-American confines of the "analytical philosophy of language"; the other emerged on the continent under such labels as "phenomenology" and "existential analysis." Despite their heterogeneity, the two developments moved toward (at least partial) convergence in regard to the role of interpretive understanding; using a shorthand formula one might say that both initiatives threw a new light not only on the much belabored issue of "psychologism" but also on the much more weighty and age-old heritage of methodological "individualism" (still prominent in Weber's case). For the sake of continuity of presentation, discussion here will focus first on the rise of linguistic analysis within the positivist camp, broadly defined, and subsequently turn to intellectual trends on the continent.

In the positivist and empiricist context, the turn toward language and language analysis signified first of all a realization that empirical reality could not be directly grasped without an adequate conceptual and linguistic framework; in the long run, however, the same turn carried with it another implication important for social inquiry: the insight that human action is social from the beginning, since the meaning of an action cannot be articulated even by the individual actor without recourse to language, that is, a shared pool of significations. Initially, it is true, language analysts—like their positivist companions—shunned all reference to purposive meaning, whether individual or social, and to the enterprise of interpretive understanding. In his *Tractatus Logico-Philosophicus*, Ludwig Wittgenstein—the pioneering leader of the group—tried to design a transparent (or "ideal") linguistic framework modeled on formal logic, a framework that would grant unobstructed access to reality, completely eluding the obscure domain of opinions, purposes, and intentions. Rigorously construed, the perspective of the *Tractatus* relegated the notions of "subject" and purposive "meaning" from the realm of concrete experience to the status of external "limits" or linguistic parameters of the world; in so doing, the study also eliminated the need for intersubjective clarification of meaning (and ultimately also the possibility of philosophical reflection).

The aversion to exegesis was continued by semanticists and linguistic pluralists dedicated to the construction of specialized language frameworks; despite the importance attached to meta-languages or meta-linguistic conventions for scientific inquiry, such conventions were treated either as simple factual premises or as arbitrary fiats of experts. The contours of a rapprochement emerged only in the writings of the later Wittgenstein, especially in his emphasis on ordinary language and the notion of "language games" embedded in commonsense conventions; once linguistic practices were seen as intimately "interwoven" with concrete "life-forms" and worldviews, the feasibility of a "cultural" interpretation became apparent. Nevertheless, Wittgenstein's own attitude in this matter remained ambivalent to the end, as he left open (or failed to block) the road to an empiricist treatment of language and the reduction of meaning to behavior.[9]

Whatever Wittgenstein's preferences may have been, a number of followers—foremost among them Peter Winch—have developed the notion of "language games" into a springboard for cultural and social analysis. Winch's

The Idea of a Social Science placed decisive stress on the task of interpretive exegesis or—in his words—on "the central role which the concept of understanding plays in the activities which are characteristic of human societies." As the study tried to show, however, the interpretation of social behavior could not rely solely on the intentions of an individual actor, since these intentions were intelligible only within a language community and in terms of the rules of conduct and language usage operative in that community. Social analysis thus was predicated on the understanding of intersubjective standards: "It is only a situation in which it makes sense to suppose that somebody else could in principle discover the rule which I am following that I can be said to follow a rule at all." Comparing these premises with traditional sociology and especially with Weber's legacy, Winch found similarities as well as divergences. In accord with Weber (at least with Weber's early formulations), Winch argued that social understanding involves "grasping the *point* or *meaning* of what is being done or said" and thus an effort "far removed from the world of statistics and causal laws" and "closer to the realm of discourse." The charge of "psychologism" was quickly dismissed by the insistence that the distinctiveness of social inquiry "does not rest on the hypothesis of an 'inner sense.' " Despite these affinities, Winch summed up the chief divergence in the statement that Weber's "characterization of *Sinn* as something 'subjectively intended' must be approached wearily"; for the understanding of meaning was possible only on the basis of rules or "where the act in question has a relation to a social context: this must be true even of the most private acts, if, that is, they are meaningful."[10]

The aspect of Winch's study that occasioned the most lively controversy among reviewers was the thesis of the uniqueness and virtual incommensurability of individual language games and life-forms. Viewing life-forms as closely knit webs of opinions and ideas, Winch considered it "nonsensical to take several systems of ideas, find an element in each which can be expressed in the same verbal form, and then claim to have discovered an idea which is common to all the systems"; rather, the "very nature" of human society was "to consist in different and competing ways of life, each offering a different account of the intelligibility of things." The thesis of uniqueness was of crucial importance to the social scientist who had to take his bearings and his criteria from "within the way of life he is studying," instead of arbitrarily imposing "his own standards from without"; in fact, science and logical analysis were themselves a particular way of life and could not be applied as criteria on "modes of social life as such." In formulating this argument, Winch seemed indebted, at least in part, to Wittgenstein's empiricist and antispeculative leanings; despite his efforts to differentiate life-forms from mere habits on the basis of the potentially "reflective" character of language rules, he was averse to the enterprise of a general, comparative reflection: "Connected with the realization that intelligibility takes many and varied forms is the realization that reality has no key." His argument on this score has been criticized from many quarters—most vocally by adepts of a "critical positivism" committed to the proposition that scientific research, although fallible and in need of constant revision, is destined ultimately to grasp objective reality independently of historical conditions and cultural variations. In subsequent writings Winch progressively modified his "relativist" assumptions; it is not entirely clear, however, how these modifications affect the basic Wittgensteinian program of social analysis.

On the continent, phenomenology was to some extent a continuation of Dilthey's and Rickert's efforts to elucidate the dimension of "meaning" as a counterpart to scientific explanation. Paralleling Rickert's initiative, Husserl's early writings launched a broad-scale attack on "psychologism" and on the reduction of thought to empirical processes; by comparison with neo-Kantianism, however, Husserl from the beginning extended the scope of inquiry beyond normative values to the full range of (natural and cultural) phenomena amenable to human cognition. His *Logical Investigations* initially sought to vindicate the integrity and constancy of logical propositions; but the force of the argument carried over to all types of meaningful statements reflecting man's understanding of the world. Although reformulating and sharpening the insights of his predecessors, Husserl at least in one respect remained heir to their perspective: in the attachment to individualism or to an individual-egological "consciousness." The phenomenological method of "bracketing," or *epoché*, in his treatment signified basically an attempt to unravel the meaningful core, or "essence," of phenomena as disclosed in (or "constituted" by) a purified consciousness. At least in this respect his approach replicated the solipsistic dilemma of early language analysis and of much of traditional philosophy: to the extent that consciousness was presented as "transcendental limit" of the world, the domain of intersubjective understanding and clarification of meaning was obliterated. In his later writings Husserl sought to overcome this dilemma by introducing the notion of the "life-world," or world of mundane experience, but the relationship between mundanity and consciousness was never fully clarified.

By that time, the thrust of phenomenological analysis had already been profoundly reshaped by Heidegger's delineation, in *Being and Time*, of a "hermeneutical phenomenology" or "existential ontology." Understanding of meaning, in Heidegger's conception, was no longer the prerogative of individual cognition or consciousness but a basic attribute of man's existential condition or *Dasein* construed as "being-in-the world." Far from occupying the role of an alien spectator, *Dasein* was seen as enmeshed in a fabric of "preunder-

standing" and "pre-predicative" experience, a fabric that was basically intersubjective and cultural in character.[12]

Neither Husserl nor Heidegger were concerned with articulating the implications of their thoughts for social inquiry. The elaboration of a "phenomenological sociology" was chiefly the accomplishment of one of Husserl's students, Alfred Schutz. In one of his first major works, *The Phenomenology of
the Social World*, Schutz tried to effect a merger of Weberian sociology and
Husserl's teachings by tracing the notion of meaningful social action to an
underlying stratum or stream of constitutive consciousness. Even in this early
study, however, Schutz was not wedded in a doctrinaire manner to the method
of bracketing; turning to the predicaments of intersubjective relations, he
replaced "transcendental reduction" with the "attitude of the natural standpoint" concerned with mundane experience. In his later writings, he grew
steadily weary of egological methodology and increasingly preoccupied with
the domain of the "life-world," the domain of "common-sense" and everyday
activity. Drawing at least in part on Heideggerian insights, he treated "understanding" not simply as an individual cognitive faculty but as a multidimen-
sional category denoting an existential or "experiential form of common-sense
knowledge of human affairs" as well as an "epistemological problem" and a
"method peculiar to the social sciences." Yet, like Husserl, Schutz ultimately
left unresolved the significance of the life-world and the respective weights of
consciousness and intersubjectivity.[13]

In a sense the same ambivalence overshadows contemporary "ethnomethodology," one of the major offshoots of phenomenological sociology. Basically
committed to the investigation of commonsense experience, or "the practical
everyday activities of men in society as they make accountable, to themselves
and others, their everyday affairs," ethnomethodologists tend to differ on
whether ordinary life reflects invariant or transcendental cognitive structures or
whether cognition is itself shaped by cultural contexts. In the first case, social
reality is in danger of being dissolved into mental or "ideal" properties; in the
second case, cognition faces the hazard of historical and cultural
contingency.[14]

The tension between invariance and contingency, individualism and intersubjectivity, are not the only predicaments besetting social inquiry today.
Conjoined with these issues, the sketched skirmishes and developments have
engendered a quandary which touches the core of cognition and the basic
structure of the republic of letters: the quandary regarding the relationship
between science and understanding, knowledge and self-knowledge. The dilemma is an outgrowth of the contemporary attack on "individualism" and
"subjectivism," construed not as a methodological ploy but as a challenge to
the pervasive subject-object legacy of the modern age. In this sense, the present

day "crisis of understanding" is also a crisis of modernity. Once the pillar of individualism is eroded, the twin seedlings of the modern era—natural science and interpretive understanding—are also bound to be affected and to be compelled to redefine their respective provinces. Once man is no longer seen as sovereign analyst and potential master of the world, his independence not only from society but also from nature is placed in jeopardy.

Although universally noted, the dilemma has been debated in recent years with particular intensity by German and French thinkers; preponderantly, these debates have centered on the proper range or scope of interpretive exegesis. One argumentative strategy, favored by representatives of the "neo-Frankfurt School" of social research, has been to maintain the integrity of traditional types of inquiry while resisting the tendency toward segregation or one-sided hegemony. Thus, dedicated to the long-range prospect of human self-understanding and emancipation but disturbed by the quasi-natural constraints of modern society, Jürgen Habermas and Karl-Otto Apel have advocated the juxtaposition of hermeneutics and scientific analysis (and also their combination for purposes of critical social inquiry).[15] On the other hand, hermeneuticists influenced by Heidegger have tended to redefine interpretive exegesis by deemphasizing the aspect of subjective purpose and intentionality; in his *Truth and Method*, Hans-Georg Gadamer presented history not so much as an emanation of individual practice but as a complex learning process in which man is able to decipher himself only through encounters with past cultural institutions. Seen in this light, the scope of hermeneutical understanding is bound to be broad and devoid of clear-cut boundary lines. In the French context, Paul Ricoeur has argued in favor not only of the coexistence but of an intimate reciprocal dialogue and symbiosis of understanding and scientific explanation.[16]

The issues underlying these debates are likely to preoccupy and trouble philosophy and social inquiry for a long time to come. This is hardly surprising. After all, the predicaments of human understanding are not like mathematical problems or crossword puzzles, which permit definitive solutions. Involving both man's relation to the world and his self-assessment, the contemporary crisis is itself part of a difficult learning process whose direction signals are hazy and whose end is by no means in sight. Can interpretive exegesis still perform a role in a situation when the individual is dislodged from his traditional preeminence? Is it possible to speak of "meaning" and the "point" of life even without reference to subjectively intended purposes? Or will understanding become defunct and be effaced by anonymous events and structures? Social inquiry cannot and should not be expected to offer ready-made answers; however, as long as they claim or desire to make a point, social scientists will have to grapple with these questions.

NOTES

1. Compare on this point Karl-Otto Apel, "Das Verstehen (eine Problemgeschichte als Begriffsgeschichte)," *Archiv für Begriffsgeschichte* 1 (1955): 142–99, esp. pp. 144–53. The essay sketches the "dual prehistory" of the contemporary notion of "understanding": the emergence of modern science and the development of hermeneutical interpretation.

2. In the words of Richard E. Palmer, hermeneutical understanding in its modern sense "emerges historically from its parentage in biblical exegesis and classical philology." See *Hermeneutics: Interpretation Theory in Schleiermacher, Dilthey, Heidegger, and Gadamer* (Evanston, Ill.: Northwestern University Press, 1969), p. 40. Palmer points also to the Greek roots of the term "hermeneutics," indicating (pp. 12–32) that these roots refer broadly to all kinds of efforts to render man or the world intelligible, including oral recitation, explanation, and translation.

3. In lieu of Weber it might also have been possible to select as starting point another "founder" of sociology, Georg Simmel. However, many or most of Simmel's arguments are also present in Weber's writings; besides, Weber's influence on sociology both in Europe and America has been vastly more pervasive. One may note that Maurice Merleau-Ponty entitled a probing essay on Weber "The Crisis of Understanding"; see *Adventures of the Dialectic*, trans. Joseph Bien (Evanston, Ill.: Northwestern University Press, 1973), pp. 9–29.

4. As Apel writes: "The accent of Schleiermacher's notion of understanding lies on the domain of individual biography—an aspect which makes him a teacher of Dilthey, Simmel, and modern biography in general. His ultimate goal is to understand the individual as completely as possible." "Das Verstehen . . . ," p. 168.

5. Compare Wilhelm Dilthey, *Gesammelte Schriften*, 5th ed. (Stuttgart: Kohlhammer, 1962), 1: 12, 5: 144, 7: 148. Compare also Herbert P. Rickman, "Reaction against Positivism and Dilthey's Concept of Understanding," *British Journal of Sociology*, 11 (1960): 307–18; Rudolf A. Makkreel, "Wilhelm Dilthey and the Neo-Kantians: The Distinction of the *Geisteswissenschaften* and the *Kulturwissenschaften*," *Journal of the History of Philosophy*, 7 (1969): 423–40.

6. See Max Weber, " 'Objectivity' in Social Science and Social Policy," in *Methodology of the Social Sciences*, ed. Edward A. Shils and Henry A. Finch (Glencoe, Ill.: Free Press, 1949), pp. 52–54; "The Fundamental Concepts of Sociology," in *Economy and Society*, ed. Guenther Roth and Claus Wittich (New York: Bedminster Press, 1968), pp. 10–16.

7. Commenting on the relationship between natural and "cultural" sciences, Parsons noted: "What Weber did was to take an enormous step in the direction of bridging the gap between the two types of science, and to make possible the treatment of social material in a systematic scientific manner rather than as an art. But he failed to complete the process, and the nature of the halfway point at which he stopped helps to account for many of the difficulties of his position." See *The Theory of Social and Economic Organization*, trans. A. M. Henderson and Talcott Parsons (Glencoe, Ill.: Free Press, 1947), "Introduction," pp. 10–11.

8. Compare Arthur W. Diquattro, "*Verstehen* as an Empirical Concept," *Sociology and Sociological Research*, 57 (1972): 35; also Thomas A. McCarthy, "On Misunderstanding 'Understanding'," *Theory and Decision*, 3 (1973): 351–70.

9. For this background compare Apel, "Wittgenstein und das Problem des hermeneutischen Verstehens," in *Transformation der Philosophie* (Frankfurt-Main: Suhr-

kamp, 1973), 1: 335–77; also his "Die Entfaltung der 'sprachanalytischen' Philosophie und das Problem der 'Geisteswissenschaften'," ibid., 2: 28–95.

10. Peter Winch, *The Idea of a Social Science and Its Relation to Philosophy* (London: Routledge and Kegan Paul, 1958), pp. 22, 30, 47, 50, 115, 119. Compare also his comment (p. 40) that "the philosophical elucidation of human intelligence, and the notions associated with this, requires that these notions be placed in the context of the relations between men in society. In so far as there has been a genuine revolution in recent years, perhaps it lies in the emphasis on that fact and in the profound working out of its consequences, which we find in Wittgenstein's work."

11. Ibid., pp. 100, 102–3, 107–8.

12. On these developments see Apel, "Die beiden Phasen der Phänomenologie in ihrer Auswirkung auf das philosophische Vorverständnis von Sprache und Dichtung in der Gegenwart" and his "Heideggers philosophische Radikalisierung der 'Hermeneutik' und das 'Sinnkriterium' der Sprache," in *Transformation der Philosophie*, 1: 79–105, 276–334. Compare also Palmer's comments: "For Heidegger, understanding is the power to grasp one's own possibilities for being, within the context of the life-world in which one exists. It is not a special capacity or gift for feeling into the situation of another person, nor is it the power to grasp the meaning of some 'expression of life' on a deeper level. Understanding is conceived not as something to be possessed but rather as a mode or constituent element of being-in-the-world." *Hermeneutics*, p. 131.

13. Compare Alfred Schutz, *The Phenomenology of the Social World*, trans. George Walsh and Frederick Lehnert (Evanston, Ill.: Northwestern University Press, 1967); also "Concept and Theory Formation in the Social Sciences," in *Collected Papers I: The Problem of Social Reality*, ed. Maurice Natanson (The Hague: Martinus Nijhoff, 1962), pp. 48–66. The ambivalence is evident in the latter essay (pp. 56, 62) when Schutz first notes that, far removed from "introspection," *Verstehen* "is a result of processes of learning or acculturation," and then endorses Weber's premise of subjective intentionality: "If the social sciences aim indeed at explaining social reality," then their constructs "must include a reference to the subjective meaning an action has for the actor. This is, I think, what Max Weber understood by his famous postulate of subjective understanding."

14. Compare Jack D. Douglas, ed., *Understanding Everyday Life: Toward the Reconstruction of Sociological Knowledge* (Chicago: Aldine Publishing Co., 1970); also George Psathas, "Ethnomethods and Phenomenology," *Social Research*, 35 (1968): 509; and Fred R. Dallmayr, "Phenomenology and Social Science: An Overview and Appraisal," in *Explorations in Phenomenology*, ed. David Carr and Edward S. Casey (The Hague: Martinus Nijhoff, 1974), pp. 133–66, esp. pp. 157–58.

15. Compare Jürgen Habermas, *Knowledge and Human Interests* (Boston: Beacon Press, 1971); Karl-Otto Apel, "Szientistik, Hermeneutik, Ideologiekritik: Entwurf einer Wissenschaftslehre in erkenntnisanthropologischer Sicht," in *Transformation der Philosophie*, 2: 96–127; also Apel et al., eds., *Hermeneutik und Ideologiekritik* (Frankfurt-Main: Suhrkamp, 1971).

16. Compare Hans-Georg Gadamer, *Wahrheit und Methode: Grundzüge einer philosophischen Hermeneutik,* 2d ed. (Tübingen: J. C. B. Mohr, 1965), English translation: *Truth and Method*, trans. Garrett Barden and John Cumming (New York: Seabury Press, 1975); Paul Ricoeur, *Freud and Philosophy: An Essay on Interpretation*, trans. Denis Savage (New Haven: Yale University Press, 1970), and *The Conflict of Interpretations: Essays in Hermeneutics*, ed. Don Ihde (Evanston, Ill.: Northwestern University Press, 1974).

Suggested Readings

BROWN, R. R. *Explanation in Social Science*. Chicago: Aldine, 1963.

BÜHL, Walter L., ed. *Verstehende Soziologie: Grundzüge und Entwicklungstendenzen*. Munich: Nymphenburger Verlagshandlung, 1972.

CHAMBERS, F. P. *Perception, Understanding, and Society: A Philosophical Essay on the Arts, Sciences, and Human Studies*. London: Sidgwick and Jackson, 1961.

HODGES, H. A. *The Philosophy of Wilhelm Dilthey*. New York: Humanities Press, 1952.

_____. *Wilhelm Dilthey: An Introduction*. London: Routledge and Kegan Paul, 1944.

MANNINEN J., and Tuomela, R., eds. *Essays on Explanation and Understanding*. Dordrecht, Holland: Reidel, 1975.

PARKINSON, G. H. R., ed. *The Theory of Meaning*. London: Oxford University Press, 1968.

RADNITZKY, Gerard. *Contemporary Schools of Metascience*. 2 vols. Göteborg, Sweden: Akademiförlaget, 1968.

RICKMAN, H. P. *Understanding and the Human Studies*. London: Heineman, 1967.

RICKMAN, H. P., ed. *Meaning in History: W. Dilthey's Thoughts on History*. London: George Allen and Unwin, 1961.

RYAN, Alan, ed. *The Philosophy of Social Explanation*. London: Oxford University Press, 1973.

SKJERVHEIM, H. *Objectivism and the Study of Man*. Oslo: Universitetsvorlaget, 1959.

TAYLOR. *The Explanation of Behavior*. London: Routledge and Kegan Paul, 1964.

TOULMIN, Stephen. *Foresight and Understanding*. London: Hutchison, 1961.

_____. *Human Understanding*. Vol. 1. Princeton, N.J.; Princeton University Press, 1972.

TRUZZI, Marcello, ed. *Verstehen: Subjective Understanding in the Social Sciences*. Reading, Mass.: Addison-Wesley Publishing Co., 1974.

VON WRIGHT, George H. *Explanation and Understanding*. Ithaca, N.Y.: Cornell University Press, 1971.

WACH, Joachim. *Das Verstehen: Grundzüge einer Geschichte der hermeneutischen Theorie*. 3 vols. Tübingen: Mohr, 1926–33.

ZIFF, Paul. *Understanding Understanding*. Ithaca, N.Y.: Cornell University Press, 1972.

PART ONE

Max Weber on *Verstehen*

Introduction

AMONG THE FOUNDERS OF CONTEMPORARY SOCIAL SCIENCE, MAX WEBER IS probably the most challenging and intellectually complex figure. His vast opus of detailed historical, economic, and social-political investigations is a stunning illustration of the "sociological imagination" at work. Intellectually, Weber was a perceptive student of the philosophical tradition and a lively participant in the major philosophical currents—especially the neo-Kantian movement—of his time. Both as a scholar and an intellectual, he was deeply imbued with the legacy of liberal individualism. From the vantage point of this legacy, it seemed eminently plausible that social life was the product of individual human activity and that a social science faithful to its subject matter had to concentrate its efforts on trying to "understand" the purposes and motivations of individual agents. From the same perspective it was imperative that the social scientist should not impose his preferences on these agents; just as the liberal "state" was assumed to function merely as umpire among competing social initiatives, the social scientist had to be tolerant of the diverse human goals and interests encountered in his studies. Scholarly objectivity and "value-neutrality" was the counterpart of unrestricted commitment in practical life. The two aspects, to be sure, could not be neatly segregated. As Weber realized, the models or theoretical constructs of social scientists—instead of simply mirroring an external reality—are themselves derived from personal insight and serendipity. Conversely, in line with the Kantian juxtaposition of moral autonomy and natural necessity, "understanding" of cultural meanings and social designs was silhouetted against nonpurposive behavior and causal chains of events.

The essay " 'Objectivity' in Social Science and Social Policy" (1904) demonstrates Weber's close affinity to neo-Kantianism and especially to its "Southwest German" branch led by Heinrich Rickert. Opposing both the identification of the human with the natural sciences and the reduction of social or historical phenomena to psychic or mental conditions, Rickert had laid the groundwork for "cultural" inquiry dealing with the normative-purposive significance of concrete events or unique constellations. Drawing on this background, Weber's essay treats knowledge of causal or analytical "laws" as at best a heuristic device or preliminary step. Properly construed, he notes, social science has to be viewed as one of the "cultural sciences," that is, disciplines "which analyze the phenomena of life in terms of their cultural significance." Such meaning or significance derives from the "value-relation" or "value-orientation" of human actions and historical events: "The concept of culture is a *value-concept*. Empirical reality becomes 'culture' to us because and insofar as we relate it to value ideas." According to Weber, a crucial instrument for grasping the significance of events or cultural patterns consists in the formulation of synthetic "mental constructs" called "ideal types," constructs that are "formed by the one-sided *accentuation* of one or more points of view and by the synthesis of a great many diffuse, discrete, more or less present and occasionally absent *concrete individual* phenomena." Such constructs, he adds, are always predicated on "subjective presuppositions," since knowledge of cultural reality is "always knowledge from *particular points of view*." The "objectivity" of ideal types resides not in their correspondence to external reality or "ideal" normative standards, but rather in their theoretical coherence and heuristic utility: "The *objective* validity of all empirical knowledge rests exclusively upon the ordering of the given reality according to categories which are *subjective* in a specific sense, namely, in that they present the *presuppositions* of our knowledge and are based on the presupposition of the *value* of those truths which empirical knowledge alone is able to give us."

By comparison with the suggestive and discursive character of the discussed essay, Weber's examination of "basic sociological terms" in part 1 of *Economy and Society* is more rigorous and systematic. In the opening paragraph, sociology is defined as "a science concerning itself with the interpretive understanding of social action"; "action" in this formula refers to behavior to which "the acting individual attaches a subjective meaning," while the term "social" denotes such action whose subjective meaning "takes account of the behavior of others and is thereby oriented in its course." By focusing on intelligible action, sociology excludes from its domain "merely reactive behavior" and all kinds of animate or inanimate processes "to which no subjective meaning is attached," although Weber recognizes that the dividing line "cannot be sharply drawn empirically" and that nonintelligible phenomena must be taken into account "in the role of stimuli, results, favoring or hindering circumstances." The presentation leaves room for the possibility that "future research may be able to discover nonunderstandable uniformities underlying what has appeared to be specifically meaningful action"; but the thrust of sociological analysis would remain unchanged by such developments. Concerning interpretive understanding (*Verstehen*), Weber distinguishes between two kinds: "direct observational understanding," where purpose or meaning is immediately apparent; and "explanatory understanding," which seeks to grasp the "motivation" or final cause of behavior by "placing the act in an intelligible and more inclusive context of meaning." Subjective meaning or purpose can be detected on different levels: either in the concrete action of a particular individual actor, in the intentional behavior of a plurality of actors, or in a theoretically constructed "pure" or "ideal type" of action ascribed to a hypothetical actor or group of actors. No matter what level or context is chosen, however, the focus is always on the behavior of "one or more *individual* human beings," since only individuals "can be treated as agents in a course of subjectively understandable action." As Weber adds, sociology is differentiated from historiography by its relative stress on "type concepts and generalized uniformities of empirical process." The second section delineates four basic "ideal types" of social action (of which the first is considered particularly useful for sociological analysis): "instrumentally rational" action directed toward "the attainment of the actor's own rationally pursued and calculated ends"; "value-rational" action guided by belief in some "value for its own sake"; "affectual" and "traditional" modes of intentional behavior.

Apart from the aspect of "generalized uniformities," *Economy and Society* pays attention to the issue of verification, in a manner that seems to involve at least a slight shift of accent from the earlier essay. In general terms, Weber writes, "verification of subjective interpretation by comparison with the concrete course of events is, as in the case of all hypotheses, indispensable." In discussing the difficulties of verification in sociological research, he distinguishes two types of tests (which ideally are linked): theoretical coherence or "adequacy on the level of meaning"; and "causal adequacy" predicated on the probability that, "according to established generalizations from experience," an action or sequence of events "will always actually occur in the same way." Some students of Weber have construed his concern with generalization and verification as guideposts pointing away from the narrow preoccupation with interpretive understanding of subjectively meaningful behavior; Talcott Parsons has exerted a leading influence in this direction.

In the introduction to his own translation of the first part of *Economy and Society* (1947),[1] Parsons treated Weber's work as a stepping stone toward a "unified science" program assimilating cultural inquiry to natural science canons. "What Weber did," he wrote, "was to take an enormous step in the direction of bridging the gap between the two types of science, and to make possible the treatment of social material in a systematic scientific manner rather than as an art. But he failed to complete the process, and the nature of the half-way point at which he stopped helps to account for many of the difficulties of his position." The basic source of these difficulties, he continued, resided "in Weber's failure to carry through a systematic functional analysis of a generalized social system of action." To remedy this gap is the chief aim of

Parson's own approach. While superior to simple versions of functionalism, this approach may still be checked against Weber's caveat that, though convenient for provisional orientation, functional analysis "can be highly dangerous" if "its cognitive value is overestimated."

Parson's later comments on Weber (1971), reproduced below, amplify his earlier observations. As he states, "value-freedom" or scientific objectivity must be considered the "foundation" of Weber's intellectual and sociological position. The term in his view designates "freedom to pursue the values of science within the relevant limits, without their being overridden by values either contradictory to or irrelevant to those of scientific investigation." In terms of sociological research, attachment to scientific values is basically synonymous with acceptance of the canons of natural science. Weber, Parsons notes, "took very seriously indeed the proposition that *knowledge* in the empirical sense clearly implied the *causal explanation* of phenomena and events" and that such knowledge could only be achieved "by means of a generalized theoretical scheme" or systematic framework: "Very bluntly, the conception of a generalized *theory* as has been developed in the great tradition of the natural science is an essential component of *all* empirical science." Subsuming Rickert's teachings under the "fallacy of historicism," he adds that "in *this* crucial sense, there is not 'natural' or 'cultural' science, there is only science or nonscience and all empirical knowledge is scientific in so far as it is valid." Given these premises, the role of "value-relation" (*Wertbeziehung*) and of interpretive understanding is bound to be limited if not marginal. According to Parsons the term has chiefly "extrascientific" status, referring either to the personal motivation of the researcher or to the cultural context in which science operates. Despite the recognition of the need to grasp or "communicate" with the values of social agents, *Verstehen* in his treatment does not involve a mutual learning process but derives entirely from the privileged perspective of the scientist whose value system "articulates both in that of the culture in which the investigator participates and in that of the objects he studies." The central point, he concludes, is the "basic *autonomy* of both the special values and the technical theory of science" and "the priority of these considerations over any particularities of *Verstehen* of particular complexes of meaning or motivation."

In his reply, Jürgen Habermas emphasizes the multiplicity or multidimensionality of Weber's cognitive concerns. Pointing to Weber's focus on the understanding of subjective motivations and the subjectively intended meaning of actions, he addresses to Parsons the question whether, "going beyond the production of knowledge which is technically usable," Weber's cognitive ambition does not embrace the explication of "the significance of social processes"? Since Parson's treatment of sociology as "empirical analytical science" tends to obscure from view the dimension of significance or rather to submerge it in the presumed "universalism" of the scientist's perspective, a second question arises: whether interpretive sociology needs to move "beyond the understanding of motivation to the dimension of a hermeneutic adoption of handed-down meaning-contents"? Intimately tied to this issue is the status of "value-relation" and its impact on the distinction between natural and social-cultural science. Does *Wertbeziehung* in sociology, Habermas asks, affect only the extrascientific "selection of problems," or does it "influence the formation of theories as such?" His last question, concerning the role of "value-freedom" and the relationship between methodological canons and social life, is addressed to Parsons and Weber alike. Weber's "militant latter-day liberalism," he suggests, can be (and has been) invoked not only to buttress scientific neutrality, but also in support of arbitrary political decisions and ideological blueprints.

NOTES

1. Max Weber, *The Theory of Social and Economic Organization*, trans. A. M. Henderson and Talcott Parsons, ed. with introduction Talcott Parsons (New York: Oxford University Press, 1947).

"Objectivity" in Social Science and Social Policy

MAX WEBER

THE TYPE OF SOCIAL SCIENCE IN WHICH WE ARE INTERESTED IS AN *empirical science* of concrete *reality (Wirklichkeitswissenschaft)*. Our aim is the understanding of the characteristic uniqueness of the reality in which we move. We wish to understand on the one hand the relationships and the cultural significance of individual events in their contemporary manifestations and on the other the causes of their being historically *so* and not *otherwise*. Now, as soon as we attempt to reflect about the way in which life confronts us in immediate concrete situations, it presents an infinite multiplicity of successively and coexistently emerging and disappearing events, both "within" and "outside" ourselves. The absolute infinitude of this multiplicity is seen to remain undiminished even when our attention is focused on a single "object," for instance, a concrete act of exchange, as soon as we seriously attempt an exhaustive description of *all* the individual components of this "individual phenomenon," to say nothing of explaining it causally. All the analysis of infinite reality which the finite human mind can conduct rests on the tacit assumption that only a finite portion of this reality constitutes the object of scientific investigation, and that only it is "important" in the sense of being "worthy of being known." But what are the criteria by which this segment is selected? It has often been thought that the decisive criterion in the cultural sciences, too, was in the last analysis, the "regular" recurrence of certain causal relationships. The "laws" which we are able to perceive in the infinitely manifold stream of events must—according to this conception—contain the scientifically "essential" aspect of reality. As soon as we have shown some causal relationship to be a "law," i.e., if we have shown it to be universally valid by means of comprehensive historical induction or have made it immediately and tangibly plausible according to our subjective experience, a great number of similar cases order themselves under the formula thus attained. Those elements in each individual event which are left unaccounted for by the selection of their elements subsumable under the "law" are considered as scientifically unintegrated residues which will be taken care of in the further perfection of the system of "laws." Alternatively they will be viewed as "accidental" and therefore scientifically unimportant *because* they do not fit into the structure of the "law"; in other words, they are not typical of the event and hence can only be the objects of "idle curiosity." Accordingly, even among the followers of the Historical School we continually find the attitude which declares that the ideal which all the sciences, including the cultural sciences, serve and towards which they should strive even in the remote future is a system of propositions from which reality can be "deduced." As is well known, a leading natural scientist believed that he could designate the (factually unattainable) ideal goal of such a treatment of cultural reality as a sort of *"astronomical"* knowledge.

Let us not, for our part, spare ourselves the trouble of examining these matters more closely—however often they have already been discussed. The first thing that impresses one is that the "astronomical" knowledge which was referred to is not a system of laws at all. On the contrary, the laws which it presupposes have been taken from other disciplines like mechanics. But it too concerns itself with the question of the *individual* consequence which the working of these laws in an unique *configuration* produces, since it is these individual configurations which are *significant* for us. Every individual constellation which it "explains" or predicts is causally explicable only as the consequence of another equally individual constellation which has preceded it. As far back as we may go into the grey mist of the far-off past, the reality to which the laws apply always remains equally *individual*, equally *undeducible* from laws. A cosmic "primeval state" which had no individual character or less individual character than the cosmic reality of the present would naturally be a meaningless notion. But is there not some trace of similar ideas in our field in those propositions sometimes derived from natural law and sometimes verified by the observation of "primitives," concerning an economic-social "primeval state" free from historical "accidents," and characterized by phenomena such as "primitive agrarian communism," sexual "promiscuity," etc., from which individual historical development emerges by a sort of fall from grace into concreteness?

The social-scientific interest has its point of departure, of course, in the *real*, i.e., concrete, individually structured configuration of our cultural life in its universal relationships which are themselves no less individually structured, and in its development out of other social cultural conditions, which themselves are obviously likewise individually structured. It is clear here that the situation which we illustrated by reference to astronomy as a limiting case (which is regularly drawn on by logicians for the same purpose) appears in a more accentuated form. Whereas in astronomy, the heavenly bodies are of interest to us only in their *quantitative* and exact aspects, the *qualitative* aspect of phenomena concerns us in the social sciences. To this should be added that in the social sciences we are concerned with psychological and intellectual (*geistig*) phenomena the empathic understanding of which is naturally a problem of a specifically different type from those which the schemes of the exact natural sciences in general can or seek to solve. Despite that, this distinction in itself is not a distinction in principle, as it seems at first glance. Aside from pure mechanics, even the exact natural sciences do not proceed without qualitative categories. Furthermore, in our own field we encounter the idea (which is obviously distorted) that at least the phenomena characteristic of a money-economy—which are basic to our culture—are quantifiable and on that account subject to formulation as "laws." Finally it depends on the breadth or narrowness of one's definition of "law" as to whether one will also include regularities which because they are not quantifiable are not subject to numerical analysis. Especially insofar as the influence of psychological and intellectual (*geistig*) factors is concerned, it does not in any case exclude the establishment of *rules* governing rational conduct. Above all, the point of view still persists which claims that the task of psychology is to play a role comparable to mathematics for the *Geisteswissenschaften* in the sense that it analyzes the complicated phenomena of social life into their psychic conditions and effects, reduces them to their most elementary possible psychic factors and then analyzes their functional interdependence. Thereby, a sort of "chemistry" if not "mechanics" of the psychic foundations of social life would be created. Whether such investigations can produce valuable and—what is something else—useful results for the cultural sciences, we cannot decide here. But this would be irrelevant to the question as to whether the aim of social-economic knowledge in our sense, i.e., knowledge of *reality* with respect to its cultural *significance* and its causal relationships can be attained through the quest for recurrent sequences. Let us assume that we have succeeded by means of psychology or otherwise in analyzing all the observed and imaginable relationships of social phenomena into some ultimate elementary "factors," that we have made an exhaustive analysis and classification of them and then formulated rigorously exact laws covering their behavior.—What would be the significance of these results for our knowledge of the *historically* given culture or any individual phase thereof, such as capitalism, in its development and cultural significance? As an analytical tool, it would be as useful as a textbook of organic chemical combinations would be for our knowledge of the biogenetic aspect of the animal and plant world. In each case, certainly an important and useful preliminary step would have been taken. In neither case can concrete reality be deduced from "laws" and "factors." This is not because some higher mysterious powers reside in living phenomena (such as "dominants," "entelechies," or whatever they might be called). This is, however, a problem in its own right. The real reason is that the analysis of reality is concerned with the *configuration* into which those (hypothetical!) "factors" are arranged to form a cultural phenomenon which is historically significant to us. Furthermore, if we wish to "explain" this individual configuration "causally" we must invoke other equally individual configurations on the basis of which we will explain it with the aid of those ((hypothetical!) "laws."

The determination of those (hypothetical) "laws" and "factors" would in any case only be the first of the many operations which would lead us to the desired type of knowledge. The analysis of the historically given individual configuration of those "factors" and their *significant* concrete interaction, conditioned by their historical context and especially the *rendering intelligible* of the basis and type of this significance would be the next task to be achieved. This task must be achieved, it is true, by the utilization of the preliminary analysis but it is nonetheless an entirely new and *distinct* task. The tracing as far into the past as possible of the individual features of these historically evolved configurations which are *contemporaneously* significant, and their historical explanation by antecedent and equally individual configurations would be the third task. Finally the prediction of possible future constellations would be a conceivable fourth task.

For all these purposes, clear concepts and the knowledge of those (hypothetical) "laws" are obviously of great value as heuristic means—but only as such. Indeed they are quite indispensable for this purpose. But even in this function their limitations become evident at a decisive point. In stating this, we arrive at the decisive feature of the method of the cultural sciences. We have designated as "cultural sciences" those disciplines which analyze the phenomena of life in terms of their cultural significance. The *significance* of a configuration of cultural phenomena and the basis of this significance cannot however be derived and rendered intelligible by a system of analytical laws (*Gesetzesbegriffen*), however perfect it may be, since the significance of cultural events presupposes a *value-orientation* towards these events. The concept of culture is a *value-concept*. Empirical reality becomes "culture" to us because and insofar as we relate it to value ideas. It includes those segments and only those segments of reality which have become significant to us because of this value-relevance. Only a small portion of existing concrete reality is colored by our value-conditioned interest and it alone is significant to us. It is significant because it reveals relationships which are important to us due to their connection with our values. Only because and to the extent that this is the case is it worthwhile for us to know it in its individual features. We cannot discover, however, what is meaningful to us by means of a "presuppositionless" investigation of empirical data. Rather perception of its meaningfulness to us is the presupposition of its becoming an *object* of investigation. Meaningfulness naturally does not coincide with laws as such, and the more general the law the less the coincidence. For the specific meaning which a phenomenon has for us is naturally *not* to be found in those relationships which it shares with many other phenomena.

The focus of attention on reality under the guidance of values which lend it significance and the selection and ordering of the phenomena which are thus affected in the light of their cultural significance is entirely different from the analysis of reality in terms of laws and general concepts. Neither of these two types of the analysis of reality has any necessary logical relationship with the other. They can coincide in individual instances but it would be most disastrous if their occasional coincidence caused us to think that they were not distinct *in principle*. The *cultural significance* of a phenomenon, e.g., the significance of exchange in a money economy, can be the fact that it exists on a mass scale as a fundamental component of modern culture. But the historical fact that it plays this role must be causally explained in order to render its cultural significance understandable. The analysis of the *general* aspects of exchange and the technique of the market is a—highly important and indispensable—*preliminary task*. For not only does this type of analysis leave unanswered the question as to how exchange historically acquired its fundamental significance in the modern world; but above all else, the fact with which we are primarily concerned, namely, the *cultural significance* of the money economy, for the sake of which we are interested in the description of exchange technique and for the sake of which alone a science exists which deals with that technique—is not derivable from any "law." The *generic features* of exchange, purchase, etc., interest the jurist—but we are concerned with the analysis of the *cultural significance* of the concrete *historical* fact that today exchange exists on a mass scale. When we require an explanation, when we wish to understand what distinguishes the social-economic aspects of our culture for instance from that of antiquity in which exchange showed precisely the same generic traits as it does today and when we raise the question as to where the significance of "money economy" lies, logical principles of quite heterogeneous derivation enter into the investigation. We will apply those concepts with which we are provided by the investigation of the general features of economic mass phenomena—indeed, insofar as they are relevant to the meaningful aspects of our culture, we shall use them as *means* of exposition. The *goal* of our investigation is not reached through the exposition of those laws and concepts, precise as it may be. The question as to what should be the object of universal conceptualization cannot be decided "presuppositionlessly" but only with reference to the *significance* which certain segments of that infinite multiplicity which we call "commerce" have for culture. We seek knowledge of an historical phenomenon, meaning by historical: significant in its individuality (*Eigenart*). And the decisive element in this is that only through the presupposition that a finite part alone of the infinite variety of phenomena is significant, does the knowledge of an individual phenomenon become logically meaningful. Even with the widest imaginable knowledge of "laws," we are helpless in the face of the question: how is the *causal explanation* of an *individual* fact possible—since a *description* of even the smallest slice of reality can never be exhaustive? The number and type of causes which have influenced any given event are always infinite and there is nothing in the things themselves to set some of them apart as alone meriting attention. A chaos of "existential judgments" about countless individual events would be the only result of a serious attempt to analyze reality "without presuppositions." And even this result is only seemingly possible, since every single perception discloses on closer examination an infinite number of constituent perceptions which can never be exhaustively expressed in a judgment. Order is brought into this chaos only on the condition that in every case only a *part* of concrete reality is interesting and *significant* to us, because only it is related to the *cultural values* with which we approach reality. Only certain sides of the infinitely complex concrete phenomenon, namely those to which we attribute a general *cultural significance*—are therefore worthwhile knowing. They alone are objects of causal explanation. And even this causal explanation evinces the same character; an *exhaustive* causal investigation of any concrete phenomenon in its full reality is not only practically impossible—it is simply nonsense. We select only those causes to which are to be imputed in the individual case, the "essential" features of an event. Where the *individuality* of a phenomenon is concerned, the question of causality is not a question of *laws* but of concrete causal *relationships*; it is not a question of the subsumption of the event under some general rubric as a representative case but of its imputation as a consequence of some constellation. It is in brief a *question of imputation*. Wherever the causal explanation of a "cultural phenomenon"—an "historical individual" is under consideration, the knowledge of causal *laws* is not the *end* of the investigation but only a *means*. It facilitates and renders possible the causal imputation to their concrete causes of those components of a phenomenon the individuality of which is culturally significant. So far and only so far as it achieves this, is it valuable for our knowledge of concrete relationships. And the more "general," i.e., the more abstract the laws, the less they can contribute to the causal imputation of *individual* phenomena and, more indirectly, to the understanding of the significance of cultural events.

What is the consequence of all this?

Naturally, it does not imply that the knowledge of *universal* propositions, the construction of abstract concepts, the knowledge of regularities and the attempt to formulate *"laws"* have no scientific justification in the cultural sciences. Quite the contrary, if the causal knowledge of the historians consists of the imputation of concrete effects to concrete causes a *valid* imputation of any individual effect without the application of *"nomological" knowledge*—i.e., the knowledge of recurrent causal sequences—would in general be impossible. Whether a single individual component of a relationship is, in a concrete case, to be assigned causal responsibility for an effect, the causal explanation of which is at issue, can in doubtful cases be determined only by estimating the effects which we *generally* expect from it and from the other components of the same complex which are relevant to the explanation. In other words, the *"adequate"* effects of the causal elements involved must be considered in arriving at any such conclusion. The extent to which the historian (in the widest sense of the word) can perform this imputation in a reasonably certain manner with his imagination sharpened by personal experience and trained in analytic methods and the extent to which he must have recourse to the aid of special disciplines which make it possible, varies with the individual case. Everywhere, however, and hence also in the sphere of complicated economic processes, the more certain and the more comprehensive our general knowledge the greater is the *certainty* of imputation. This proposition is not in the least affected by the fact that even in the case of all so-called "economic laws" without exception, we are concerned here not with "laws" in the narrower exact natural science sense, but with *adequate* causal relationships expressed in rules and with the application of the category of "objective possibility." The establishment of such regularities is not the *end* but rather the *means* of knowledge. It is entirely a question of expediency, to be settled separately for each individual case, whether a regularly recurrent causal relationship of everyday experience should be formulated into a "law." Laws are important and valuable in the exact natural sciences, in the measure that those sciences are *universally valid*. For the knowledge of historical phenomena in their concreteness, the most general laws, because they are most devoid of content are also the least valuable. The more comprehensive the validity—or scope—of a term, the more it leads us away from the richness of reality since in order to include the common elements of the largest possible number of phenomena, it must necessarily be as abstract as possible and hence *devoid* of content. In the cultural sciences, the knowledge of the universal or general is never valuable in itself.

The conclusion which follows from the above is that an "objective" analysis of cultural events, which proceeds according to the thesis that the ideal of science is the reduction of empirical reality of "laws," is meaningless. It is not meaningless, as is often maintained, because cultural or psychic events for instance are "objectively" less governed by laws. It is meaningless for a number of other reasons. Firstly, because the knowledge of social laws is not knowledge of social reality but is rather one of the various aids used by our minds for attaining this end; secondly, because knowledge of *cultural* events is inconceivable except on a basis of the *significance* which the concrete constellations of reality have for us in certain *individual* concrete situations. In *which* sense and in *which* situations this is the case is not revealed to us by any law; it is decided according to the *value-ideas* in the light of which we view "culture" in each individual case. "Culture" is a finite segment of the meaningless infinity of the world process, a segment on which *human beings* confer meaning and significance. This is true even for the human being who views a *particular* culture as a mortal enemy and who seeks to "return to nature." He can attain this point of view only after viewing the culture in which he lives from the standpoint of his values, and finding it "too soft." This is the purely logical-formal fact which is involved when we speak of the logically necessary rootedness of all historical entities (*historische Individuen*) in "evaluative ideas." The transcendental presupposition of every *cultural science* lies not in our finding a certain culture or any "culture" in general to be *valuable* but rather in the fact that we are *cultural beings*, endowed with the capacity and the will to take a deliberate attitude towards the world and to lend it *significance*. Whatever this significance may be, it will lead us to judge certain phenomena of human existence in its light and to respond to them as being (positively or negatively) meaningful. Whatever may be the content of this attitude—these phenomena have cultural significance for us and on this significance alone rests its scientific interest. Thus when we speak here of the conditioning of cultural knowledge through *evaluative* ideas (*Wertideen*) (following the terminology of modern logic), it is done in the hope that we will not be subject to crude misunderstandings such as the opinion that cultural significance should be attributed only to *valuable* phenomena. Prostitution is a *cultural* phenomenon just as much as religion or money. All three are cultural phenomena *only* because and *only* insofar as their existence and the form which they historically assume touch directly or indirectly on our cultural *interests* and arouse our striving for knowledge concerning problems brought into focus by the evaluative ideas which give *significance* to the fragment of reality analyzed by those concepts.

All knowledge of cultural reality, as may be seen, is always knowledge from *particular points of view*. When we require from the historian and social research worker as an elementary presupposition that they distinguish the important from the trivial and that they should have the necessary "point of view" for this distinction, we mean that they must understand how to relate the events of the real world consciously or unconsciously to universal "cultural values" and to select out those relationships which are significant for us. If the notion that those standpoints can be derived from the "facts themselves" continually recurs, it is due to the naive self-deception of the specialist who is unaware that it is due to the evaluative ideas with which he unconsciously approaches his subject matter, that he has selected from an absolute infinity a tiny portion with the study of which he *concerns* himself. In connection with this selection of individual special "aspects" of the event which always and everywhere occurs, consciously or unconsciously, there also occurs that element of cultural-scientific work which is referred to by the often-heard assertion that the "personal" element of a scientific work is what is really valuable in it, and that personality must be expressed in every work if its existence is to be justified. To be sure, without the investigator's evaluative ideas, there would be no principle of selection of subject-matter and no meaningful knowledge of the concrete reality. Just as without the investigator's conviction regarding the significance of particular cultural facts, every attempt to analyze concrete reality is absolutely meaningless, so the direction of his personal belief, the refraction of values in the prism of his mind, gives direction to his work. And the values to which the scientific genius relates the object of his inquiry may determine, i.e., decide the "conception" of a whole epoch, not only concerning what is regarded as "valuable" but also concerning what is significant or insignificant, "important" or "unimportant" in the phenomena.

Accordingly, cultural science in our sense involves "subjective" presuppositions insofar as it concerns itself only with those components of reality which have some relationship, however indirect, to events to which we attach cultural *significance*. Nonetheless, it is entirely *causal* knowledge exactly in the same sense as the knowledge of significant concrete (*individueller*) natural events which have a qualitative character. . . .

Undoubtedly, all evaluative ideas are "subjective." Between the "historical" interest in a family chronicle and that in the development of the greatest conceivable cultural phenomena which were and are common to a nation or to mankind over long epochs, there exists an infinite gradation of "significance" arranged into an order which differs for each of us. And they are, naturally, historically variable in accordance with the character of the culture and the ideas which rule men's minds. But it obviously does not follow from this that research in the cultural sciences can only have results which are "subjective" in the sense that they are *valid* for one person and not for others. Only the degree to which they interest different persons varies. In other words, the choice of the object of investigation and the extent or depth to which this investigation attempts to penetrate into the infinite causal web are determined by the evaluative ideas which dominate the investigator and his age. In the *method* of investigation, the guiding "point of view" is of great importance for the *construction* of the conceptual scheme which will be used in the investigation. In the mode of their *use*, however, the investigator is obviously bound by the norms of our thought just as much here as elsewhere. For scientific truth is precisely what is *valid* for all who *seek* the truth.

However, there emerges from this the meaninglessness of the idea which prevails occasionally even among historians, namely, that the goal of the cultural sciences, however far it may be from realization, is to construct a closed system of concepts, in which reality is synthesized in some sort of *permanently* and *universally* valid classification and from which it can again be deduced. The stream of immeasurable events flows unendingly towards eternity. The cultural problems which move men form themselves ever anew and in different colors, and the boundaries of that area in the infinite stream of concrete events which acquires meaning and significance for us, i.e., which becomes an "historical individual," are constantly subject to change. The intellectual contexts from which it is viewed and scientifically analyzed shift. The points of departure of the cultural sciences remain changeable throughout the limitless future as long as a Chinese ossification of intellectual life does not render mankind incapable of setting new questions to the eternally inexhaustible flow of life. A systematic science of culture, even only in the sense of a definitive, objectively valid, systematic fixation of the problems which it should treat, would be senseless in itself. Such an attempt could only produce a collection of numerous, specifically particularized, heterogeneous and disparate viewpoints in the light of which reality becomes "culture" through being significant in its unique character.

Having now completed this lengthy discussion, we can finally turn to the question which is *methodologically* relevant in the consideration of the "objectivity" of cultural knowledge. The question is: what is the logical function and structure of the *concepts* which our science, like all others, uses? Restated with special reference to the decisive problem, the question is: what is the significance of *theory* and theoretical conceptualization (*theoretische Begriffsbildung*) for our knowledge of cultural reality? . . .

In the establishment of the propositions of abstract theory, it is only apparently a matter of "deductions" from fundamental psychological motives. Actually, the former are a special case of a kind of concept-construction which is peculiar and to a certain extent, indispensable, to the cultural sciences. It is worthwhile at this point to describe it in further detail since we can thereby approach more closely the fundamental question of the significance of theory in the social sciences. Therewith we leave undiscussed, once and for all, whether *the* particular analytical concepts which we cite or to which we allude as illustrations correspond to the purposes they are to serve, i.e., whether in fact they are well-adapted. The question as to how far, for example, contemporary "abstract theory" should be further elaborated is ultimately also a question of the strategy of science, which must, however concern itself with other problems as well. Even the "theory of marginal utility" is subsumable under a "law of marginal utility."

We have in abstract economic theory an illustration of those synthetic constructs which have been designated as "*ideas*" of historical phenomena. It offers us an ideal picture of events on the commodity-market under conditions of a society organized on the principles of an exchange economy, free competition and rigorously rational conduct. This conceptual pattern brings together certain relationships and events of historical life into a complex, which is conceived as an internally consistent system. Substantively, this construct in itself is like a *utopia* which has been arrived at by the analytical accentuation of certain elements of reality. Its relationship to the empirical data consists solely in the fact that where market-conditioned relationships of the type referred to by the abstract construct are discovered or suspected to exist in reality to some extent, we can make the *characteristic* features of this relationship pragmatically *clear* and *understandable* by reference to an *ideal type*. This procedure can be indispensable for heuristic as well as expository purposes. The ideal typical concept will help to develop our skill in imputation in *research*: it *is* no "hypothesis" but it offers guidance to the construction of hypotheses. It is not a *description* of reality but it aims to give unambiguous means of expression to such a description. It is thus the "idea" of the *historically* given modern society, based on an exchange economy, which is developed for us by quite the same logical principles as are used in constructing the idea of the medieval "city economy" as a "genetic" concept. When we do this, we construct the concept "city economy" not as an average of the economic structures actually existing in all the cities observed but as an *ideal type*. An ideal type is formed by the one-sided *accentuation* of one or more points of view and by the synthesis of a great many diffuse, discrete, more or less present and occasionally absent *concrete individual* phenomena, which are arranged according to those one-sidedly emphasized viewpoints into a unified *analytical* construct (*Gedankenbild*). In its conceptual purity, this mental construct (*Gedankenbild*) cannot be found empirically anywhere in reality. It is a *utopia*. Historical research faces the task of determining in each individual case the extent to which this ideal construct approximates to or diverges from reality, to what extent for example, the economic structure of a certain city is to be classified as a "city economy." When carefully applied, those concepts are particularly useful in research and exposition. In very much the same way one can work the "idea" of "handicraft" into a utopia by arranging certain traits, actually found in an unclear, confused state in the industrial enterprises of the most diverse epochs and countries, into a consistent ideal construct by an accentuation of their essential tendencies. This ideal type is then related to the idea (*Gedankenausdruck*) which one finds expressed there. One can further delineate a society in which all branches of economic and even intellectual activity are governed by maxims which appear to be applications of the same principle which characterizes the ideal-typical "handicraft" system. Furthermore, one can juxtapose alongside the ideal-typical "handicraft" system the antithesis of a correspondingly ideal-typical capitalistic productive system, which has been abstracted out of certain features of modern large scale industry. On the basis of this, one can delineate the utopia of a "capitalistic" culture, i.e., one in which the governing principle is the investment of private capital. This procedure would accentuate certain individual concretely diverse traits of modern material and intellectual culture in its unique aspects into an ideal construct which from our point of view would be completely self-consistent. This would then be the delineation of an *"idea"* of *capitalistic culture*. We must disregard for the moment whether and how this procedure could be carried out. It is possible, or rather, it must be accepted as certain that numerous, indeed a very great many, utopias of this sort can be worked out, of which *none* is like another, and *none* of which can be observed in empirical reality as an actually existing economic system, but *each* of which claims that it is a representation of the "idea" of capitalistic culture. *Each* of these can claim to be a representation of the "idea" of capitalistic culture to the extent that it has really taken certain traits, meaningful in their essential features, from the empirical reality of our culture and brought them together into a unified ideal construct. For those phenomena which interest us as cultural phenomena are interesting to us with respect to very different kinds of evaluative ideas to which we relate them. Inasmuch as the "points of view" from which they can become significant for us are very diverse, the most varied criteria can be applied to the selection of the traits which are to enter into the construction of an ideal-typical view of a particular culture. . . .

The attempts to determine the "real" and the "true" meaning of historical concepts always reappear and never succeed in reaching their goal. Accordingly the synthetic concepts used by historians are either imperfectly defined or, as soon as the elimination of ambiguity is sought for, the concept becomes an abstract ideal type and reveals itself therewith as a theoretical and hence "one-sided" viewpoint which illuminates the aspect of reality with which it can be related. But these concepts are shown to be obviously inappropriate as schema into which reality could be completely *integrated*. For none of those systems of ideas, which are absolutely indispensable in the understanding of those segments of reality which are meaningful at a particular moment, can exhaust its infinite richness. They are all attempts, on the basis of the present state of our knowledge and the available conceptual patterns, to bring order into the chaos of those facts which we have drawn into the field circumscribed by our *interest*. The intellectual apparatus which the past has developed through the analysis, or more truthfully, the analytical rearrangement of the immediately given reality, and through the latter's integration by concepts which correspond to the state of its knowledge and the focus of its interest, is in constant tension with the new knowledge which we can and *desire* to wrest from reality. The progress of cultural science occurs through this conflict. Its result is the perpetual reconstruction of those concepts through which we seek to comprehend reality. The history of the social sciences is and remains a continuous process passing from the attempt to order reality analytically through the construction of concepts—the dissolution of the analytical constructs so constructed through the expansion and shift of the scientific horizon—and the reformulation anew of concepts on the foundations thus transformed. It is not the error of the attempt to construct conceptual systems *in general* which is shown by this process—every science, even simple descriptive history, operates with the conceptual stock-in-trade of its time. Rather, this process shows that in the cultural sciences concept-construction depends on the setting of the problem, and the latter varies with the content of culture itself. The relationship between concept and reality in the cultural sciences involves the transitoriness of all such syntheses. The great attempts at theory-construction in our science were always useful for revealing the limits of the significance of those points of view which provided their foundations. The greatest advances in the sphere of the social sciences are substantively tied up with the shift in practical cultural problems and take the guise of a critique of concept-construction. Adherence to the purpose of this critique and therewith the investigation of the *principles of syntheses* in the social sciences shall be among the primary tasks of our journal. . . .

We are now at the end of this discussion, the only purpose of which was to trace the course of the hair-line which separates science from faith and to make explicit the *meaning* of the quest for social and economic knowledge. The *objective* validity of all empirical knowledge rests exclusively upon the ordering of the given reality according to categories which are *subjective* in a specific sense, namely, in that they present the *presuppositions* of our knowledge and are based on the presupposition of the *value* of those *truths* which empirical knowledge alone is able to give us. The means available to our science offer nothing to those persons to whom this truth is of no value. It should be remembered that the belief in the value of scientific truth is the product of certain cultures and is not a product of man's original nature. Those for whom scientific truth is of no value will seek in vain for some other truth to take the place of science in just those respects in which it is unique, namely, in the provision of concepts and judgments which are neither empirical reality nor reproductions of it but which facilitate its analytical ordering in a valid manner. In the empirical social sciences, as we have seen, the possibility of meaningful knowledge of what is essential for us in the infinite richness of events is bound up with the unremitting application of viewpoints of a specifically particularized character, which, in the last analysis, are oriented on the basis of evaluative ideas. These evaluative ideas are for their part empirically discoverable and analyzable as elements of meaningful human conduct, but their validity can *not* be deduced from empirical data as such. The "objectivity" of the social sciences depends rather on the fact that the empirical data are always related to those evaluative ideas which alone make them worth knowing and the significance of the empirical data is derived from these evaluative ideas. But these data can never become the foundation for the empirically impossible proof of the validity of the evaluative ideas. The belief which we all have in some form or other, in the meta-empirical validity of ultimate and final values, in which the meaning of our existence is rooted, is not incompatible with the incessant changefulness of the concrete viewpoints, from which empirical reality gets its significance. Both these views are, on the contrary, in harmony with each other. Life with its irrational reality and its store of possible meanings is inexhaustible. The *concrete* form in which value-relevance occurs remains perpetually in flux, ever subject to change in the dimly seen future of human culture. The light which emanates from those highest evaluative ideas always falls on an ever changing finite segment of the vast chaotic stream of events, which flows away through time.

Now all this should not be misunderstood to mean that the proper task of the social sciences should be the continual chase for new viewpoints and new analytical constructs. *On the contrary:* nothing should be more sharply emphasized than the proposition that the knowledge of the *cultural significance* of *concrete historical events and patterns* is exclusively and solely the final end which, among other means, concept-construction and the criticism of constructs also seek to serve.

Basic Sociological Terms

MAX WEBER

1. The definition of sociology and of social action

SOCIOLOGY (IN THE SENSE IN WHICH THIS HIGHLY AMBIGUOUS WORD is used here) is a science concerning itself with the interpretive understanding of social action and thereby with a causal explanation of its course and consequences. We shall speak of "action" insofar as the acting individual attaches a subjective meaning to his behavior—be it overt or covert, omission or acquiescence. Action is "social" insofar as its subjective meaning takes account of the behavior of others and is thereby oriented in its course.

A. Methodological Foundations

1. "Meaning" may be of two kinds. The term may refer first to the actual existing meaning in the given concrete case of a particular actor, or to the average or approximate meaning attributable to a given plurality of actors; or secondly to the theoretically conceived *pure type* of subjective meaning attributed to the hypothetical actor or actors in a given type of action. In no case does it refer to an objectively "correct" meaning or one which is "true" in some metaphysical sense. It is this which distinguishes the empirical sciences of action, such as sociology and history, from the dogmatic disciplines in that area, such as jurisprudence, logic, ethics, and esthetics, which seek to ascertain the "true" and "valid" meanings associated with the objects of their investigation.

2. The line between meaningful action and merely reactive behavior to which no subjective meaning is attached, cannot be sharply drawn empirically. A very considerable part of all sociologically relevant behavior, especially

Max Weber, "Basic Sociological Terms," in *Economy and Society*, ed. Guenther Roth and Claus Wittich (New York: Bedminster Press, 1968), 1:4–15, 17–23, 24–26.

purely traditional behavior, is marginal between the two. In the case of some psychophysical processes, meaningful, i.e., subjectively understandable, action is not to be found at all, in others it is discernible only by the psychologist. Many mystical experiences which cannot be adequately communicated in words are, for a person who is not susceptible to such experiences, not fully understandable. At the same time the ability to perform a similar action is not a necessary prerequisite to understanding; "one need not have been Caesar in order to understand Caesar." "Recapturing an experience" is important for accurate understanding, but not an absolute precondition for its interpretation. Understandable and non-understandable components of a process are often intermingled and bound up together.

3. All interpretation of meaning, like all scientific observations, strives for clarity and verifiable accuracy of insight and comprehension (*Evidenz*). The basis for certainty in understanding can be either rational, which can be further subdivided into logical and mathematical, or it can be of an emotionally empathic or artistically appreciative quality. Action is rationally evident chiefly when we attain a completely clear intellectual grasp of the action-elements in their intended context of meaning. Empathic or appreciative accuracy is attained when, through sympathetic participation, we can adequately grasp the emotional context in which the action took place. The highest degree of rational understanding is attained in cases involving the meanings of logically or mathematically related propositions; their meaning may be immediately and unambiguously intelligible. We have a perfectly clear understanding of what it means when somebody employs the proposition $2 \times 2 = 4$ or the Pythagorean theorem in reasoning or argument, or when someone correctly carries out a logical train of reasoning according to our accepted modes of thinking. In the same way we also understand what a person is doing when he tries to achieve certain ends by choosing appropriate means on the basis of the facts of the situation, as experience has accustomed us to interpret them. The interpretation of such rationally purposeful action possesses, for the understanding of the choice of means, the highest degree of verifiable certainty. With a lower degree of certainty, which is, however, adequate for most purposes of explanation, we are able to understand errors, including confusion of problems of the sort that we ourselves are liable to, or the origin of which we can detect by sympathetic self-analysis.

On the other hand, many ultimate ends or values toward which experience shows that human action may be oriented, often cannot be understood completely, though sometimes we are able to grasp them intellectually. The more radically they differ from our own ultimate values, however, the more difficult it is for us to understand them empathically. Depending upon the circumstances of the particular case we must be content either with a purely intellectual understanding of such values or when even that fails, sometimes we must simply accept them as given data. Then we can try to understand the action motivated by them on the basis of whatever opportunities for approximate emotional and intellectual interpretation seem to be available at different points in its course. These difficulties confront, for instance, people not susceptible to unusual acts of religious and charitable zeal, or persons who abhor extreme rationalist fanaticism (such as the fanatic advocacy of the "rights of man").

The more we ourselves are susceptible to such emotional reactions as anxiety, anger, ambition, envy, jealousy, love, enthusiasm, pride, vengeful-ness, loyalty, devotion, and appetites of all sorts, and to the "irrational" conduct which grows out of them, the more readily can we empathize with them. Even when such emotions are found in a degree of intensity of which the observer himself is completely incapable, he can still have a significant degree of emotional understanding of their meaning and can interpret intellectually their influence on the course of action and the selection of means.

For the purposes of a typological scientific analysis it is convenient to treat all irrational, affectually determined elements of behavior as factors of devia-tion from a conceptually pure type of rational action. For example a panic on the stock exchange can be most conveniently analysed by attempting to deter-mine first what the course of action would have been if it had not been influenced by irrational affects; it is then possible to introduce the irrational components as accounting for the observed deviations from this hypothetical course. Similarly, in analysing a political or military campaign it is convenient to determine in the first place what would have been a rational course, given the ends of the participants and adequate knowledge of all the circumstances. Only in this way is it possible to assess the causal significance of irrational factors as accounting for the deviations from this type. The construction of a purely rational course of action in such cases serves the sociologist as a type (ideal type) which has the merit of clear understandability and lack of ambiguity. By comparison with this it is possible to understand the ways in which actual action is influenced by irrational factors of all sorts, such as affects and errors, in that they account for the deviation from the line of conduct which would be expected on the hypothesis that the action were purely rational.

Only in this respect and for these reasons of methodological convenience is the method of sociology "rationalistic." It is naturally not legitimate to inter-pret this procedure as involving a rationalistic bias of sociology, but only as a methodological device. It certainly does not involve a belief in the actual predominance of rational elements in human life, for on the question of how far this predominance does or does not exist, nothing whatever has been said. That there is, however, a danger of rationalistic interpretations where they are out of place cannot be denied. All experience unfortunately confirms the existence of this danger.

4. In all the sciences of human action, account must be taken of processes

and phenomena which are devoid of subjective meaning, in the role of stimuli, results, favoring or hindering circumstances. To be devoid of meaning is not identical with being lifeless or non-human; every artifact, such as for example a machine, can be understood only in terms of the meaning which its production and use have had or were intended to have; a meaning which may derive from a relation to exceedingly various purposes. Without reference to this meaning such an object remains wholly unintelligible. That which is intelligible or understandable about it is thus its relation to human action in the role either of means or of end; a relation of which the actor or actors can be said to have been aware and to which their action has been oriented. Only in terms of such categories is it possible to "understand" objects of this kind. On the other hand processes or conditions, whether they are animate or inanimate, human or non-human, are in the present sense devoid of meaning in so far as they cannot be related to an intended purpose. That is to say they are devoid of meaning if they cannot be related to action in the role of means or ends but constitute only the stimulus, the favoring or hindering circumstances. It may be that the flooding of the Dollart [at the mouth of the Ems river near the Dutch-German border] in 1277 had historical significance as a stimulus to the beginning of certain migrations of considerable importance. Human mortality, indeed the organic life cycle from the helplessness of infancy to that of old age, is naturally of the very greatest sociological importance through the various ways in which human action has been oriented to these facts. To still another category of facts devoid of meaning belong certain psychic or psychophysical phenomena such as fatigue, habituation, memory, etc.; also certain typical states of euphoria under some conditions of ascetic mortification; finally, typical variations in the reactions of individuals according to reaction-time, precision, and other modes. But in the last analysis the same principle applies to these as to other phenomena which are devoid of meaning. Both the actor and the sociologist must accept them as data to be taken into account.

It is possible that future research may be able to discover noninterpretable uniformities underlying what has appeared to be specifically meaningful action, though little has been accomplished in this direction thus far. Thus, for example, differences in hereditary biological constitution, as of "races," would have to be treated by sociology as given data in the same way as the physiological facts of the need of nutrition or the effect of senescence on action. This would be the case if, and insofar as, we had statistically conclusive proof of their influence on sociologically relevant behavior. The recognition of the causal significance of such factors would not in the least alter the specific task of sociological analysis or of that of the other sciences of action, which is the interpretation of action in terms of its subjective meaning. The effect would be only to introduce certain noninterpretable data of the same order as others which are already present, into the complex of subjectively understandable motivation at certain points. (Thus it may come to be known that there are typical relations between the frequency of certain types of teleological orientation of action or of the degree of certain kinds of rationality and the cephalic index or skin color or any other biologically inherited characteristic.)

5. Understanding may be of two kinds: the first is the direct observational understanding of the subjective meaning of a given act as such, including verbal utterances. We thus understand by direct observation, in this case, the meaning of the proposition $2 \times 2 = 4$ when we hear or read it. This is a case of the direct rational understanding of ideas. We also understand an outbreak of anger as manifested by facial expression, exclamations or irrational movements. This is direct observational understanding of irrational emotional reactions. We can understand in a similar observational way the action of a woodcutter or of somebody who reaches for the knob to shut a door or who aims a gun at an animal. This is rational observational understanding of actions.

Understanding may, however, be of another sort, namely explanatory understanding. Thus we understand in terms of *motive* the meaning an actor attaches to the proposition twice two equals four, when he states it or writes it down, in that we understand what makes him do this at precisely this moment and in these circumstances. Understanding in this sense is attained if we know that he is engaged in balancing a ledger or in making a scientific demonstration, or is engaged in some other task of which this particular act would be an appropriate part. This is rational understanding of motivation, which consists in placing the act in an intelligible and more inclusive context of meaning. Thus we understand the chopping of wood or aiming of a gun in terms of motive in addition to direct observation if we know that the woodchopper is working for a wage or is chopping a supply of firewood for his own use or possibly is doing it for recreation. But he might also be working off a fit of rage, an irrational case. Similarly we understand the motive of a person aiming a gun if we know that he has been commanded to shoot as a member of a firing squad, that he is fighting against an enemy, or that he is doing it for revenge. The last is affectually determined and thus in a certain sense irrational. Finally we have a motivational understanding of the outburst of anger if we know that it has been provoked by jealousy, injured pride, or an insult. The last examples are all affectually determined and hence derived from irrational motives. In all the above cases the particular act has been placed in an understandable sequence of motivation, the understanding of which can be treated as an explanation of the actual course of behavior. Thus for a science which is concerned with the subjective meaning of action, explanation requires a grasp of the complex of meaning in which an actual course of understandable action thus interpreted belongs. In all such cases, even where the processes are largely affectual, the subjective meaning of the action, including that also of the relevant meaning complexes, will be called the intended meaning. (This involves a departure from ordinary usage, which speaks of intention in this sense only in the case of rationally purposive action.)

6. In all these cases understanding involves the interpretive grasp of the meaning present in one of the following contexts: (a) as in the historical approach, the actually intended meaning for concrete individual action; or (b) as in cases of sociological mass phenomena, the average of, or an approximation to, the actually intended meaning; or (c) the meaning appropriate to a scientifically formulated pure type (an ideal type) of a common phenomenon. The concepts and "laws" of pure economic theory are examples of this kind of ideal type. They state what course a given type of human action would take if it were strictly rational, unaffected by errors or emotional factors and if, furthermore, it were completely and unequivocally directed to a single end, the maximization of economic advantage. In reality, action takes exactly this course only in unusual cases, as sometimes on the stock exchange; and even then there is usually only an approximation to the ideal type.

Every interpretation attempts to attain clarity and certainty, but no matter how clear an interpretation as such appears to be from the point of view of meaning, it cannot on this account claim to be the causally valid interpretation. On this level it must remain only a peculiarly plausible hypothesis. In the first place the "conscious motives" may well, even to the actor himself, conceal the various "motives" and "repressions" which constitute the real driving force of his action. Thus in such cases even subjectively honest self-analysis has only a relative value. Then it is the task of the sociologist to be aware of this motivational situation and to describe and analyse it, even though it has not actually been concretely part of the conscious intention of the actor; possibly not at all, at least not fully. This is a borderline case of the interpretation of meaning. Secondly, processes of action which seem to an observer to be the same or similar may fit into exceedingly various complexes of motive in the case of the actual actor. Then even though the situations appear superficially to be very similar we must actually understand them or interpret them as very different, perhaps, in terms of meaning, directly opposed. (Simmel, in his *Probleme der Geschichtsphilosophie*, gives a number of examples.) Third, the actors in any given situation are often subject to opposing and conflicting impulses, all of which we are able to understand. In a large number of cases we know from experience it is not possible to arrive at even an approximate estimate of the relative strength of conflicting motives and very often we cannot be certain of our interpretation. Only the actual outcome of the conflict gives a solid basis of judgment.

More generally, verification of subjective interpretation by comparison with the concrete course of events is, as in the case of all hypotheses, indispensable. Unfortunately this type of verification is feasible with relative accuracy only in the few very special cases susceptible of psychological experimentation. In very different degrees of approximation, such verification is also feasible in the limited number of cases of mass phenomena which can be statistically described and unambiguously interpreted. For the rest there remains only the possibility of comparing the largest possible number of historical or contemporary processes which while otherwise similar differ in the one decisive point of their relation to the particular motive or factor the role of which is being investigated. This is a fundamental task of comparative sociology. Often, unfortunately, there is available only the uncertain procedure of the "imaginary experiment" which consists in thinking away certain elements of a chain of motivation and working out the course of action which would then probably ensue, thus arriving at a causal judgment.

For example, the generalization called Gresham's Law is a rationally clear interpretation of human action under certain conditions and under the assumption that it will follow a purely rational course. How far any actual course of action corresponds to this can be verified only by the available statistical evidence for the actual disappearance of under-valued monetary units from circulation. In this case our information serves to demonstrate a high degree of accuracy. The facts of experience were known before the generalization, which was formulated afterwards; but without this successful interpretation our need for causal understanding would evidently be left unsatisfied. On the other hand, without the demonstration that what can here be assumed to be a theoretically adequate interpretation also is in some degree relevant to an actual course of action, a "law," no matter how fully demonstrated theoretically, would be worthless for the understanding of action in the real world. In this case the correspondence between the theoretical interpretation of motivation and its empirical verification is entirely satisfactory and the cases are numerous enough so that verification can be considered established. But to take another example, Eduard Meyer has advanced an ingenious theory of the causal significance of the battles of Marathon, Salamis, and Platea for the development of the cultural peculiarities of Greek, and hence, more generally, Western civilization. This is derived from a meaningful interpretation of certain symptomatic facts having to do with the attitudes of the Greek oracles and prophets towards the Persians. It can only be directly verified by reference to the examples of the conduct of the Persians in cases where they were victorious, as in Jerusalem, Egypt, and Asia Minor, and even this verification must necessarily remain unsatisfactory in certain respects. The striking rational plausibility of the hypothesis must here necessarily be relied on as a support. In very many cases of historical interpretation which seem highly plausible, however, there is not even a possibility of the order of verification which was feasible in this case. Where this is true the interpretation must necessarily remain a hypothesis.

7. A motive is a complex of subjective meaning which seems to the actor himself or to the observer an adequate ground for the conduct in question. The

interpretation of a coherent course of conduct is "subjectively adequate" (or "adequate on the level of meaning"), insofar as, according to our habitual modes of thought and feeling, its component parts taken in their mutual relation are recognized to constitute a "typical" complex of meaning. It is more common to say "correct." The interpretation of a sequence of events will on the other hand be called *causally* adequate insofar as, according to established generalizations from experience, there is a probability that it will always actually occur in the same way. An example of adequacy on the level of meaning in this sense is what is, according to our current norms of calculation or thinking, the correct solution of an arithmetical problem. On the other hand, a causally adequate interpretation of the same phenomenon would concern the statistical probability that, according to verified generalizations from experience, there would be a correct or an erroneous solution of the same problem. This also refers to currently accepted norms but includes taking account of typical errors or of typical confusions. Thus causal explanation depends on being able to determine that there is a probability, which in the rare ideal case can be numerically stated, but is always in some sense calculable, that a given observable event (overt or subjective) will be followed or accompanied by another event.

A correct causal interpretation of a concrete course of action is arrived at when the overt action and the motives have both been correctly apprehended and at the same time their relation has become meaningfully comprehensible. A correct causal interpretation of typical action means that the process which is claimed to be typical is shown to be both adequately grasped on the level of meaning and at the same time the interpretation is to some degree causally adequate. If adequacy in respect to meaning is lacking, then no matter how high the degree of uniformity and how precisely its probability can be numerically determined, it is still an incomprehensible statistical probability, whether we deal with overt or subjective processes. On the other hand, even the most perfect adequacy on the level of meaning has causal significance from a sociological point of view only insofar as there is some kind of proof for the existence of a probability that action in fact normally takes the course which has been held to be meaningful. For this there must be some degree of determinable frequency of approximation to an average or a pure type.

Statistical uniformities constitute understandable types of action, and thus constitute sociological generalizations, only when they can be regarded as manifestations of the understandable subjective meaning of a course of social action. Conversely, formulations of a rational course of subjectively understandable action constitute sociological types of empirical processes only when they can be empirically observed with a significant degree of approximation. By no means is the actual likelihood of the occurrence of a given course of overt action always directly proportional to the clarity of subjective interpretation.

Only actual experience can prove whether this is so in a given case. There are statistics of processes devoid of subjective meaning, such as death rates, phenomena of fatigue, the production rate of machines, the amount of rainfall, in exactly the same sense as there are statistics of meaningful phenomena. But only when the phenomena are meaningful do we speak of sociological statistics. Examples are such cases as crime rates, occupational distributions, price statistics, and statistics of crop acreage. Naturally there are many cases where both components are involved, as in crop statistics.

8. Processes and uniformities which it has here seemed convenient not to designate as sociological phenomena or uniformities because they are not "understandable," are naturally not on that account any the less important. This is true even for sociology in our sense which is restricted to subjectively understandable phenomena—a usage which there is no intention of attempting to impose on anyone else. Such phenomena, however important, are simply treated by a different method from the others; they become conditions, stimuli, furthering or hindering circumstances of action.

9. Action in the sense of subjectively understandable orientation of behavior exists only as the behavior of one or more *individual* human beings. For other cognitive purposes it may be useful or necessary to consider the individual, for instance, as a collection of cells, as a complex of bio-chemical reactions, or to conceive his psychic life as made up of a variety of different elements, however these may be defined. Undoubtedly such procedures yield valuable knowledge of causal relationships. But the behavior of these elements, as expressed in such uniformities, is not subjectively understandable. This is true even of psychic elements because the more precisely they are formulated from a point of view of natural science, the less they are accessible to subjective understanding. This is never the road to interpretation in terms of subjective meaning. On the contrary, both for sociology in the present sense, and for history, the object of cognition is the subjective meaning-complex of action. The behavior of physiological entities such as cells, or of any sort of psychic elements, may at least in principle be observed and an attempt made to derive uniformities from such observations. It is further possible to attempt, with their help, to obtain a causal explanation of individual phenomena, that is, to subsume them under uniformities. But the subjective understanding of action takes the same account of this type of fact and uniformity as of any others not capable of subjective interpretation. (This is true, for example, of physical, astronomical, geological, meteorological, geographical, botanical, zoological, and anatomical facts, of those aspects of psycho-pathology which are devoid of subjective meaning, or of the natural conditions of technological processes.)

For still other cognitive purposes—for instance, juristic ones—or for practical ends, it may on the other hand be convenient or even indispensable to treat social collectivities, such as states, associations, business corporations, foundations, as if they were individual persons. Thus they may be treated as the subjects of rights and duties or as the performers of legally significant actions. But for the subjective interpretation of action in sociological work these collectivities must be treated as *solely* the resultants and modes of organization of the particular acts of individual persons since these alone can be treated as agents in a course of subjectively understandable action. Nevertheless, the sociologist cannot for his purposes afford to ignore these collective concepts derived from other disciplines. For the subjective interpretation of action has at least three important relations to these concepts. In the first place it is often necessary to employ very similar collective concepts, indeed often using the same terms, in order to obtain an intelligible terminology. Thus both in legal terminology and in everyday speech the term "state" is used both for the legal concept of the state and for the phenomena of social action to which its legal rules are relevant. For sociological purposes, however, the phenomenon "the state" does not consist necessarily or even primarily of the elements which are relevant to legal analysis; and for sociological purposes there is no such thing as a collective personality which "acts." When reference is made in a sociological context to a state, a nation, a corporation, a family, or an army corps, or to similar collectivities, what is meant is, on the contrary, *only* a certain kind of development of actual or possible social actions of individual persons. Both because of its precision and because it is established in general usage the juristic concept is taken over, but is used in an entirely different meaning.

Secondly, the subjective interpretation of action must take account of a fundamentally important fact. These concepts of collective entities which are found both in common sense and in juristic and other technical forms of thought, have a meaning in the minds of individual persons, partly as of something actually existing, partly as something with normative authority. This is true not only of judges and officials, but of ordinary private individuals as well. Actors thus in part orient their action to them, and in this role such ideas have a powerful, often a decisive, causal influence on the course of action of real individuals. This is above all true where the ideas involve normative prescription or prohibition. Thus, for instance, one of the important aspects of the existence of a modern state, precisely as a complex of social interaction of individual persons, consists in the fact that the action of various individuals is oriented to the belief that it exists or should exist, thus that its acts and laws are valid in the legal sense. This will be further discussed below. Though extremely pedantic and cumbersome, it would be possible, if purposes of sociological terminology alone were involved, to eliminate such terms entirely, and substitute newly-coined words. This would be possible even though the word "state" is used ordinarily not only to designate the legal concept but also the real process of action. But in the above important connexion, at least, this would naturally be impossible.

Thirdly, it is the method of the so-called "organic" school of sociology —classical example: Schäffle's brilliant work, *Bau und Leben des sozialen Körpers*—to attempt to understand social interaction by using as a point of departure the "whole" within which the individual acts. His action and behavior are then interpreted somewhat in the way that a physiologist would treat the role of an organ of the body in the "economy" of the organism, that is from the point of view of the survival of the latter. (Compare the famous dictum of a well-known physiologist: "Sec. 10. The spleen. Of the spleen, gentlemen, we know nothing. So much for the spleen." Actually, of course, he knew a good deal about the spleen—its position, size, shape, etc.; but he could say nothing about its function, and it was his inability to do this that he called "ignorance.") How far in other disciplines this type of functional analysis of the relation of "parts" to a "whole" can be regarded as definitive cannot be discussed here; but it is well known that the bio-chemical and bio-physical modes of analysis of the organism are on principle opposed to stopping there. For purposes of sociological analysis two things can be said. First this functional frame of reference is convenient for purposes of practical illustration and for provisional orientation. In these respects it is not only useful but indispensable. But at the same time if its cognitive value is overestimated and its concepts illegitimately "reified," it can be highly dangerous. Secondly, in certain circumstances this is the only available way of determining just what processes of social action it is important to understand in order to explain a given phenomenon. But this is only the beginning of sociological analysis as here understood. In the case of social collectivities, precisely as distinguished from organisms, we are in a position to go beyond merely demonstrating functional relationships and uniformities. We can accomplish something which is never attainable in the natural sciences, namely the subjective understanding of the action of the component individuals. The natural sciences on the other hand cannot do this, being limited to the formulation of causal uniformities in objects and events and the explanation of individual facts by applying them. We do not "understand" the behavior of cells, but can only observe the relevant functional relationships and generalize on the basis of these observations. This additional achievement of explanation by interpretive understanding, as distinguished from external observation, is of course attained only at a price—the more hypothetical and fragmentary character of its results. Nevertheless, subjective understanding is the specific characteristic of sociological knowledge. . . .

. . . It is true that we must know what kind of action is functionally necessary for "survival," but even more so for the maintenance of a cultural type and the continuity of the corresponding modes of social action, before it is possible even to inquire how this action has come about and what motives determine it. It is necessary to know what a "king," an "official," an "entrepreneur," a "procurer," or a "magician" does, that is, what kind of typical action, which justifies classifying an individual in one of these categories, is important and relevant for an analysis, before it is possible to undertake the analysis itself. (This is what Rickert means by *Wertbezogenheit*). But it is only this analysis itself which can achieve the sociological understanding of the actions of typically differentiated human (and only human) individuals, and which hence constitutes the specific function of sociology. It is a tremendous misunderstanding to think that an "individualistic" *method* should involve what is in any conceivable sense an individualistic system of *values*. It is as important to avoid this error as the related one which confuses the unavoidable tendency of sociological concepts to assume a rationalistic character with a belief in the predominance of rational motives, or even a positive valuation of rationalism. Even a socialistic economy would have to be understood sociologically in exactly the same kind of "individualistic" terms; that is, in terms of the action of individuals, the types of officials found in it, as would be the case with a system of free exchange analysed in terms of the theory of marginal utility (or a "better," but in this respect similar theory). The real empirical sociological investigation begins with the question: What motives determine and lead the individual members and participants in this socialistic community to behave in such a way that the community came into being in the first place and that it continues to exist? Any form of functional analysis which proceeds from the whole to the parts can accomplish only a preliminary preparation for this investigation—a preparation, the utility and indispensability of which, if properly carried out, is naturally beyond question.

10. It is customary to designate various sociological generalizations, as for example "Gresham's Law," as "laws." These are in fact typical probabilities confirmed by observation to the effect that under certain given conditions an expected course of social action will occur, which is understandable in terms of the typical motives and typical subjective intentions of the actors. These generalizations are both understandable and definite in the highest degree insofar as the typically observed course of action can be understood in terms of the purely rational pursuit of an end, or where for reasons of methodological convenience such a theoretical type can be heuristically employed. In such cases the relations of means and end will be clearly understandable on grounds of experience, particularly where the choice of means was "inevitable." In such cases it is legitimate to assert that insofar as the action was rigorously rational it could not have taken any other course because for technical reasons, given their clearly defined ends, no other means were available to the actors. This very case demonstrates how erroneous it is to regard any kind of psychology as the ultimate foundation of the sociological interpretation of action. The term psychology, to be sure, is today understood in a wide variety of senses. For certain quite specific methodological purposes the type of treatment which attempts to follow the procedures of the natural sciences employs a distinction

between "physical" and "psychic" phenomena which is entirely foreign to the disciplines concerned with human action, at least in the present sense. The results of a type of psychological investigation which employs the methods of the natural sciences in any one of various possible ways may naturally, like the results of any other science, have outstanding significance for sociological problems; indeed this has often happened. But this use of the results of psychology is something quite different from the investigation of human behavior in terms of its subjective meaning. Hence sociology has no closer relationship on a general analytical level to this type of psychology than to any other science. The source of error lies in the concept of the "psychic." It is held that everything which is not physical is *ipso facto* psychic. However, the *meaning* of a train of mathematical reasoning which a person carries out is not in the relevant sense "psychic." Similarly the rational deliberation of an actor as to whether the results of a given proposed course of action will or will not promote certain specific interests, and the corresponding decision, do not become one bit more understandable by taking "psychological" considerations into account. But it is precisely on the basis of such rational assumptions that most of the laws of sociology, including those of economics, are built up. On the other hand, in explaining the irrationalities of action sociologically, that form of psychology which employs the method of subjective understanding undoubtedly can make decisively important contributions. But this does not alter the fundamental methodological situation.

11. We have taken for granted that sociology seeks to formulate type concepts and generalized uniformities of empirical process. This distinguishes it from history, which is oriented to the causal analysis and explanation of individual actions, structures, and personalities possessing cultural significance. The empirical material which underlies the concepts of sociology consists to a very large extent, though by no means exclusively, of the same concrete processes of action which are dealt with by historians. An important consideration in the formulation of sociological concepts and generalizations is the contribution that sociology can make toward the causal explanation of some historically and culturally important phenomenon. As in the case of every generalizing science the abstract character of the concepts of sociology is responsible for the fact that, compared with actual historical reality, they are relatively lacking in fullness of concrete content. To compensate for this disadvantage, sociological analysis can offer a greater precision of concepts. This precision is obtained by striving for the highest possible degree of adequacy on the level of meaning. It has already been repeatedly stressed that this aim can be realized in a particularly high degree in the case of concepts and generalizations which formulate rational processes. But sociological investigation attempts to include in its scope various irrational phenomena, such as prophetic, mystic, and affectual modes of action, formulated in terms of

theoretical concepts which are adequate on the level of meaning. In *all* cases, rational or irrational, sociological analysis both abstracts from reality and at the same time helps us to understand it, in that it shows with what degree of approximation a concrete historical phenomenon can be subsumed under one or more of these concepts. For example, the same historical phenomenon may be in one aspect feudal, in another patrimonial, in another bureaucratic, and in still another charismatic. In order to give a precise meaning to these terms, it is necessary for the sociologist to formulate pure ideal types of the corresponding forms of action which in each case involve the highest possible degree of logical integration by virtue of their complete adequacy on the level of meaning. But precisely because that is true, it is probably seldom if ever that a real phenomenon can be found which corresponds exactly to one of these ideally constructed pure types. The case is similar to a physical reaction which has been calculated on the assumption of an absolute vacuum. Theoretical differentiation (*Kasuistik*) is possible in sociology only in terms of ideal or pure types. It goes without saying that in addition it is convenient for the sociologist from time to time to employ average types of an empirical statistical character, concepts which do not require methodological discussion. But when reference is made to "typical" cases, the term should always be understood, unless otherwise stated, as meaning *ideal* types, which may in turn be rational or irrational as the case may be (thus in economic theory they are always rational), but in any case are always constructed with a view to adequacy on the level of meaning.

It is important to realize that in the sociological field as elsewhere, averages, and hence average types, can be formulated with a relative degree of precision only where they are concerned with differences of degree in respect to action which remains qualitatively the same. Such cases do occur, but in the majority of cases of action important to history or sociology the motives which determine it are qualitatively heterogeneous. Then it is quite impossible to speak of an "average" in the true sense. The ideal types of social action which for instance are used in economic theory are thus unrealistic or abstract in that they always ask what course of action would take place if it were purely rational and oriented to economic ends alone. This construction can be used to aid in the understanding of action not purely economically determined but which involves deviations arising from traditional restraints, affects, errors, and the intrusion of other than economic purposes or considerations. This can take place in two ways. First, in analysing the extent to which in the concrete case, or on the average for a class of cases, the action was in part economically determined along with the other factors. Secondly, by throwing the discrepancy between the actual course of events and the ideal type into relief, the analysis of the non-economic motives actually involved is facilitated. The procedure would be very similar in employing an ideal type of mystical orientation, with its appropriate attitude of indifference to worldly things, as a tool for analysing its consequences for the actor's relation to ordinary life—for instance, to political or economic affairs. The more sharply and precisely the ideal type has been constructed, thus the more abstract and unrealistic in this sense it is, the better it is able to perform its functions in formulating terminology, classifications, and hypotheses. In working out a concrete causal explanation of individual events, the procedure of the historian is essentially the same. Thus in attempting to explain the campaign of 1866, it is indispensable both in the case of Moltke and of Benedek to attempt to construct imaginatively how each, given fully adequate knowledge both of his own situation and of that of his opponent, would have acted. Then it is possible to compare with this the actual course of action and to arrive at a causal explanation of the observed deviations, which will be attributed to such factors as misinformation, strategical errors, logical fallacies, personal temperament, or considerations outside the realm of strategy. Here, too, an ideal-typical construction of rational action is actually employed even though it is not made explicit.

The theoretical concepts of sociology are ideal types not only from the objective point of view, but also in their application to subjective processes. In the great majority of cases actual action goes on in a state of inarticulate half-consciousness or actual unconsciousness of its subjective meaning. The actor is more likely to "be aware" of it in a vague sense than he is to "know" what he is doing or be explicitly self-conscious about it. In most cases his action is governed by impulse or habit. Only occasionally and, in the uniform action of large numbers, often only in the case of a few individuals, is the subjective meaning of the action, whether rational or irrational, brought clearly into consciousness. The ideal type of meaningful action where the meaning is fully conscious and explicit is a marginal case. Every sociological or historical investigation, in applying its analysis to the empirical facts, must take this fact into account. But the difficulty need not prevent the sociologist from systematizing his concepts by the classification of possible types of subjective meaning. That is, he may reason as if action actually proceeded on the basis of clearly self-conscious meaning. The resulting deviation from the concrete facts must continually be kept in mind whenever it is a question of this level of concreteness, and must be carefully studied with reference both to degree and kind. It is often necessary to choose between terms which are either clear or unclear. Those which are clear will, to be sure, have the abstractness of ideal types, but they are none the less preferable for scientific purposes. (On all these questions see " 'Objectivity' in Social Science and Social Policy.")

B. Social Action

1. Social action, which includes both failure to act and passive acquiescence, may be oriented to the past, present, or expected future behavior of

others. Thus it may be motivated by revenge for a past attack, defence against present, or measures of defence against future aggression. The "others" may be individual persons, and may be known to the actor as such, or may constitute an indefinite plurality and may be entirely unknown as individuals. (Thus, money is a means of exchange which the actor accepts in payment because he orients his action to the expectation that a large but unknown number of individuals he is personally unacquainted with will be ready to accept it in exchange on some future occasion.)

2. Not every kind of action, even of overt action, is "social" in the sense of the present discussion. Overt action is non-social if it is oriented solely to the behavior of inanimate objects. Subjective attitudes constitute social action only so far as they are oriented to the behavior of others. For example, religious behavior is not social if it is simply a matter of contemplation or of solitary prayer. The economic activity of an individual is social only if it takes account of the behavior of someone else. Thus very generally it becomes social insofar as the actor assumes that others will respect his actual control over economic goods. Concretely it is social, for instance, if in relation to the actor's own consumption the future wants of others are taken into account and this becomes one consideration affecting the actor's own saving. Or, in another connexion, production may be oriented to the future wants of other people.

3. Not every type of contact of human beings has a social character; this is rather confined to cases where the actor's behavior is meaningfully oriented to that of others. For example, a mere collision of two cyclists may be compared to a natural event. On the other hand, their attempt to avoid hitting each other, or whatever insults, blows, or friendly discussion might follow the collision, would constitute "social action." . . .

2. Types of Social Action

Social action, like all action, may be oriented in four ways. It may be:

(1) *instrumentally rational (zweckrational)*, that is, determined by expectations as to the behavior of objects in the environment and of other human beings; these expectations are used as "conditions" or "means" for the attainment of the actor's own rationally pursued and calculated ends;

(2) *value-rational (wertrational)*, that is, determined by a conscious belief in the value for its own sake of some ethical, aesthetic, religious, or other form of behavior, independently of its prospects of success;

(3) *affectual* (especially emotional), that is, determined by the actor's specific affects and feeling states;

(4) *traditional*, that is, determined by ingrained habituation.

1. Strictly traditional behavior, like the reactive type of imitation discussed above, lies very close to the borderline of what can justifiably be called meaningfully oriented action, and indeed often on the other side. For it is very often a matter of almost automatic reaction to habitual stimuli which guide behavior in a course which has been repeatedly followed. The great bulk of all everyday action to which people have become habitually accustomed approaches this type. Hence, its place in a systematic classification is not merely that of a limiting case because, as will be shown later, attachment to habitual forms can be upheld with varying degrees of self-consciousness and in a variety of senses. In this case the type may shade over into value rationality (*Wertrationalität*).

2. Purely affectual behavior also stands on the borderline of what can be considered "meaningfully" oriented, and often it, too, goes over the line. It may, for instance, consist in an uncontrolled reaction to some exceptional stimulus. It is a case of sublimation when affectually determined action occurs in the form of conscious release of emotional tension. When this happens it is usually well on the road to rationalization in one or the other or both of the above senses.

3. The orientation of value-rational action is distinguished from the affectual type by its clearly self-conscious formulation of the ultimate values governing the action and the consistently planned orientation of its detailed course to these values. At the same time the two types have a common element, namely that the meaning of the action does not lie in the achievement of a result ulterior to it, but in carrying out the specific type of action for its own sake. Action is affectual if it satisfies a need for revenge, sensual gratification, devotion, contemplative bliss, or for working off emotional tensions (irrespective of the level of sublimation).

Examples of pure value-rational orientation would be the actions of persons who, regardless of possible cost to themselves, act to put into practice their convictions of what seems to them to be required by duty, honor, the pursuit of beauty, a religious call, personal loyalty, or the importance of some "cause" no matter in what it consists. In our terminology, value-rational action always involves "commands" or "demands" which, in the actor's opinion, are binding on him. It is only in cases where human action is motivated by the fulfillment of such unconditional demands that it will be called value-rational. This is the case in widely varying degrees, but for the most part only to a relatively slight extent. Nevertheless, it will be shown that the occurrence of this mode of action is important enough to justify its formulation as a distinct type; though it may be remarked that there is no intention here of attempting to formulate in any sense an exhaustive classification of types of action.

4. Action is instrumentally rational (*zweckrational*) when the end, the means, and the secondary results are all rationally taken into account and weighed. This involves rational consideration of alternative means to the end, of the relations of the end to the secondary consequences, and finally

of the relative importance of different possible ends. Determination of action either in affectual or in traditional terms is thus incompatible with this type. Choice between alternative and conflicting ends and results may well be determined in a value-rational manner. In that case, action is instrumentally rational only in respect to the choice of means. On the other hand, the actor may, instead of deciding between alternative and conflicting ends in terms of a rational orientation to a system of values, simply take them as given subjective wants and arrange them in a scale of consciously assessed relative urgency. He may then orient his action to this scale in such a way that they are satisfied as far as possible in order of urgency, as formulated in the principle of "marginal utility." Value-rational action may thus have various different relations to the instrumentally rational action. From the latter point of view, however, value-rationality is always irrational. Indeed, the more the value to which action is oriented is elevated to the status of an absolute value, the more "irrational" in this sense the corresponding action is. For, the more unconditionally the actor devotes himself to this value for its own sake, to pure sentiment or beauty, to absolute goodness or devotion to duty, the less is he influenced by considerations of the consequences of his action. The orientation of action wholly to the rational achievement of ends without relation to fundamental values is, to be sure, essentially only a limiting case.

5. It would be very unusual to find concrete cases of action, especially of social action, which were oriented *only* in one or another of these ways. Furthermore, this classification of the modes of orientation of action is in no sense meant to exhaust the possibilities of the field, but only to formulate in conceptually pure form certain sociologically important types to which actual action is more or less closely approximated or, in much the more common case, which constitute its elements. The usefulness of the classification for the purposes of this investigation can only be judged in terms of its results.

Value-Freedom and Objectivity

TALCOTT PARSONS

MAX WEBER'S INTELLECTUAL HOME, OF COURSE, LAY IN THE 'HISTORISTIC' aftermath of German Idealism as this worked out in the historical schools of jurisprudence, economics, and more generally of culture, e.g. in the work of Dilthey, and of religion as in the work of Troeltsch. The trend was, of course, to stress the internal integration and the historical individuality and uniqueness of the particular cultural system, such as Roman Law, or Renaissance Culture, or indeed 'rational bourgeois capitalism'. The way in which this was done tended to accentuate the dualism already present in the Kantian position between the world of Nature and the world of *Kultur* or *Geist*, involving Kant's 'practical reason', human values and problems of meaning. The cultural and social sciences, dealing with the latter realms, were thereby sharply set off against the natural, not only in terms of empirical subject-matter but also of basic method and mode of conceptualization.

This position not only accentuated a distinction between the two groups of sciences. It went further to structure the relation in favour of protecting the historical-cultural sphere against the encroachments of natural science perspectives and methods. The implication that these were dangerous to human values was certainly present. Closely related to this problem in turn was that of the relation between the individual observer and his subject-matter. As became perhaps particularly clear in the philosophy of Dilthey, the relativity inherent in the conception of the socio-cultural historical individual came to involve the individual because of his involvement in it. There was then, the threat of a socio-cultural solipsism which in some respects was more profound than the individual version propounded by Bishop Berkeley.

The crucial problem from one point of view was that of the source of leverage whereby the individual scholar or scientist, and the scholarly community of which he was a part, could avoid involvement in a closed system from which

Talcott Parsons, "Value-Freedom and Objectivity," in *Max Weber and Sociology Today*, ed. Otto Stammer (New York: Harper & Row, 1971), pp. 29–39.

there was no escape. From some perspectives the difficulty seemed to be insuperable because the understanding of motives and meanings (*Verstehen*), which were shared between observer and object, seemed to be the essence of the cultural disciplines which separated them from the natural. This was, of course, perhaps the most central point at which Weber made his proposals for reformation.

The citing of these difficulties in German historicism—which incidentally have tended to be repeated a half century later in American cultural anthropology—is by no means meant to belittle the major substantive contributions made under the aegis of the 'historical schools' in various disciplines during the relevant period. They did, however, create tensions which were the starting points for Weber's special contribution.

Before attempting to characterize this, I think it will be helpful to sketch briefly the two principal alternatives to historicism which seemed to be most readily available in the intellectual situation of Weber's time. The first of these was relatively foreign to the main German tradition, though constantly close to its centre of awareness. Indeed there was a strong tendency to define the main axis of the differences between German and 'Western' culture in terms of the contrast between the complex just sketched and Western 'rationalism', atomism and various other terms.

In intellectual history this contrast presents too many complexities to enter into here. The most salient elements for present purposes, however, were those centring in British social thought—and American, though the United States was not at the time a very prominent focus of major intellectual movements to a central European. Here the main focus, I think, lies in the broad Utilitarian movement, which had two particularly important characteristics for purposes of the present analysis. The first of these is that it tended to assimilate the natural and the socio-cultural fields to each other rather than, in the German tradition, separating them. The most prominent movement in this direction centred about the development of economics as a theoretical discipline, which had become firmly established in Britain. The same general intellectual framework had much to do with the beginnings of psychology as a science. The level of economics was clearly one of the *Verstehen* of human motives, of the relations of the 'wants' of individuals to the measures taken to secure their satisfaction. In theoretical terms, however, this was a sharply limited range of motives and utilitarianism also remained 'atomistic'—which is to say that it had no theoretical way of establishing relations among individuals other than at the level of means and the situation of action. As such it was unstable and subject to pressures to 'reductionism', the purport of which was that the relevance of the theoretical model of 'natural science' tended to cover over the reduction of man to what was in fact a biological organism or even a physical particle. Considerations such as these seem to be related to the common German tendency to derogate the intellectual merits of utilitarian thought by treating it as merely an ideological expression of the 'materialistic' interest of its proponents. There were, however, profoundly important intellectual problems underlying the difference between German historicism and English utilitarianism.

French social and cultural thought of the time is much more difficult to characterize. On the one hand both positivism and rationalism of important sorts flourished in France. This circumstance is related to the German tendency at that time to treat French *Civilization* as somehow inferior to German *Kultur*. At the same time, as developments of special interest to the sociologist have made clear, there were more readily available openings for a sociological type of development in France than in England, in the more 'collectivistic' strain of French radical rather than conservative thought, i.e. from Rousseau, through St. Simon and Comte to Durkheim and other contemporaries of Weber. It seems fair to say that on the whole the French situation was intermediate between the German and the British and subsequently, though not in Weber's lifetime, came to be an essential intellectual bridge between them.

The second major movement toward which Weber had to assume a position was socialist thought. As by far the most philosophical version and over the long run the most influential, it seems justified to confine attention here to Marxism. Moreover, it was the version dominant in the German intellectual situation of Weber's time, though it should not be forgotten that the split between the Communist and the Social Democratic wings did not occur in time to affect Weber's basic orientation.

In the present frame of reference, Marx presented a peculiar synthesis between the German and British patterns of thinking just outlined, which he could achieve by, in his famous phrase, 'standing Hegel on his head'. I understand this to mean that Marx remained basically within the main frame of reference of German philosophy in this respect, above all in that he accepted a dichotomy which was not identical to that between the cultural and the natural science, but obviously very closely related to it, namely between the two categories of factors operating in the field of human behavior, the *Idealfaktoren* and the *Realfaktoren*. Hegel, as idealist, clearly thought the former to be paramount whereas standing him on his head asserted the primacy of the other set, of the 'material' interests. This could even bring Marx closer to the natural sciences as in a sense the concept 'scientific socialism' suggested, but it still remained within the idealist-historicist frame of reference. It could also make possible a positive use of utilitarian economics, as a scheme for analysing the internal dynamics of the capitalistic system in modified Ricardian terms —though remaining true to historicism, by insisting that economic theory in anything like that sense applied *only* to capitalism. To be sure, finally, Marx stopped short of pure historicism in that he shared with Hegel a teleologically orientated scheme of the evolution of human society and culture as a whole.

My thesis is that these three intellectual movements, with reference in all cases to the problem of the sciences of human social and cultural affairs, defined the co-ordinates of Weber's problem. In fact he achieved a synthesis which, though refusing to accept any one of them on its own terms, ended by incorporating essential elements from all of them into a single frame of reference, and leaning on this, the beginnings of a theory, which was clearly on a level much higher than could be offered by any of these antecedents. Weber's innovations—in which he was not alone, but certainly in most respects pre-eminent, can I think best be put in terms of his 'methodological' conceptions on the one hand, his substantive contribution to social science on the other. This distinction, it seems to me, is roughly equivalent to that between frame of reference and theory in the broad scientific sense.

Weber's Methodology of Social Science

I. Wertfreiheit

The concept of *value-freedom* may be said to be the foundation of his position. It stands in sharp contrast to all three of the above views from which Weber differed. From the historicist perspective the investigator was so firmly ascribed to his cultural position that capacity to transcend it in favour of a new level of objectivity was certainly problematical. From the Marxist point of view this embeddedness in a socio-cultural system, here the class-system, remained, but this time was compounded by the movement's commitment to political action in the name of the implementation of the doctrine's views of the iniquity of capitalism and the prospective glories of socialism. The case of utilitarianism is a bit more complex, for here no clear line was drawn between the grounds of objectivity in empirical judgment on the one hand, and of advocacy of policies on the other, since the latter problem was so far reduced to the level of merely individual preferences.

By contrast with all three, Weber's position is one of a much higher level of differentiation. It is not an advocacy that the social scientist abstain from all value-commitments—for example the position taken in *Wissenschaft als Beruf* makes that entirely clear. The point is rather that *in his role* as scientist a particular subvalue system must be paramount for the investigator, that in which conceptual clarity, consistency and generality on the one hand, empirical accuracy and verifiability on the other are the valued outputs of the process of investigation. But the scientist is never the whole man, and the scientific community is never a whole society. It is as inconceivable that either a person or a society should be exhausted in these terms as that there should be a totally 'economic' man of society. Other value-components are naturally paramount in other roles of individuals and in other subsystems of the society. Value-freedom I thus interpret as freedom to pursue the values of science within the relevant limits, without their being overridden by values either contradictory to or irrelevant to those of scientific investigation. At the same time it involved the renunciation of any claims that the scientist *qua* scientist speaks for a value-position, on a broader basis of social or cultural significance than that of his science. Thus from Weber's point of view such a phrase as 'scientific socialism' is just as unacceptable as 'Christian Science' would be if the term science there were meant in an empirical sense. The policy-orientations of political movements are *never* simple applications of scientific knowledge, but always involve value-components analytically independent of the sciences, natural or social. Value-freedom, furthermore, implies that a science need not be bound to the values of any particular historic culture.

2. Wertbeziehung

Secondly, there is a sense in which the doctrine of *Wertbeziehung* is the obverse of that of *Wertfreiheit*. The latter I have interpreted in the sense of stressing the independence of the role of scientists from other roles. The former may be interpreted as stressing their *inter*dependence. This, above all, seems to be directed against the kind of naïve empiricism, according to which scientific knowledge is held to be simply a 'reflection' of the reality of the external world, whether this empiricism be understood in the more historicist sense of involvement in the particular cultural system itself, or in that of British empiricism with its relations to utilitarianism and to cultural trait-atomism. It is an implication of the differentiation of roles between scientist and other bases of participation in both the cultural and the social systems, that the bases of interest for the posing of problems for a science should be carefully distinguished from the canons of procedure in the solution of those problems, and of the validity of propositions arrived at through following those procedures. Scientific investigation is never purely an occupation of the ivory tower and its products are not 'immaculately conceived'. Values for Weber may in this context be said to constitute the extrascientific source of the scientific 'paternity' by virtue of which 'mother-science' can be fruitful. This doctrine is of course related to a number of considerations. First it may be noted that the scientist himself, as a total human being, must find his commitment to his science meaningful in terms of *his* values—it must be his calling (*Beruf*). But, secondly, science is only in a limiting case a purely individual isolated activity—it must in the nature of the case be socially organized. In this connection it is essential that it should be integrated to a degree to the value-consensus of the community in which it takes place, not totally absorbed, but accorded the kind of place which is essential to its support in a broadly political sense. Without such consensus for example anything like a modern university system would be unthinkable. Contrary, then, to much näive cultural 'isolationism' we can then say that *of course* science, including the socio-cultural science, is oriented in terms of and dependent on the total value systems of the society and culture of the time. This almost follows from the fundamental fact that science is a human enterprise. But as noted, the interdependence is not incompatible with its essential independence.

3. *Causal Explanation and Generalized Theory*

In the above two primary references of Weber's methodology of social science the problem has been that of relation to the wider culture. The next problem I wish to take up concerns a problem internal to the sciences, namely the relation between the status of natural and of cultural science. Here it seems to me that the crucial points are essentially very simple. Weber took very seriously indeed the proposition that *knowledge* in the empirical sense clearly implied the *causal explanation* of phenomena and events. Causal explanation, in turn, is simply not possible unless the particular facts are related, not merely in an historical sequence, but through analysis by means of a generalized theoretical scheme which is in the nature of the case abstract. Very bluntly, the conception of generalized *theory* as has been developed in the great tradition of the natural science is an essential component of *all* empirical science. This includes not merely definitions of generalized concepts, and classificatory schemes, but substantive propositions about the *relations* among abstractly defined variables.

The basic fallacy of 'historicism', if I am correct in interpreting what I take to be Weber's view, was the idea that, through emphatic 'understanding' of the cultural orientations of a system alone, either it was possible to *explain* action within it without reference to any analysis in terms of generalized theory, or explanation itself was thought irrelevant. Weber's position in repudiating both doctrines means that, in *this* crucial sense, there is not 'natural' or 'cultural' science, there is only science or nonscience and all empirical knowledge is scientific in so far as it is valid. It is not possible here to take the space to ground this view—only to state that it was very clearly asserted by Weber, and is of the very first importance. In particular it may be noted that Marxism still adheres basically to a position of historical relativity which is incompatible with Weber's position.

The new thing in Weber, beyond this position itself, was the claim that not only was it methodologically essential, if causal knowledge of value-oriented human action was to be achieved, to develop general analytical theory in the social sciences, but it was entirely feasible, a proposition which had been vehemently denied in the historicist tradition. Indeed Weber himself tackled this task at its very core. This seems to me to have been one primary aspect of the significance of his embarking in the famous series of comparative studies in the sociology of religion. In the essay on the Protestant Ethic he cut into the centre of a major problem of 'historical' explanation. In the older tradition the indicated procedure would have been to delve even more deeply into the specific historical antecedents both of Protestantism and of capitalism in the West. Instead, Weber quite deliberately chose to develop an 'experimental design' by which he studied the negative cases where 'capitalism' had failed, under what he showed to be comparative circumstances,[1] to develop. My essential point is that Weber chose this method not only in order to help to demonstrate his thesis about the relation between Protestantism and capitalism, but *also* to show the importance and the feasibility of generalized analytical theory in the cultural sphere. His most developed product in this respect was the section on the Sociology of Religion in *Wirtschaft und Gesellschaft*. This is elementary theory, but for more than a generation it has been far in advance of anything else in the field. Such propositions as that stating the intimate relations between a religious ethic and the phenomenon of prophecy, or with reference to the dispositions of different kinds of social strata to different religious orientations are examples of the propositional content of this scheme. Indeed there is a sense in which this was the major 'pay-off' of Weber's new orientation, the commitment to and development of a generalized analytical science in the field precisely of the cultural content which the historicist tradition had declared completely inaccessible to such methods. This, essentially, was what Weber meant by sociology as a theoretical discipline.

4. Verstehen

There was, however, one essential component of his methodology which has not yet been treated. Weber, that is to say, had to cope with the doctrine that the methodological dichotomy between nomothetic and ideographic orientations coincided with that between observation of 'external' realities in almost the physical sense and participation with the object of observation through *Verstehen*. It is necessary to discuss this problem briefly in order to complete the methodological picture.

It can, I think, correctly be said that Weber dealt with this problem area as an integral part of his general methodology. First it was essential that he should make clear that *both* the understanding of cultural meaning-systems as such—e.g. mathematical propositions—and of motivational meanings 'intended' by individual actors should be included. Without clarity on this point the essential bridge between cultural levels and those of the concrete actions of individuals could not have been built. The concept of *Verstehen* was, however, also intimately connected with all three of the other methodological doctrines which have just been reviewed.

First, let me suggest an important relation to the concept of *Wertbeziehung*. Not only are the non-scientific values of the investigator himself and his culture involved, but also those of the persons and collectivities which are the object of his investigation. At the level of *Verstehen* scientific investigation is basically a process of meaningful *communication*, even though, where for example the objects are dead, it is a one-way process. In principle, however, it would always be desirable to have the object available for interviews, and taking his written expressions, accounts of him by others, etc., is always second best —thus to be able to interview Brutus about Caesar's death would, from the point of view of certain definitions of that event as an 'historical individual', have been highly desirable.

We can now say that effective communication in human cultural-symbolic terms *always* involved the sharing of values at some level and in some respects. At the same time, however, the values shared in the nature of the case cannot be those of a total cultural *Gestalt*. If this were the case the investigator would be enclosed within a basically solipsistic system, as that problem has been outlined above. What must be conceived to be shared are value-components, which are relevant to the particular investigative problems and are in principle isolable from others of the investigator's own culture. If anything Weber seems to have underestimated the possibilities of extension of understanding on these bases, as some of his remarks on the impossibility of understanding very primitive peoples seem, in the light of the development of anthropology, to indicate. From this point of view *Verstehen*, of course, is both a method and a result of the investigative process. As method it is as noted inherently dependent on the sharing of values and motivational meanings between investigator and object.

The relation of these conditions to value-freedom in turn is patent. *Only* the investigator who is capable of differentiating his role from that of simply a participant in his general culture can attain the perspective and the objectivity necessary to select out those elements which are essential to his scientific purposes from those of his own culture which are irrelevant to it. The science itself, that is, must have its *own* value-system which articulates both in that of the culture in which the investigator participates and in that of the objects he studies. The clear implication is that of a basic *universalism* of values involved in social science, which are not particular to any cultural complex. This seems to point to the grain of truth in Karl Mannheim's well-known doctrine about the special status of the 'free intelligentsia' who were not fully bound into their cultures—however inadequate Mannheim's analysis of this phenomenon. This is a crucial sense in which Weber, as comparative sociologist, *could not* be a radical relativist with respect to values.[2]

If, however, the *Wertbeziehung* of the social-scientific investigator is emancipated from boundness to any particular cultural complex, how is it to be conceived to be controlled by standards of genuine relevance? There is an entirely clear answer in Weber's scheme, namely by virtue of the generality of theoretical conceptualization and of the canons of empirical validity. Science is, precisely, one of the primary elements of a generalized cultural system which is most specifically governed by general norms, the familiar norms of objectivity both in verification of statements of empirical facts, and in logical inference and analysis. Thus once again the central importance of Weber's break with the particularism of the historicist tradition becomes evident. The general loosening up of his methodological position through differentiation keeps leading him back to the view that, if the values of science are to be differentiated from the diffused general value complex, then if their inter-dependence with others in defining relevance, both in the direction of the object observed and the observer himself, is taken into account, and finally if the crucial facts are to be accessible through *Verstehen*, then the process as a whole must be subject to control through general theory of the *logical* type already established in the natural sciences. In *this* crucial respect Weber aligned himself with the basic 'utilitarian' tradition, especially with British economic theory, against both historicism and Marxism. The essential point is the basic *autonomy* of both the special values and the technical theory of science, relative both to the general culture and to the other value-commitments of the investigator, and the priority of these considerations over any particularities of *Verstehen* of particular complexes of meaning or motivation.

In conclusion of this all-too-brief sketch of some problems of Weber's methodological position, I would like to endorse emphatically the view so clearly stated by Professor Henrich that these conceptions of Weber's are couched at the level of the methodology of science, not that of epistemology. Basically Weber is not concerned with the problem of the grounds on which valid empirical science in the field of human meaning and motivated action is or is not possible. He fundamentally takes this for granted. What he presented was an ordered account of the structure of such knowledge and certain of its relations to the more general culture of which it is a part. He was no more concerned with the epistemological problem than is the modern physicist with the question of whether the physical world 'really' exists, or the biologist of whether there is any ultimate difference between living organism and lifeless 'matter'. This is perhaps the most fundamental of all the respects in which Weber carried through a basic *differentiation* of the intellectual tradition from which he started. . . .

NOTES

1. The two studies of religion and society in China and India respectively. The study of Ancient Judaism belongs in a different category.

2. Cf. Dieter Henrich, *Die Einheit der Wissenschaftslehre Max Webers* (Tübingen, 1952).

Discussion

JÜRGEN HABERMAS

IN THE ARGUMENT ABOUT VALUE-JUDGMENTS, MAX WEBER TOOK UP A position which unmistakably allots to the social sciences the task of producing knowledge capable of being utilized technically. Like all strict empirical analytical sciences they should provide information which can be translated into technical recommendations for a choice of means to a particular end. Conditional prognosis or causal explanations presuppose the knowledge of empirical uniformities. A social science suitable for that purpose will develop theories and test the validity of hypotheses with the aim of finding out reliable general rules of social behaviour. As far as required by the subject, the analysis can be facilitated by an understanding of motivation. The aim of this knowledge is however not the understanding of social facts but the causal explanation by means of ordered relationships. In this respect Max Weber accords methodologically subordinate status to the understanding of meaning. Parsons therefore claims with good reason that Weber was interested in knowledge as a part of a general theory of social behaviour. But Weber's interest in knowledge was wider than this.

For the student of Rickert, a cultural science cannot derive its interest from the investigation of empirical regularities. Its questions are not only directed to the analysis of the relative nature of cultural phenomena but also to the explanation of their significance. From this point of view the deduction and verification of hypotheses concerned with laws, from which technical recommendations can be made, lose their value: they form preliminary studies, which as such do not lead us straight to the 'knowledge we are striving for'. The analysis and orderly presentation of the historically given, individual grouping of those factors and the concrete interaction determined by them and significant in its own way, and above all the clarification of the basis and the nature of this significance would be the first task, admittedly to be solved by application of

Jürgen Habermas, "Discussion," in *Max Weber and Sociology Today,* ed. Otto Stammer (New York: Harper & Row, 1971), pp. 59–66.

this preliminary work, but 'completely new and independent of it'.[1] Here it is not the understanding of the meaning, but the explanation which is given a methodologically subordinate status.

My first question to Professor Parsons is this: Does not Max Weber's interest in knowledge, going beyond the production of knowledge which is technically usable, also aim at the explanation of the significance of social processes? Three further questions may clarify this first one. They are concerned in order with the methodological meaning of the three categories which Professor Parsons has rightly distinguished: understanding, value-relativity and value-freedom.

Understanding. Max Weber distinguished the motivational understanding of a subjectively intentioned sense of action from the so-called value-interpretation, related to the significance objectivized in cultural values. In this sense single texts and entire epochs both have 'significance'. Value-interpretation comprises not a real linking but the ideal relationships proper to an evaluated cultural object. It reveals in them the areas capable of objective evaluation and discovers the concrete value-relationships to which an historic object owes its individual meaning. Max Weber can leave this task to the historic-philological sciences, for sociology can find another approach to social realities. It approaches subjectively the meaning of actions and in so doing tends to select hypothetically purposeful actions, governed according to pure maxims of behaviour. A strict social science which 'seeks to observe and understand behaviour and thereby explains its course causally',[2] proceeds by normative analysis, as shown by the example of the theory of mathematical economics.

If, on the contrary, one makes sociology as Parsons does, a strictly empirical analytical science, social roles no longer coincide with a subjectively intended meaning which can be reconstructed in the form of pure maxims. Value-structures and chains of motivation go their separate ways. The understanding of motivation cannot open up the way to these value-structures. Approach to social realities of this kind can only be provided by a hermeneutic understanding in the manner of value-interpretation. If this is so, then the social sciences are burdened with the problem of *Verstehen* inherited from historicism. Parsons supersedes this problem by demanding a universalism of values: the meaning-contents objectivized in value-systems are to consist of elementary value-components, valid for all cultures and all epochs. Therefore my second question to Professor Parsons is this: does a *Verstehende* social science extend beyond the understanding of motivation to the dimension of a hermeneutic adoption of handed-down meaning-contents, for which Max Weber had provided something like value-interpretation?

Wertbeziehung. Rickert tried with the help of this concept to separate culture as the object of the historic-interpretative sciences from the concept of nature.

The historian certainly does not communicate with his subject at sight alone: he fits it inevitably into the value-relationships of his own cultural situation. The transcendental sense of this category is also present in Max Weber: it is not related in the first place to the *choice* of scientific problems, but to the *constitution* of possible objects of cultural-scientific knowledge. Otherwise a firm distinction could not be made between natural and the cultural sciences.

Parsons, who rejects this distinction with regard to sociology, understands the methodological *Wertbeziehung* of the social researcher simply as obligation to the value-system of science. This dictates a strict division between the role of the investigator and the role of the member of a certain society. The cultural-specific values should guide the investigator in the choice of problems but not in the method of their treatment. Obviously in Weber's conception *Wertbeziehung* enters more radically into the methods of the cultural sciences. In the natural sciences the theoretical points of view which guide the course of research are subject to control by the outcome of the research itself: they prove heuristically fruitful or yield nothing from which to educe useful hypotheses. The value-relationships, however, as guides to method in the cultural sciences remain transcendental to research as such: they cannot be corrected by the outcome of the investigation. When the light which had fallen from value-ideas onto the great problems of culture retreats, then the cultural sciences prepare to change their position and their apparatus of concepts, and make towards 'those constellations which alone are capable of giving meaning and direction to their work' (W.L. 214). Sociology owes to this constitutive *Wertbeziehung* its ability to place the causal-analytical knowledge of empirical stereotypes at the service of a more extensive interest in knowledge. 'We want to understand the nature of the reality of environment: the cultural significance of its various phenomena on the one hand, and the reasons for its having historically become thus and not otherwise' (W.L. 170 ff.). Max Weber himself was guided in his historical-sociological research by an idea which was decisive in his construction of concepts and his formation of theories: the idea of the rationalization of all social fields. It has often been remarked that the ideal types for the forms of authority, for the order of procedure in economy and law, for urban settlements and the forms of education are always formed and arranged in accordance with the private philosophy of history, from whose visual angle Weber interprets the whole development of society. This also explains the central position, emphasized by Parsons, of the sociology of law, which displays above all the concept of formal law: a system of general and abstract norms mediates between the purposive exchange between private owners of goods and the bureaucratic exercise of authority of a rational state institution. Even the preference in method, accorded by Max Weber on logical grounds to the model of purposive action, only has any prospect of making empirically substantial hypotheses possible beyond normative-analytical purposes, if that tendency is realized as a general rationalization.

My third question to Professor Parsons therefore is this: does the *Wertbeziehung* which is inevitable in the social sciences in regard to method, extend only to the selection of problems, or does it influence the formation of theories as such?

Value-freedom. Even if we start from the point that the bases of social scientific theories are dependent on general interpretations, without these being refutable according to criteria existing in the empirical sciences, such presuppositions can be explained. *Wertbeziehungen* are at one and the same time methodologically unavoidable and objectively not binding. We are therefore bound to declare the dependence of descriptive pronouncements on premises of normative content. In particular Weber explains the meaning of value-freedom in method in connection with the sociotechnical devaluation of empirical-analytical knowledge. The knowledge of empirical ascertained patterns in social activity lends itself to technical recommendations for a purposeful choice of means, wherein the purposes themselves are merely hypothetical. The postulate of value-freedom is to be taken for granted in scientific theory. There is obvious ground for discussion in the scientific and political aspects connected by Weber with this postulate. He used it in order to restrict the social sciences to a cognitive interest, valid for the production of knowledge which can be utilized technically. The meta-theoretical assertion that this knowledge must have an exclusively descriptive content is scarcely worth our notice. The positivists' claim, however, that sociology's scope should be limited to this, has evoked doubts and protests. I will limit myself here to asking how this scientific-political claim is explained by Weber himself, although it contradicts the type of his own investigation, for instance the hermeneutic intention repeatedly stated: that is, to clarify the cultural significance of historical connections and from them to make the present social situation understandable.

It seems to me that we cannot separate Max Weber's methodology from his general interpretation of the tendencies in development which are relevant for the present time. In this respect we can learn from older researchers into Weber's work, from Löwith, Landshut, and Freyer.[3] Weber took the increasing rational reorganization of the conditions of living as the guide for his analysis: A capitalist economic order, formalized legal procedures and bureaucratic hierarchy form the structures of a society, the institutionally independent spheres of which uniformly comprehend social behaviour. You know how Weber judged the steel-rigid container of this rationalized world we live in. It is precisely the form of organization intended to ensure the purposefulness of behaviour, i.e. to allow an optimal use of means for autonomously posited purposes, which limits the autonomy of individual choice. Max Weber finds the irrationalities of rationalization all collected in bureaucratization. The autocracy of bureaucratic ideals of life lead to the 'dividing up of the soul',[4] to the professional man without intellect and the pleasure-seeker without heart,[5] Weber conjured up a vision of a house of bondage, 'in which man will perhaps be forced to submit weakly, like the fellaheen in the Egyptian state'[6] and then formulated the cultural problem of the present-day thus: 'in view of this overwhelming power of the tendency towards bureaucratization, how is it at all possible to save any remnants of any kind of individual freedom of movement?' Weber's philosophical answer is this: decisionist self-assertion in the midst of a rationalized world: his political answer: scope for a leader, strong-willed and with an instinct for power—scope for the strong politician whose use of the expert civil servant is both authoritarian and rational, and for the private employer, who uses his business similarly.

The 'leader with a machine' is thus the social role which in a partially rationalized society appears to allow subjective purposefulness without the price of a heteronomy of aim. In this context the scientific-political claim of value-freedom also deserves a place. The experiential sciences are in an ambiguous way part of the general process of rationalization. They have disenchanted the world, and have taken away their claim to objective validity from the values and norms which orientate behaviour. Thus they make way first of all for an individual discrimination between subjectivized forces of belief. On the other hand, they too, like bureaucracy, follow the tendency to usurp the scope of decision, having first cleared the way. They must therefore be restricted to function as technical aids. So far as the postulate of value-freedom aims at restricting the social sciences to the production of technically utilizable knowledge, it is analogous to the political claim for protection of the decision-making authority from the competent expert's arrogance.

It is ironical, however, that, as we have seen, this recommendation of a restrictive concept of science rests on an interpretation of developments in the whole of society: an interpretation which, if it is to have validity, presupposes a more pretentious concept of sociology. In his own work Max Weber did not keep within the limits set by positivism: he was, however, in agreement with the Neo-Kantians, positivistic enough not to allow himself to reflect upon the connection between his methodological perspectives and rules, and the results of his social analysis.

My fourth question to Professor Parsons is therefore: how far can methodological decisions, which are obligatory for empirical analytical procedures in the social sciences, be discussed in connection with social processes?

In the same connection I should like to put a further question to the previous speaker, Professor Albert. He stressed the point that the value-free operation of social science not only produces knowledge of empirical patterns but can also be utilized for purposes of criticism. It is beyond doubt that the social sciences can examine accepted value-systems logically, and, in a given situation, also technologically. But does a normative definition of science, in this case in its application to social criticism, depend on the choice made by an individual scholar, or, as Popper thinks, on a choice influenced by a critical tradition—or does it arise simply from natural interest? However that may be, we are always obliged to account for such methodological principles and decisions. As sociologists we should not be afraid of judging those who determine the rules of analysis together with the social process that they analyse. Statements of this kind are not to be found within the bounds of strict empirical science. The business of an ideologically critical examination of the methodology of sociology cannot be relegated to the sociology of knowledge.

Please allow me a final intellectual historical observation. Professor Parsons has claimed that Max Weber's teaching is a development towards bringing about the end of ideology. Weber is said to have broken the trilemma of historicism, utilitarianism and Marxism, and to have led the way into the free field of discussion beyond the European fronts of civil war. I envy our American colleagues their political traditions which permit such a generous and (in the best sense of the word) liberal interpretation of Max Weber.[7] We here in Germany, who are still seeking for alibis, would only too gladly follow them. But Weber's political sociology has had a different history here. At the time of the First World War he outlined a sketch of Caesar-like leader-democracy on the contemporary basis of a national-state imperialism.[8] This militant latter-day liberalism had consequences in the Weimar period which we, and not Weber, must answer for. If we are to judge Weber here and now, we cannot overlook the fact that Carl Schmitt was a 'legitimate pupil' of Weber's.[9] Viewed in the light of the history of influences, the decisionist element in Weber's sociology did not break the spell of ideology, but strengthened it.

NOTES

1. *Gesammelte Aufsätze zur Wissenschaftslehre,* 2nd revised and enlarged edition (Tübingen, 1951; subsequently quoted as W.L.), pp. 174 f.

2. *Grundriss der Sozialökonomik,* vol. III, *Wirtschaft und Gesellschaft,* 2nd enlarged edition, 1st half-volume (Tübingen, 1925), p. 1.

3. K. Löwith, 'Max Weber and Karl Marx', in *Ges. Abhandlungen* (Stuttgart, 1960), pp. 1 ff.; S. Landshut, *Kritik der Soziologie* (Leipzig, 1928); H. Freyer, *Soziologie als Wirklichkeitswissenschaft* (Berlin, 1930).

4. *Gesammelte Aufsätze zur Soziologie und Sozialpolitik* (Tübingen, 1924), p. 414.

5. *Gesammelte Aufsätze zur Religionssoziologie,* vol. I (Tübingen, 1920), p. 204 (cited hereafter as R.S.)

6. *Gesammelte politische Schriften,* 2nd enlarged ed. (Tübingen, 1958), p. 320 (cited hereafter as G.P.S.).

7. Cf. R. Bendix, *Max Weber—An Intellectual Portrait* (New York, 1960).

8. Cf. W. J. Mommsen, *Max Weber und die deutsche Politik* (Tübingen, 1959).

9. Following a friendly piece of advice Professor Habermas said he thought afterwards 'a natural son' of Weber's to be a more appropriate expression.

Suggested Readings

ABEL, Theodore F. *Systematic Sociology in Germany*. New York: Columbia University Press, 1929.

ANDRESKI, Stanislav. "Method and Substantive Theory in Max Weber." *British Journal of Sociology* 15 (1964): 1–18.

BAAR, Carl. "Max Weber and the Process of Social Understanding." *Sociology and Social Research* 51 (1967): 337–46.

BECKER, Howard. *Through Values to Social Interpretation: Essays on Social Contexts, Actions, Types, and Prospects*. Durham, N.C.: Duke University Press, 1950.

BENDIX, Reinhard. *Max Weber: An Intellectual Portrait*. Garden City, N.Y.: Doubleday & Co., 1960.

BENDIX, Reinhard, and Roth, Guenther, eds. *Scholarship and Partisanship: Essays on Max Weber*. Berkeley: University of California Press, 1971.

FREUND, Julien. *The Sociology of Max Weber*. New York: Random House, 1968.

GERTH, H. H., and Mills, C. Wright, eds. *From Max Weber: Essays in Sociology*. New York: Oxford University Press, 1946.

GIDDENS, Anthony. *Politics and Sociology in the Thought of Max Weber*. London: Macmillan, 1972.

HENRICH, Dieter. *Die Einheit der Wissenschaftslehre Max Webers*. Tübingen: Mohr, 1952.

KÖHLER, Wolfgang. *The Place of Value in a World of Facts*. New York: Liveright, 1938.

LOEWENSTEIN, Karl. *Max Weber's Political Ideas in the Perspective of Our Time*. Amherst: University of Massachusetts Press, 1966.

MAYER, J. P. *Max Weber and German Politics: A Study in Political Sociology*. London: Faber and Faber, 1943.

PARSONS, Talcott. *The Social System*. New York: Free Press, 1951.

_____. *The Structure of Social Action*. New York: McGraw-Hill Book Co., 1937.

PARSONS, Talcott, and Shils, Edward A., eds. *Toward a General Theory of Action*. Cambridge, Mass.: Harvard University Press, 1951.

RUNCIMAN, W. G. *A Critique of Max Weber's Philosophy of Social Science*. Cambridge: At the University Press, 1972.

STARK, Werner. "Max Weber and the Heterogony of Purposes." *Social Research* 34 (1967): 249–64.

STRAUSS, Leo. *Natural Right and History*. Chicago: University of Chicago Press, 1953.

SYMPOSIUM. "Max Weber Today." *The International Social Science Journal* 17 (1965): 9–70.

SYMPOSIUM. "Papers on Max Weber." *American Sociological Review* 30 (1965): 171–223.

TUCKER, William T. "Max Weber's *Verstehen.*" *Sociological Quarterly* 6 (1965): 157–65.

WEBER, Max. *The Methodology of the Social Sciences*. Translated and edited by Edward A. Shils and Henry A. Finch. Glencoe, Ill.: Free Press, 1949.

—————. *The Protestant Ethic and the Spirit of Capitalism*. Translated by Talcott Parsons. New York: Scribner's, 1930.

—————. *The Theory of Social and Economic Organization*. Edited with introduction by Talcott Parsons, translated by A. M. Henderson and Talcott Parsons. New York: Oxford University Press, 1947.

PART TWO

The Positivist Reception

Introduction

THE TERM "POSITIVISM" NOW FUNCTIONS MORE AS A POLEMICAL EPITHET than as a designation for a distinct philosophical movement. Even if we leave aside the positive philosophy of Saint-Simon and Comte, the evolutionary positivism of Spencer and Haeckel, and the phenomenalism of Mach and Avenarius, and concentrate on the "logical positivism" of the Vienna Circle and its descendents, it is difficult to specify a common "positivist" perspective. For the subsequent development of the more or less unified program of the original members of the circle has led to its disintegration as a *distinct* philosophical movement. This is not to say that logical positivism has disappeared without a trace; on the contrary, it has been absorbed into such influential traditions as empiricism, pragmatism, and linguistic analysis. The net result is that the "legacy of logical positivism"—a legacy of convictions and attitudes, problems and techniques, concepts and theories—pervades contemporary thought. Methodological positions are most easily identified—because they so identify themselves—with respect to this legacy, pro or con. For our purposes it will be sufficient to indicate a few of the central "positivist" tenets regarding the nature of social inquiry.

The striking developments in the systematic study of the human world —from historiography and philology to sociology and anthropology—that took place in the course of the nineteenth century were generally viewed against the background of the established natural sciences. One or the other of these was usually taken as a paradigm of "scientificity" and a standard against which progress in the human sciences was to be measured. This perspective is also characteristic of the logical positivism of the twentieth century. The original members of the Vienna Circle were, for the most part, neither social scientists nor pure philosophers, but they "had devoted a large part of their academic studies—often including their doctoral work—to logic and mathematics, to physics, or to a combination of these subjects."[1] It was, then, quite natural that their attention was focused for the most part on logic, the foundations of mathematics, and the methodology of the physical sciences and that the social sciences received comparatively little attention from them. While the focus of neopositivism gradually expanded to include the latter, the original commitment to the paradigmatic status of the "exact" sciences remained firm. The characteristic tenets of its approach to social inquiry derive from this commitment.[2]

(1) Regarding the *unity of scientific method*, despite differences in the specific concepts and techniques proper to diverse domains of inquiry, the *methodological procedures* of natural science are applicable to the sciences of man; the *logic* of inquiry is in both cases the same.

(2) More particularly, the goals of inquiry—*explanation and prediction*—are identical, as is the form in which they are realized: *the subsumption of individual cases under hypothetically proposed general laws*. Scientific investigation, whether of social or nonsocial phenomena, aims at the discovery of "law-like" generalizations that can function as premises in deductive explanations and predictions. An event is explained by showing that it occurred in accordance with certain laws of nature as a result of certain particular circumstances. If the laws and circumstances are known, an event can be predicted by employing the same deductive form of argument.

(3) The relation of theory to practice is primarily *technical*. If the appropriate general laws are known and the relevant initial conditions are manipulable, we can produce a desired state of affairs, natural or social. But the question as to which states of affairs are to be produced cannot itself be scientifically resolved. It is ultimately a matter of decision, for no "ought" can be derived from an "is," no "value" from a "fact." Scientific inquiry is itself "*value-free*"; it strives only for objective (that is, intersubjectively testable, value-neutral) results.

(4) The hallmark of scientific knowledge is precisely its *testability* (in principle). To test an hypothesis, we apply deductive logic in order to derive singular observation statements whose falsehood would refute it. Thus the *empirical basis* of science is composed of observation statements (that is, statements referring to publicly observable objects or events) that can be said either to report *perceptual experiences* or, at least, to be motivated by them.

In recent decades, the applicability of these tenets to social inquiry has become a subject of prolonged controversy. Questions concerning the nature and role of interpretive understanding have proved to be of fundamental importance at every point in these epistemological and methodological debates. Those who argue for the distinctiveness of the social from the natural sciences—whether in respect to the existence of general laws, the nature of explanation, the relation to values, the access to data, and so forth—typically base their arguments on the necessity in social inquiry of procedures designed to grasp the "meaning" of social phenomena. Conversely, those defending the methodological unity of the sciences typically proffer a rather low estimate of the importance of *Verstehen* for the logic of the social sciences. It is either rejected as un- or pre-scientific, or analyzed as a "heuristic device" that, while useful, belongs in the anteroom of science proper. The selections by Abel and Rudner exemplify this approach. Despite their different emphases, these authors share a particular conception of the role and nature of *Verstehen* and arrive at similar conclusions regarding its scientific status.

1. *Verstehen* is a procedure employed to gain understanding of individual or group behavior. Faced with an observed sequence of behavior, the social scientist imputes to the agent certain "psychological states" (motives, beliefs, values, emotions) that might account for it. This is basically a matter of postulating "an intervening process 'located' inside the human organism" (Abel), or of "recreating psychological states" (Rudner) in order to make the observed behavior comprehensible.

2. The procedure itself is based on acts of "sympathetic imagination" or "empathetic identification." The social scientist attempts to put himself in his subject's shoes. In his now classic article of 1948, which set the terms for much of the later discussion, Abel breaks this down into three steps: a) internalizing the stimulus, b) internalizing the response, and c) applying a behavior maxim to connect them. Each step is "based on the application of personal experience to observed behavior."

3. This definition of the problem goes a long way toward its resolution. With few exceptions—Scriven, for example—methodologists in this tradition are not prepared to attribute a fundamental methodological role to psychological acts of empathy. So defined, *Verstehen* would, argues Abel, depend upon "personal experience" and "introspective capacity." It could not be a "method of verification," but, at best, a heuristic "aid in preliminary explorations of a subject," with perhaps the additional capacity "to relieve us of a sense of apprehension in connection with behavior that is unfamiliar or unexpected." In the last analysis, the "probability of a connection" can be established "only by means of objective, experimental, and statistical tests." In a similar vein, Rudner assigns the "technique" of *Verstehen* to the heuristic realm of hypothesis formulation or the "context of discovery"; it is not a "method" relevant to the "context of validation." The common result of these analyses is, then, that the employment of interpretive understanding does not affect the *logic* of social inquiry; as a merely heuristic device it furnishes no grounds for distinguishing the latter from the logic of the natural sciences.

Charles Taylor's discussion of interpretation challenges this account at every point. *Verstehen* has to do not with "inner-organic," "psychological" states, but with "intersubjective meanings" that are constitutive of social life. These are not grasped through acts of empathy, but through procedures not unlike those employed in the hermeneutic interpretation of texts. And the logic of such interpretation is markedly different from that obtaining in the investigation of nonsocial phenomena. In particular, hermeneutic understanding is inextricably involved in a "circle" of readings (of texts or expressions), a circle that cannot be broken by appeal to "brute data" of any kind. A reading can be corrected only by other readings. Thus, interpretive understanding "cannot meet the requirements of intersubjective, non-arbitrary verification" that the neopositivists consider essential to science.

The student of social life is not confronted merely with observable sequences of uninterpreted behavior which he must then subsume under general laws. Since man is a "self-interpreting" animal, "what is interpreted is itself an interpretation; a self-interpretation which is embedded in a stream of action." The agent experiences his situation "in terms of certain meanings"; the "explanation" we seek is "one which 'makes sense' of his behavior, which shows a coherence of meaning." But these meanings are not merely subjective meanings "located" in the mind of the agent; they are in large part "the common property of the society," "intersubjective meanings which are constitutive of the social matrix in which individuals find themselves and act." They cannot be grasped with the methods analyzed and universalized in the positivist tradition. Rather, they are the object of a hermeneutic science that requires of its practitioners "a certain measure of insight." And insights may differ, not only owing to divergent theoretical positions, but as a result of "different fundamental options in life" as well. Taylor's hermeneutic interpreter has little in common with the value-neutral observer of behavioral science.[3]

NOTES

1. Carl G. Hempel, "Logical Positivism and the Social Sciences," in *The Legacy of Logical Positivism*, ed. Peter Achinstein and Stephen F. Barker (Baltimore: Johns Hopkins Press, 1969), p. 163.

2. The sketch that follows ignores the controversies that have developed around most of the points mentioned, in particular questions concerning the structure of explanation and its relation to prediction, issues in confirmation theory, and difficulties in specifying the nature and function of the empirical basis. But the position presented here has served as the point of reference for these controversies and is no less influential for having been the subject of prolonged debate.

3. Cf. Karl-Otto Apel's essay in Part 5 for additional critical reflections on the neopositivist logic of "unified science."

The Operation Called *Verstehen*[1]

THEODORE ABEL

ABSTRACT

The postulate of *Verstehen* is the main argument of social theorists who assert the existence of a dichotomy between the physical and the social sciences. An analysis of the operation of *Verstehen* shows that it does not provide new knowledge and that it cannot be used as a means of verification. Lacking the fundamental attributes of scientific method, even though it does perform some auxiliary functions in research, the fact of *Verstehen* cannot be used to validate the assumption of a dichotomy of the sciences.

THE ADVOCATES OF VERSTEHEN DEFINE IT AS A SINGULAR FORM OF operation which we perform whenever we attempt to explain human behavior. The idea behind this claim is by no means of German origin. Long before Dilthey and Weber, Vico acclaimed mathematics and human history as subjects about which we have a special kind of knowledge. This he attributed to the fact that the abstractions and fictions of mathematics are created by us, while history, too, is "made by men." He claimed that human beings can possess a type of knowledge concerning things they themselves produce which is not obtainable about the phenomena of nature.

Comte, too, implied that a special procedure is involved in the interpretation of human behavior. He held that the methods used in sociology embrace not only observation and experiment but a further process of verification which makes use of what he vaguely referred to as "our knowledge of human nature." According to him, empirical generalizations about human behavior are not valid unless they are in accord with our knowledge of human nature. Comte was the first to establish what may be termed "the postulate of *Verstehen*" for

Theodore Abel, "The Operation Called *Verstehen*," *The American Journal of Sociology* 54 (1948): 211–18. © 1948 by the University of Chicago. All rights reserved.

sociological research, for he asserted that no sociological demonstration is complete until the conclusions of historical and statistical analyses are in harmony with the "laws of human nature."

In the American sociological field Cooley is the outstanding protagonist of the idea that we understand the human and the social in ways different from those in which we understand the material. His theory is that we can understand the behavior of human beings by being able to share their "state of mind." This ability to share other people's minds is a special knowledge, distinct from the kind of perception gleaned from tests and statistics. Statistical knowledge without "emphatic" knowledge is superficial and unintelligent. Between the two, Cooley claims, "there is a difference in kind which it would be fatuous to overlook."[2]

The notion of *Verstehen* is included in Znaniecki's concept of the "humanistic coefficient" and particularly in the role he ascribes to "vicarious experience" as a source of sociological data. According to Znaniecki, vicarious experience enables the student of human behavior "to gain a specific kind of information which the natural experimenter . . . ignores altogether."[3]

Similarly, Sorokin stresses the need for *Verstehen* when he insists that the causal-functional method is not applicable to the interpretation of cultural phenomena. He points out that the social sciences must employ the logico-meaningful method which enables us to perceive connections which "are much more intimately comprehensible, more readily perceived, than are causal-functional unities."[4]

MacIver, too, speaks of a special method which must be used whenever we study social causation. He calls this process "imaginative reconstruction." He claims the causal formula of classical mechanics cannot be applied to human behavior. However, the student of human behavior will find this compensated for by "the advantage that some of the factors operative in social causation are understandable as causes; are validated as causal by our own experience."[5]

As these brief references indicate, there is no dearth of tradition and authority behind the idea of *Verstehen*.[6] It is, therefore, surprising to find that, while many social scientists have eloquently discoursed on the existence of a special method in the study of human behavior, none has taken the trouble to describe the nature of this method. They have given it various names; they have insisted on its use; they have pointed to it as a special kind of operation which has no counterpart in the physical sciences; and they have extolled its superiority as a process of giving insight unobtainable by any other methods. Yet the advocates of *Verstehen* have continually neglected to specify how this operation of "understanding" is performed—and what is singular about it. What, exactly, do we do when we say we practice *Verstehen*? What significance can we give to results achieved by *Verstehen*? Unless the operation is clearly defined, *Verstehen* is but a vague notion, and, without being dogmatic, we are unable to ascertain how much validity can be attributed to the results achieved by it.

I. The Operation Illustrated

Our first task is to ascertain the formula according to which the operation of *Verstehen* is performed. To do so, we had best examine a few illustrations of behavior analysis. For this purpose we shall use three examples: the first will deal with a single case; the second, with a generalization; and the third, with a statistical regularity.

Case I.—Last April 15 a freezing spell suddenly set in, causing a temperature drop from 60 to 34 degrees. I saw my neighbor rise from his desk by the window, walk to the woodshed, pick up an ax, and chop some wood. I then observed him carrying the wood into the house and placing it in the fireplace. After he had lighted the wood, he sat down at his desk and resumed his daily task of writing.

From these observations I concluded that, while working, my neighbor began to feel chilly and, in order to get warm, lighted a fire. This conclusion has all the earmarks of an "obvious fact." Yet it is obvious only because I have fitted the action of my neighbor into a sequential pattern by assuming that the stimulus "drop in temperature" induced the response "making a fire." Since I recognize a relevant connection between the response and the stimulus, I state that I understand the behavior of my neighbor. I may even say that I am certain of it ("The case is obvious"), provided I note carefully to what this certainty refers. I *cannot* be certain that this is the *correct* or true explanation of his conduct. To be sure my explanation is correct, I need additional information. I can go over to him and ask him why he lighted the fire. He may confirm my interpretation. However, I cannot stop there. Suppose he has another, hidden, intention? He may be expecting a guest and wish to show off his fireplace. Or suppose he himself is not aware of the "true" motive? Perhaps he was impelled by a subconscious motive of wanting to burn down his house so as to punish the fellow who harasses him about paying off the mortgage. If so, his lighting the fire would have a symbolic function. Of what, then, am I certain? I am certain only that my interpretation *could* be correct.

Hence, *Verstehen* gives me the certainty that a given interpretation of behavior is a possible one. I *know* that it can happen this way, even though I cannot be certain that such was the case in this instance. My interpretation in itself is not a hypothesis; only its application to the stated case is hypothetical.

Whence comes this certainty that I achieve through *Verstehen*? Since the case is simple, the answer is simple: I have enacted it myself. Feeling chilled, I have gathered wood and lighted a fire; therefore, I *know*. The sense of relevance is the result of personal experience; the connection has been established by me before, so I am *certain* of its possibility.

However, the answer as stated does not give us a clear picture of the operation the act of *Verstehen* involves. It will, therefore, be necessary to schematize the evidence and show the steps taken to perform the operation.

Two sets of observations are given in our example. First, there is a sequence of bodily movement (chopping wood, lighting a fire, etc.); second, there is a thermometer reading of a near-freezing temperature. The act of *Verstehen* links these two facts into the conclusion that the freezing weather was the stimulus which set off the response "making a fire." An elementary examination shows that three items of information are utilized to reach this conclusion:

1. Low temperature (A) reduces the temperature of the body (B).
2. Heat is produced (C) by making a fire (D).
3. A person "feeling cold" (B') will "seek warmth" (C').

Through this interpretation the three items are linked together as follows:

$$A\!-\!B \qquad C\!-\!D$$
$$B'\!-\!C'$$

We immediately recognize the third item as the significant element of the interpretation. The two conditions (A–B), together with their known consequences (C–D), are disparate facts. We link them into a sequence and state that C–D is the consequence of A–B by "translating" B and C into feeling-states of a human organism, namely, B' and C'. Introducing these intervening factors enables us to apply a generalization concerning the function of the organism (behavior maxim), from which we deduce the drop in temperature as a possible "cause" of my neighbor's behavior.

By specifying the steps which are implicit in the interpretation of our case, we have brought out two particulars which are characteristic of the act of *Verstehen*. One is the "internalizing" of observed factors in a given situation; the other is the application of a behavior maxim which makes the connection between these factors relevant. Thus we "understand" a given human action if we can apply to it a generalization based upon personal experience. We can apply such a rule of behavior if we are able to "internalize" the facts of the situation.

These propositions require further elucidation, but, before we attempt this, let us consider two other examples of behavior analysis.

Case 2.—In one of Lundberg's articles we find the following generalization:

> Faced by the insecurity of a changing and hostile world, we seek security by creating "eternal verities" in our thoughts. The more inadequate we feel, the more we indulge in this type of wishful thinking. Conversely, as the clergy has always complained, in times of prosperity and security, man tends to neglect his gods. It has been suggested that the Platonic preference for the changeless may be due to the fact that the Greeks did not have a mathematical technique such as the calculus for dealing with modes and rates of change.[7]

The opening sentence of this quotation asserts a relevant connection between "belief in eternal verities" (verbal response) and "a changing and hostile world" (stimulus). The subsequent sentences hint at a possible statistical basis for the generalization and cite two historical examples as illustrations. Clearly there is insufficient evidence to substantiate the validity of the interpretation as a tendency in some of us toward idealistic philosophy. We can recognize, though, that the connection asserted by the generalization is relevant; that is, we "understand" it, and so consider it possible.

The act of *Verstehen* which is implied here involves the same operation we have observed in the first example. We internalize "change and hostility" (B), which we observe to be an attribute of "the world" (A), into "feeling of inadequacy" (B'). The connotation "changeless" (C), which the concept "eternal verities" (D) implies, we internalize into "feeling of security" (C'). Having thus internalized the situation, we can now apply the behavior maxim that a person who feels inadequate (when facing change) will seek security (in something changeless). This procedure provides the mediating links $B'-C'$, which enable us to "understand," or recognize, the relevancy of the causal connection brought out in the generalization.

Case 3.—Competent statistical research has established a high correlation $(r=.93)$ between the annual rate of crop production and the rate of marriage in a given year. There are, of course, statistical methods for proving whether or not this correlation is spurious. In this case, however, we feel that we can forego such tests because the correlation as such does not present a problem to us. We regard the connection as relevant; in short, we say we "understand" why the rate of marriage in farming districts closely follows the rate of crop production.

The act of *Verstehen* which this reasoning implies can be shown to involve the same procedure we have observed in the other examples. We use as items of information the fact that failure of crops (A) materially lowers the farmer's income (B) and the fact that one is making new commitments (C) when one marries (D). We then internalize B into "feeling of anxiety" (B'), and C—since the behavior in question is "postponement of marriage"—into "fear of new commitments" (C'). We are now able to apply the behavior maxim: "People who experience anxiety will fear new commitments" $(B'-C')$. Since we can fit the fact of fewer marriages when crops fail into this rule, we say we "understand" the correlation.

II. The Operation Analyzed

The examples show that the characteristic feature of the operation of *Verstehen* is the postulation of an intervening process "located" inside the human organism, by means of which we recognize an observed—or assumed—connection as relevant or "meaningful." *Verstehen*, then, consists of the act of bringing to the foreground the inner-organic sequence intervening between a stimulus and a response.

The examples also suggest that there are special conditions which determine the need for making the intervening process explicit. Some connections appear to be obvious; that is, we recognize their relevancy instantaneously and without any awareness of the implicit assumptions upon which the recognition is based. These are usually connections of which we have direct knowledge, because we ourselves established such connections in the past; or they are connections we have previously examined, so that their occurrence is accepted as an expected or familiar happening.

The need for making the intervening process explicit arises whenever behavior is not routine or commonplace. This is clearly the case when we are puzzled. For example, when we were confronted with the evidence that in army units in which promotion was easy there was much more griping about "injustice" than in those units in which very few were promoted, we were puzzled. We would expect the contrary. It is only by internalizing the situation—namely, by introducing the intervening factor of "expectation"—that we are able to understand the connection. If we then assume that in units in which promotion is easy there will be greater expectation of promotion, we can apply the behavior maxim: "The higher one's expectations, the greater one's disappointment if those expectations are not fulfilled." This enables us to "understand" the seemingly paradoxical behavior.

Another condition for making the intervening inner-organic sequence explicit arises whenever we are called upon to explain the reason for asserting a connection between occurrences. This is particularly so when no experimental or statistical data are available and recourse is taken to arguments in support of an interpretation. This happens frequently when interpretations of individual historical events are attempted, as, for example, establishing the cause of a war. Here the behavior in question can be related to earlier events solely on the basis that in terms of assumed feeling-states such a relation is a plausible one.

As has been indicated, the operation of *Verstehen* involves three steps: (1) internalizing the stimulus, (2) internalizing the response, and (3) applying behavior maxims. The questions now arise as to how to go about the process of internalizing and where we get our knowledge of behavior maxims.

1. Internalizing the Stimulus

To the best of my knowledge, no one has yet specified a technique by which we can objectively attribute certain feeling-states to persons faced by a particular situation or event. The arbitrary procedure we employ to internalize a stimulus consists of *imagining* what emotions may have been aroused by the impact of a given situation or event. Sometimes we are able to employ definite clues which we have gathered while observing the impact. These may have been gestures, facial expressions, or exclamations or comments. Where there are no such clues, we note the effect produced by an event or situation. Then we imagine how we would have been affected by such an impact. For example, not being a farmer, I never experienced the consequence of crop failure. However, observing that its effect is a curtailment of income, I attribute to the farmer a feeling of anxiety which I recall having felt—or imagine I might feel—under similar circumstances. Thus the internalizing of a stimulus depends largely upon our ability to describe a situation or event by categorizing it and evoking a personal experience which fits into that category.

2. Internalizing the Response

Here, too, no specific techniques are known which permit a definite association between feeling-states and observed behavior. All that can again be said is that we use our imagination when we ascribe a motive to a person's behavior— for example, "fear of new commitments" as the reason for postponing marriage; or, in another instance, when we view the behavior as expressive of some emotion—namely, when we infer that the "griping" of soldiers over promotions evokes a feeling of disappointment. We generally infer the motive of an act from the known or observed modification it produces. If we express this consequence of an act in general terms, we can utilize our personal experience with motives or feelings we had when we ourselves acted in order to produce a similar result.

In cases where both stimulus and response are stated, imagination is facilitated by the fact that both can be viewed as part of a complete situation. This enables us to relate to each other whatever inferences we make about the stimulus and the response. We then select the inferences which "fit" one another in such a way that the given behavior can be recognized as the "solution" (release of tension) of the "problem" (tension experience) created by the impact of the stated event.

3. Behavior Maxims

The generalizations which we call "behavior maxims" link two feeling-states together in a uniform sequence and imply a functional dependence between them. In the cases cited it can be seen that the functional dependence consists of the fact that the feeling-state we ascribe to a given human action is *directed* by the feeling-state we presume is evoked by an impinging situation or event. Anxiety directs caution; a feeling of cold, the seeking of warmth; a feeling of insecurity, a desire for something that will provide reassurance.

Behavior maxims are not recorded in any textbooks on human behavior. In fact, they can be constructed *ad hoc* and be acceptable to us as propositions even though they have not been established experimentally. The relation asserted appears to us as self-evident.

This peculiarity of behavior maxims can be accounted for only by the assumption that they are generalizations of direct personal experience derived from introspection and self-observation. Such personal experiences appear originally in the form of what Alexander has called "emotional syllogisms." He has this to say about them:

> Our understanding of psychological connections is based on the tacit recognition of certain causal relationships which we know from everyday experience and the validity of which we accept as self-evident. We understand anger and aggressive behavior as a reaction to an attack; fear and guilt as results of aggressiveness; envy as an outgrowth of the feeling of weakness and inadequacy. Such self-evident connections as "I hate him because he attacks me" I shall call emotional syllogisms. The feeling of the self-evident validity of these emotional connections is derived from daily introspective experiences as we witness the emotional sequences in ourselves . . . Just as the logic of intellectual thinking is based on repeated and accumulated experiences of relations in the external world, the logic of emotions is based on the accumulated experiences of our own emotional reactions.[8]

Emotional syllogisms when stated in the form of general propositions are behavior maxims. This explains their familiar ring and accounts for the facility with which they can be formulated. In generalizing emotional syllogisms we proceed on the assumption that the emotions of others function similarly to our own.

We find, then, that in all its essential features the operation of *Verstehen* is based upon the application of personal experience to observed behavior. We "understand" an observed or assumed connection if we are able to parallel either one with something we know through self-observation does happen. Furthermore, since the operation consists of the application of knowledge we already possess, it cannot serve as a means of discovery. At best it can only confirm what we already know.

III. The Operation Evaluated

From the foregoing description of the operation of *Verstehen* we can draw several inferences as to its limitations and possibilities. The most obvious limitation of the operation is its dependence upon knowledge derived from personal experience. The ability to define behavior will vary with the amount and quality of the personal experience and the introspective capacity of the interpreter. It will also depend upon his ability to generalize his experiences. In some cases it may be possible to secure objective data on the basis of which the verification of an interpretation can be approximated. However, owing to the relative inaccessibility of emotional experiences, most interpretations will remain mere expressions of opinion, subject only to the "test" of plausibility.

Regardless of the relative ability of people to use it, a second limitation to the use of the operation itself lies in the fact that it is *not a method of verification*. This means that what in the realm of scientific research we consider a quality of crucial importance is not an attribute of the operation of *Verstehen*.

When we say we "understand" a connection, we imply nothing more than recognizing it as a possible one. We simply affirm that we have at least once in direct experience observed and established the connection or its equivalent. But from the affirmation of a possible connection we cannot conclude that it is also probable. From the point of view of *Verstehen* alone, any connection that is possible is *equally* certain. In any given case the test of the actual probability calls for the application of objective methods of observation; e.g., experiments, comparative studies, statistical operations of mass data, etc. We do not accept the fact that farmers postpone intended marriages when faced with crop failures because we can "understand" the connection. It is acceptable to us because we have found through reliable statistical operations that the correlation between the rate of marriage and the rate of crop production is extremely high. We would continue to accept the fact even if we could not "understand" it. In this instance the operation of *Verstehen* does no more than relieve us of a sense of apprehension which would undoubtedly haunt us if we were unable to understand the connection.

The postulate of *Verstehen* can now be viewed from a proper perspective. It cannot be made to imply that if we do not "understand" a connection it surely, or most probably, is false. It does, however, imply that our curiosity concerning human behavior does not rest until we have in some way been able to relate it to our personal experience. The satisfaction of curiosity produces subjective increment but adds nothing to the objective validity of a proposition. Thus, all assertions based solely on the evidence of "understandability" can be viewed as cases of "misplaced familiarity."

These limitations virtually preclude the use of the operation of *Verstehen* as a scientific tool of analysis. Still there is one positive function which the operation can perform in scientific investigations: It can serve as an aid in preliminary explorations of a subject. Furthermore, the operation can be particularly helpful in setting up hypotheses, even though it cannot be used to test them.

In dealing with human behavior, we create hypotheses whenever we ask for the "stimulus" which produced a given response, or when we attempt to predict what "response" will follow from a given occurrence. It is an accepted fact that, in formulating hypotheses, we start with some "hunch" or "intuition." Now it appears highly probable that the hunches which lead us to certain hypotheses concerning human behavior originate from the application of the operation of *Verstehen*. This follows from the fact that the operation—in addition to using the stated stimulus or response—allows the use of another item of knowledge (a behavior maxim), which permits us to "reach out" from a given observation to its unknown counterpart. The diagram representing the reasoning about the neighbor seen chopping wood clearly indicates how behavior maxims can serve as a source of "hunches." Suppose C–D were given as an item of observation. By internalizing C, we obtain C', to which we can then apply a behavior maxim, which gives us B'. B', in turn, provides a clue to the nature of the situation or event which may be the possible stimulus (A–B) to the behavior in question. Lundberg's generalization (Case 2) is an example of a hypothesis derived in this fashion. By postulating that people who assert "eternal verities" are seeking security, he inferred a strong feeling of anxiety as the counterpart to this motive. He then surmised that the "changing and hostile world" might be the anxiety-producing condition. A "hunch" similarly reached was used by Durkheim in his study of suicide. When he found the rate of suicide varying in different groups, he was confronted by the problem of selecting the most likely determinant from a multitude of attributes of group life. From Merton's statement of the "paradigm of Durkheim's theoretic analysis," we can infer that Durkheim first internalized rates of suicide as "functions of unrelieved anxieties and stresses to which persons are subjected."[9] He then viewed such emotional states as the result of a lack of "psychic support," such as is provided by intimate associations with others. This suggested the possibility of social cohesion being the crucial factor which determines the characteristic rate of suicide in a group. Subsequent investigations established a high degree of probability for this inference because Durkheim was able to show that the rate of suicide varies consistently in inverse ratio with the degree of group coherence.

By reversing the procedure, we arrive at hunches about possible responses to given or expected occurrences. That is, we internalize the situation by projecting it as a problem experience and then, by means of a behavior maxim, infer the problem-solving response (intention). However, to guess the particular form the response will take requires information which the operation of *Verstehen* does not provide. It would not, for example, be of use in trying to conjecture specific ways and means of aggression which may be employed by a group in response to a provocation by another group. The operation gives us "hunches," and it points out the general character of possible factors, but it does not enable us to evaluate probabilities.

The findings with regard to the operation of *Verstehen* may be summarized in the following propositions:

The operation of *Verstehen* is performed by analyzing a behavior situation in such a way—usually in terms of general "feeling-states" —that it parallels some personal experience of the interpreter.

Primarily the operation of *Verstehen* does two things: It relieves us of a sense of apprehension in connection with behavior that is unfamiliar or unexpected and it is a source of "hunches," which help us in the formulation of hypotheses.

The operation of *Verstehen* does not, however, add to our store of knowledge, because it consists of the application of knowledge already validated by personal experience; nor does it serve as a means of verification. The probability of a connection can be ascertained only by means of objective, experimental, and statistical tests.

NOTES

1. To avoid confusion, we prefer to use the German term instead of its English equivalent, which is "understanding." Understanding is a general term approximating the German *Begreifen* and does not convey the specific meaning intended by the term *Verstehen*, which implies a particular kind of understanding, applicable primarily to human behavior. Understanding is synonymous with comprehension, and Lundberg is perfectly right when he asserts (in *Foundations of Sociology* [New York: Macmillan Co., 1939], p. 51) that "understanding is the end at which all methods aim, rather than a method in itself." In this sense "understanding" is the goal of all sciences. *Verstehen*, on the other hand, is viewed by its proponents as a method by means of which we can explain human behavior. The purpose of this paper is to clarify this point and evaluate its significance.

2. H. E. Cooley, *Sociological Theory and Social Research* (New York: Scribner's, 1930), p. 290.

3. Florian Znaniecki, *The Method of Sociology* (New York: Farrar & Rinehart, 1934), p. 167.

4. Pitirim Sorokin, *Social and Cultural Dynamics* (New York: American Book Co., 1937), p. 26.

5. R. M. MacIver, *Social Causation* (Boston: Ginn & Co., 1942), p. 263.

6. The more important works dealing with *Verstehen* are K. Bühler, *Die Krise der Philosophie* (Jena: Fischer, 1927); W. Dilthey, *Ideen ueber eine beschreibende und zergliedcrnde Psychologie* (Leipzig: Teubner, 1894); T. Erisman, *Die Eigenart des Geistigen* (Leipzig: Quelle, 1924); P. Häberlin, *Der Geist und die Triebe* (Berlin: Springer, 1924); K. Jaspers, *Allgemeine Psychopathologie* (Berlin: Springer, 1920); H. Rickert, *Die Grenzen der naturwissenschaflichen Begriffsbildung* (Tübingen: Mohr, 1913); E. Rothacker, *Logik und Systematik der Geisteswissenschaften* (Bonn: Bouvier, 1947); G. Simmel, *Geschichtsphilosophic* (Berlin: Duncan, 1920); E. Spranger, *Lebensformen* (Halle: Niemeyer, 1924); and Max Weber, *Gesammelte Aufsaetze zur Wissenschaftslehre* (Tübingen: Mohr, 1920).

7. "Thoughtways of Contemporary Sociology," *American Sociological Review*, I (1936), 703.

8. Franz Alexander, "The Logic of Emotions and Its Dynamic Background," *International Journal of Psychoanalysis*, XVI (October, 1935), 399.

9. R. K. Merton, "Sociological Theory," *American Journal of Sociology*, L (May, 1945), 470.

On the Objectivity of Social Science

RICHARD RUDNER

VERSTEHEN. NO SERIOUS DISCUSSION OF THE VARIOUS GROUNDS ON THE basis of which social phenomena have been held *not* amenable to scientific investigation could reasonably omit mention of the issue of *Verstehen*, or empathic understanding. As in the cases mentioned above, here too we find proponents of the view that the methodology of the social sciences be radically different from that of the other sciences.

In this case it is especially important to keep the distinctions between methodology and technique, and validation and discovery, clearly in mind. The issue is not whether achieving empathic understanding of some subject of inquiry (presumably by an imaginative act of psychologically "putting oneself into the place of" the subject) is a helpful, fruitful, or indispensable technique for discovering hypotheses, or means for testing hypotheses. The issue is not even whether such techniques of discovery are peculiarly techniques of the social scientist. What is at issue is whether empathic understanding constitutes an indispensable method for the validation of hypotheses about social phenomena. This question had best be considered in two stages: First, in what sense, if any, is *Verstehen* a validational method? Second, is it an indispensable methodological recourse of the social sciences alone?

Concerning the first question, it is clear that some serious and influential students of the methodology of the social sciences have thought the aim of social inquiry to be a kind of *understanding* of the phenomena investigated, which can be gained or validated by empathic, or empathy-like, or other participatory acts of the investigator. For several proponents of the view, this thesis is connected with the assertion that social activities have a "significance" or "meaning" and that hypotheses about this significance can be validated *through* the empathy of the investigator. . . . we shall have something further

Richard Rudner, "On the Objectivity of Social Science," in *Philosophy of Social Science,* © 1966, pp. 71–73, 78–83. Reprinted by permission of Prentice-Hall, Inc., Englewood Cliffs, New Jersey.

to say about problems posed by what is termed the 'meaningfulness' of social phenomena. For the present, however, let us assume that meaningfulness is an unproblematic concept and confine our attention solely to the analysis of the empathic part of the current question.

Max Weber and other proponents of the methodological use of empathy have maintained that coming to the kind of understanding required in social science of, say, the phenomenon of religious martyrdom, is through empathy with martyrs. In order really to understand Christian martyrdom, to validate hypotheses about its sociocultural character, to accomplish the requisite task of capturing the "meaning" that martyrdom had for the martyr, we imagine ourselves in the place of, or "recreate" the psychological states of, the martyr—and thus, presumably, come to the requisite understanding and effect the requisite validation. (For Weber and others, not only is this empathic method a means for the social scientist to "capture" the significance of Christian martyrdom, but it is the only, and hence, indispensable, means for doing so. It is, moreover, peculiar to social science by its very nature.)

The above will suffice perhaps to give something of the flavor of the proponents' arguments—which arguments we may now examine. To begin, even if we waive consideration of the vagueness of 'meaningfulness' and 'understanding' in this context, there is still a residual oddness about this thesis that makes it something less than compelling. The question that arises on reflection is this: What check does the empathizer have on whether his empathic state is veridical (i.e., reliable)? We need not argue against empathy or discard it as a validational step, but clearly, in order to accept some specific empathic act as validational, we must presuppose an investigation establishing the hypothesis that this act is veridical. In short, to provide the empathizer with a reliable basis for accepting or rejecting his hypotheses about the phenomenon he is investigating, we must have established independently that the empathy is sufficiently like the state of which it is an empathy.

But how can we establish independently the reliability of such an empathic act without having had previous knowledge of (i.e., without having previously accepted a hypothesis about the character of) the very psychological state that is the object of empathy? And if we do have this presupposed knowledge (i.e., if we have already accepted a hypothesis about the nature of the target psychological state) what more could be methodologically required? If further confirmation of the investigator's hypotheses about the character of the target psychological state *is* in order, then the logic of the situation just outlined entails that some means are available, independent of empathy, for acquiring it.

A little reflection will show that these considerations answer the second question about empathy posed earlier, as well as the first. The answer to the first question is that if we waive (temporarily) difficulties about such terms as 'meaningfulness' and 'understanding', it is possible to accept empathy as a validational method in those cases where its veridicalness or reliability has been independently established in such a way as to have made it redundant. The answer to the second question is, therefore, that empathy is *not* an indispensable methodological device of the social sciences. The very logic of its methodological employment precludes this by guaranteeing that there will be independent means for validating the hypotheses its use is intended to validate. . . .

Weber offers a variety of arguments for his position on the irremediable (methodological) subjectivity of the social sciences, some of which were mentioned in the last part. But two further and closely related arguments deserve detailed consideration. These begin with premises about the character of social phenomena and the aim of social inquiry and proceed to conclusions about the inadequacy of the scientific method to fulfill this aim, the need to supplement the scientific method by special methodological adjuncts peculiar to social science, and end with the claim that these special but indispensable adjuncts render social science methodologically nonobjective.

What (according to Weber and others) renders social phenomena idiosyncratic is the quality of *meaningfulness* that typically attaches to such phenomena. Moreover, according to proponents of this view, it is an essential aim of social inquiry to come to an understanding of the specific meaningfulness attaching to each such phenomenon studied. To appreciate the force of this kind of argument we must, at the outset, attempt to clarify the concept of meaningfulness. One of the chief difficulties involving this is that in English, as in several other natural languages, words like 'meaningful' and 'significant' and their cognates occur with a certain systematic ambiguity.

These particular words and their cognates can be used, first, in a *semantical (nonevaluational)* sense—a sense in which we are explicitly addressing ourselves to the semantical (i.e., referential or significatory) aspects of language itself. Thus, when we ask "What is the meaning of the word 'elephant'?" we need not be asking for an evaluation—in the sense of a judgment about importance—of the word 'elephant' or its referent. In the second place, there are many contexts in which our questions about the meanings of things are not, or not *merely*, inquiries concerning semantical (evaluationally neutral) characteristics. Rather, they are primarily questions about the importance or value those things may have. It is this sense of 'meaning' that is at stake when we ask "What is the meaning of (i.e., what is the importance of, or what are important consequences of) France's refusal to sign the test-ban treaty so far as the Atlantic Alliance is concerned?" or when we assert "The state visit of Greek royalty to England last year was an empty gesture—a gesture without meaning."

We are, then, confronted in these arguments with a key word that is systematically ambiguous; it behooves us therefore to distinguish carefully between the two versions of the arguments as determined by the two meanings of 'meaningful.' To facilitate the discussion we shall use the term 'meaning$_1$' (or 'significance$_1$') for indications of the semantical sense, and 'meaning$_2$' (or 'significance$_2$') for indications of the evaluational sense. In assessing the arguments we must keep the two senses distinct, even though it is not always clear that the parties to the controversy have succeeded in doing so.

Consider first the argument based upon the meaningfulness$_2$, or significance$_2$, of social phenomena. We may grant at once that not only do objects and acts that have value or importance come within the purview of social inquiry, but also that acts *of* valuing (whether or not such acts have value) are likewise suitable objects of investigation for the social scientist. The issue that arises is whether such phenomena necessitate a special methodology for their study. Is there any reason to believe that a hypothesis like (a) 'X is valued or judged to be important by Y' is *logically* impervious to validation through the scientific method?

It is crucial to notice here that this is an issue in the context of validation and not in the context of discovery—it is a question of method or logic or the rationale of validation, and not one of technique of investigation. Incidentally, the Weberian position cannot be construed as merely technological on pain of instant trivialization—it would become simply the uninteresting claim that different techniques need to be employed in different disciplines. On the other hand, from the methodological point of view, the arguments that purport to show that hypotheses like (a) are not amenable to the scientific method of validation, are singularly uncompelling. Generally speaking, these arguments are of two sorts, one being to the effect that value phenomena require that the inquirer himself make a value judgment in order to validate hypotheses concerning their occurrence or some characteristic they may have. The reason advanced to support this claim seems simply to be the presupposition that in order for us to determine, say, that X is regarded as important by Y, or that Y regards X as having some other valuationally relevant characteristic, it is necessary for us, through some empathic act, "to put ourselves in the place of" the evaluating subject of the inquiry. If we do not do this, the argument appears to claim, it will be impossible for us to tell (i.e., to validate the hypothesis) that X is valued, or to ascertain how it is valued.

The second argument, closely related to the first, holds that there is no sort of observable, or empirically testable, *behavior* whose occurrence is both necessary and sufficient for the applicability of any valuational predicates; and that, accordingly, it is impossible to employ the standard validational steps of the scientific method to test hypotheses about valuations. . . . this amounts to the claim that valuational predicates that occur in social-science theories or hypotheses are not definable by any set of observation predicates, not even introspective or empathic ones.

This last contention, and others related to it, are among the most vexed problems in current analytical philosophy and it would be quite outside the province of this discussion to attempt to settle it and them here. But we do not have to settle these problems in order to reject both of the arguments just considered. For the scientific validation of the types of hypothesis involved is not dependent on the *synonymy* of valuational predicates with any set of observational (or introspective) ones. All that is required for scientific validation of the relevant hypothesis is that *some* observable state of affairs be a *likely concomitant* of the value phenomenon in question and not that any observable state of affairs be both a necessary and sufficient condition for it. To be sure, in taking the observable concomitant—or its absence—simply as evidence relevant to the hypothesis, we can never know with certainty whether the hypothesis is true or false; but certainty cannot attach to the results of *any* empirical inquiry, and our position of having to accept or reject a valuational hypothesis in the absence of absolutely conclusive evidence is simply the very condition of scientific inquiry. (Indeed, one suspects that it is the very urgency of some atavistic "quest for certainty" in empirical inquiry that has blinded otherwise perspicacious philosophers and scientists to this point.) At any rate, here we need neither accept the second argument that standard validational procedures are inapplicable to value phenomena nor, a fortiori, the stronger first argument that some substitute (empathylike) method is indispensable to their validation. It just *doesn't* take a fat cowherd to drive fat kine!

We have been examining the view that what has been called the meaning$_2$ of social phenomena necessitates a peculiar methodological divorce of social science from the rest of science. Though we have not couched the arguments at issue in just the terminology of Weber's own discussion, the arguments examined (or ones having substantially their import) do put in an appearance in one guise or another in his works on the objectivity of social science.

But Weber also seems at times to be arguing from the meaningfulness$_1$ (i.e., semantical meaningfulness) of phenomena to the same conclusion. And more recently, several extremely acute analytical philosophers, apparently under the influence of Wittgenstein's later writings, have also put forward subtle and profound arguments toward an even more radical (if closely related) conclusion. The work of Peter Winch is especially challenging.

Winch (and doubtless Weber too) would hold that the concept of a social phenomenon or act must be coextensive with (i.e., refer to just the same things as) that of a meaningful$_1$ act. He holds that it is a definitory or essential characteristic of social acts that they should have meaning in what we have been calling the semantical (or significatory) sense of the term. He explicates his use of 'meaningful' (i.e., our 'meaningful$_1$') by equating meaningful behavior with *rule-governed behavior*. He then contends that we must surely fail as students of the character of social phenomena unless we come to understand the meaning$_1$ of such phenomena. Yet, to do this we must understand what it is to behave in conformity with a rule or what it is to "follow a rule." In particular, we must understand what it is to follow the particular rule(s) governing the meaningful₁ phenomenon in question.

The explication given by Winch of what it is to follow a rule is attributed by him to Wittgenstein. Winch tells us that to follow a rule is to act in such a manner that one's action commits one to, and is a sign of commitment to, some further act that it portends and whose nonrealization would presumably constitute a violation of the rule. Rule violation is indeed the key notion involved. We are said to know what it is to follow the rule (and thus, presumably, to "understand" the social phenomena involved) only if we know what would constitute a violation of it. Hence, we know the rule only if we can cogently make judgments of correctness or incorrectness about the act in question.

Having established this much (at least to his own ostensible satisfaction) Winch then raises the question of how an inquirer (or indeed anyone) can come to know or learn what it is to follow a rule, and thus come to know or learn the meaning₁ of any social phenomenon. This question brings us to the nub of the matter. For Winch's answer is that the method of science is *wholly irrelevant* to the acquisition of this kind of knowledge; consequently, the scientific method is held to be inappropriate in attempting to consummate the essential task of social science—namely, the task of gaining an understanding of meaningful₁ phenomena. It is, according to this view, at best misleading and ineffectual to employ the method used by the rest of the sciences in an area that belongs uniquely to social science. The method Winch claims actually to be appropriate is that of *philosophical analysis* (which for Winch is a task of learning the relevant rules). Sociology (in particular) is thus held by him to be a branch of philosophy rather than an empirical science. The kind of methodology Winch is advocating would give us, in contrast to the scientific method, just the sort of understanding of the meaning₁ of a social act that the subject agent, i.e., the follower of the appropriate rule, himself has.

Now this is a complex argument, and it has ramifications for other areas of philosophy that again cannot appropriately be brought within the scope of this discussion. We are, however, fortunately in a position to assess its worth for our own context without having to explore these extraneous ramifications. . . .

Suppose we were to grant both Winch's contention that all social phenomena are meaningful₁ phenomena and also that meaningful₁ phenomena are rule-governed phenomena. Even granting this much, Winch's argument seems to fail. Whatever plausibility it has stems from a disguised equivocation over the term 'understanding.' It is hard to cavil at the precept that a social scientist must gain an understanding of the phenomena he investigates, or at the apparent truism that a phenomenon is susceptible of being understood if, and only if, it is intelligible (i.e., understandable). But the next move in Winch's argument, a move that consists in adopting the precept that a meaningful phenomenon is not intelligible or understandable unless its meaning can be understood, makes a pivotal use of the equivocation.

For there are at least two senses of 'understanding' at issue, one of which warrants the application of the term only if the individual to whom it applies has had certain *direct* experiences of the subject matter being "understood." 'Understand,' in the other sense, does not have the occurrence of such experiences as a necessary condition. For example, with respect to the natural sciences it is generally agreed that a scientific understanding or knowledge of things or events of a given kind does not necessarily presuppose direct experience of such things or events. Indeed, as Winch himself points out, we have acquired the understanding appropriate in *natural* science when we have achieved, say, a causal explanation of the type of event being investigated.

Still, there have always been philosophers (Bergson and Whitehead are notable examples) who, while agreeing that causal or scientific explanations of physical phenomena are as much as can be understood by physical science, have nevertheless taken this very fact to be symptomatic of the deficiency or limitations of the scientific method—even as employed in physics. A typical claim maintains that science distorts (through abstraction from) physical reality. It is held, for example, that a scientific description of a tornado conveys in only a feeble, truncated manner what is, on the other hand, conveyed with overpowering richness and fullness by the direct experience of a tornado.

. . . The shortcomings of this view should be clear. We need but to remember Einstein's remark that it is not the function of science to give the taste of the soup. It is the function of science to describe the world, not to reproduce it. Of course a description of a tornado is *not* the same thing as a tornado! And incidentally, the description does not "fail" to be a tornado on account of being incomplete, truncated, generalized, or abstract. Even if it were a "complete" description of a tornado—whatever that might be—it would still be a *description* of a tornado and not a tornado. Moreover, a description of a tornado no more *fails* to be a tornado than does a tornado fail to be a description.

How, in the end, does all of this bear on Winch's argument? The answer is that Winch's argument commits a rather subtle form of the "reproductive fallacy"—reminding ourselves of the character of the fallacy in the more neutral context of physical science (e.g., illustratively using tornados) allows us to discuss it more easily here. The claim that the only understanding appropriate to social science is one that consists of a reproduction of the conditions or states of affairs being studied is logically the same as the claim that the only understanding appropriate to the investigation of tornados is that gained in the direct experience of tornados.

We can scarcely entertain the idea that the only kind of understanding at which we can aim in the investigation of tornados must come from the experiencing of tornados. Notice that in rejecting Winch's thesis, it is not necessary to deny that *some sort* of knowledge or understanding of, say, religion is gained in "playing" the "religious game," any more than it is necessary to deny that some sort of knowledge or understanding is gained in experiencing tornados. The point is that nothing whatever in such a concession implies that these direct understandings are either the only ones possible for the social scientist or that they are a substitute for a scientific understanding of social phenomena.

Neither Weber's arguments nor the more contemporary but still rather Weberian arguments of Winch are decisive, then, in compelling the conclusion either that social science must fail of achieving the methodological objectivity of the rest of science or that social science must employ a radically distinct methodology.

Interpretation and the Sciences of Man

CHARLES TAYLOR

I

i

IS THERE A SENSE IN WHICH INTERPRETATION IS ESSENTIAL TO explanation in the sciences of man? The view that it is, that there is an unavoidably "hermeneutical" component in the sciences of man, goes back to Dilthey. But recently the question has come again to the fore, for instance, in the work of Gadamer,[1] in Ricoeur's interpretation of Freud,[2] and in the writings of Habermas.[3]

Interpretation, in the sense relevant to hermeneutics, is an attempt to make clear, to make sense of an object of study. This object must, therefore, be a text, or a text-analogue, which in some way is confused, incomplete, cloudy, seemingly contradictory—in one way or another, unclear. The interpretation aims to bring to light an underlying coherence or sense.

This means that any science which can be called "hermeneutical," even in an extended sense, must be dealing with one or another of the confusingly interrelated forms of meaning. Let us try to see a little more clearly what this involves.

1) We need, first, an object or field of objects, about which we can speak in terms of coherence or its absence, of making sense or nonsense.

2) Second, we need to be able to make a distinction, even if only a relative one, between the sense or coherence made, and its embodiment in a particular field of carriers or signifiers. For otherwise, the task of making clear what is fragmentary or confused would be radically impossible. No sense could be given to this idea. We have to be able to make for our interpretations claims of

Charles Taylor, "Interpretation and the Sciences of Man," *Review of Metaphysics* 25 (1971): 3–34, 45–51.

the order: the meaning confusedly present in this text or text-analogue is clearly expressed here. The meaning, in other words, is one which admits of more than one expression, and, in this sense, a distinction must be possible between meaning and expression.

The point of the above qualification, that this distinction may be only relative, is that there are cases where no clear, unambiguous, nonarbitrary line can be drawn between what is said and its expression. It can be plausibly argued (I think convincingly although there isn't space to go into it here) that this is the normal and fundamental condition of meaningful expression, that exact synonymy, or equivalence of meaning, is a rare and localized achievement of specialized languages or uses of civilization. But this, if true (and I think it is), doesn't do away with the distinction between meaning and expression. Even if there is an important sense in which a meaning re-expressed in a new medium can not be declared identical, this by no means entails that we can give no sense to the project of expressing a meaning in a new way. It does of course raise an interesting and difficult question about what can be meant by expressing it in a clearer way: what is the "it" which is clarified if equivalence is denied? I hope to return to this in examining interpretation in the sciences of man.

Hence the object of a science of interpretation must be describable in terms of sense and nonsense, coherence and its absence; and must admit of a distinction between meaning and its expression.

3) There is also a third condition it must meet. We can speak of sense or coherence, and of their different embodiments, in connection with such phenomena as gestalts, or patterns in rock formations, or snow crystals, where the notion of expression has no real warrant. What is lacking here is the notion of a subject for whom these meanings are. Without such a subject, the choice of criteria of sameness and difference, the choice among the different forms of coherence which can be identified in a given pattern, among the different conceptual fields in which it can be seen, is arbitrary.

In a text or text-analogue, on the other hand, we are trying to make explicit the meaning expressed, and this means expressed by or for a subject or subjects. The notion of expression refers us to that of a subject. The identification of the subject is by no means necessarily unproblematical, as we shall see further on; it may be one of the most difficult problems, an area in which prevailing epistemological prejudice may blind us to the nature of our object of study. I think this has been the case, as I will show below. And moreover, the identification of a subject does not assure us of a clear and absolute distinction between meaning and expression as we saw above. But any such distinction, even a relative one, is without any anchor at all, is totally arbitrary, without appeal to a subject.

The object of a science of interpretation must thus have: sense, distinguishable from its expression, which is for or by a subject.

ii

Before going on to see in what way, if any, these conditions are realized in the sciences of man, I think it would be useful to set out more clearly what rides on this question, why it matters whether or not we think of the sciences of man as hermeneutical, what the issue is at stake here.

The issue here is at root an epistemological one. But it is inextricable from an ontological one, and, hence, cannot but be relevant to our notions of science and of the proper conduct of inquiry. We might say that it is an ontological issue which has been argued ever since the seventeenth century in terms of epistemological considerations which have appeared to some to be unanswerable.

The case could be put in these terms: what are the criteria of judgment in a hermeneutical science? A successful interpretation is one which makes clear the meaning originally present in a confused, fragmentary, cloudy form. But how does one know that this interpretation is correct? Presumably because it makes sense of the original text: what is strange, mystifying, puzzling, contradictory is no longer so, is accounted for. The interpretation appeals throughout to our understanding of the "language" of expression, which understanding allows us to see that this expression is puzzling, that it is in contradiction to that other, etc., and that these difficulties are cleared up when the meaning is expressed in a new way.

But this appeal to our understanding seems to be crucially inadequate. What if someone does not "see" the adequacy of our interpretation, does not accept our reading? We try to show him how it makes sense of the original non- or partial sense. But for him to follow us he must read the original language as we do, he must recognize these expressions as puzzling in a certain way, and hence be looking for a solution to our problem. If he does not, what can we do? The answer, it would seem, can only be more of the same. We have to show him through the reading of other expressions why this expression must be read in the way we propose. But success here requires that he follow us in these other readings, and so on, it would seem, potentially forever. We cannot escape an ultimate appeal to a common understanding of the expressions, of the "language" involved. This is one way of trying to express what has been called the "hermeneutical circle." What we are trying to establish is a certain reading of text or expressions, and what we appeal to as our grounds for this reading can only be other readings. The circle can also be put in terms of part-whole relations: we are trying to establish a reading for the whole text, and for this we appeal to readings of its partial expressions; and yet because we are dealing with meaning, with making sense, where expressions only make sense or not in relation to others, the readings of partial expressions depend on those of others, and ultimately of the whole.

Put in forensic terms, as we started to do above, we can only convince an interlocutor if at some point he shares our understanding of the language concerned. If he does not, there is no further step to take in rational argument; we can try to awaken these intuitions in him, or we can simply give up; argument will advance us no further. But of course the forensic predicament can be transferred into my own judging: if I am this ill-equipped to convince a stubborn interlocutor, how can I convince myself? how can I be sure? Maybe my intuitions are wrong or distorted, maybe I am locked into a circle of illusion.

Now one, and perhaps the only sane response to this would be to say that such uncertainty is an ineradicable part of our epistemological predicament. That even to characterize it as "uncertainty" is to adopt an absurdly severe criterion of "certainty," which deprives the concept of any sensible use. But this has not been the only or even the main response of our philosophical tradition. And it is another response which has had an important and far-reaching effect on the sciences of man. The demand has been for a level of certainty which can only be attained by breaking beyond the circle.

There are two ways in which this break-out has been envisaged. The first might be called the "rationalist" one and could be thought to reach a culmination in Hegel. It does not involve a negation of intuition, or of our understanding of meaning, but rather aspires to attainment of an understanding of such clarity that it would carry with it the certainty of the undeniable. In Hegel's case, for instance, our full understanding of the whole in "thought" carries with it a grasp of its inner necessity, such that we see how it could not be otherwise. No higher grade of certainty is conceivable. For this aspiration the word "break-out" is badly chosen; the aim is rather to bring understanding to an inner clarity which is absolute.

The other way, which we can call "empiricist," is a genuine attempt to go beyond the circle of our own interpretations, to get beyond subjectivity. The attempt is to reconstruct knowledge in such a way that there is no need to make final appeal to readings or judgments which can not be checked further. That is why the basic building block of knowledge on this view is the impression, or sense-datum, a unit of information which is not the deliverance of a judgment, which has by definition no element in it of reading or interpretation, which is a brute datum. The highest ambition would be to build our knowledge from such building blocks by judgments which could be anchored in a certainty beyond subjective intuition. This is what underlies the attraction of the notion of the association of ideas, or if the same procedure is viewed as a method, induction. If the original acquisition of the units of information is not the fruit of judgment or interpretation, then the constatation that two such elements occur together need not either be the fruit of interpretation, of a reading or intuition which cannot be checked. For if the occurrence of a single element is a brute datum, then so is the co-occurrence of two such elements. The path to true knowledge would then repose crucially on the correct recording of such co-occurrences.

This is what lies behind an ideal of verification which is central to an important tradition in the philosophy of science, whose main contemporary protagonists are the logical empiricists. Verification must be grounded ultimately in the acquisition of brute data. By "brute data," I mean here and throughout data whose validity cannot be questioned by offering another interpretation or reading, data whose credibility cannot be confounded or undermined by further reasoning.[4] If such a difference of interpretation can arise over given data, then it must be possible to structure the argument so as to distinguish the basic, brute data from the inferences made on the basis of them.

The inferences themselves, of course, to be valid must similarly be beyond the challenge of a rival interpretation. Here the logical empiricists added to the rival interpretation. Here the logical empiricists added to the armory of traditional empiricism which set great store by the method of induction, the whole domain of logical and mathematical inference which had been central to the rationalist position (with Leibniz at least, although not with Hegel), and which offered another brand of unquestionable certainty.

Of course, mathematical inference and empirical verification were combined in such a way that two theories or more could be verified of the same domain of facts. But this was a consequence to which logical empiricism was willing to accommodate itself. As for the surplus meaning in a theory which could not be rigorously co-ordinated with brute data, it was considered to be quite outside the logic of verification.

As a theory of perception, this epistemology gave rise to all sorts of problems, not least of which was the perpetual threat of skepticism and solipsism inseparable from a conception of the basic data of knowledge as brute data, beyond investigation. As a theory of perception, however, it seems largely a thing of the past, in spite of a surprising recrudescence in the Anglo-Saxon world in the 'thirties and 'forties. But there is no doubt that it goes marching on, among other places, as a theory of how the human mind and human knowledge actually function.

In a sense, the contemporary period has seen a better, more rigorous statement of what this epistemology is about in the form of computer-influenced theories of intelligence. These try to model intelligence as consisting of operations on machine-recognizable input which could themselves be matched by programs which could be run on machines. The machine criterion provides us with our assurance against an appeal to intuition or interpretations which cannot be understood by fully explicit procedures operating on brute data—the input.[5]

The progress of natural science has lent great credibility to this epistemology, since it can be plausibly reconstructed on this model, as for instance has been done by the logical empiricists. And, of course, the temptation has been overwhelming to reconstruct the sciences of man on the same model; or rather to launch them in lines of inquiry that fit this paradigm, since they are constantly said to be in their "infancy." Psychology, where an earlier vogue of behaviorism is being replaced by a boom of computer-based models, is far from the only case.

The form this epistemological bias—one might say obsession—takes is different for different sciences. Later I would like to look at a particular case, the study of politics, where the issue can be followed out. But in general, the empiricist orientation must be hostile to a conduct of inquiry which is based on interpretation, and which encounters the hermeneutical circle as this was characterized above. This cannot meet the requirements of intersubjective, non-arbitrary verification which it considers essential to science. And along with the epistemological stance goes the ontological belief that reality must be susceptible to understanding and explanation by science so understood. From this follows a certain set of notions of what the sciences of man must be.

On the other hand, many, including myself, would like to argue that these notions about the sciences of man are sterile, that we cannot come to understand important dimensions of human life within the bounds set by this epistemological orientation. This dispute is of course familiar to all in at least some of its ramifications. What I want to claim is that the issue can be fruitfully posed in terms of the notion of interpretation as I began to outline it above.

I think this way of putting the question is useful because it allows us at once to bring to the surface the powerful epistemological beliefs which underlie the orthodox view of the sciences of man in our academy, and to make explicit the notion of our epistemological predicament implicit in the opposing thesis. This is in fact rather more way-out and shocking to the tradition of scientific thought than is often admitted or realized by the opponents of narrow scientism. It may not strengthen the case of the opposition to bring out fully what is involved in a hermeneutical science as far as convincing waverers is concerned, but a gain in clarity is surely worth a thinning of the ranks—at least in philosophy.

iii

Before going on to look at the case of political science, it might be worth asking another question: why should we even pose the question whether the sciences of man are hermeneutical? What gives us the idea in the first place that men and their actions constitute an object or a series of objects which meet the conditions outlined above?

The answer is that on the phenomenological level or that of ordinary speech (and the two converge for the purposes of this argument) a certain notion of meaning has an essential place in the characterization of human behavior. This is the sense in which we speak of a situation, an action, a demand, a prospect having a certain meaning for a person.

Now it is frequently thought that "meaning" is used here in a sense which is a kind of illegitimate extension from the notion of linguistic meaning. Whether it can be considered an extension or not is another matter; it certainly differs from linguistic meaning. But it would be very hard to argue that it is an illegitimate use of the term.

When we speak of the "meaning" of a given predicament, we are using a concept which has the following articulation. a) Meaning is for a subject: it is not the meaning of the situation *in vacuo*, but its meaning for a subject, a specific subject, a group of subjects, or perhaps what its meaning is for the human subject as such (even though particular humans might be reproached with not admitting or realizing this). b) Meaning is of something; that is, we can distinguish between a given element—situation, action, or whatever—and its meaning. But this is not to say that they are physically separable. Rather we are dealing with two descriptions of the element, in one of which it is characterized in terms of its meaning for the subject. But the relations between the two descriptions are not symmetrical. For, on the one hand, the description in terms of meaning cannot be unless descriptions of the other kind apply as well; or put differently, there can be no meaning without a substrate. But on the other hand, it may be that the same meaning may be borne by another substrate—e.g., a situation with the same meaning may be realized in different physical conditions. There is a necessary role for a potentially substitutable substrate; or all meanings are of something.

And thirdly, c) things only have meaning in a field, that is, in relation to the meanings of other things. This means that there is no such thing as a single, unrelated meaningful element; and it means that changes in the other meanings in the field can involve changes in the given element. Meanings can't be identified except in relation to others, and in this way resemble words. The meaning of a word depends, for instance, on those words with which it contrasts, on those which define its place in the language (e.g., those defining "determinable" dimensions, like color, shape), on those which define the activity or "language game" it figures in (describing, invoking, establishing communion), and so on. The relations between meanings in this sense are like those between concepts in a semantic field.

Just as our color concepts are given their meaning by the field of contrast they set up together, so that the introduction of new concepts will alter the boundaries of others, so the various meanings that a subordinate's demeanor can have for us, as deferential, respectful, cringing, mildly mocking, ironical, insolent, provoking, downright rude, are established by a field of contrast; and as with finer discrimination on our part, or a more sophisticated culture, new possibilities are born, so other terms of this range are altered. And as the meaning of our terms "red," "blue," "green" is fixed by the definition of a field of contrast through the determinable term "color," so all these alternative demeanors are only available in a society which has, among other types, hierarchical relations of power and command. And corresponding to the underlying language game of designating colored objects is the set of social practices which sustain these hierarchical structures and are fulfilled in them.

Meaning in this sense—let us call it experiential meaning—thus is for a subject, of something, in a field. This distinguishes it from linguistic meaning which has a four and not three-dimensional structure. Linguistic meaning is for subjects and in a field, but it is the meaning of signifiers and it is about a world of referents. Once we are clear about the likenesses and differences, there should be little doubt that the term "meaning" is not a misnomer, the product of an illegitimate extension into this context of experience and behavior.

There is thus a quite legitimate notion of meaning which we use when we speak of the meaning of a situation for an agent. And that this concept has a place is integral to our ordinary consciousness and hence speech about our actions. Our actions are ordinarily characterized by the purpose sought and explained by desires, feelings, emotions. But the language by which we describe our goals, feelings, desires is also a definition of the meaning things have for us. The vocabulary defining meaning—words like "terrifying," "attractive"—is linked with that describing feeling—"fear," "desire"—and that describing goals—"safety," "possession."

Moreover, our understanding of these terms moves inescapably in a hermeneutical circle. An emotion term like "shame," for instance, essentially refers us to a certain kind of situation, the "shameful," or "humiliating," and a certain mode of response, that of hiding oneself, of covering up, or else "wiping out" the blot. That is, it is essential to this feeling's being identified as shame that it be related to this situation and give rise to this type of disposition. But this situation in its turn can only be identified in relation to the feelings which it provokes; and the disposition is to a goal which can similarly not be understood without reference to the feelings experienced: the "hiding" in question is one which will cover up my shame; it is not the same as hiding from an armed pursuer; we can only understand what is meant by "hiding" here if we understand what kind of feeling and situation is being talked about. We have to be within the circle.

An emotion term like "shame" can only be explained by reference to other concepts which in turn cannot be understood without reference to shame. To understand these concepts we have to be in on a certain experience, we have to understand a certain language, not just of words, but also a certain language of mutual action and communication, by which we blame, exhort, admire, esteem each other. In the end we are in on this because we grow up in the ambit of certain common meanings. But we can often experience what it is like to be on the outside when we encounter the feeling, action, and experiential meaning language of another civilization. Here there is no translation, no way of explaining in other, more accessible concepts. We can only catch on by getting somehow into their way of life, if only in imagination. Thus if we look at human behavior as action done out of a background of desire, feeling, emotion, then we are looking at a reality which must be characterized in terms of meaning. But does this mean that it can be the object of a hermeneutical science as this was outlined above?

There are, to remind ourselves, three characteristics that the object of a science of interpretation has: it must have sense or coherence; this must be distinguishable from its expression, and this sense must be for a subject.

Now insofar as we are talking about behavior as action, hence in terms of meaning, the category of sense or coherence must apply to it. This is not to say that all behavior must "make sense," if we mean by this be rational, avoid contradiction, confusion of purpose, and the like. Plainly a great deal of our action falls short of this goal. But in another sense, even contradictory, irrational action is "made sense of," when we understand why it was engaged in. We make sense of action when there is a coherence between the actions of the agent and the meaning of his situation for him. We find his action puzzling until we find such a coherence. It may not be bad to repeat that this coherence in no way implies that the action is rational: the meaning of a situation for an agent may be full of confusion and contradiction; but the adequate depiction of this contradiction makes sense of it.

Making sense in this way through coherence of meaning and action, the meanings of action and situation cannot but move in a hermeneutical circle. Our conviction that the account makes sense is contingent on our reading of action and situation. But these readings cannot be explained or justified except by reference to other such readings, and their relation to the whole. If an interlocutor does not understand this kind of reading, or will not accept it as valid, there is nowhere else the argument can go. Ultimately, a good explanation is one which makes sense of the behavior; but then to appreciate a good explanation, one has to agree on what makes good sense; what makes good sense is a function of one's readings; and these in turn are based on the kind of sense one understands.

But how about the second characteristic, that sense should be distinguishable from its embodiment? This is necessary for a science of interpretation because interpretation lays a claim to make a confused meaning clearer; hence there must be some sense in which the "same" meaning is expressed, but differently.

This immediately raises a difficulty. In talking of experiential meaning above, I mentioned that we can distinguish between a given element and its meaning, between meaning and substrate. This carried the claim that a given meaning *may* be realized in another substrate. But does this mean that we can *always* embody the same meaning in another situation? Perhaps there are some situations, standing before death, for instance, which have a meaning which can't be embodied otherwise.

But fortunately this difficult question is irrelevant for our purposes. For here we have a case in which the analogy between text and behavior implicit in the notion of a hermeneutical science of man only applies with important modifications. The text is replaced in the interpretation by another text, one which is clearer. The text-analogue of behavior is not replaced by another such text analogue. When this happens we have revolutionary theatre or terrorist acts designed to make propaganda of the deed, in which the hidden relations of a society are supposedly shown up in a dramatic confrontation. But this is not scientific understanding, even though it may perhaps be based on such understanding, or claim to be.

But in science the text-analogue is replaced by a text, an account. Which might prompt the question, how we can even begin to talk of interpretation here, of expressing the same meaning more clearly, when we have two such utterly different terms of comparison, a text and a tract of behavior? Is the whole thing not just a bad pun?

This question leads us to open up another aspect of experiential meaning which we abstracted from earlier. Experiential meanings are defined in fields of contrast, as words are in semantic fields.

But what was not mentioned above is that these two kinds of definition aren't independent of each other. The range of human desires, feelings, emotions, and hence meanings is bound up with the level and type of culture, which in turn is inseparable from the distinctions and categories marked by the language people speak. The field of meanings in which a given situation can find its place is bound up with the semantic field of the terms characterizing these meanings and the related feelings, desires, predicaments.

But the relationship involved here is not a simple one. There are two simple types of models of relation which could be offered here, but both are inadequate. We could think of the feeling vocabulary as simply describing pre-existing feelings, as marking distinctions which would be there without them. But this is not adequate because we often experience in ourselves or others how achieving, say, a more sophisticated vocabulary of the emotions makes our emotional life more sophisticated and not just our descriptions of it. Reading a good, powerful novel may give me the picture of an emotion which I had not previously been aware of. But we can't draw a neat line between an increased ability to identify and an altered ability to feel emotions which this enables.

The other simple inadequate model of the relationship is to jump from the above to the conclusion that thinking makes it so. But this clearly won't do either, since not just any new definition can be forced on us, nor can we force it on ourselves; and some which we do gladly take up can be judged inauthentic, or in bad faith, or just wrong-headed by others. These judgments may be wrong, but they are not in principle illicit. Rather we make an effort to be lucid about ourselves and our feelings, and admire a man who achieves this.

Thus, neither the simple correspondence view is correct, nor the view that thinking makes it so. But both have prima facie warrant. There is such a thing as self-lucidity, which points us to a correspondence view; but the achievement of such lucidity means moral change, that is, it changes the object known. At the same time, error about oneself is not just an absence of correspondence; it is also in some form inauthenticity, bad faith, self-delusion, repression of one's human feelings, or something of the kind; it is a matter of the quality of what is felt just as much as what is known about this, just as self-knowledge is.

If this is so, then we have to think of man as a self-interpreting animal. He is necessarily so, for there is no such thing as the structure of meanings for him independently of his interpretation of them; for one is woven into the other. But then the text of our interpretation is not that heterogeneous from what is interpreted; for what is interpreted is itself an interpretation; a self-interpretation which is embedded in a stream of action. It is an interpretation of experiential meaning which contributes to the constitution of this meaning. Or to put it another way: that of which we are trying to find the coherence is itself partly constituted by self-interpretation.

Our aim is to replace this confused, incomplete, partly erroneous self-interpretation by a correct one. And in doing this we look not only to the self-interpretation but to the stream of behavior in which it is set; just as in interpreting a historical document we have to place it in the stream of events which it relates to. But of course the analogy is not exact, for here we are interpreting the interpretation and the stream of behavior in which it is set together, and not just one or the other.

There is thus no utter heterogeneity of interpretation to what it is about; rather there is a slide in the notion of interpretation. Already to be a living agent is to experience one's situation in terms of certain meanings; and this in a sense can be thought of as a sort of proto-"interpretation." This is in turn interpreted and shaped by the language in which the agent lives these meanings. This whole is then at a third level interpreted by the explanation we proffer of his actions.

In this way the second condition of a hermeneutical science is met. But this account poses in a new light the question mentioned at the beginning whether the interpretation can ever express the same meaning as the interpreted. And in this case, there is clearly a way in which the two will not be congruent. For if the explanation is really clearer than the lived interpretation then it will be such that it would alter in some way the behavior if it came to be internalized by the agent as his self-interpretation. In this way a hermeneutical science which achieves its goal, that is, attains greater clarity than the immediate understanding of agent or observer, must offer us an interpretation which is in this way crucially out of phase with the explicandum.

Thus, human behavior seen as action of agents who desire and are moved, who have goals and aspirations, necessarily offers a purchase for descriptions in terms of meaning—what I have called "experiential meaning." The norm of explanation which it posits is one which "makes sense" of the behavior, which shows a coherence of meaning. This "making sense of" is the proffering of an interpretation; and we have seen that what is interpreted meets the conditions of a science of interpretation: first, that we can speak of its sense or coherence; and second, that this sense can be expressed in another form, so that we can speak of the interpretation as giving clearer expression to what is only implicit in the explicandum. The third condition, that this sense be for a subject, is obviously met in this case, although who this subject is is by no means an unproblematical question as we shall see later on.

This should be enough to show that there is a good prima facie case to the effect that men and their actions are amenable to explanation of a hermeneutical kind. There is, therefore, some reason to raise the issue and challenge the epistemological orientation which would rule interpretation out of the sciences of man. A great deal more must be said to bring out what is involved in the hermeneutical sciences of man. But before getting on to this, it might help to clarify the issue with a couple of examples drawn from a specific field, that of politics.

II

i

In politics, too, the goal of a verifiable science has led to the concentration on features which can supposedly be identified in abstraction from our understanding or not understanding experiential meaning. These—let us call them brute data identifications—are what supposedly enable us to break out from the hermeneutical circle and found our science four square on a verification procedure which meets the requirements of the empiricist tradition.

But in politics the search for such brute data has not gone to the lengths which it has in psychology, where the object of science has been thought of by many as behavior qua "colorless movement," or as machine-recognizable properties. The tendency in politics has been to stop with something less basic, but—so it is thought—the identification of which cannot be challenged by the offering of another interpretation or reading of the data concerned. . . .This is what is referred to as "behavior" in the rhetoric of political scientists, but it has not the rock bottom quality of its psychological homonym.

Political behavior includes what we would ordinarily call actions, but ones that are supposedly brute data identifiable. How can this be so? Well, actions are usually described by the purpose or end-state realized. But the purposes of some actions can be specified in what might be thought to be brute data terms; some actions, for instance, have physical end-states, like getting the car in the garage or climbing the mountain. Others have end-states which are closely tied by institutional rules to some unmistakable physical movement; thus, when I raise my hand in the meeting at the appropriate time, I am voting for the motion. The only questions we can raise about the corresponding actions, given such movements or the realization of such end-states, are whether the agent was aware of what he was doing, was acting as against simply emitting reflex behavior, knew the institutional significance of his movement, etc. Any worries on this score generally turn out to be pretty artificial in the contexts political scientists are concerned with; and where they do arise they can be checked by relatively simple devices, e.g., asking the subject: did you mean to vote for the motion?

Hence, it would appear that there are actions which can be identified beyond fear of interpretative dispute; and this is what gives the foundation for the category of "political behavior." Thus, there are some acts of obvious political relevance which can be specified thus in physical terms, such as killing, sending tanks into the streets, seizing people and confining them to cells; and there is an immense range of others which can be specified from physical acts by institutional rules, such as voting for instance. These can be the object of a science of politics which can hope to meet the stringent requirements of verification. The latter class particularly has provided matter for study in recent decades—most notably in the case of voting studies.

But of course a science of politics confined to such acts would be much too narrow. For on another level these actions also have meaning for the agents which is not exhausted in the brute data descriptions, and which is often crucial to understanding why they were done. Thus, in voting for the motion I am also saving the honor of my party, or defending the value of free speech, or vindicating public morality, or saving civilization from breakdown. It is in such terms that the agents talk about the motivation of much of their political action, and it is difficult to conceive a science of politics which doesn't come to grips with it.

Behavioral political science comes to grips with it by taking the meanings involved in action as facts about the agent, his beliefs, his affective reactions, his "values," as the term is frequently used. For it can be thought verifiable in the brute data sense that men will agree to subscribe or not to a certain form of words (expressing a belief, say); or express a positive or negative reaction to certain events, or symbols; or agree or not with the proposition that some act is right or wrong. We can thus get at meanings as just another form of brute data by the techniques of the opinion survey and content analysis.

An immediate objection springs to mind. If we are trying to deal with the meanings which inform political action, then surely interpretive acumen is unavoidable. Let us say we are trying to understand the goals and values of a certain group, or grasp their vision of the polity; we might try to probe this by a questionnaire asking them whether they assent or not to a number of propositions, which are meant to express different goals, evaluations, beliefs. But how did we design the questionnaire? How did we pick these propositions? Here we relied on our understanding of the goals, values, vision involved. But then this understanding can be challenged, and hence the significance of our results questioned. Perhaps the finding of our study, the compiling of proportions of assent and dissent to these propositions is irrelevant, is without significance for understanding the agents or the polity concerned. This kind of attack is frequently made by critics of mainstream political science, or for that matter social science in general.

To this proponents of this mainstream reply with a standard move of logical empiricism: distinguishing the process of discovery from the logic of verification. Of course, it is our understanding of these meanings which enables us to draw up the questionnaire which will test people's attitudes in respect to them. And, of course, interpretive dispute about these meanings is potentially endless; there are no brute data at this level, every affirmation can be challenged by a rival interpretation. But this has nothing to do with verifiable science. What is firmly verified is the set of correlations between, say, the assent to certain propositions and certain behavior. We discover, for instance, that people who are active politically (defined by participation in a certain set of institutions) are more likely to consent to certain sets of propositions supposedly expressing the values underlying the system.[6] This finding is a firmly verified correlation no matter what one thinks of the reasoning, or simple hunches, that went into designing the research which established it. Political science as a body of knowledge is made up of such correlations; it does not give a truth value to the background reasoning or hunch. A good interpretive nose may be useful in hitting on the right correlations to test, but science is never called on to arbitrate the disputes between interpretations.

Thus, in addition to those overt acts which can be defined physically or institutionally, the category of political behavior can include assent or dissent to verbal formulae, or the occurrence or not of verbal formulae in speech, or expressions of approval or rejection of certain events or measures as observed in institutionally-defined behavior (for instance, turning out for a demonstration).

Now there are a number of objections which can be made to this notion of political behavior; one might question in all sorts of ways how interpretation-free it is in fact. But I would like to question it from another angle. One of the basic characteristics of this kind of social science is that it reconstructs reality in line with certain categorial principles. These allow for an intersubjective social reality which is made up of brute data, identifiable acts and structures, certain institutions, procedures, actions. It allows for beliefs, affective reactions, evaluations as the psychological properties of individuals. And it allows for correlations between these two orders or reality: e.g., that certain beliefs go along with certain acts, certain values with certain institutions, etc.

To put it another way, what is objectively (intersubjectively) real is brute data identifiable. This is what social reality *is*. Social reality described in terms of its meaning for the actors, such that disputes could arise about interpretation which couldn't be settled by brute data (e.g., are people rioting to get a hearing, or are they rioting to redress humiliation, out of blind anger, because they recover a sense of dignity in insurrection?), this is given subjective reality, that is, there are certain beliefs, affective reactions, evaluations which individuals make or have about or in relation to social reality. These beliefs or reactions can have an effect on this reality; and the fact that such a belief is held is a fact of objective social reality. But the social reality which is the object of these attitudes, beliefs, reactions can only be made up of brute data. Thus any description of reality in terms of meanings which is open to interpretive question is only allowed into this scientific discourse if it is placed, as it were, in quotes and attributed to individuals as their opinion, belief, attitude. That this opinion, belief, etc. is held is thought of as a brute datum, since it is redefined as the respondent's giving a certain answer to the questionnaire.

This aspect of social reality which concerns its meanings for the agents has been taken up in a number of ways, but recently it has been spoken of in terms of political culture. Now the way this is defined and studied illustrates clearly the categorial principles above. For instance, political cultural is referred to by Almond and Powell[7] as the "psychological dimension of the political system" (23). Further on they state: "Political culture is the pattern of individual attitudes and orientations towards politics among the members of a political system. It is the subjective realm which underlies and gives meaning to political actions" (50). The authors then go on to distinguish three different kinds of orientations, cognitive (knowledge and beliefs), affective (feelings), and evaluative (judgments and opinions).

From the point of view of empiricist epistemology, this set of categorial principles leaves nothing out. Both reality and the meanings it has for actors are coped with. But what it in fact cannot allow for are intersubjective meanings, that is, it cannot allow for the validity of descriptions of social reality in terms of meanings, hence not as brute data, which are not in quotation marks and attributed as opinion, attitude, etc. to individual(s). Now it is this exclusion that

I would like to challenge in the name of another set of categorial principles, inspired by a quite other epistemology.

ii

We spoke earlier about the brute data identification of acts by means of institutional rules. Thus, putting a cross beside someone's name on a slip of paper and putting this in a box counts in the right context as voting for that person; leaving the room, saying or writing a certain form of words, counts as breaking off the negotiations; writing one's name on a piece of paper counts as signing the petition, etc. But what is worth looking at is what underlies this set of identifications. These identifications are the application of a language of social life, a language which marks distinctions among different possible social acts, relations, structures. But what underlies this language?

Let us take the example of breaking off negotiations above. The language of our society recognizes states or actions like the following: entering into negotiation, breaking off negotiations, offering to negotiate, negotiating in good (bad) faith, concluding negotiations, making a new offer, etc. In other more jargon-infested language, the semantic "space" of this range of social activity is carved up in a certain way, by a certain set of distinctions which our vocabulary marks; and the shape and nature of these distinctions is the nature of our language in this area. These distinctions are applied in our society with more or less formalism in different contexts.

But of course this is not true of every society. Our whole notion of negotiation is bound up for instance with the distinct identity and autonomy of the parties, with the willed nature of their relations; it is a very contractual notion. But other societies have no such conception. It is reported about the traditional Japanese village that the foundation of its social life was a powerful form of consensus, which put a high premium on unanimous decision.[8] Such a consensus would be considered shattered if two clearly articulated parties were to separate out, pursuing opposed aims and attempting either to vote down the opposition or push it into a settlement on the most favorable possible terms for themselves. Discussion there must be, and some kind of adjustment of differences. But our idea of bargaining, with the assumption of distinct autonomous parties in willed relationship, has no place there; nor does a series of distinctions, like entering into and leaving negotiation, or bargaining in good faith (sc. with the genuine intention of seeking agreement).

Now the difference between our society and one of the kind just described could not be well expressed if we said we have a vocabulary to describe negotiation which they lack. We might say, for instance, that we have a vocabulary to describe the heavens that they lack, viz., that of Newtonian mechanics; for here we assume that they live under the same heavens as we do, only understand it differently. But it is not true that they have the same kind of bargaining as we do. The word, or whatever word of their language we translate as "bargaining," must have an entirely different gloss, which is marked by the distinctions their vocabulary allows in contrast to those marked by ours. But this different gloss is not just a difference of vocabulary, but also one of social reality.

But this still may be misleading as a way of putting the difference. For it might imply that there is a social reality which can be discovered in each society and which might exist quite independently of the vocabulary of that society, or indeed of any vocabulary, as the heavens would exist whether men theorized about them or not. And this is not the case; the realities here are practices; and these cannot be identified in abstraction from the language we use to describe them, or invoke them, or carry them out. That the practice of negotiation allows us to distinguish bargaining in good or bad faith, or entering into or breaking off negotiations, presupposes that our acts and situation have a certain description for us, e.g., that we are distinct parties entering into willed relations. But they cannot have these descriptions for us unless this is somehow expressed in our vocabulary of this practice; if not in our descriptions of the practices (for we may as yet be unconscious of some of the important distinctions) in the appropriate language for carrying them on. (Thus, the language marking a distinction between public and private acts or contexts may exist even where these terms or their equivalents are not part of this language; for the distinction will be marked by the different language which is appropriate in one context and the other, be it perhaps a difference of style, or dialect, even though the distinction is not designated by specific descriptive expressions.)

The situation we have here is one in which the vocabulary of a given social dimension is grounded in the shape of social practice in this dimension; that is, the vocabulary wouldn't make sense, couldn't be applied sensibly, where this range of practices didn't prevail. And yet this range of practices couldn't exist without the prevalence of this or some related vocabulary. There is no simple one-way dependence here. We can speak of mutual dependence if we like, but really what this points up is the artificiality of the distinction between social reality and the language of description of that social reality. The language is constitutive of the reality, is essential to its being the kind of reality it is. To separate the two and distinguish them as we quite rightly distinguish the heavens from our theories about them is forever to miss the point.

This type of relation has been recently explored, e.g., by John Searle, with his concept of a constitutive rule. As Searle points out,[9] we are normally induced to think of rules as applying to behavior which could be available to us whether or not the rule existed. Some rules are like this, they are regulative like commandments: don't take the goods of another. But there are other rules, e.g., that governing the Queen's move in chess, which are not so separable. If one suspends these rules, or imagines a state in which they have not yet been introduced, then the whole range of behavior in question, in this case, chess playing, would not be. There would still, of course, be the activity of pushing a wood piece around on a board made of squares 8 by 8; but this is not chess any longer. Rules of this kind are constitutive rules. By contrast again, there are other rules of chess, such as that one say "j'adoube" when one touches a piece without intending to play it, which are clearly regulative.[10]

I am suggesting that this notion of the constitutive be extended beyond the domain of rule-governed behavior. That is why I suggest the vaguer word 'practice'. Even in an area where there are no clearly defined rules, there are distinctions between different sorts of behavior such that one sort is considered the appropriate form for one action or context, the other for another action or context, e.g., doing or saying certain things amounts to breaking off negotiations, doing or saying other things amounts to making a new offer. But just as there are constitutive rules, i.e., rules such that the behavior they govern could not exist without them, and which are in this sense inseparable from that behavior, so I am suggesting that there are constitutive distinctions, constitutive ranges of language which are similarly inseparable, in that certain practices are not without them.

We can reverse this relationship and say that all the institutions and practices by which we live are constituted by certain distinctions and hence a certain language which is thus essential to them. We can take voting, a practice which is central to large numbers of institutions in a democratic society. What is essential to the practice of voting is that some decision or verdict be delivered (a man elected, a measure passed), through some criterion of preponderance (simple majority, two-thirds majority, or whatever) out of a set of micro-choices (the votes of the citizens, MPs, delegates). If there is not some such significance attached to our behavior, no amount of marking and counting pieces of paper, raising hands, walking out into lobbies amounts to voting. From this it follows that the institution of voting must be such that certain distinctions have application: e.g., that between someone being elected, or a measure passed, and their failing of election, or passage; that between a valid vote and an invalid one which in turn requires a distinction between a real choice and one which is forced or counterfeited. For no matter how far we move from the Rousseauian notion that each man decide in full autonomy, the very institution of the vote requires that in some sense the enfranchised choose. For there to be voting in a sense recognizably like ours, there must be a distinction in men's self-interpretations between autonomy and forced choice.

This is to say that an activity of marking and counting papers has to bear intentional descriptions which fall within a certain range before we can agree to call it voting, just as the intercourse of two men or teams has to bear descriptions of a certain range before we will call it negotiation. Or in other words, that some practice is voting or negotiation has to do in part with the vocabulary established in a society as appropriate for engaging in it or describing it.

Hence implicit in these practices is a certain vision of the agent and his relation to others and to society. We saw in connection with negotiation in our society that it requires a picture of the parties as in some sense autonomous, and as entering into willed relations. And this picture carries with it certain implicit norms, such as that of good faith mentioned above, or a norm of rationality, that agreement correspond to one's goals as far as attainable, or the norm of continued freedom of action as far as attainable. These practices require that one's actions and relations be seen in the light of this picture and the accompanying norms, good faith, autonomy, and rationality. But men do not see themselves in this way in all societies, nor do they understand these norms in all societies. The experience of autonomy as we know it, the sense of rational action and the satisfactions thereof, are unavailable to them. The meaning of these terms is opaque to them because they have a different structure of experiential meaning open to them.

We can think of the difference between our society and the simplified version of the traditional Japanese village as consisting in this, that the range of meaning open to the members of the two societies is very different. But what we are dealing with here is not subjective meaning which can fit into the categorial grid of behavioral political science, but rather intersubjective meanings. It is not just that the people in our society all or mostly have a given set of ideas in their heads and subscribe to a given set of goals. The meanings and norms implicit in these practices are not just in the minds of the actors but are out there in the practices themselves, practices which cannot be conceived as a set of individual actions, but which are essentially modes of social relation, of mutual action.

The actors may have all sorts of beliefs and attitudes which may be rightly thought of as their individual beliefs and attitudes, even if others share them; they may subscribe to certain policy goals or certain forms of theory about the polity, or feel resentment at certain things, and so on. They bring these with them into their negotiations, and strive to satisfy them. But what they do not bring into the negotiations is the set of ideas and norms constitutive of negotiation themselves. These must be the common property of the society before there can be any question of anyone entering into negotiation or not. Hence they are not subjective meanings, the property of one or some individuals, but rather intersubjective meanings, which are constitutive of the social matrix in which individuals find themselves and act.

The intersubjective meanings which are the background to social action are often treated by political scientists under the heading "consensus." By this is meant convergence of beliefs on certain basic matters, or of attitude. But the two are not the same. Whether there is consensus or not, the condition of there being either one or the other is a certain set of common terms of reference. A society in which this was lacking would not be a society in the normal sense of the term, but several. Perhaps some multi-racial or multi-tribal states approach this limit. Some multi-national states are bedevilled by consistent cross-purposes, e.g., my own country. But consensus as a convergence of beliefs or values is not the opposite of this kind of fundamental diversity. Rather the opposite of diversity is a high degree of intersubjective meanings. And this can go along with profound cleavage. Indeed, intersubjective meanings are a condition of a certain kind of very profound cleavage, such as was visible in the Reformation, or the American Civil War, or splits in left wing parties, where the dispute is at fever pitch just because both sides can fully understand the other.

In other words, convergence of belief or attitude or its absence presupposes a common language in which these beliefs can be formulated, and in which these foundations can be opposed. Much of this common language in any society is rooted in its institutions and practices; it is constitutive of these institutions and practices. It is part of the intersubjective meanings. To put the point another way, apart from the question of how much people's beliefs converge is the question of how much they have a common language of social and political reality in which these beliefs are expressed. This second question cannot be reduced to the first; intersubjective meaning is not a matter of converging beliefs or values. When we speak of consensus we speak of beliefs and values which could be the property of a single person, or many, or all; but intersubjective meanings could not be the property of a single person because they are rooted in social practice.

We can perhaps see this if we envisage the situation in which the ideas and norms underlying a practice are the property of single individuals. This is what happens when single individuals from one society interiorize the notions and values of another, e.g., children in missionary schools. Here we have a totally different situation. We *are* really talking now about subjective beliefs and attitudes. The ideas are abstract, they are mere social "ideals." Whereas in the original society, these ideas and norms are rooted in their social relations, and are that on the basis of which they can formulate opinions and ideals.

We can see this in connection with the example we have been using all along, that of negotiations. The vision of a society based on negotiation is coming in for heavy attack by a growing segment of modern youth, as are the attendant norms of rationality and the definition of autonomy. This is a dramatic failure of "consensus." But this cleavage takes place in the ambit of this intersubjective meaning, the social practice of negotiation as it is lived in our society. The rejection wouldn't have the bitter quality it has if what is rejected were not understood in common, because it is part of a social practice which we find it hard to avoid, so pervasive is it in our society. At the same time there is a reaching out for other forms which have still the "abstract" quality of ideals which are subjective in this sense, that is, not rooted in practice; which is what makes the rebellion look so "unreal" to outsiders, and so irrational.

iii

Intersubjective meanings, ways of experiencing action in society which are expressed in the language and descriptions constitutive of institutions and practices, do not fit into the categorial grid of mainstream political science. This allows only for an intersubjective reality which is brute data identifiable. But social practices and institutions which are partly constituted by certain ways of talking about them are not so identifiable. We have to understand the language, the underlying meanings, which constitute them.

We can allow, once we accept a certain set of institutions or practices as our starting point and not as objects of further questioning, that we can easily take as brute data that certain acts are judged to take place or certain states judged to hold within the semantic field of these practices. For instance, that someone has voted Liberal, or signed the petition. We can then go on to correlate certain subjective meanings—beliefs, attitudes, etc.—with this behavior or its lack. But this means that we give up trying to define further just what these practices and institutions are, what the meanings are which they require and hence sustain. For these meanings do not fit into the grid; they are not subjective beliefs or values, but are constitutive of social reality. In order to get at them we have to drop the basic premise that social reality is made up of brute data alone. For any characterization of the meanings underlying these practices is open to question by someone offering an alternative interpretation. The negation of this is what was meant as brute data. We have to admit that intersubjective social reality has to be partly defined in terms of meanings; that meanings as subjective are not just in causal interaction with a social reality made up of brute data, but that as intersubjective they are constitutive of this reality.

We have been talking here of intersubjective meanings. And earlier I was contrasting the question of intersubjective meaning with that of consensus as convergence of opinions. But there is another kind of nonsubjective meaning which is also often inadequately discussed under the head of "consensus." In a society with a strong web of intersubjective meanings, there can be a more or less powerful set of common meanings. By these I mean notions of what is significant which are not just shared in the sense that everyone has them, but are also common in the sense of being in the common reference world. Thus, almost everyone in our society may share a susceptibility to a certain kind of feminine beauty, but this may not be a common meaning. It may be known to no one, except perhaps market researchers, who play on it in their advertisements. But the survival of a national identity as francophones is a common meaning of *Québecois*; for it is not just shared, and not just known to be shared, but its being a common aspiration is one of the common reference points of all debate, communication, and all public life in the society.

We can speak of a shared belief, aspiration, etc. when there is convergence between the subjective beliefs, aspirations, of many individuals. But it is part of the meaning of a common aspiration, belief, celebration, etc. that it be not just shared but part of the common reference world. Or to put it another way, its being shared is a collective act, it is a consciousness which is communally sustained, whereas sharing is something we do each on his own, as it were, even if each of us is influenced by the others.

Common meanings are the basis of community. Intersubjective meaning gives a people a common language to talk about social reality and a common understanding of certain norms, but only with common meanings does this common reference world contain significant common actions, celebrations, and feelings. These are objects in the world that everybody shares. This is what makes community.

Once again, we cannot really understand this phenomenon through the usual definition of consensus as convergence of opinion and value. For what is meant here is something more than convergence. Convergence is what happens when our values are shared. But what is required for common meanings is that this shared value be part of the common world, that this sharing be shared. But we could also say that common meanings are quite other than consensus, for they can subsist with a high degree of cleavage; this is what happens when a common meaning comes to be lived and understood differently by different groups in a society. It remains a common meaning, because there is the reference point which is the common purpose, aspiration, celebration. Such is for example the American Way, or freedom as understood in the USA. But this common meaning is differently articulated by different groups. This is the basis of the bitterest fights in a society, and this we are also seeing in the U.S. today. Perhaps one might say that a common meaning is very often the cause of the most bitter lack of consensus. It thus must not be confused with convergence of opinion, value, attitude.

Of course, common meanings and intersubjective meanings are closely interwoven. There must be a powerful net of intersubjective meanings for there to be common meanings; and the result of powerful common meanings is the development of a greater web of intersubjective meanings as people live in community.

On the other hand, when common meanings wither, which they can do through the kind of deep dissensus we described earlier, the groups tend to grow apart and develop different languages of social reality, hence to share less intersubjective meanings.

Hence, to take our above example again, there has been a powerful common meaning in our civilization around a certain vision of the free society in which bargaining has a central place. This has helped to entrench the social practice of negotiation which makes us participate in this intersubjective meaning. But there is a severe challenge to this common meaning today, as we have seen. Should those who object to it really succeed in building up an alternative society, there would develop a gap between those who remain in the present type of society and those who had founded the new one.

Common meanings, as well as intersubjective ones, fall through the net of mainstream social science. They can find no place in its categories. For they are not simply a converging set of subjective reactions, but part of the common world. What the ontology of mainstream social science lacks is the notion of meaning as not simply for an individual subject; of a subject who can be a "we" as well as an "I." The exclusion of this possibility, of the communal, comes once again from the baleful influence of the epistemological tradition for which all knowledge has to be reconstructed from the impressions imprinted on the individual subject. But if we free ourselves from the hold of these prejudices, this seems a wildly implausible view about the development of human consciousness; we are aware of the world through a "we" before we are through an "I." Hence we need the distinction between what is just shared in the sense that each of us has it in our individual worlds, and that which is in the common world. But the very idea of something which is in the common world in contradistinction to what is in all the individual worlds is totally opaque to empiricist epistemology. Hence it finds no place in mainstream social science. What this results in must now be seen.

III

Thus, to sum up the last pages: a social science which wishes to fulfill the requirements of the empiricist tradition naturally tries to reconstruct social reality as consisting of brute data alone. These data are the acts of people (behavior) as identified supposedly beyond interpretation either by physical descriptions or by descriptions clearly defined by institutions and practices; and secondly, they include the subjective reality of individuals' beliefs, attitudes, values, as attested by their responses to certain forms of words, or in some cases their overt non-verbal behavior.

What this excludes is a consideration of social reality as characterized by intersubjective and common meanings. It excludes, for instance, an attempt to understand our civilization, in which negotiation plays such a central part both in fact and in justificatory theory, by probing the self-definitions of agent, other and social relatedness which it embodies. Such definitions which deal with the meaning for agents of their own and others' action, and of the social relations in which they stand, do not in any sense record brute data, in the sense that this term is being used in this argument; that is, they are in no sense beyond challenge by those who would quarrel with our interpretations of these meanings.

Thus, I tried to adumbrate above the vision implicit in the practice of negotiation by reference to certain notions of autonomy and rationality. But this reading will undoubtedly be challenged by those who have different fundamental conceptions of man, human motivation, the human condition; or even by those who judge other features of our present predicament to have greater importance. If we wish to avoid these disputes, and have a science grounded in verification as this is understood by the logical empiricists, then we have to avoid this level of study altogether and hope to make do with a correlation of behavior which is brute data identifiable.

A similar point goes for the distinction between common meanings and shared subjective meanings. We can hope to identify the subjective meanings of individuals if we take these in the sense in which there are adequate criteria for them in people's dissent or assent to verbal formulae or their brute data identifiable behavior. But once we allow the distinction between such subjective meanings which are widely shared and genuine common meanings, then we can no longer make do with brute data indentification. We are in a domain where our definitions can be challenged by those with another reading.

The profound option of mainstream social scientists for the empiricist conception of knowledge and science makes it inevitable that they should accept the verification model of political science and the categorial principles that this entails. This means in turn that a study of our civilization in terms of its intersubjective and common meanings is ruled out. Rather this whole level of study is made invisible.

On the mainstream view, therefore, the different practices and institutions of different societies are not seen as related to different clusters of intersubjective or common meanings, rather, we should be able to differentiate them by different clusters of "behavior" and/or subjective meaning. The comparison between societies requires on this view that we elaborate a universal vocabulary of behavior which will allow us to present the different forms and practices of different societies in the same conceptual web.

Now present day political science is contemptuous of the older attempt at comparative politics via a comparison of institutions. An influential school of our day has therefore shifted comparison to certain practices, or very general classes of practices, and proposes to compare societies according to the different ways in which these practices are carried on. Such are the "functions" of the influential "developmental approach."[11] But it is epistemologically crucial that such functions be identified independently of those intersubjective meanings which are different in different societies; for otherwise, they will not be genuinely universal; or will be universal only in the loose and unilluminating sense that the function-name can be given application in every society but with varying, and often widely varying meaning—the same term being "glossed" very differently by different sets of practices and intersubjective meanings. The danger that such universality might not hold is not even suspected by mainstream political scientists since they are unaware that there is such a level of description as that which defines intersubjective meanings and are convinced that functions and the various structures which perform them can be identified in terms of brute data behavior.

But the result of ignoring the difference in intersubjective meanings can be disastrous to a science of comparative politics, viz., that we interpret all other societies in the categories of our own. Ironically, this is what seems to have happened to American political science. Having strongly criticized the old institution-focussed comparative politics for its ethnocentricity (or Western bias), it proposes to understand the politics of all society in terms of such functions, for instance, as "interest articulation" and "interest aggregation" whose definition is strongly influenced by the bargaining culture of our civilization, but which is far from being guaranteed appropriateness elsewhere. The not surprising result is a theory of political development which places the Atlantic-type polity at the summit of human political achievement. . . .

IV

It can be argued then, that mainstream social science is kept within certain limits by its categorial principles which are rooted in the traditional epistemology of empiricism; and secondly, that these restrictions are a severe handicap and prevent us from coming to grips with important problems of our day which should be the object of political science. We need to go beyond the bounds of a science based on verification to one which would study the intersubjective and common meanings embedded in social reality.

But this science would be hermeneutical in the sense that has been developed in this paper. It would not be founded on brute data; its most primitive data would be readings of meanings, and its object would have the three properties mentioned above: the meanings are for a subject in a field or fields; they are moreover meanings which are partially constituted by self-definitions, which are in this sense already interpretations, and which can thus be reexpressed or made explicit by a science of politics. In our case, the subject may be a society or community; but the intersubjective meanings, as we saw, embody a certain self-definition, a vision of the agent and his society, which is that of the society or community.

But then the difficulties which the proponents of the verification model foresee will arise. If we have a science which has no brute data, which relies on readings, then it cannot but move in a hermeneutical circle. A given reading of the intersubjective meanings of a society, or of given institutions or practices, may seem well founded, because it makes sense of these practices or the development of that society. But the conviction that it does make sense of this history itself is founded on futher related readings. Thus, what I said above on the identity-crisis which is generated by our society makes sense and holds together only if one accepts this reading of the intersubjective meanings of our society, and if one accepts this reading of the rebellion against our society by many young people (sc. the reading in terms of identity-crisis). These two readings make sense together, so that in a sense the explanation as a whole reposes on the readings, and the readings in their turn are strengthened by the explanation as a whole.

But if these readings seem implausible, or even more, if they are not understood by our interlocutor, there is no verification procedure which we can fall back on. We can only continue to offer interpretations; we are in an interpretative circle.

But the ideal of a science of verification is to find an appeal beyond differences of interpretation. Insight will always be useful in discovery, but should not have to play any part in establishing the truth of its findings. This ideal can be said to have been met by our natural sciences. But a hermeneutic science cannot but rely on insight. It requires that one have the sensibility and understanding necessary to be able to make and comprehend the readings by which we can explain the reality concerned. In physics we might argue that if someone does not accept a true theory, then either he has not been shown enough (brute data) evidence (perhaps not enough is yet available), or he cannot understand and apply some formalized language. But in the sciences of man conceived as hermeneutical, the nonacceptance of a true or illuminating theory may come from neither of these, indeed is unlikely to be due to either of these, but rather from a failure to grasp the meaning field in question, an inability to make and understand readings of this field.

In other words, in a hermeneutical science, a certain measure of insight is indispensable, and this insight cannot be communicated by the gathering of brute data, or initiation in modes of formal reasoning or some combination of these. It is unformalizable. But this is a scandalous result according to the authoritative conception of science in our tradition, which is shared even by many of those who are highly critical of the approach of mainstream psychology, or sociology, or political science. For its means that this is not a study in which anyone can engage, regardless of their level of insight; that some claims of the form: "if you don't understand, then your intuitions are at fault, are blind or inadequate," some claims of this form will be justified; that some differences will be nonarbitrable by further evidence, but that each side can only make appeal to deeper insight on the part of the other. The superiority of one position over another will thus consist in this, that from the more adequate position one can understand one's own stand and that of one's opponent, but not the other way around. It goes without saying that this argument can only have weight for those in the superior position.

Thus, a hermeneutical science encounters a gap in intuitions, which is the other side, as it were, of the hermeneutical circle. But the situation is graver than this; for this gap is bound up with our divergent options in politics and life.

We speak of a gap when some cannot understand the kind of self-definition which others are proposing as underlying a certain society or set of institutions. Thus some positivistically-minded thinkers will find the language of identity-theory quite opaque; and some thinkers will not recognize any theory which does not fit with the categorial presuppositions of empiricism. But self-definitions are not only important to us as scientists who are trying to understand some, perhaps distant, social reality. As men we are self-defining beings, and we are partly what we are in virtue of the self-definitions which we have accepted, however we have come by them. What self-definitions we understand and what ones we don't understand, is closely linked with the self-definitions which help to constitute what we are. If it is too simple to say that one only understands an "ideology" which one subscribes to, it is nevertheless hard to deny that we have great difficulty grasping definitions whose terms structure the world in ways which are utterly different from, incompatible with our own.

Hence the gap in intuitions doesn't just divide different theoretical positions, it also tends to divide different fundamental options in life. The practical and the theoretical are inextricably joined here. It may not just be that to understand a certain explanation one has to sharpen one's intuitions, it may be that one has to change one's orientation—if not in adopting another orientation, at least in living one's own in a way which allows for greater comprehension of others. Thus, in the sciences of man insofar as they are hermeneutical there can be a valid response to "I don't understand" which takes the form, not only "develop your intuitions," but more radically "change yourself." This puts an end to any aspiration to a value-free or "ideology-free" science of man. A study of the science of man is inseparable from an examination of the options between which men must choose.

This means that we can speak here not only of error, but of illusion. We speak of "illusion" when we are dealing with something of greater substance than error, error which in a sense builds a counterfeit reality of its own. But errors of interpretation of meaning, which are also self-definitions of those who interpret and hence inform their lives, are more than errors in this sense: they are sustained by certain practices of which they are constitutive. It is not implausible to single out as examples two rampant illusions in our present society. One is that of the proponents of the bargaining society who can recognize nothing but either bargaining gambits or madness in those who rebel against this society. Here the error is sustained by the practices of the bargaining culture, and given a semblance of reality by the refusal to treat any protests on other terms; it hence acquires the more substantive reality of illusion. The second example is provided by much "revolutionary" activity in our society which in desperate search for an alternative mode of life purports to see its situation in that of an Andean guerilla or Chinese peasants. Lived out, this passes from the stage of laughable error to tragic illusion. One illusion cannot recognize the possibility of human variation, the other cannot see any limits to man's ability to transform itself. Both make a valid science of man impossible.

In face of all this, we might be so scandalized by the prospect of such a hermeneutical science, that we will want to go back to the verification model. Why can we not take our understanding of meaning as part of the logic of discovery, as the logical empiricists suggest for our unformalizable insights, and still found our science on the exactness of our predictions? Our insightful understanding of the intersubjective meanings of our society will then serve to elaborate fruitful hypotheses, but the proof of these puddings will remain in the degree they enable us to predict.

The answer is that if the epistemological views underlying the science of interpretation are right, such exact prediction is radically impossible. This, for three reasons of ascending order of fundamentalness.

The first is the well-known "open system" predicament, one shared by human life and meteorology, that we cannot shield a certain domain of human events, the psychological, economic, political, from external interference; it is impossible to delineate a closed system.

The second, more fundamental, is that if we are to understand men by a science of interpretation, we cannot achieve the degree of fine exactitude of a science based on brute data. The data of natural science admit of measurement to virtually any degree of exactitude. But different interpretations cannot be judged in this way. At the same time different nuances of interpretation may lead to different predictions in some circumstances, and these different outcomes may eventually create widely varying futures. Hence it is more than easy to be wide of the mark.

But the third and most fundamental reason for the impossibility of hard prediction is that man is a self-defining animal. With changes in his self-definition go changes in what man is, such that he has to be understood in different terms. But the conceptual mutations in human history can and frequently do produce conceptual webs which are incommensurable, that is, where the terms can't be defined in relation to a common stratum of expressions. The entirely different notions of bargaining in our society and in some primitive ones provide an example. Each will be glossed in terms of practices, institutions, ideas in each society which have nothing corresponding to them in the other.

The success of prediction in the natural sciences is bound up with the fact that all states of the system, past and future, can be described in the same range of concepts, as values, say, of the same variables. Hence all future states of the solar system can be characterized, as past ones are, in the language of Newtonian mechanics. This is far from being a sufficient condition of exact prediction, but it is a necessary one in this sense, that only if past and future are brought under the same conceptual net can one understand the states of the latter as some function of the states of the former, and hence predict.

This conceptual unity is vitiated in the sciences of man by the fact of conceptual innovation which in turn alters human reality. The very terms in which the future will have to be characterized if we are to understand it properly are not all available to us at present. Hence we have such radically unpredictable events as the culture of youth today, the Puritan rebellion of the sixteenth and seventeenth centuries, the development of Soviet society, etc.

And thus, it is much easier to understand after the fact than it is to predict. Human science is largely *ex post* understanding. Or often one has the sense of impending change, of some big reorganization, but is powerless to make clear what it will consist in: one lacks the vocabulary. But there is a clear assymetry here, which there is not (or not supposed to be) in natural science, where events are said to be predicted from the theory with exactly the same ease with which one explains past events and by exactly the same process. In human science this will never be the case.

Of course, we strive *ex post* to understand the changes, and to do this we try to develop a language in which we can situate the incommensurable webs of concepts. We see the rise of Puritanism, for instance, as a shift in man's stance to the sacred; and thus, we have a language in which we can express both stances—the earlier mediaeval Catholic one and the Puritan rebellion—as "glosses" on this fundamental term. We thus have a language in which to talk of the transition. But think how we acquired it. This general category of the sacred is acquired not only from our experience of the shift which came in the Reformation, but from the study of human religion in general, including primitive religion, and with the detachment which came with secularization. It would be conceivable, but unthinkable, that a mediaeval Catholic could have this conception—or for that matter a Puritan. These two protagonists only had a language of condemnation for each other: "heretic," "idolator." The place for such a concept was pre-empted by a certain way of living the sacred. After a big change has happened, and the trauma has been resorbed, it is possible to try to understand it, because one now has available the new language, the transformed meaning world. But hard prediction before just makes one a laughing stock. Really to be able to predict the future would be to have explicited so clearly the human condition that one would already have pre-empted all cultural innovation and transformation. This is hardly in the bounds of the possible.

Sometimes men show amazing prescience: the myth of Faust, for instance, which is treated several times at the beginning of the modern era. There is a kind of prophesy here, a premonition. But what characterizes these bursts of foresight is that they see through a glass darkly, for they see in terms of the old language: Faust sells his soul to the devil. They are in no sense hard predictions. Human science looks backward. It is inescapably historical.

There are thus good grounds both in epistemological arguments and in their greater fruitfulness for opting for hermeneutical sciences of man. But we cannot hide from ourselves how greatly this option breaks with certain commonly held notions about our scientific tradition. We cannot measure such sciences against the requirements of a science of verification: we cannot judge them by their predictive capacity. We have to accept that they are founded on intuitions which all do not share, and what is worse that these intuitions are closely bound up with our fundamental options. These sciences cannot be "*wertfrei*"; they are moral sciences in a more radical sense than the eighteenth century understood. Finally, their successful prosecution requires a high degree of self-knowledge, a freedom from illusion, in the sense of error which is rooted and expressed in one's way of life; for our incapacity to understand is rooted in our own self-definitions, hence in what we are. To say this is not to say anything new: Aristotle makes a similar point in Book I of the *Ethics*. But it is still radically shocking and unassimilable to the mainstream of modern science.

NOTES

1. Cf. e.g., H. G. Gadamer, *Wahrheit und Methode*, Tübingen, 1960.
2. Cf. Paul Ricoeur, *De L'interprétation*, Paris, 1965.
3. Cf. e.g., J. Habermas, *Erkenntnis und Interesse*, Frankfurt, 1968.
4. The notion of brute data here has some relation to, but is not at all the same as the "brute facts" discussed by Elizabeth Anscombe, "On Brute Facts," *Analysis*, v. 18, 1957–1958, pp. 69–72, and John Searle, *Speech Acts,* Cambridge, 1969, pp. 50–53. For Anscombe and Searle, brute facts are contrasted to what may be called 'institutional facts', to use Searle's term, i.e., facts which presuppose the existence of certain institutions. Voting would be an example. But, as we shall see below in part II, some institutional facts, such as X's having voted Liberal, can be verified as brute data in the sense used here, and thus find a place in the category of political behavior. What cannot

as easily be described in terms of brute data are the institutions themselves. Cf. the discussion below in part II.

5. Cf. discussion in M. Minsky, *Computation,* Englewood Cliffs, N.J., 1967, pp. 104–107, where Minsky explicitly argues that an effective procedure, which no longer requires intuition or interpretation, is one which can be realized by a machine.

6. Cf. H. McClosky, "Consensus and Ideology in American Politics," *American Political Science Review*, v. 58, 1964, pp. 361–382.

7. Gabriel A. Almond and G. Bingham Powell, *Comparative Politics: A Developmental Approach*, Boston and Toronto, 1966. Page references in my text here and below are to this work.

8. Cf. Thomas C. Smith, *The Agrarian Origins of Modern Japan*. Stanford, 1959, ch. 5. This type of consensus is also found in other traditional societies. Cf. for instance, the *desa* system of the Indonesian village.

9. J. Searle, *Speech Acts: An Essay in the Philosophy of Language,* Cambridge, 1969, pp. 33–42.

10. Cf. the discussion in Stanley Cavell, *Must We Mean What We Say?* New York, 1969, pp. 21–31.

11. Cf. Almond and Powell, *op. cit.*

Suggested Readings

ABEL, Theodore. "Verstehen I and Verstehen II." *Theory and Decision* 6 (1975):99–102.

APEL, Karl-Otto. *Analytic Philosophy of Language and the Geisteswissenschaften.* Dordrecht, Holland: Reidel, 1967.

BRAITHWAITE, R. B. *Scientific Explanation.* Cambridge: At the University Press, 1953.

BRAUDE, Lee. "Die Verstehende Soziologie: A New Look at an Old Problem." *Sociology and Social Research* 50 (1966):230–35.

BRAYBROOKE, David. *Philosophical Problems of the Social Sciences.* New York: Macmillan, 1965.

BRODBECK, May. "Meaning and Action." *Philosophy of Science* 30 (1964):309–24; reprinted in *Readings in the Philosophy of the Social Sciences,* edited by Brodbeck, pp. 58–78. New York: Macmillan, 1968.

COHEN, Carl. "Naturalism and the Method of Verstehen." *Journal of Philosophy* 51 (1954):220–25.

COULTER, Jeff. "Decontextualized Meanings: Current Approaches to *Verstehende* Investigations." *Sociological Review* 19 (1971):301–23.

CUNNINGHAM, Frank U. "More on Understanding in the Social Sciences." *Inquiry* 10 (1967):321–28.

DIESING, Paul. "Subjectivity and Objectivity in the Social Sciences." *Philosophy of the Social Sciences* 2 (1972):147–65.

DIQUATTRO, Arthur W. "*Verstehen* as an Empirical Concept." *Sociology and Social Research* 57 (1972):32–42.

DRAY, William H. *Laws and Explanation in History.* London: Oxford University Press, 1957.

GIDDENS, Anthony, ed. *Positivism and Sociology.* London: Heinemann, 1974.

GRUNER, Rolf. "The Notion of Understanding: Replies to Cunningham and Van Evra." *Inquiry* 12 (1969):349–56.

_____. "Understanding in the Social Sciences and in History." *Inquiry* 10 (1967):151–63.

HAYEK, F. A. von. *The Counter-Revolution of Science.* Glencoe, Ill.: Free Press, 1952.

HEMPEL, Carl G. *Aspects of Scientific Explanation and Other Essays in the Philosophy of Science.* New York: Free Press, 1965; especially "Typological Methods in the Natural and Social Sciences," "The Function of General Laws in History," "Studies in the Logic of Explanation," and "Aspects of Scientific Explanation," especially section 10 of the latter: "The Concept of Rationality and the Logic of Explanation by Reasons."

LEAT, Diana. "Misunderstanding *Verstehen.*" *Sociological Review* 20 (1972):29–38.

McCARTHY, Thomas A. "On Misunderstanding Understanding." *Theory and Decision* 3 (1973):351–70.

MARKOVIĆ, Mihailo. "The Problem of Reification and the *Verstehen-Erklären* Controversy." *Acta Sociologica* 15 (1972):27–38.

MARTIN, Jane R. "Another look at the Doctrine of Verstehen." *British Journal of the Philosophy of Science* 20 (1969):53–67.

POPPER, Karl R. *The Poverty of Historicism.* London: Routledge and Kegan Paul, 1957.

RADNITZKY, Gerard. *Anglo-Saxon Schools of Metascience.* Contemporary Schools of Metascience, vol. 1. Göteborg, Sweden: Akademiförlaget, 1968.

SCRIVEN, Michael. "Logical Positivism and the Behavioral Sciences." In *The Legacy of Logical Positivism*, edited by Peter Achinstein and Stephen F. Barker, pp. 195–210. Baltimore: Johns Hopkins Press, 1969.

_____. "Verstehen Again." *Theory and Decision* 1 (1971):382–86.

TAYLOR, Charles. "Explaining Action." *Inquiry* 13 (1970):54–89.

_____. *The Explanation of Behavior.* London: Routledge and Kegan Paul, 1964.

_____. "Neutrality in Political Science." In *Philosophy, Politics, and Society,* edited by Peter Laslett and W. G. Runciman, pp. 25–57. Third series. Oxford: Basil Blackwell, 1967.

TRUZZI, Marcello, ed. *Verstehen: Subjective Understanding in the Social Sciences.* Reading, Mass.: Addison-Wesley Publishing Co., 1974.

VAN EVRA, James W. "Understanding in the Social Sciences Revisited." *Inquiry* 12 (1969):347–49.

WARRINER, Charles K. "Social Action, Behavior, and *Verstehen.*" *Sociological Quarterly* 10 (1969):501–11.

WAX, Murray L. "On Misunderstanding Verstehen: A Reply to Abel" (with a rejoinder). *Sociology and Social Research* 51 (1967):323–36.

PART THREE

The Wittgensteinian Reformulation

Introduction

THE NEOPOSITIVIST ANALYSIS OF VERSTEHEN AS A HEURISTIC DEVICE based on empathetic identification is certainly relevant to some of the earlier versions in which the theory of understanding was historically propounded —for instance, to the psychologically oriented conceptions of Schleiermacher and the early Dilthey. Less obvious is its relevance to other versions—for instance, to the neo-Kantian approaches derived from a transcendental conception of culture as constituted by certain *Wertbeziehungen*, or value-relations (Rickert); to approaches incorporating Hegel's notion of objective spirit (later Dilthey); or to approaches based on a hermeneutics of language (Heidegger, Gadamer). But it is not necessary to look to Germany for significantly different theories of interpretive understanding. Serious challenges to the positivist analysis can also be found within Anglo-Saxon thought. There is, for example, the current flowing from the writings of Michael Oakeshott and R. G. Collingwood—two thinkers quite familiar with the German tradition of the *Geisteswissenschaften*—and which presently numbers William Dray among its chief spokesmen. The principal challenge, however, has emerged from one of the nerve centers of analytic philosophy itself: from the work of Ludwig Wittgenstein.

Wittgenstein's early study, the *Tractatus Logico-Philosophicus,* has been referred to as a "bible of logical positivism"; together with Bertrand Russell's logical atomism and the thought of the Vienna Circle, it is a principal source of this brand of analytic philosophy. In the *Tractatus* Wittgenstein attempts to fix the limits of language (and of thought and of the world) by disclosing its uniform logical structure. The universal structure of language, its "essence," is to be found in the logical form concealed beneath the surface of everyday discourse. This form, he asserts, mirrors the structure of the world: "Logic pervades the world: the limits of the world are also its limits." (5.61) "The fact that the propositions of logic are tautologies *shows* the formal-logical properties of language and the world." (6.12) In Wittgenstein's later work, most importantly his *Philosophical Investigations*, this transcendental analysis of lan-

137

guage is explicitly rejected in favor of an analysis of concrete "language games" as "forms of life." And this rejection set in motion a second main stream of analytic philosophy, usually referred to as "ordinary language analysis."

Although Wittgenstein did not himself focus on the problem of sociological understanding and although his own analyses of human action may have tended in a more or less behavioristic direction, the importance of his later ideas for the theory of *Verstehen* are evident. Language is no longer thought of as a logically rigid essence. Rather, words have meanings only within diverse language games that are forms of life—complexes of speech and action, intentions and emotions, interests and attitudes. In Wittgenstein's view, these polymorphous arrays of language and practice are not without their own structures or "grammars." The activities that comprise a language game proceed according to definite rules (although they are not everywhere circumscribed by rules). In learning to play a language game we come to engage in agreed common practices and to share agreed common criteria for their performance. These networks of conventions, or forms of life, are the foundation of intersubjectivity and interaction, of meaningful communication and meaningful practice.

Ideas of this kind seem to point philosophy in the direction of a general sociology or anthropology of conceptual systems. But Wittgenstein himself was inspired by much more ascetic ideals: philosophers were not called upon to propound theories, even descriptive theories of language; their task, rather, was to describe facts about language that were already perfectly familiar, in order to break the hold upon our minds of philosophical confusions and paradoxes—to "assemble reminders" for the therapeutic purpose of dispelling the latter. However, in 1958 Peter Winch attempted to draw out the consequences of Wittgenstein's theory of language games for the foundations of social inquiry. His little book, *The Idea of a Social Science and Its Relation to Philosophy*, has ever since been the subject of controversy. For Winch not only makes explicit the latent challenge of Wittgenstein's ideas to the neopositivist logic of unified science; he uses them to withdraw social inquiry from the realm of science and to locate it in the immediate vicinity of philosophy. In doing so he develops a conception of interpretive understanding that is much closer to that of hermeneutics than to the empathy theory of neopositivism.

In the second chapter of his book Winch characterizes meaningful behavior as behavior that is "*ipso facto* rule-governed." (p. 52)[1] This is not to say that it is simply a putting into effect of preexisting principles. Rather, principles and rules "arise in the course of conduct and are intelligible only in relation to the conduct out of which they arise." (p. 63) On the other hand, "the nature of the conduct out of which they arise can only be grasped as an embodiment of those principles." (p. 63) From this perspective the problem of understanding human action arises already at the level of observation and description. The characterization of a sequence of movements as an action of a certain sort involves interpreting the behavior as having a certain point and as situated within a system of rules, norms, standards and the like. It essentially *presupposes* an understanding of the concepts and rules of the agent as well as the criteria for their application. In other words, the agents whose behavior the social scientist seeks to understand have themselves an understanding of that behavior, ideas about what they are doing and why they are doing it. The heuristic application of empathetic identification discussed by the neopositivists presupposes *Verstehen* in a more fundamental sense, that is, understanding the language game or form of life in which the behavior to be explained is located. In Winch's terms: "Any more reflective understanding [of social phenomena] must necessarily presuppose, if it is to count as genuine understanding at all, the participant's unreflective understanding." (p. 89)

Contrary to what Rudner implies in his critique of Winch's "reproductive fallacy" (see Part 2), Winch does not deny the possibility of developing and employing sociological categories other than those of the participant. His claim is rather that the social scientist's access to his data, his formulation of the "more reflective" categories, and his application of them must be mediated through the participant's way of viewing his world; he must understand the "language game" that is being "played." And this, says Winch, is much more akin to "tracing the internal relations" of a system of ideas than to "the application of generalizations and theories to particular instances." (p. 133) For "social relations between men and the ideas which men's actions embody are really the same thing considered from different points of view." (p. 121)

Winch's argument has been the object of repeated criticism—from Ernest Gellner's charges that it amounts to a "new idealism" and that it dismisses on a priori grounds a number of things that social scientists actually and successfully do to Leon Goldstein's argument that it makes it impossible to explain the historical emergence and development of conceptual systems and A. R. Louch's critique of the idea that understanding social action amounts to understanding the concepts embedded in it and is, therefore, a philosophical and not an empirical undertaking.[2]

One of the most interesting controversies concerns the apparently relativistic implications of Winch's views on *Verstehen*. Although he does not call for "recreating" the thoughts of others in the usual sense of the word, he does insist that the fundamental criteria for identifying actions are taken not from the rules governing the sociologist's investigation but from the rules according to which the activity under investigation is itself carried out. Thus, to take one of his examples, the criteria according to which the social researcher must decide whether two utterances belong to the same class of religious activity—say prayer—are not taken from sociology but from religion itself. Hence, Winch argues, the relation of the sociologist to the performances of religious activity "cannot be that of the observer to the observed" (p. 87); it is rather analogous to the participation of a member of a social group in the activities of that group. This replacement of the empathy model with a participation analogy raises obvious problems. What language game is the sociologist playing? What is the relationship of his language game to that under investigation? Are they simply the same? The reference to the participant's unreflective understanding may or may not suffice for Wittgenstein's therapeutic purposes; it certainly does not suffice as an explication of the logic of *Verstehen*. For Winch's social scientist is not simply "assembling reminders" *in and about the language in question*; he is offering an interpretation of one language game or form of life *in terms of another language game*, his own. The proper analogy seems to be *not participation but translation*.

In a later article, "Understanding a Primitive Society," Winch takes up precisely this issue. The article focuses on the "strain inherent in the situation of the anthropologist" who has to present an account of alien beliefs and practices that is intelligible according to the criteria of the culture to which he and his readers belong. This "strain" involved in translating meanings constituted in one universe of discourse into another raises problems regarding the commensurability of different systems of concepts and practices. Is such "translation" at all possible, and if so, how? Winch defends what has been called "the principle of charity in interpretation." In explicit opposition to the "intellectualism" of earlier generations of anthropologists, he argues that the investigator may not simply assume that he and his culture are paradigms of rationality and intelligibility—this inevitably leads to equating cultural difference with cultural inferiority, that is, to *misunderstanding* other ways of life. He proposes instead that the anthropologist must seek contextually given criteria according to which the alien beliefs and practices appear rational. And this demands a sort of dialectical process in which, by somehow bringing the alien conception of intelligible behavior into relation with our own, we create a new unity for the concept of intelligibility: "Seriously to study another way of life is necessarily to seek to extend our own—not simply to bring the other way of life within the existing boundaries of our own."

This reaction to the practice of anthropologists (for example Frazer and Tylor) who understand societies in terms of the opposition between rationality and irrationality—or more precisely, in terms of the opposition between "our scientific rationality" and "primitive irrationality"—has seemed to many an overreaction. Jarvie accuses Winch of a relativism that undermines all hopes of developing forms of social inquiry deserving of the titles "scientific" or "critical." Winch, he argues, tends to place differing conceptions of reality and rationality on a par. Beliefs and actions cannot be criticized, but must always be understood within their own context; the imposition of alien criteria is always and necessarily a mistake. According to Jarvie this leads to disastrous consequences: there could be no generalizing social science, nor could one legiti- mately evaluate the beliefs of an alien culture either from the point of view of standards current in one's own culture or from the point of view of objective, critical conceptions of reality and rationality. The exchange between Jarvie and Winch brings home with full force the *normative* dimensions of the problem of *Verstehen* that were suggested by Charles Taylor (Part 2). *The inseparability of interpretation from critique* becomes the central issue.[3]

NOTES

1. The pages in parentheses refers to page numbers of Winch's book.
2. For the appropriate references, see the list of suggested readings below.
3. This controversy is amply documented in the volume edited by Bryan R. Wilson, *Rationality*; see suggested readings below.

The Idea of a Social Science

PETER WINCH

Meaningful Behaviour

WITTGENSTEIN'S ACCOUNT OF WHAT IT IS TO FOLLOW A RULE IS, FOR obvious reasons, given principally with an eye to elucidating the nature of language. I have now to show how this treatment may shed light on other forms of human interaction besides speech. The forms of activity in question are, naturally, those to which analogous categories are applicable: those, that is, of which we can sensibly say that they have a *meaning, a symbolic* character. In the words of Max Weber, we are concerned with human behaviour 'if and in so far as the agent or agents associate a subjective *sense (Sinn)* with it'. [*Economy and Society,* Chapter 1.] I want now to consider what is involved in this idea of meaningful behaviour.

Weber says that the 'sense' of which he speaks is something which is 'subjectively intended'; and he says that the notion of meaningful behaviour is closely associated with notions like *motive* and *reason.* ' "Motive" means a meaningful configuration of circumstances which, to the agent or observer, appears as a meaningful "reason" (*Grund*) of the behaviour in question.'

Let us consider some examples of actions which are performed *for a reason.* Suppose that it is said of a certain person, *N*, that he voted Labour at the last General Election because he thought that a Labour government would be the most likely to preserve industrial peace. What kind of explanation is this? The clearest case is that in which *N*, prior to voting, has discussed the pros and cons of voting Labour and has explicitly come to the conclusion: 'I will vote Labour because that is the best way to preserve industrial peace.' That is a paradigm case of someone performing an action for a reason. To say this is not to deny that in some cases, even where *N* has gone through such an explicit process of

Peter Winch, "The Idea of a Social Science," in *The Idea of a Social Science and Its Relation to Philosophy* (London: Routledge and Kegan Paul, 1958), pp. 45–50, 83–91, 103–16, 123–26.

reasoning, it may be possible to dispute whether the reason he has given is in fact the real reason for his behaviour. But there is very often no room for doubt; and if this were not so, the idea of *a reason for an action* would be in danger of completely losing its sense. (This point will assume greater importance subsequently, when I come to discuss the work of Pareto.)

The type of case which I have taken as a paradigm is not the only one covered by Weber's concept. But the paradigm exhibits clearly one feature which I believe to have a more general importance. Suppose that an observer, O, is offering the above explanation for N's having voted Labour: then it should be noted that the force of O's explanation rests on the fact that the concepts which appear in it must be grasped not merely by O and his hearers, but also *by N himself*. N must have some idea of what it is to 'preserve industrial peace' and of a connection between this and the kind of government which he expects to be in power if Labour is elected. (For my present purposes it is unnecessary to raise the question whether N's beliefs in a particular instance are true or not.)

Not all cases of meaningful behaviour are as clearcut as this. Here are some intermediate examples. N may not, prior to casting his vote, have formulated any reason for voting as he does. But this does not necessarily preclude the possibility of saying that he has a reason for voting Labour and of specifying that reason. And in this case, just as much as in the paradigm, the acceptability of such an explanation is contingent on N's grasp of the concepts contained in it. If N does not grasp the concept of industrial peace it must be senseless to say that his reason for doing anything is a desire to see industrial peace promoted.

A type of case even farther removed from my paradigm is that discussed by Freud in *The Psychopathology of Everday Life*. N forgets to post a letter and insists, even after reflection, that this was 'just an oversight' and had no reason. A Freudian observer might insist that N 'must have had a reason' even though it was not apparent to N: suggesting perhaps that N unconsciously connected the posting of the letter with something in his life which is painful and which he wants to suppress. In Weberian terms, Freud classifies as 'meaningfully directed' (*sinnhaft orientiert*) actions which have no sense at all to the casual observer. Weber seems to refer to cases of this sort when, in his discussion of borderline cases, he speaks of actions the sense of which is apparent only 'to the expert'. This means that his characterization of *Sinn* as something 'subjectively intended' must be approached warily: more warily, for instance than it is approached by Morris Ginsberg, who appears to assume that Weber is saying that the sociologist's understanding of the behaviour of other people must rest on an analogy with his own introspective experience. [*On the Diversity of Morals*, pp. 153 ff.] This misunderstanding of Weber is very common both among his critics and among his vulgarizing followers; I will say more about it at a later stage. But Weber's insistence on the importance of the subjective point of view can be interpreted in a way which is not open to Ginsberg's objections:

he can be taken as meaning that even explanations of the Freudian type, if they are to be acceptable, must be in terms of concepts which are familiar to the agent as well as to the observer. It would make no sense to say that N's omission to post a letter to X (in settlement, say, of a debt) was an expression of N's unconscious resentment against X for having been promoted over his head, if N did not himself understand what was meant by 'obtaining promotion over somebody's head'. It was worth mentioning here too that, in seeking explanations of this sort in the course of psychotherapy, Freudians try to get the patient himself to recognize the validity of the proffered explanation; that this indeed is almost a condition of its being accepted as the 'right' explanation.

The category of meaningful behaviour extends also to actions for which the agent has no 'reason' or 'motive' at all in any of the senses so far discussed. In the first chapter of *Wirtschaft und Gesellschaft* Weber contrasts meaningful action with action which is 'purely reactive' (*bloss reaktiv*) and says that purely *traditional* behaviour is on the borderline between these two categories. But, as Talcott Parsons points out, Weber is not consistent in what he says about this. Sometimes he seems to regard traditional behaviour as simply a species of habit, whereas at other times he sees it as 'a type of social action, its traditionalism consisting in the fixity of certain essentials, their immunity from rational or other criticism'. [*The Structure of Social Action*, chapter 16.] Economic behaviour related to a fixed standard of living is cited as an example: behaviour, that is, where a man does not exploit an increase in the productive capacities of his labour in order to raise his standard of living but does less work instead. Parsons remarks that tradition in this sense is not to be equated with mere habit, but has a *normative* character. That is, the tradition is regarded as a standard which directs choices between alternative actions. As such it clearly falls within the category of the *sinnhaft*.

Suppose that N votes Labour without deliberating and without subsequently being able to offer any reasons, however hard he is pressed. Suppose that he is simply following without question the example of his father and his friends, who have always voted Labour. (This case must be distinguished from that in which N's *reason* for voting Labour is that his father and friends have always done so.) Now although N does not act here for any reason, his act still has a definite sense. What he does is not *simply* to make a mark on a piece of paper; he is *casting a vote*. And what I want to ask is, what gives his action *this* sense, rather than, say, that of being a move in a game or part of a religious ritual. More generally, by what criteria do we distinguish acts which have a sense from those which do not?

In the paper entitled *R. Stammlers 'Ueberwindung' der materialistischen Geschichtsauffassung*, Weber considers the hypothetical case of two 'non-social' beings meeting and, in a purely physical sense, 'exchanging' objects. This occurrence, he says, is conceivable as an act of *economic* exchange only if it has a sense. He expands this by saying that the present actions of the two men must carry with them, or represent, a regulation of their future behaviour. Action with a sense is symbolic: it goes together with certain other actions in the sense that it *commits* the agent to behaving in one way rather than another in the future. This notion of 'being committed' is most obviously appropriate where we are dealing with actions which have an immediate social significance, like economic exchange or promise keeping. But it applies also to meaningful behaviour of a more 'private' nature. Thus, to stay with examples used by Weber, if *N* places a slip of paper between the leaves of a book he can be said to be 'using a bookmark' only if he acts with the idea of using the slip to determine where he shall start re-reading. This does not mean that he must necessarily *actually* so use it in the future (though that is the paradigm case); the point is that if he does not, some special explanation will be called for, such that he forgot, changed his mind, or got tired of the book.

The notion of being committed by what I do now to doing something else in the future is identical in form with the connection between a definition and the subsequent use of the word defined. . . . It follows that I can only be committed in the future by what I do now if my present act is the *application of a rule*. Now according to the argument of the last chapter, this is possible only where the act in question has a relation to a social context: this must be true even of the most private acts, if, that is, they are meaningful. . . .

The Investigation of Regularities

A follower of Mill might concede that explanations of human behaviour must appeal not to causal generalizations about the individual's reaction to his environment but to our knowledge of the institutions and ways of life which give his acts their meaning. But he might argue that this does not damage the fundamentals of Mill's thesis, since understanding social institutions is still a matter of grasping empirical generalizations which are logically on a footing with those of natural science. For an institution is, after all, a certain kind of uniformity, and a uniformity can only be grasped in a generalization. I shall now examine this argument.

A regularity or uniformity is the constant recurrence of the same kind of event on the same kind of occasion; hence statements of uniformities presuppose judgements of identity. But this takes us right back to the argument . . . according to which criteria of identity are necessarily relative to some rule: with the corollary that two events which count as qualitatively similar from the point of view of one rule would count as different from the point of view of another. So to investigate the type of regularity studied in a given kind of enquiry is to examine the nature of the rule according to which judgements of identity are made in that enquiry. Such judgements are intelligible only relatively to a given mode of human behaviour, governed by its own rules.[1] In a physical science the relevant rules are those governing the procedures of investigators in the science in question. For instance, someone with no understanding of the problems and procedures of nuclear physics would gain nothing from being present at an experiment like the Cockcroft-Walton bombardment of lithium by hydrogen; indeed even the description of what he saw in those terms would be unintelligible to him, since the term 'bombardment' does not carry the sense in the context of the nuclear physicists' activities that it carries elsewhere. To understand what was going on in this experiment he would have to learn the nature of what nuclear physicists do; and this would include learning the criteria according to which they make judgements of identity.

Those rules, like all others, rest on a social context of common activity. So to understand the activities of an individual scientific investigator we must take account of two sets of relations: first, his relation to the phenomena which he investigates; second, his relation to his fellow-scientists. Both of these are essential to the sense of saying that he is 'detecting regularities' or 'discovering uniformities'; but writers on scientific 'methodology' too often concentrate on the first and overlook the importance of the second. That they must belong to different types is evident from the following considerations.—The phenomena being investigated present themselves to the scientist as an *object* of study; he observes them and notices certain facts about them. But to say of a man that he does this presupposes that he already has a mode of communication in the use of which rules are already being observed. For to notice something is to identify relevant characteristics, which means that the noticer must have some *concept* of such characteristics; this is possible only if he is able to use some symbol according to a rule which makes it refer to those characteristics. So we come back to his relation to his fellow-scientists, in which context alone he can be spoken of as following such a rule. Hence the relation between N and his fellows in virtue of which we say that N is following the same rule as them cannot be simply a relation of observation: it cannot consist in the fact that N has noticed how his fellows behave and has decided to take that as a norm for his own behaviour. For this would presuppose that we could give some account of the notion of 'noticing how his fellows behave' *apart from* the relation between N and his fellows which we are trying to specify; and that, as has been shown, is untrue. . . .

In the course of his investigation the scientist applies and develops the concepts germane to his particular field of study. This application and modification are 'influenced' both by the phenomena *to* which they are applied and also by the fellow-workers *in participation with* whom they are applied. But the two kinds of 'influence' are different. Whereas it is on the basis of his observation of the phenomena (in the course of his experiments) that he develops his concepts as he does, he is able to do this only in virtue of his participation in an established form of activity with his fellow-scientists. (When I speak of 'participation' here I do not necessarily imply any direct physical conjunction or even any direct communication between fellow-participants. What is important is that they are all taking part in the same general kind of activity, which they have all *learned* in similar ways; that they are, therefore, *capable* of communicating with each other about what they are doing; that what any one of them is doing is in principle intelligible to the others.)

Understanding Social Institutions

On Mill's account, understanding a social institution consists in observing regularities in the behaviour of its participants and expressing these regularities in the form of generalizations. Now if the position of the sociological investigator (in a broad sense) can be regarded as comparable, in its main logical outlines, to that of the natural scientist, the following must be the case. The concepts and criteria according to which the sociologist judges that, in two situations, the same thing has happened, or the same action performed, must be understood *in relation to the rules governing sociological investigations*. But here we run against a difficulty; for whereas in the case of the natural scientist we have to deal with only one set of rules, namely those governing the scientist's investigation itself, here *what the sociologist is studying,* as well as his study of it, is a human activity and is therefore carried on according to rules. And it is these rules, rather than those which govern the sociologist's investigation, which specify what is to count as 'doing the same kind of thing' in relation to that kind of activity.

An example may make this clearer. Consider the parable of the Pharisee and the Publican (*Luke*, 18, 9). Was the Pharisee who said 'God, I thank Thee that I am not as other men are' doing the same kind of thing as the Publican who prayed 'God be merciful unto me a sinner'? To answer this one would have to start by considering what is involved in the idea of prayer; and that is a *religious* question. In other words, the appropriate criteria for deciding whether the actions of these two men were of the same kind or not belong to religion itself. Thus the sociologist of religion will be confronted with an answer to the question: Do these two acts belong to the same kind of activity?; and this answer is given according to criteria which are not taken from sociology, but from religion itself.

But if the sociologist of religion's judgments of identity—and hence his generalizations—rest on criteria taken from religion, then his relation to the performers of religious activity cannot be just that of observer to observed. It must rather be analogous to the participation of the natural scientist with his fellow-workers in the activities of scientific investigation. Putting the point generally, even if it is legitimate to speak of one's understanding of a mode of social activity as consisting in a knowledge of regularities, the nature of this knowledge must be very different from the nature of knowledge of physical regularities. So it is quite mistaken in principle to compare the activity of a student of a form of social behaviour with that of, say, an engineer studying the workings of a machine; and one does not advance matters by saying, with Mill, that the machine in question is of course immensely more complicated than any physical machine. If we are going to compare the social student to an engineer, we shall do better to compare him to an apprentice engineer who is studying what engineering—that is, the activity of engineering—is all about. His understanding of social phenomena is more like the engineer's understanding of his colleagues' activities than it is like the engineer's understanding of the mechanical systems which he studies.

This point is reflected in such common-sense considerations as the following: that a historian or sociologist of religion must himself have some religious feeling if he is to make sense of the religious movement he is studying and understand the considerations which govern the lives of its participants. A historian of art must have some aesthetic sense if he is to understand the problems confronting the artists of his period; and without this he will have left out of his account precisely what would have made it a history of *art*, as opposed to a rather puzzling external account of certain motions which certain people have been perceived to go through.

I do not wish to maintain that we must stop at the unreflective kind of understanding of which I gave as an instance the engineer's understanding of the activities of his colleagues. But I do want to say that any more reflective understanding must necessarily presuppose, if it is to count as genuine understanding at all, the participant's unreflective understanding. And this in itself makes it misleading to compare it with the natural scientist's understanding of his scientific data. Similarly, although the reflective student of society, or of a particular mode of social life, may find it necessary to use concepts which are not taken from the forms of activity which he is investigating, but which are taken rather from the context of his own investigations, still these technical concepts of his will imply a previous understanding of those other concepts which belong to the activities under investigation.

For example, liquidity preference is a technical concept of economics: it is not generally used by businessmen in the conduct of their affairs but by the economist who wishes to *explain* the nature and consequences of certain kinds of business behaviour. But it is logically tied to concepts which do enter into business activity, for its use by the economist presupposes his understanding of what it is to conduct a business, which in turn involves an understanding of such business concepts as money, profit, cost, risk, etc. It is only the relation between his account and these concepts which makes it an account of economic activity as opposed, say, to a piece of theology.

Again, a psychoanalyst may explain a patient's neurotic behaviour in terms of factors unknown to the patient and of concepts which would be unintelligible to him. Let us suppose that the psychoanalyst's explanation refers to events in the patient's early childhood. Well, the description of those events will presuppose an understanding of the concepts in terms of which family life, for example, is carried on in our society; for these will have entered, however rudimentarily, into the relations between the child and his family. A psychoanalyst who wished to give an account of the aetiology of neuroses amongst, say, the Trobriand Islanders, could not just apply without further reflection the concepts developed by Freud for situations arising in our own society. He would have first to investigate such things as the idea of fatherhood amongst the islanders and take into account any relevant aspects in which their idea differed from that current in his own society. And it is almost inevitable that such an investigation would lead to some modification in the psychological theory appropriate for explaining neurotic behaviour in this new situation.

These considerations also provide some justification for the sort of historical scepticism which that underestimated philosopher, R. G. Collingwood, expresses in *The Idea of History*. Although they need not be brought to the foreground where one is dealing with situations in one's own society or in societies with whose life one is reasonably familiar, the practical implications become pressing where the object of study is a society which is culturally remote from that of the investigator. This accounts for the weight which the Idealists attached to concepts like 'empathy' and 'historical imagination' (which is not to deny that these concepts give rise to difficulties of their own). It is also connected with another characteristic doctrine of theirs: that the understanding of a human society is closely connected with the activities of the philosopher. . . .

Pareto: Residues and Derivations

. . . I now turn to the second of Pareto's distinctions: between *residues* and *derivations*. This distinction is supposed to perform two functions. In the first place it is supposed to provide *recurring* features in our observation of human societies, which will be a suitable subject for scientific generalization. Pareto argues that if one looks at a wide variety of different societies at different historical periods, one is struck by the fact that whereas certain kinds of conduct occur again and again with very little variation, other kinds are very unstable, changing constantly with time and differing considerably from one society to another. He calls the constant, recurring element 'residues'; (they are what remains when the changeable features are left out of account). The variable elements are 'derivations', a term which refers to a fact about such kinds of conduct which Pareto claims to have discovered empirically: namely, that the main occupants of this category are the theories in terms of which people try to explain why they behave as they do. The derivation 'represents the work of the mind in accounting for [the residue]. That is why [it] is much more variable, as reflecting the play of the imagination'. [*The Mind and Society*, Section 850.] Because the derivations are so unstable and variable in comparison with the residues, Pareto urges, we must accept that the ideas and theories which people embrace have little real influence on the way they otherwise behave; embracing the theories cannot be a necessary condition of behaving in the appropriate way, for that behaviour goes on even after the theories have been abandoned. The concept of a derivation obviously offers many points of comparison with, for example, the Marxian concept of an 'ideology' and the Freudian concept of a 'rationalization'. The point I should like to emphasize here, however, is that it is only by way of this conceptual distinction that Pareto succeeds in finding common features of different societies of a sort which appear suitable as a subject for scientific generalizations. That is, the claim that there are sociological uniformities goes hand in hand with the claim that human intelligence is much overrated as a real influence on social events.

I will now quote an example of Pareto's detailed application of the distinction.

> Christians have the custom of baptism. If one knew the Christian procedure only one would not know whether and how it could be analysed. Moreover, we have an explanation of it: we are told that the rite of baptism is celebrated in order to remove original sin. That still is not enough. If we had no other facts of the same class to go by, we should find it difficult to isolate the elements in the complex phenomenon of baptism. But we do have other facts of that type. The pagans too had lustral water, and they used it for purposes of purification. If we stopped at that we might associate the idea of water with the fact of purification. But other cases of baptism show that the use of water is not a constant element. Blood may be used for purification, and other substances as well. Nor is that all; there are numbers of rites that effect the same result . . . The given case, therefore, is made up of that constant element, a, and a variable element, b, the latter comprising the means that are used for restoring the individual's integrity and the reasonings by which the efficacy of the means is presumably explained. The human being has a vague feeling that water somehow cleanses moral as well as material pollution. However, he does not, as a rule, justify his conduct in that manner. The explanation would be far too simple. So he goes looking for

something more complicated, more pretentious, and readily finds what he is looking for. *(Ibid.,* Section 863.)

Now there are well-known philosophical difficulties which arise from the attempt to reject as nugatory whole classes of reasonings as opposed to particular appeals to that kind of reasoning within an accepted class. Consider, for instance, the often discussed difficulties involved in casting *general* doubt on the reliability of the senses, or of memory. But Pareto would no doubt maintain that his thesis is saved from this kind of vacuity by the mass of empirical evidence on which it rests. However, his thesis concerning the relative variability of derivations and constancy of residues is not, as he thinks, a straightforward report of the results of observation; it involves a conceptual misinterpretation of those results. The constant element, a, and the variable element, b, are not distinguished by observation but only as the result of an (illegitimate) abstraction. In the example quoted of the purification residues, the unvarying element is not just a straightforward set of physical movements for it may take a multitude of different physical forms (as Pareto himself is at pains to point out). The mere act of washing one's hands would not be an instance of it; it would become one only if performed with *symbolic* intent, as a sign of moral or religious purification. This point is so important that I will illustrate it with another example, the 'sex residues'. Pareto does not, as might be expected, mean to refer to the common factor of simple biological sexual intercourse which is found amidst all the multifarious social customs and moral ideas connected with sexual relations at different times and in different societies. He explicitly rules this out. To qualify as a residue a form of behaviour must have a quasi-intellectual, or symbolic content. 'Mere sexual appetite, though powerfully active in the human race, is no concern of ours here . . . We are interested in it only in so far as it influences theories, modes of thinking'. *(Ibid.,* Section 1,324.) For example, one dominant residue which Pareto discusses is the ascetic attitude to sexual relations: the idea that they are to be avoided as something evil or at least morally debilitating. But this constant factor, as in the previous example, is not something that Pareto has *observed* separately from the highly various moral and theological systems of ideas in terms of which sexual asceticism is justified or explained in different societies. It is something that he has analysed out of those systems of ideas by means of a conceptual analysis.

But ideas cannot be torn out of their context in that way; the relation between idea and context is an *internal* one. The idea gets its sense from the role it plays in the system. It is nonsensical to take several systems of ideas, find an element in each which can be expressed in the same verbal form, and then claim to have discovered an idea which is common to all the systems. This would be like observing that both the Aristotelian and Galilean systems of mechanics use a notion of force, and concluding that they therefore make use of the same notion. One can imagine the howl of rage which Pareto would send up at the philistinism of such a proceeding; but he is guilty of exactly the same kind of philistinism when, for instance, he compares the social relation between 'an American millionaire and a plain American' to that between an Indian of high caste and one of low caste. (See Section 1,044.) And this sort of comparison is essential to his whole method of procedure.

The same point may be expressed as follows. Two things may be called 'the same' or 'different' only with reference to a set of criteria which lay down what is to be regarded as a relevant difference. When the 'things' in question are purely physical the criteria appealed to will of course be those of the observer. But when one is dealing with intellectual (or, indeed, any kind of social) 'things', that is not so. For their *being* intellectual or social, as opposed to physical, in character depends entirely on their belonging in a certain way to a system of ideas or mode of living. It is only by reference to the criteria governing that system of ideas or mode of life that they have any existence as intellectual or social events. It follows that if the sociological investigator wants to regard them *as* social events (as, *ex hypothesi*, he must), he has to take seriously the criteria which are applied for distinguishing 'different' kinds of actions and identifying the 'same' kinds of actions within the way of life he is studying. It is not open to him arbitrarily to impose his own standards from without. In so far as he does so, the events he is studying lose altogether their character as *social* events. A Christian would strenuously deny that the baptism rites of his faith were really the same in character as the acts of a pagan sprinkling lustral water or letting sacrificial blood. Pareto, in maintaining the contrary, is inadvertently removing from his subject-matter precisely that which gives them sociological interest: namely their internal connection with a way of living.

Miss G. E. M. Anscombe has remarked, in an unpublished paper, how there are certain activities—she mentions arithmetic as an example—which, unlike other activities, such as acrobatics, cannot be understood by an observer unless he himself possesses the ability to perform the activities in question. She notes that any description of activities like arithmetic which is not based on arithmetical (or whatever) capacities is bound to seem pointless and arbitrary, and also compulsive in the sense that the steps no longer appear as meaningful choices. This is precisely the impression of social activities which is given by Pareto's account of them as residues; but the impression is not a well-founded one, it is an optical illusion based on a conceptual misunderstanding.

This shows, I think, that the whole presupposition of Pareto's procedure is absurd: namely that it is possible to treat propositions and theories as 'experimental facts' on a par with any other kind of such fact. (See *The Mind and*

Society, Section 7.) It is a presupposition which is certainly not peculiar to him: it is contained, for instance, in Emile Durkheim's first rule of sociological method: 'to consider social facts as things'. Pareto's statement, and the others like it, are absurd because they involve a contradiction: in so far as a set of phenomena is being looked at 'from the outside', 'as experimental facts', it cannot at the same time be described as constituting a 'theory' or set of 'propositions'. In a sense Pareto has not carried his empiricism far enough. For what the sociological observer has presented *to his senses* is not at all people holding certain theories, believing in certain propositions, but people making certain movements and sounds. (Indeed, even describing them as 'people' really goes too far, which may explain the popularity of the sociological and social psychological jargon word 'organism': but organisms, as opposed to people, do not believe propositions or embrace theories.) To describe what is observed by the sociologist in terms of notions like 'proposition' and 'theory' is already to have taken the decision to apply a set of concepts incompatible with the 'external', 'experimental' point of view. To refuse to describe what is observed in such terms, on the other hand, involves not treating it as having *social* significance. It follows that the understanding of society cannot be observational and experimental in one widely accepted sense.

What I am saying needs qualification. I do not mean, of course, that it is impossible to take as a datum that a certain person, or group of people, holds a certain belief—say that the earth is flat—without subscribing to it oneself. And this is all Pareto thinks he is doing: but actually he is doing more than this. He is not just speaking of particular beliefs *within* a given mode of discourse, but of whole modes of discourse. What he misses is that a mode of discourse has to be *understood* before anyone can speak of theories and propositions within it which could constitute data for him. He does not really consider the fundamental problem of what it is to understand a mode of discourse. In so far as he thinks anything about it he regards it as simply a matter of establishing generalizations on the basis of observation; a view which was disposed of [above]. . . .

Max Weber: Verstehen and Causal Explanation

It is Max Weber who has said most about the peculiar sense which the word 'understand' bears when applied to modes of social life. I have already referred to his account of meaningful behaviour and propose in the next two sections to say something about his conception of sociological understanding (*Verstehen*). (See *Economy and Society*, Chapter 1.) The first issue on which I mean to concentrate is Weber's account of the relation between acquiring an 'interpretive understanding' (*deutend verstehen*) of the meaning (*Sinn*) of a piece of behaviour and providing a causal explanation (*kausal erklären*) of what brought the behaviour in question about and what its consequences are.

Now Weber never gives a clear account of the *logical* character of interpretive understanding. He speaks of it much of the time as if it were simply a psychological technique: a matter of putting oneself in the other fellow's position. This has led many writers to allege that Weber confuses what is simply a technique for framing hypotheses with the logical character of the evidence for such hypotheses. Thus Popper argues that although we may use our knowledge of our own mental processes in order to frame hypotheses about the similar processes of other people, 'these hypotheses must be tested, they must be submitted to the method of selection by elimination. (By their intuition, some people are prevented from even imagining that anybody can possibly dislike chocolate).' [*The Poverty of Historicism*, Section 29.]

However applicable such criticisms may be to Weber's vulgarizers, however, they cannot justly be used against his own views, for he is very insistent that mere 'intuition' is not enough and must be tested by careful observation. However, what I think can be said against Weber is that he gives a wrong account of the process of checking the validity of suggested sociological interpretations. But the correction of Weber takes us farther away from, rather than closer to, the account which Popper, Ginsberg, and the many who think like them, would like to substitute.

Weber says:

> Every interpretation aims at self-evidence or immediate plausibility (*Evidenz*). But an interpretation which makes the meaning of a piece of behaviour as self-evidently obvious as you like cannot claim *just* on that account to be the causally *valid* interpretation as well. In itself it is nothing more than a particularly plausible hypothesis. [*Economy and Society*, Chapter 1.]

He goes on to say that the appropriate way to verify such an hypothesis is to establish statistical laws based on observation of what happens. In this way he arrives at the conception of a sociological law as 'a statistical regularity which corresponds to an intelligible intended meaning'.

Weber is clearly right in pointing out that the obvious interpretation need not be the right one. R. S. Lynd's interpretation of West Indian voodoo magic as 'a system of imputedly true and reliable causal sequences' is a case in point [*Knowledge for What?* p. 121]; and there is a plethora of similar examples in Frazer's *The Golden Bough*. But I want to question Weber's implied suggestion that *Verstehen* is something which is logically incomplete and needs supplementing by a different method altogether, namely the collection of statistics. Against this, I want to insist that if a proffered interpretation is wrong, statistics, though they may suggest that that is so, are not the decisive and ultimate court of appeal for the validity of sociological interpretations in the way Weber suggests. What is then needed is a better interpretation, not something different in kind. The compatibility of an interpretation with the statistics does not prove its validity. Someone who interprets a tribe's magical rites as a form of misplaced scientific activity will not be corrected by statistics about what members of that tribe are likely to do on various kinds of occasion (though this might form *part* of the argument); what is ultimately required is a *philosophical* argument like, e.g., Collingwood's in *The Principles of Art*. (Book 1, Chapter IV.) For a mistaken interpretation of a form of social activity is closely akin to the type of mistake dealt with in philosophy.

Wittgenstein says somewhere that when we get into philosophical difficulties over the use of some of the concepts of our language, we are like savages confronted with something from an alien culture. I am simply indicating a corollary of this: that sociologists who misinterpret an alien culture are like philosophers getting into difficulties over the use of their own concepts. There will be differences of course. The philosopher's difficulty is usually with something with which he is perfectly familiar but which he is for the moment failing to see in its proper perspective. The sociologist's difficulty will often be over something with which he is not at all familiar; he may have no suitable perspective to apply. This may sometimes make his task more difficult than the philosopher's, and it may also sometimes make it easier. But the analogy between their problems should be plain.

Some of Wittgenstein's procedures in his philosophical elucidations reinforce this point. He is prone to draw our attention to certain features of our own concepts by comparing them with those of an imaginary society, in which our own familiar ways of thinking are subtly distorted. For instance, he asks us to suppose that such a society sold wood in the following way: They 'piled the timber in heaps of arbitrary, varying height and then sold it at a price proportionate to the area covered by the piles. And what if they even justified this with the words: "Of course, if you buy more timber, you must pay more"?' (*Remarks on the Foundations of Mathematics*, Chapter I, p. 142–151.) The important question for us is: in what circumstances could one say that one had *understood* this sort of behaviour? As I have indicated, Weber often speaks as if the ultimate test were our ability to formulate statistical laws which would enable us to *predict* with fair accuracy what people would be likely to do in given circumstances. In line with this is his attempt to define a 'social role' in terms of the probability (*Chance*) of actions of a certain sort being performed in given circumstances. But with Wittgenstein's example we might well be able to make predictions of great accuracy in this way and still not be able to claim any real understanding of what those people were doing. The difference is precisely analogous to that between being able to formulate statistical laws about the likely occurrences of words in a language and being able to understand what was being *said* by someone who spoke the language. The latter can never be reduced to the former; a man who understands Chinese is not a man who has a firm grasp of the statistical probabilities for the occurrence of the various words in the Chinese language. (Indeed, he could have that without knowing that he was dealing with a language at all; and anyway, the knowledge that he was dealing with a language is not itself something that could be formulated statistically.) 'Understanding', in situations like this, is grasping the *point* or *meaning* of what is being done or said. This is a notion far removed from the world of statistics and causal laws: it is closer to the realm of discourse and to the internal relations that link the parts of a realm of discourse. The notion of *meaning* should be carefully distinguished from that of *function*, which is popular with certain sociologists. The latter is a quasi-causal notion, which it is perilous to apply to social institutions. . . .

The Internality of Social Relations

. . . To give an account of the meaning of a word is to describe how it is used; and to describe how it is used is to describe the social intercourse into which it enters.

If social relations between men exist only in and through their ideas, then, since the relations between ideas are internal relations, social relations must be a species of internal relation too. This brings me into conflict with a widely accepted principle of Hume's: 'There is no object, which implies the existence of any other if we consider these objects in themselves, and never look beyond the ideas which we form of them'. There is no doubt that Hume intended this to apply to human actions and social life as well as to the phenomena of nature. Now to start with, Hume's principle is not unqualifiedly true even of our knowledge of natural phenomena. If I hear a sound and recognize it as a clap of thunder, I already commit myself to believing in the occurrence of a number of other events—e.g. electrical discharges in the atmosphere—even in calling what I have heard 'thunder'. That is, from 'the idea which I have formed' of what I heard I *can* legitimately infer 'the existence of other objects'. If I subsequently find that there was no electrical storm in the vicinity at the time I heard the sound I shall have to retract my claim that what I heard was thunder. To use a phrase of Gilbert Ryle's, the word 'thunder' is theory-impregnated; statements affirming the occurrence of thunder have logical connections with statements affirming the occurrence of other events. To say this, of course, is not to reintroduce any mysterious causal nexus *in rebus*, of a sort to which Hume could legitimately object. It is simply to point out that Hume overlooked the fact that 'the idea we form of an object' does not just consist of elements drawn from our observation of that object in isolation, but includes the idea of connections between it and other objects. (And one could scarcely form a conception of a language in which this was not so.)

Consider now a very simple paradigm case of a relation between actions in a human society: that between an act of command and an act of obedience to that command. A sergeant calls 'Eyes right!' and his men all turn their eyes to the right. Now, in describing the men's act in terms of the notion of obedience to a command, one is of course committing oneself to saying that a command has been issued. So far the situation looks precisely parallel to the relation between thunder and electrical storms. But now one needs to draw a distinction. An event's character as an act of obedience is *intrinsic* to it in a way which is not true of an event's character as a clap of thunder; and this is in general true of human acts as opposed to natural events. In the case of the latter, although human beings can think of the occurrences in question only in terms of the concepts they do in fact have of them, yet the events themselves have an existence independent of those concepts. There existed electrical storms and thunder long before there were human beings to form concepts of them or establish that there was any connection between them. But it does not make sense to suppose that human beings might have been issuing commands and obeying them before they came to form the concept of command and obedience. For their performance of such acts is itself the chief manifestation of their possession of those concepts. An act of obedience itself contains, as an essential element, a recognition of what went before as an order. But it would of course be senseless to suppose that a clap of thunder contained any recognition of what went before as an electrical storm; it is our recognition of the sound, rather than the sound itself, which contains that recognition of what went before.

Part of the opposition one feels to the idea that men can be related to each other through their actions in at all the same kind of way as can propositions be related to each other is probably due to an inadequate conception of what logical relations between propositions themselves are. One is inclined to think of the laws of logic as forming a *given* rigid structure to which men try, with greater or less (but never complete) success, to make what they say in their actual linguistic and social intercourse conform. One thinks of propositions as something ethereal, which just because of their ethereal, non-physical nature, can fit together more tightly than can be conceived in the case of anything so grossly material as flesh-and-blood men and their actions. In a sense one is right in this; for to treat of logical relations in a formal systematic way is to think at a very high level of abstraction, at which all the anomalies, imperfections and crudities which characterize men's actual intercourse with each other in society have been removed. But, like any abstraction not recognized as such, this can be misleading. It may make one forget that it is only from their roots in this actual flesh-and-blood intercourse that those formal systems draw such life as they have; for the whole idea of a logical relation is only possible by virtue of the sort of agreement between men and their actions which is discussed by Wittgenstein in the *Philosophical Investigations*. Collingwood's remark on formal grammar is apposite: 'I likened the grammarian to a butcher; but if so, he is a butcher of a curious kind. Travellers say that certain African peoples will cut a steak from a living animal and cook it for dinner, the animal being not much the worse. This may serve to amend the original comparison'. (*The Principles of Art*, p. 259.) It will seem less strange that social relations should be like logical relations between propositions once it is seen that logical relations between propositions themselves depend on social relations between men. . . .

NOTES

1. Cf. Hume: *A Treatise of Human Nature,* Introduction—"'Tis evident, that all the sciences have a relation, greater or less, to human nature; and that however wide any of them may seem to run from it, they still return back by one passage or another." Hume's remark is a further reminder of the close relation between the subject of this monograph and one of the most persistent and dominant *motifs* in the history of modern philosophy.

Understanding a Primitive Society

PETER WINCH

THIS ESSAY WILL PURSUE FURTHER SOME QUESTIONS RAISED IN MY book, *The Idea of a Social Science*.[1] That book was a general discussion of what is involved in the understanding of human social life. I shall here be concerned more specifically with certain issues connected with social anthropology. In the first part I raise certain difficulties about Professor E. E. Evans-Pritchard's approach in his classic, *Witchcraft, Oracles and Magic among the Azande*.[2] In the second part, I attempt to refute some criticisms recently made by Mr. Alasdair MacIntyre of Evans-Pritchard and myself, to criticize in their turn MacIntyre's positive remarks, and to offer some further reflections of my own on the concept of learning from the study of a primitive society.

I. The Reality of Magic

Like many other primitive people, the African Azande hold beliefs that we cannot possibly share and engage in practices which it is peculiarly difficult for us to comprehend. They believe that certain of their members are witches, exercising a malignant occult influence on the lives of their fellows. They engage in rites to counteract witchcraft; they consult oracles and use magic medicines to protect themselves from harm.

An anthropologist studying such a people wishes to make those beliefs and practices intelligible to himself and his readers. This means presenting an account of them that will somehow satisfy the criteria of rationality demanded by the culture to which he and his readers belong: a culture whose conception of rationality is deeply affected by the achievements and methods of the sciences, and one which treats such things as a belief in magic or the practice of

Peter Winch, "Understanding a Primitive Society," *American Philosophical Quarterly* 1 (1964): 307–24.

consulting oracles as almost a paradigm of the irrational. The strains inherent in this situation are very likely to lead the anthropologist to adopt the following posture: *We* know that Zande beliefs in the influence of witchcraft, the efficacy of magic medicines, the role of oracles in revealing what is going on and what is going to happen, are mistaken, illusory. Scientific methods of investigation have shown conclusively that there are no relations of cause and effect such as are implied by these beliefs and practices. All we can do then is to show how such a system of mistaken beliefs and inefficacious practices can maintain itself in the face of objections that seem to us so obvious.[3]

Now although Evans-Pritchard goes a very great deal further than most of his predecessors in trying to present the sense of the institutions he is discussing as it presents itself to the Azande themselves, still, the last paragraph does, I believe, pretty fairly describe the attitude he himself took at the time of writing this book. There is more than one remark to the effect that "obviously there are no witches"; and he writes of the difficulty he found, during his field work with the Azande, in shaking off the "unreason" on which Zande life is based and returning to a clear view of how things really are. This attitude is not an unsophisticated one but is based on a philosophical position ably developed in a series of papers published in the 1930's in the unhappily rather inaccessible *Bulletin of the Faculty of Arts* of the University of Egypt. Arguing against Lévy-Bruhl, Evans-Pritchard here rejects the idea that the scientific understanding of causes and effects which leads us to reject magical ideas is evidence of any superior intelligence on our part. Our scientific approach, he points out, is as much a function of our culture as is the magical approach of the "savage" a function of his.

> The fact that we attribute rain to meteorological causes alone while savages believe that Gods or ghosts or magic can influence the rainfall is no evidence that our brains function differently from their brains. It does not show that we "think more logically" than savages, at least not if this expression suggests some kind of hereditary psychic superiority. It is no sign of superior intelligence on my part that I attribute rain to physical causes. I did not come to this conclusion myself by observation and inference and have, in fact, little knowledge of the meteorological processes that lead to rain. I merely accept what everybody else in my society accepts, namely that rain is due to natural causes. This particular idea formed part of my culture long before I was born into it and little more was required of me than sufficient linguistic ability to learn it. Likewise a savage who believes that under suitable natural and ritual conditions the rainfall can be influenced by use of appropriate magic is not on account of this belief to be considered of inferior intelligence. He did not build up this belief from his own observations and inferences but adopted it in the same way as he adopted the rest of his cultural heritage, namely, by being

born into it. He and I are both thinking in patterns of thought provided for us by the societies in which we live.

It would be absurd to say that the savage is thinking mystically and that we are thinking scientifically about rainfall. In either case like mental processes are involved and, moreover, the content of thought is similarly derived. But we can say that the social content of our thought about rainfall is scientific, is in accord with objective facts, whereas the social content of savage thought about rainfall is unscientific since it is not in accord with reality and may also be mystical where it assumes the existence of supra-sensible forces.[4]

In a subsequent article on Pareto, Evans-Pritchard distinguishes between "logical" and "scientific."

> Scientific notions are those which accord with objective reality both with regard to the validity of their premises and to the inferences drawn from their propositions. . . . Logical notions are those in which according to the rules of thought inferences would be true were the premises true, the truth of the premises being irrelevant. . . .
>
> A pot has broken during firing. This is probably due to grit. Let us examine the pot and see if this is the cause. That is logical and scientific thought. Sickness is due to witchcraft. A man is sick. Let us consult the oracles to discover who is the witch responsible. That is logical and unscientific thought.[5]

I think that Evans-Pritchard is right in a great deal of what he says here, but wrong, and crucially wrong, in his attempt to characterize the scientific in terms of that which is "in accord with objective reality." Despite differences of emphasis and phraseology, Evans-Pritchard is in fact hereby put into the same metaphysical camp as Pareto: for both of them the conception of "reality" must be regarded as intelligible and applicable *outside* the context of scientific reasoning itself, since it is that to which scientific notions do, and unscientific notions do not, have a relation. Evans-Pritchard, although he emphasizes that a member of scientific culture has a different conception of reality from that of a Zande believer in magic, wants to go beyond merely registering this fact and making the differences explicit, and to say, finally, that the scientific conception agrees with what reality actually is like, whereas the magical conception does not.

It would be easy, at this point, to say simply that the difficulty arises from the use of the unwieldy and misleadingly comprehensive expression "agreement with reality"; and in a sense this is true. But we should not lose sight of the fact that the idea that men's ideas and beliefs must be checkable by reference to something independent—some reality—is an important one. To abandon it is to plunge straight into an extreme Protagorean relativism, with all the paradoxes that involves. On the other hand great care is certainly necessary in fixing the precise role that this conception of the independently real does play in men's thought. There are two related points that I should like to make about it at this stage.

In the first place we should notice that the check of the independently real is not peculiar to science. The trouble is that the fascination science has for us makes it easy for us to adopt its scientific form as a paradigm against which to measure the intellectual respectability of other modes of discourse. Consider what God says to Job out of the whirlwind: "Who is this that darkeneth counsel by words without knowledge? . . . Where wast thou when I laid the foundations of the earth? declare, if thou hast understanding. Who hath laid the measures thereof, if thou knowest? or who hath stretched the line upon it. . . . Shall he that contendeth with the Almighty instruct him? he that reproveth God, let him answer it." Job is taken to task for having gone astray by having lost sight of the reality of God; this does not, of course, mean that Job has made any sort of theoretical mistake, which could be put right, perhaps, by means of an experiment.[6] God's reality is certainly independent of what any man may care to think, but what that reality amounts to can only be seen from the religious tradition in which the concept of God is used, and this use is very unlike the use of scientific concepts, say of theoretical entities. The point is that it is *within* the religious use of language that the conception of God's reality has its place, though, I repeat, this does not mean that it is at the mercy of what anyone cares to say; if this were so, God would have no reality.

My second point follows from the first. Reality is not what gives language sense. What is real and what is unreal shows itself *in* the sense that language has. Further, both the distinction between the real and the unreal and the concept of agreement with reality themselves belong to our language. I will not say that they are concepts of the language like any other, since it is clear that they occupy a commanding, and in a sense a limiting, position there. We can imagine a language with no concept of, say, wetness, but hardly one in which there is no way of distinguishing the real from the unreal. Nevertheless we could not in fact distinguish the real from the unreal without understanding the way this distinction operates in the language. If then we wish to understand the significance of these concepts, we must examine the use they actually do have—*in* the language.

Evans-Pritchard, on the contrary, is trying to work with a conception of reality which is *not* determined by its actual use in language. He wants something against which that use can itself be appraised. But this is not possible; and no more possible in the case of scientific discourse than it is in any other. We may ask whether a particular scientific hypothesis agrees with reality and test this by observation and experiment. Given the experimental methods, and the established use of the theoretical terms entering into the hypothesis, then the question whether it holds or not is settled by reference to something independent of what I, or anybody else, care to think. But the general nature of the data revealed by the experiment can only be specified in terms of criteria built into the methods of experiment employed and these, in turn, make sense only to someone who is conversant with the kind of scientific activity within which they are employed. A scientific illiterate, asked to describe the results of an experiment which he "observes" in an advanced physics laboratory, could not do so in terms relevant to the hypothesis being tested; and it is really only in such terms that we can sensibly speak of the "results of the experiment" at all. What Evans-Pritchard wants to be able to say is that the criteria applied in scientific experimentation constitute a true link between our ideas and an independent reality, whereas those characteristic of other systems of thought—in particular, magical methods of thought—do not. It is evident that the expressions "true link" and "independent reality" in the previous sentence cannot themselves be explained by reference to the scientific universe of discourse, as this would beg the question. We have then to ask how, by reference to what established universe of discourse, the use of those expressions *is* to be explained; and it is clear that Evans-Pritchard has not answered this question.

Two questions arise out of what I have been saying. First, is it in fact the case that a primitive system of magic, like that of the Azande, constitutes a coherent universe of discourse like science, in terms of which an intelligible conception of reality and clear ways of deciding what beliefs are and are not in agreement with this reality can be discerned? Second, what are we to make of the possibility of understanding primitive social institutions, like Zande magic, if the situation is as I have outlined? I do not claim to be able to give a satisfactory answer to the second question. It raises some very important and fundamental issues about the nature of human social life, which require conceptions different from, and harder to elucidate, than those I have hitherto introduced. I shall offer some tentative remarks about these issues in the second part of this essay. At present I shall address myself to the first question.

It ought to be remarked here that an affirmative answer to my first question would not commit me to accepting as rational all beliefs couched in magical concepts or all procedures practiced in the name of such beliefs. This is no more necessary than is the corresponding proposition that all procedures "justified" in the name of science are immune from rational criticism. A remark of Collingwood's is apposite here:

> Savages are no more exempt from human folly than civilized men, and are no doubt equally liable to the error of thinking that they, or the persons they regard as their superiors, can do what in fact cannot be done. But this

error is not the essence of magic; it is a perversion of magic. And we should be careful how we attribute it to the people we call savages, who will one day rise up and testify against us.[7]

It is important to distinguish a system of magical beliefs and practices like that of the Azande, which is one of the principal foundations of their whole social life and, on the other hand, magical beliefs that might be held, and magical rites that might be practiced, by persons belonging to our own culture. These have to be understood rather differently. Evans-Pritchard is himself alluding to the difference in the following passage: "When a Zande speaks of witchcraft he does not speak of it as we speak of the weird witchcraft of our own history. Witchcraft is to him a commonplace happening and he seldom passes a day without mentioning it. . . . To us witchcraft is something which haunted and disgusted our credulous forefathers. But the Zande expects to come across witchcraft at any time of the day or night. He would be just as surprised if he were not brought into daily contact with it as we would be if confronted by its appearance. To him there is nothing miraculous about it."[8]

The difference is not merely one of degree of familiarity, however, although, perhaps, even this has more importance than might at first appear. Concepts of witchcraft and magic in our culture, at least since the advent of Christianity, have been parasitic on, and a perversion of other orthodox concepts, both religious and, increasingly, scientific. To take an obvious example, you could not understand what was involved in conducting a Black Mass, unless you were familiar with the conduct of a proper Mass and, therefore, with the whole complex of religious ideas from which the Mass draws its sense. Neither would you understand the relation between these without taking account of the fact that the Black practices are rejected as *irrational* (in the sense proper to religion) in the system of beliefs on which these practices are thus parasitic. Perhaps a similar relation holds between the contemporary practice of astrology and astronomy and technology. It is impossible to keep a discussion of the rationality of Black Magic or of astrology within the bounds of concepts peculiar to them; they have an essential reference to something outside themselves. The position is like that which Socrates, in Plato's *Gorgias*, showed to be true of the Sophists' conception of rhetoric: namely, that it is parasitic on rational discourse in such a way that its irrational character can be shown in terms of this dependence. Hence, when we speak of such practices as "superstitious," "illusory," "irrational," we have the weight of our culture behind us; and this is not just a matter of being on the side of the big battalions, because those beliefs and practices belong to, and derive such sense as they seem to have, from that same culture. This enables us to show that the sense is only apparent, in terms which are culturally relevant.

It is evident that our relation to Zande magic is quite different. If we wish to understand it, we must seek a foothold elsewhere. And while there may well be room for the use of such critical expressions as "superstition" and "irrationality," the kind of rationality with which such terms might be used to point a contrast remains to be elucidated. The remarks I shall make in Part II will have a more positive bearing on this issue. In the rest of this Part, I shall develop in more detail my criticisms of Evans-Pritchard's approach to the Azande.

Early in this book he defines certain categories in terms of which his descriptions of Zande customs are couched.

> MYSTICAL NOTIONS . . . are patterns of thought that attribute to phenomena supra-sensible qualities which, or part of which, are not derived from observation or cannot be logically inferred from it, *and which they do not possess.*[9] COMMON-SENSE NO-TIONS . . . attribute to phenomena only what men observe in them or what can logically be inferred from observation. So long as a notion does not assert something which has not been observed, it is not classed as mystical even though it is mistaken on account of incomplete observation. . . . SCIENTIFIC NOTIONS. Science has developed out of common-sense but is far more methodical and has better techniques of observation and reasoning. Common sense uses experience and rules of thumb. Science uses experiment and rules of Logic. . . . *Our body of scientific knowledge and Logic are the sole arbiters of what are mystical, common sense, and scientific notions.* Their judgments are never absolute. RITUAL BEHAVIOUR. Any behaviour that is accounted for by mystical notions. *There is no objective nexus* between the behaviour and the event it is intended to cause. Such behaviour is usually intelligible to us only when we know the mystical notions associated with it. EMPIRI-CAL BEHAVIOUR. Any behaviour that is accounted for by common-sense notions.[10]

It will be seen from the phrases which I have italicized that Evans-Pritchard is doing more here than just defining certain terms for his own use. Certain metaphysical claims are embodied in the definitions: identical in substance with the claims embodied in Pareto's way of distinguishing between "logical" and "non-logical" conduct.[11] There is a very clear implication that those who use mystical notions and perform ritual behaviour are making some sort of mistake, detectable with the aid of science and logic. I shall now examine more closely some of the institutions described by Evans-Pritchard to determine how far his claims are justified.

Witchcraft is a power possessed by certain individuals to harm other individuals by "mystical" means. Its basis is an inherited organic condition, "witch-craft-substance" and it does not involve any special magical ritual or medicine. It is constantly appealed to by Azande when they are afflicted by misfortune, not so as to exclude explanation in terms of natural causes, which Azande are perfectly able to offer themselves within the limits of their not inconsiderable natural knowledge, but so as to supplement such explanations. "Witchcraft explains *why*[12] events are harmful to man and not *how*[12] they happen. A Zande perceives how they happen just as we do. He does not see a witch charge a man, but an elephant. He does not see a witch push over the granary, but termites gnawing away its supports. He does not see a psychical flame igniting thatch, but an ordinary lighted bundle of straw. His perception of how events occur is as clear as our own."[13]

The most important way of detecting the influence of witchcraft and of identifying witches is by the revelations of oracles, of which in turn the most important is the "poison oracle." This name, though convenient, is significantly misleading insofar as, according to Evans-Pritchard, Azande do not have our concept of a poison and do not think of, or behave toward, *benge*—the substance administered in the consultation of the oracle—as we do of and toward poisons. The gathering, preparation, and administering of *benge* is hedged with ritual and strict taboos. At an oracular consultation *benge* is administered to a fowl, while a question is asked in a form permitting a yes or no answer. The fowl's death or survival is specified beforehand as giving the answer "yes" or "no." The answer is then checked by administering *benge* to another fowl and asking the question the other way round. "Is Prince Ndoruma responsible for placing bad medicines in the roof of my hut? The fowl DIES giving the answer 'Yes.' . . . Did the oracle speak truly when it said that Ndoruma was responsible? The fowl SURVIVES giving the answer 'Yes'." The poison oracle is all-pervasive in Zande life and all steps of any importance in a person's life are settled by reference to it.

A Zande would be utterly lost and bewildered without his oracle. The mainstay of his life would be lacking. It is rather as if an engineer, in our society, were to be asked to build a bridge without mathematical calculation, or a military commander to mount an extensive co-ordinated attack without the use of clocks. These analogies are mine, but a reader may well think that they beg the question at issue. For, he may argue, the Zande practice of consulting the oracle, unlike my technological and military examples, is completely unintelligible and rests on an obvious illusion. I shall now consider this objection.

First I must emphasize that I have so far done little more than note the *fact*, conclusively established by Evans-Pritchard, that the Azande *do* in fact conduct their affairs to their own satisfaction in this way and are at a loss when forced to abandon the practice—when, for instance, they fall into the hands of European courts. It is worth remarking too that Evans-Pritchard himself ran his household in the same way during his field researches and says: "I found this as satisfactory a way of running my home and affairs as any other I know of."

Further, I would ask in my turn: *to whom* is the practice alleged to be unintelligible? Certainly it is difficult for us to understand what the Azande are about when they consult their oracles; but it might seem just as incredible to them that the engineer's motions with his slide rule could have any connection with the stability of his bridge. But this riposte of course misses the intention behind the objection, which was not directed to the question whether anyone in fact understands, or claims to understand, what is going on, but rather whether what is going on actually does make sense: i.e., in itself. And it may seem obvious that Zande beliefs in witchcraft and oracles cannot make any sense, however satisfied the Azande may be with them.

What criteria have we for saying that something does, or does not, make sense? A partial answer is that a set of beliefs and practices cannot make sense insofar as they involve contradictions. Now it appears that contradictions are bound to arise in at least two ways in the consultation of the oracle. On the one hand two oracular pronouncements may contradict each other; and on the other hand a self-consistent oracular pronouncement may be contradicted by future experience. I shall examine each of these apparent possibilities in turn.

Of course, it does happen often that the oracle first says "yes" and then "no" to the same question. This does not convince a Zande of the futility of the whole operation of consulting oracles: obviously, it cannot, since otherwise the practice could hardly have developed and maintained itself at all. Various explanations may be offered, whose possibility, it is important to notice, is built into the whole network of Zande beliefs and may, therefore, be regarded as belonging to the concept of an oracle. It may be said, for instance, that bad *benge* is being used; that the operator of the oracle is ritually unclean; that the oracle is being itself influenced by witchcraft or sorcery; or it may be that the oracle is showing that the question cannot be answered straightforwardly in its present form, as with "Have you stopped beating your wife yet?" There are various ways in which the behaviour of the fowl under the influence of *benge* may be ingeniously interpreted by those wise in the ways of the poison oracle. We might compare this situation perhaps with the interpretation of dreams.

In the other type of case: where an internally consistent oracular revelation is apparently contradicted by subsequent experience, the situation may be dealt with in a similar way, by references to the influence of witchcraft, ritual uncleanliness, and so on. But there is another important consideration we must take into account here too. The chief function of oracles is to reveal the presence of "mystical" forces—I use Evans-Pritchard's term without committing myself to his denial that such forces really exist. Now though there are indeed ways of determining whether or not mystical forces are operating, these ways do not correspond to what we understand by "empirical" confirmation or refutation. This indeed is a tautology, since such differences in "confirmatory" procedures are the main criteria for classifying something as a mystical force in the first place. Here we have one reason why the possibilities of "refutation by experience" are very much fewer than might at first sight be supposed.

There is also another closely connected reason. The spirit in which oracles are consulted is very unlike that in which a scientist makes experiments. Oracular revelations are not treated as hypotheses and, since their sense derives from the way they are treated in their context, they therefore *are not* hypotheses. They are not a matter of intellectual interest but the main way in which Azande decide how they should act. If the oracle reveals that a proposed course of action is fraught with mystical dangers from witchcraft or sorcery, that course of action will not be carried out; and then the question of refutation or confirmation just does not arise. We might say that the revelation has the logical status of an unfulfilled hypothetical, were it not that the context in which this logical term is generally used may again suggest a misleadingly close analogy with scientific hypotheses.

I do not think that Evans-Pritchard would have disagreed with what I have said so far. Indeed, the following comment is on very similar lines:

> Azande observe the action of the poison oracle as we observe it, but their observations are always subordinated to their beliefs and are incorporated into their beliefs and made to explain them and justify them. Let the reader consider any argument that would utterly demolish all Zande claims for the power of the oracle. If it were translated into Zande modes of thought it would serve to support their entire structure of belief. For their mystical notions are eminently coherent, being interrelated by a network of logical ties, and are so ordered that they never too crudely contradict sensory experience but, instead, experience seems to justify them. The Zande is immersed in a sea of mystical notions, and if he speaks about his poison oracle he must speak in a mystical idiom.[14]

To locate the point at which the important philosophical issue does arise, I shall offer a parody, composed by changing round one or two expressions in the foregoing quotation.

> Europeans observe the action of the poison oracle just as Azande observe it, but their observations are always subordinated to their beliefs and are incorporated into their beliefs and made to explain them and justify them. Let a Zande consider any argument that would utterly refute all European scepticism about the power of the oracle. If it were translated into European modes of thought it would serve to support their entire structure of belief. For their scientific notions are eminently coherent, being interrelated by a network of logical ties, and are so ordered that they never too crudely contradict mystical experience but, instead, experience seems to justify them. The European is immersed in a sea of scientific notions, and if he speaks about the Zande poison oracle he must speak in a scientific idiom.

Perhaps this too would be acceptable to Evans-Pritchard. But it is clear from other remarks in the book to which I have alluded, that at the time of writing it he would have wished to add: and the European is right and the Zande wrong. This addition I regard as illegitimate and my reasons for so thinking take us to the heart of the matter.

It may be illuminating at this point to compare the disagreement between Evans-Pritchard and me to that between the Wittgenstein of the *Philosophical Investigations* and his earlier *alter ego* of the *Tractatus Logico-Philosophicus*. In the *Tractatus* Wittgenstein sought "the general form of propositions": what made propositions possible. He said that this general form is: "This is how things are"; the proposition was an articulated model, consisting of elements standing in a definite relation to each other. The proposition was true when there existed a corresponding arrangement of elements in reality. The proposition was capable of saying something because of the identity of structure, of logical form, in the proposition and in reality.

By the time Wittgenstein composed the *Investigations* he had come to reject the whole idea that there must be a general form of propositions. He emphasized the indefinite number of different uses that language may have and tried to show that these different uses neither need, nor in fact do, all have something in common, in the sense intended in the *Tractatus*. He also tried to show that what counts as "agreement or disagreement with reality" takes on as many different forms as there are different uses of language and cannot, therefore, be taken as given *prior* to the detailed investigation of the use that is in question.

The *Tractatus* contains a remark strikingly like something that Evans-Pritchard says.

> *The limits of my language mean the limits of my world.* Logic fills the world: the limits of the world are also its limits. We cannot therefore say in logic: This and this there is in the world, and that there is not.
>
> For that would apparently presuppose that we exclude certain possibilities, and this cannot be the case since otherwise logic must get outside the limits of the world: that is, if it could consider these limits from the other side also.[15]

Evans-Pritchard discusses the phenomena of belief and scepticism, as they appear in Zande life. There *is* certainly widespread scepticism about certain things, for instance, about some of the powers claimed by witchdoctors or about the efficacy of certain magic medicines. But, he points out, such scepticism does not begin to overturn the mystical way of thinking, since it is necessarily expressed in terms belonging to that way of thinking.

> In this web of belief every strand depends on every other strand, and a Zande cannot get outside its meshes because this is the only world he

knows. The web is not an external structure in which he is enclosed. It is the texture of his thought and he cannot think that his thought is wrong.[16]

Wittgenstein and Evans-Pritchard are concerned here with much the same problem, though the difference in the directions from which they approach it is important too. Wittgenstein, at the time of the *Tractatus,* spoke of "language," as if all language is fundamentally of the same kind and must have the same kind of "relation to reality"; but Evans-Pritchard is confronted by two languages which he recognizes as fundamentally different in kind, such that much of what may be expressed in the one has no possible counterpart in the other. One might, therefore, have expected this to lead to a position closer to that of the *Philosophical Investigations* than to that of the *Tractatus.* Evans-Pritchard is not content with elucidating the differences in the two concepts of reality involved; he wants to go further and say: our concept of reality is the correct one, the Azande are mistaken. But the difficulty is to see what "correct" and "mistaken" can mean in this context.

Let me return to the subject of contradictions. I have already noted that many contradictions we might expect to appear in fact do not in the context of Zande thought, where provision is made for avoiding them. But there are some situations of which this does not seem to be true, where what appear to us as obvious contradictions are left where they are, apparently unresolved. Perhaps this may be the foothold we are looking for, from which we can appraise the "correctness" of the Zande system.[17]

Consider Zande notions about the inheritance of witchcraft. I have spoken so far only of the role of oracles in establishing whether or not someone is a witch. But there is a further and, as we might think, more "direct" method of doing this, namely by post-mortem examination of a suspect's intestines for "witchcraft-substance." This may be arranged by his family after his death in an attempt to clear the family name of the imputation of witchcraft. Evans-Pritchard remarks: "to our minds it appears evident that if a man is proven a witch the whole of his clan are *ipso facto* witches, since the Zande clan is a group of persons related biologically to one another through the male line. Azande see the sense of this argument but they do not accept its conclusions, and it would involve the whole notion of witchcraft in contradiction were they to do so."[18] Contradiction would presumably arise because a few positive results of post-mortem examinations, scattered among all the clans, would very soon prove that everybody was a witch, and a few negative results, scattered among the same clans, would prove that nobody was a witch. Though, in particular situations, individual Azande may avoid personal implications arising out of the presence of witchcraft-substance in deceased relatives, by imputations of bastardy and similar devices, this would not be enough to save the generally contradictory situation I have sketched. Evans-Pritchard comments: "Azande do not perceive the contradiction as we perceive it because they have no theoretical interest in the subject, and those situations in which they express their belief in witchcraft do not force the problem upon them."[19]

It might now appear as though we had clear grounds for speaking of the superior rationality of European over Zande thought, insofar as the latter involves a contradiction which it makes no attempt to remove and does not even recognize: one, however, which is recognizable as such in the context of European ways of thinking. But does Zande thought on this matter really involve a contradiction? It appears from Evans-Pritchard's account that Azande do not press their ways of thinking about witches to a point at which they would be involved in contradictions.

Someone may now want to say that the irrationality of the Azande in relation to witchcraft shows itself in the fact that they do not press their thought about it "to its logical conclusion." To appraise this point we must consider whether the conclusion we are trying to force on them is indeed a logical one; or perhaps better, whether someone who does press this conclusion is being more rational than the Azande, who do not. Some light is thrown on this question by Wittgenstein's discussion of a game,

> such that whoever begins can always win by a particular simple trick. But this has not been realized—so it is a game. Now someone draws our attention to it—and it stops being a game.
>
> What turn can I give this, to make it clear to myself?—For I want to say: "and it stops being a game"—not: "and now we see that it wasn't a game."
>
> That means, I want to say, it can also be taken like this: the other man did not *draw our attention* to anything; he taught us a different game in place of our own. But how can the new game have made the old one obsolete? We now see something different, and can no longer naively go on playing.
>
> On the one hand the game consisted in our actions (our play) on the board; and these actions I could perform as well now as before. But on the other hand it was essential to the game that I blindly tried to win; and now I can no longer do that.[20]

There are obviously considerable analogies between Wittgenstein's example and the situation we are considering. But there is an equally important difference. Both Wittgenstein's games: the old one without the trick that enables the starter to win and the new one with the trick, are in an important sense on the same level. They are both *games*, in the form of a contest where the aim of a player is to beat his opponent by the exercise of skill. The new trick makes this situation impossible and this is why it makes the old game obsolete. To be sure, the situation could be saved in a way by introducing a new rule, forbidding the use by the starter of the trick which would ensure his victory. But our intellectual habits are such as to make us unhappy about the artificiality of such a device, rather as logicians have been unhappy about the introduction of a Theory of Types as a device for avoiding Russell's paradoxes. It is noteworthy in my last quotation from Evans-Pritchard, however, that the Azande, when the possibility of this contradiction about the inheritance of witchcraft is pointed out to them, do *not* then come to regard their old beliefs about witchcraft as obsolete. "They have no theoretical interest in the subject." This suggests strongly that the context from which the suggestion about the contradiction is made, the context of our scientific culture, is not on the same level as the context in which the beliefs about witchcraft operate. Zande notions of witchcraft do not constitute a theoretical system in terms of which Azande try to gain a quasi-scientific understanding of the world.[21] This in its turn suggests that it is the European, obsessed with presssing Zande thought where it would not naturally go—to a contradiction—who is guilty of misunderstanding, not the Zande. The European is in fact committing a category-mistake.

Something else is also suggested by this discussion: the forms in which rationality expresses itself in the culture of a human society cannot be elucidated *simply* in terms of the logical coherence of the rules according to which activities are carried out in that society. For, as we have seen, there comes a point where we are not even in a position to determine what is and what is not coherent in such a context of rules, without raising questions about the point which following those rules has in the society. No doubt it was a realization of this fact which led Evans-Pritchard to appeal to a residual "correspondence with reality" in distinguishing between "mystical" and "scientific" notions. The conception of reality is indeed indispensable to any understanding of the point of a way of life. But it is not a conception which can be explicated as Evans-Pritchard tries to explicate it, in terms of what science reveals to be the case; for a form of the conception of reality must already be presupposed before we can make any sense of the expression "what science reveals to be the case."

II. Our Standards and Theirs

In Part I, I attempted, by analyzing a particular case, to criticize by implication a particular view of how we can understand a primitive institution. In this Part, I shall have two aims. First, I shall examine in a more formal way a general philosophical argument, which attempts to show that the approach I have been criticizing is in principle the right one. This argument has been advanced by Mr. Alasdair MacIntyre in two places: (a) in a paper entitled *Is Understanding Religion Compatible with Believing?* read to the Sesquicentennial Seminar of the Princeton Theological Seminar in 1962.[22] (b) In a contribution to *Philosophy, Politics and Society (Second Series)*,[23] entitled *A Mistake about Causality in Social Science*. Next, I shall make some slightly more positive suggestions about how to overcome the difficulty from which I started: how to make intelligible in our terms institutions belonging to a primitive culture, whose standards of rationality and intelligibility are apparently quite at odds with our own.

The relation between MacIntyre, Evans-Pritchard, and myself is a complicated one. MacIntyre takes Evans-Pritchard's later book, *Nuer Religion,* as an application of a point of view like mine in *The Idea of a Social Science*; he regards it as an object lesson in the absurd results to which such a position leads, when applied in practice. My own criticisms of Evans-Pritchard, on the other hand, have come from precisely the opposite direction. I have tried to show that Evans-Pritchard did not at the time of writing *The Azande* agree with me *enough*; that he did not take seriously enough the idea that the concepts used by primitive peoples can only be interpreted in the context of the way of life of those peoples. Thus I have in effect argued that Evans-Pritchard's account of the Azande is unsatisfactory precisely to the extent that he agrees with MacIntyre and not me.

The best point at which to start considering MacIntyre's position is that at which he agrees with me—in emphasizing the importance of possibilities of *description* for the concept of human action. An agent's action "is identified fundamentally as what it is by the description under which he deems it to fall." Since, further, descriptions must be intelligible to other people, an action "must fall under some description which is socially recognizable as the description of an action."[24] "To identify the limits of social action in a given period," therefore, "is to identify the stock of descriptions current in that age."[25] MacIntyre correctly points out that descriptions do not exist in isolation, but occur "as constituents of beliefs, speculations and projects." As these in turn "are continually criticized, modified, rejected, or improved, the stock of descriptions changes. The changes in human action are thus intimately linked to the thread of rational criticism in human history."

This notion of rational criticism, MacIntyre points out, requires the notion of choice between alternatives, to explain which "is a matter of making clear what the agent's criterion was and why he made use of this criterion rather than another and to explain why the use of this criterion appears rational to those who invoke it."[26] Hence "in explaining the rules and conventions to which action in a given social order conform (*sic*) we cannot omit reference to the rationality or otherwise of those rules and conventions." Further, "the beginning of an explanation of why certain criteria are taken to be rational in some societies is that they *are* rational. And since this has to enter into our explanation we cannot explain social behaviour independently of our own norms of rationality."

I turn now to criticism of this argument. Consider first MacIntyre's account of changes in an existing "stock" of available descriptions of actions. How does a candidate for inclusion *qualify* for admission to the stock? Unless there are limits, all MacIntyre's talk about possibilities of description circumscribing possibilities of action becomes nugatory, for there would be nothing to stop anybody inventing some arbitrary verbal expression, applying it to some arbitrary bodily movement, and thus adding that expression to the stock of available descriptions. But of course the new description must be an *intelligible* one. Certainly, its intelligibility cannot be decided by whether or not it belongs to an *existing* stock of descriptions, since this would rule out precisely what is being discussed: the addition of *new* descriptions to the stock. "What can intelligibly be said" is not equivalent to "what has been intelligibly said," or it would never be possible to say anything new. *Mutatis mutandis* it would never be possible to *do* anything new. Nevertheless the intelligibility of anything new said or done does depend in a certain way on what already has been said or done and understood. The crux of this problem lies in how we are to understand that "in a certain way."

In *Is Understanding Religion Compatible with Believing?* MacIntyre asserts that the development through criticism of the standards of intelligibility current in a society is ruled out by my earlier account (in *The Idea of a Social Science*) of the origin in social institutions themselves of such standards. I shall not now repeat my earlier argument, but simply point out that I did, in various passages,[27] emphasize the *open* character of the "rules" which I spoke of in connection with social institutions: i.e., the fact that in changing social situations, reasoned decisions have to be made about what is to count as "going on in the same way." MacIntyre's failure to come to terms with this point creates difficulties for him precisely analogous to those which he mistakenly attributes to my account.

It is a corollary of his argument up to this point, as well as being intrinsically evident, that a new description of action must be intelligible to the members of the society in which it is introduced. On my view the point is that what determines this is the further development of rules and principles already implicit in the previous ways of acting and talking. To be emphasized are not the actual members of any "stock" of descriptions; but the *grammar* which they express. It is through this that we understand their structure and sense, their mutual relations, and the sense of new ways of talking and acting that may be introduced. These new ways of talking and acting may very well at the same time involve modifications in the grammar, but we can only speak thus if the new grammar is (to its users) intelligibly related to the old.

But what of the intelligibility of such changes to observers from another society with a different culture and different standards of intelligibility? MacIntyre urges that such observers must make clear "what the agent's criterion was and why he made use of this criterion rather than another and why the use of this criterion appears rational to those who invoke it." Since what is at issue is the precise relation between the concepts of rationality current in these different societies it is obviously of first importance to be clear about *whose* concept of rationality is being alluded to in this quotation. It seems that it must be that which is current in the society in which the criterion is invoked. Something can appear rational to someone only in terms of *his* understanding of what is and is not rational. If *our* concept of rationality is a different one from his, then it makes no sense to say that anything either does or does not appear rational to *him* in *our* sense.

When MacIntyre goes on to say that the observer "cannot omit reference to the rationality or otherwise of those rules and conventions" followed by the alien agent, whose concept of rationality is now in question: ours or the agent's? Since the observer must be understood now as addressing himself to members of his own society, it seems that the reference must here be to the concept of rationality current in the observer's society. Thus there is a *non sequitur* in the movement from the first to the second of the passages just quoted.

MacIntyre's thought here and in what immediately follows, seems to be this. The explanation of why, in Society *S*, certain actions are taken to be rational, has got to be an explanation for *us*; so it must be in terms of concepts intelligible to us. If then, in the explanation, we say that in fact those criteria *are* rational, we must be using the word *"rational"* in *our* sense. For this explanation would require that we had previously carried out an independent investigation into the actual rationality or otherwise of those criteria, and we could do this only in terms of an understood concept of rationality—*our* understood concept of rationality. The explanation would run: members of Society *S* have seen to be the case something that we know to be the case. If "what is seen to be the case" is common to us and them, it must be referred to under the same concept for each of us.

But obviously this explanation is not open to us. For we start from the position that standards of rationality in different societies do not always coincide; from the possibility, therefore, that the standards of rationality current in *S* are different from our own. So we cannot assume that it will make sense to speak of members of *S* as discovering something which we have also discovered; such discovery presupposes initial conceptual agreement.

Part of the trouble lies in MacIntyre's use of the expression, "the rationality of criteria," which he does not explain. In the present context to speak thus is to cloak the real problem, since what we are concerned with are differences in *criteria of rationality*. MacIntyre seems to be saying that certain standards are taken as criteria of rationality because they *are* criteria of rationality. But whose?

There are similar confusions in MacIntyre's other paper: *Is Understanding Religion Compatible with Believing?* There he argues that when we detect an internal incoherence in the standards of intelligibility current in an alien society and try to show why this does not appear, or is made tolerable to that society's members, "we have already invoked our standards." In what sense is this true? Insofar as *we* "detect" and "show" something, obviously we do so in a sense intelligible to us; so we are limited by what *counts* (for us) as "detecting," "showing" something. Further, it may well be that the interest in showing and detecting such things is peculiar to our society—that we are doing something in which members of the studied society exhibit no interest, because the institutions in which such an interest could develop are lacking. Perhaps too the pursuit of that interest in our society has led to the development of techniques of inquiry and modes of argument which again are not to be found in the life of the studied society. But it cannot be guaranteed in advance that the methods and techniques we have used in the past—e.g., in elucidating the logical structure of arguments in our own language and culture—are going to be equally fruitful in this new context. They will perhaps need to be extended and modified. No doubt, if they are to have a logical relation to our previous forms of investigation, the new techniques will have to be recognizably continuous with previously used ones. But they must also so extend our conception of intelligibility as to make it possible for us to see what intelligibility amounts to in the life of the society we are investigating.

The task MacIntyre says we must undertake is to make intelligible (a) (to us) why it is that members of *S* think that certain of their practices are intelligible (b) (to them), when in fact they are not. I have introduced differentiating letters into my two uses of "intelligible," to mark the complexity that MacIntyre's way of stating the position does not bring out: the fact that we are dealing with two different senses of the word "intelligible." The relation between these is precisely the question at issue. MacIntyre's task is not like that of making intelligible a natural phenomenon, where we are limited only by what counts as intelligibility for us. We must somehow bring *S*'s conception of intelligibility (b) into (intelligible!) relation with our own conception of intelligibility (a). That is, we have to create a new unity for the concept of intelligibility, having a certain relation to our old one and perhaps requiring a considerable realignment of our categories. We are not seeking a state in which things will appear to us just as they do to members of *S*, and perhaps such a state is unattainable anyway. But we *are* seeking a way of looking at things which goes beyond our previous way in that it has in some way taken account of and incorporated the other way that members of *S* have of looking at things. Seriously to study another way of life is necessarily to seek to extend our own—not simply to bring the other way within the already existing boundaries of our own, because the point about the latter in their present form, is that they *ex hypothesi* exclude that other.

There is a dimension to the notions of rationality and intelligibility which may make it easier to grasp the possibility of such an extension. I do not think that MacIntyre takes sufficient account of this dimension and, indeed, the way he talks about "norms of rationality" obscures it. Rationality is not *just* a concept *in* a language like any other; it is this too, for, like any other concept it must be circumscribed by an established use: a use, that is, established in the language. But I think it is not a concept which a language may, as a matter of fact, have and equally well may not have, as is, for instance, the concept of politeness. It is a concept necessary to the existence of any language: to say of a society that it has a language[28] is also to say that it has a concept of rationality. There need not perhaps be any *word* functioning in its language as "rational" does in ours, but at least there must be features of its members' use of language analogous to those features of *our* use of language which are connected with our use of the word "rational." Where there is language it must make a difference what is said and this is only possible where the saying of one thing rules out, on pain of failure to communicate, the saying of something else. So in one sense MacIntyre is right in saying that we have already invoked our concept of rationality in saying of a collection of people that they constitute a society with a language: in the sense, namely, that we imply formal analogies between their behavior and that behavior in our society which we refer to in distinguishing between rationality and irrationality. This, however, is so far to say nothing about what in particular constitutes rational behavior in that society; that would require more particular knowledge about the norms they appeal to in living their lives. In other words, it is not so much a matter of invoking "our own norms of rationality" as of invoking our notion of rationality in speaking of their behavior in terms of "conformity to norms." But how precisely this notion is to be applied to them will depend on our reading of their conformity to norms —what counts for them as conformity and what does not.

Earlier I criticized MacIntyre's conception of a "stock of available descriptions." Similar criticisms apply to his talk about "our norms of rationality," if these norms are taken as forming some finite set. Certainly we learn to think, speak, and act rationally *through* being trained to adhere to particular norms. But having learned to speak, etc., rationally does not *consist* in having been trained to follow those norms; to suppose that would be to overlook the importance of the phrase "and so on" in any description of what someone who follows norms does. We must, if you like, be open to new possibilities of what could be invoked and accepted under the rubric of "rationality"—possibilities which are perhaps suggested and limited by what we have hitherto so accepted, but not uniquely determined thereby.

This point can be applied to the possibilities of our grasping forms of rationality different from ours in an alien culture. First, as I have indicated, these possibilities are limited by certain formal requirements centering round the demand for consistency. But these formal requirements tell us nothing about what in particular is to *count* as consistency, just as the rules of the propositional calculus limit, but do not themselves determine, what are to be proper values of *p, q*, etc. We can only determine this by investigating the wider context of the life in which the activities in question are carried on. This investigation will take us beyond merely specifying the rules governing the carrying out of those activities. For, as MacIntyre quite rightly says, to note that certain rules are followed is so far to say nothing about the *point* of the rules; it is not even to decide whether or not they have a point at all.

MacIntyre's recipe for deciding this is that "in bringing out this feature of the case one shows also whether the use of this concept is or is not a possible one for people who have the standards of intelligibility in speech and action which we have."[29] It is important to notice that his argument, contrary to what he supposes, does not in fact show that our *own* standards of rationality occupy a peculiarly central position. The appearance to the contrary is an optical illusion engendered by the fact that MacIntyre's case has been advanced in the English language and in the context of 20th Century European culture. But a formally similar argument could be advanced in *any* language containing concepts playing a similar role in that language to those of "intelligibility" and "rationality" in ours. This shows that, so far from overcoming relativism, as he claims, MacIntyre himself falls into an extreme form of it. He disguises this from himself by committing the very error of which, wrongly as I have tried to show, he accuses me: the error of overlooking the fact that "criteria and concepts have a history." While he emphasizes this point when he is dealing with the concepts and criteria governing action in particular social contexts, he forgets it when he comes to talk of the *criticism* of such criteria. Do not the criteria appealed to in the criticism of existing institutions equally have a history? And in whose society do they have that history? MacIntyre's implicit answer is that it is in ours; but if we are to speak of difficulties and incoherencies appearing and being detected in the way certain practices have hitherto been carried on in a society, surely this can only be understood in connection with problems arising *in* the carrying on of the activity. Outside that context we could not begin to grasp what was problematical.

Let me return to the Azande and consider something which MacIntyre says about them, intended to support the position I am criticizing.

> The Azande believe that the performance of certain rites in due form affects their common welfare; this belief cannot in fact be refuted. For they also believe that if the rites are ineffective it is because someone present at them had evil thoughts. Since this is always possible, there is never a year when it is unavoidable for them to admit that the rites were duly performed, but they did not thrive. Now the belief of the Azande is not unfalsifiable in principle (we know perfectly well what would falsify it—the conjunction of the rite, no evil thoughts and disasters). But in fact

it cannot be falsified. Does this belief stand in need of rational criticism? And if so by what standards? It seems to me that one could only hold the belief of the Azande rational *in the absence of* any practice of science and technology in which criteria of effectiveness, ineffectiveness and kindred notions had been built up. But to say this is to recognize the appropriateness of scientific criteria of judgment from our standpoint. The Azande do not intend their belief either as a piece of science or as a piece of non-science. They do not possess these categories. It is only *post eventum,* in the light of later and more sophisticated understanding that their belief and concepts can be classified and evaluated at all.[30]

Now in one sense classification and evaluation of Zande beliefs and concepts does require "a more sophisticated understanding" than is found in Zande culture; for the sort of classification and evaluation that are here in question are sophisticated philosophical activities. But this is not to say that Zande forms of life are to be classified and evaluated in the way MacIntyre asserts: in terms of certain specific forms of life to be found in our culture, according as they do or do not measure up to what is required within these. MacIntyre confuses the sophistication of the interest in classification with the sophistication of the concepts employed in our classificatory work. It is of interest to us to understand how Zande magic is related to science; the concept of such a comparison is a very sophisticated one; but this does not mean that we have to see the unsophisticated Zande practice in the light of more sophisticated practices in our own culture, like science—as perhaps a more primitive form of it. MacIntyre criticizes, justly, Sir James Frazer for having imposed the image of his own culture on more primitive ones: but that is exactly what MacIntyre himself is doing here. It is extremely difficult for a sophisticated member of a sophisticated society to grasp a very simple and primitive form of life: in a way he must jettison his sophistication, a process which is itself perhaps the ultimate in sophistication. Or, rather, the distinction between sophistication and simplicity becomes unhelpful at this point.

It may be true, as MacIntyre says, that the Azande do not have the categories of science and non-science. But Evans-Pritchard's account shows that they do have a fairly clear working distinction between the technical and the magical. It is neither here nor there that individual Azande may sometimes confuse the categories, for such confusions may take place in any culture. A much more important fact to emphasize is that *we* do not initially have a category that looks at all like the Zande category of magic. Since it is we who want to understand the Zande category, it appears that the onus is on us to extend our understanding so as to make room for the Zande category, rather than to insist on seeing it in terms of our own ready-made distinction between science and non-science. Certainly the sort of understanding we seek requires that we see the Zande category in relation to our own already understood categories. But this neither means that it is right to "evaluate" magic in terms of criteria belonging to those other categories; nor does it give any clue as to *which* of our existing categories of thought will provide the best point of reference from which we can understand the point of the Zande practices.

MacIntyre has no difficulty in showing that *if* the rites which the Azande perform in connection with their harvests are "classified and evaluated" by reference to the criteria and standards of science or technology, then they are subject to serious criticism. He thinks that the Zande "belief" is a sort of *hypothesis* like, e.g., an Englishman's belief that all the heavy rain we have been having is due to atomic explosions.[31] MacIntyre believes that he is applying as it were a neutral concept of "*A* affecting *B*," equally applicable to Zande magic and western science. In fact, however, he is applying the concept with which *he* is familiar, one which draws is significance from its use in scientific and technological contexts. There is no reason to suppose that the Zande magical concept of "*A* affecting *B*" has anything like the same significance. On the contrary, since the Azande do, in the course of their practical affairs, apply something very like our technical concept—though perhaps in a more primitive form—and since their attitude to and thought about their magical rites are quite different from those concerning their technological measures, there is every reason to think that their concept of magical "influence" is quite different. This may be easier to accept if it is remembered that, even in our own culture, the concept of causal influence is by no means monolithic: when we speak, for example, of "what made Jones get married," we are not saying the same kind of thing as when we speak of "what made the aeroplane crash"; I do not mean simply that the events of which we speak are different in kind but that the relation between the events is different also. It should not then be difficult to accept that in a society with quite different institutions and ways of life from our own, there may be concepts of "causal influence" which behave even more differently.

But I do not want to say that we are quite powerless to find ways of thinking in our own society that will help us to see the Zande institution in a clearer light. I only think that the direction in which we should look is quite different from what MacIntyre suggests. Clearly the nature of Zande life is such that it is of very great importance to them that their crops should thrive. Clearly too they take all kinds of practical "technological" steps, within their capabilities, to ensure that they *do* thrive. But that is no reason to see their magical rites as a further, misguided such step. A man's sense of the importance of something to him shows itself in all sorts of ways: not merely in precautions to safeguard that thing. He may want to come to terms with its importance to him in quite a different way: to contemplate it, to gain some sense of his life in relation to it. He may wish thereby, in a certain sense, to *free* himself from dependence on it. I do not mean by making sure that it does not let him down, because the point is that, *whatever* he does, he may still be let down. The important thing is that he should understand *that* and come to terms with it. Of course, merely to understand that is not to come to terms with it, though perhaps it is a necessary condition for so doing, for a man may equally well be transfixed and terrorized by the contemplation of such a possibility. He must see that he can still go on even if he is let down by what is vitally important to him; and he must so order his life that he still *can* go on in such circumstances. I stress once again that I do not mean this in the sense of becoming "technologically independent," because from the present point of view technological independence is yet another form of dependence. Technology destroys some dependencies but always creates new ones, which may be fiercer—because harder to understand—than the old. This should be particularly apparent to *us*.[32]

In Judaeo-Christian cultures the conception of "If it be Thy Will," as developed in the story of Job, is clearly central to the matter I am discussing. Because this conception is central to Christian prayers of supplication, they may be regarded from one point of view as freeing the believer from dependence on what he is supplicating for.[33] Prayers cannot play this role if they are regarded as a means of influencing the outcome for in that case the one who prays is still dependent on the outcome. He frees himself from this by acknowledging his complete dependence on God; and this is totally unlike any dependence on the outcome precisely because God is eternal and the outcome contingent.

I do not say that Zande magical rites are at all like Christian prayers of supplication in the positive attitude to contingencies which they express. What I do suggest is that they are alike in that they do, or may, express an attitude to contingencies; one, that is, which involves recognition that one's life is subject to contingencies, rather than an attempt to control these. To characterize this attitude more specifically one should note how Zande rites emphasize the importance of certain fundamental features of their life which MacIntyre ignores. MacIntyre concentrates implicitly on the relation of the rites to consumption, but of course they are also fundamental to social relations and this seems to be emphasized in Zande notions of witchcraft. We have a drama of resentments, evil-doing, revenge, expiation, in which there are ways of dealing (symbolically) with misfortunes and their disruptive effect on a man's relations with his fellows, with ways in which life can go on despite such disruptions.

How is my treatment of this example related to the general criticisms I was making of MacIntyre's account of what it is for us to see the *point* of the rules and conventions followed in an alien form of life? MacIntyre speaks as though our own rules and conventions are somehow a paradigm of what it is for rules and conventions to have a point, so that the only problem that arises is in accounting for the point of the rules and conventions in some other society. But in fact, of course, the problem is the same in relation to our own society as it is in relation to any other; no more than anyone else's are *our* rules and conventions immune from the danger of being or becoming pointless. So an account of this matter cannot be given simply in terms of any set of rules and conventions at all: our own or anyone else's; it requires us to consider the relation of a set of rules and conventions to something else. In my discussion of Zande magical rites just now what I tried to relate the magical rites to was a sense of the significance of human life. This notion is, I think, indispensable to any account of what is involved in understanding and learning from an alien culture; I must now try to say more about it.

In a discussion of Wittgenstein's philosophical use of language games[34] Mr. Rush Rhees points out that to try to account for the meaningfulness of language solely in terms of isolated language games is to omit the important fact that ways of speaking are not insulated from each other in mutually exclusive systems of rules. What can be said in one context by the use of a certain expression depends for its sense on the uses of that expression in other contexts (different language games). Language games are played by men who have lives to live—lives involving a wide variety of different interests, which have all kinds of different bearings on each other. Because of this, what a man says or does may make a difference not merely to the performance of the activity upon which he is at present engaged, but to his *life* and to the lives of other people. Whether a man sees point in what he is doing will then depend on whether he is able to see any unity in his multifarious interests, activities, and relations with other men; what sort of sense he sees in his life will depend on the nature of this unity. The ability to see this sort of sense in life depends not merely on the individual concerned, though this is not to say it does not depend on him at all; it depends also on the possibilities for making such sense which the culture in which he lives does, or does not, provide.

What we may learn by studying other cultures are not merely possibilities of different ways of doing things, other techniques. More importantly we may learn different possibilities of making sense of human life, different ideas about the possible importance that the carrying out of certain activities may take on for a man, trying to contemplate the sense of his life as a whole. This dimension of the matter is precisely what MacIntyre misses in his treatment of Zande magic: he can see in it only a (misguided) technique for producing consumer goods. But a Zande's crops are not just potential objects of consumption: the life he lives, his relations with his fellows, his chances for acting decently or doing evil, may all spring from his relation to his crops. Magical rites constitute a form of expression in which these possibilities and dangers may be contemplated and reflected on—and perhaps also thereby transformed and deepened. The difficulty we find in understanding this is not merely its remoteness from science, but an aspect of the general difficulty we find, illustrated by

MacIntyre's procedure, of thinking about such matters at all except in terms of "efficiency of production"—production, that is, for consumption. This again is a symptom of what Marx called the "alienation" characteristic of man in industrial society, though Marx's own confusions about the relations between production and consumption are further symptoms of that same alienation. Our blindness to the point of primitive modes of life is a corollary of the pointlessness of much of our own life.

I have now explicitly linked my discussion of the "point" of a system of conventions with conceptions of good and evil. My aim is not to engage in moralizing, but to suggest that the concept of *learning from* which is involved in the study of other cultures is closely linked with the concept of *wisdom*. We are confronted not just with different techniques, but with new possibilities of good and evil, in relation to which men may come to terms with life. An investigation into this dimension of a society may indeed require a quite detailed inquiry into alternative techniques (e.g., of production), but an inquiry conducted for the light it throws on those possibilities of good and evil. A very good example of the kind of thing I mean is Simone Weil's analysis of the techniques of modern factory production in *Oppression and Liberty*, which is not a contribution to business management, but part of an inquiry into the peculiar form which the evil of oppression takes in our culture.

In saying this, however, I may seem merely to have lifted to a new level the difficulty raised by MacIntyre of how to relate our own conceptions of rationality to those of other societies. Here the difficulty concerns the relation between our own conceptions of good and evil and those of other societies. A full investigation would thus require a discussion of ethical relativism at this point. I have tried to show some of the limitations of relativism in an earlier paper.[35] I shall close the present essay with some remarks which are supplementary to that.

I wish to point out that the very conception of human life involves certain fundamental notions—which I shall call "limiting notions"—which have an obvious ethical dimension, and which indeed in a sense determine the "ethical space," within which the possibilities of good and evil in human life can be exercised. The notions which I shall discuss very briefly here correspond closely to those which Vico made the foundation of his idea of natural law, on which he thought the possibility of understanding human history rested: birth, death, sexual relations. Their significance here is that they are inescapably involved in the life of all known human societies in a way which gives us a clue where to look, if we are puzzled about the point of an alien system of institutions. The specific forms which these concepts take, the particular institutions in which they are expressed, vary very considerably from one society to another; but their central position within a society's institutions is and must be a constant factor. In trying to understand the life of an alien society, then, it will be of the utmost importance to be clear about the way in which these notions enter into it. The actual practice of social anthropologists bears this out, although I do not know how many of them would attach the same kind of importance to them as I do.

I speak of a "limit" here because these notions, along no doubt with others, give shape to what we understand by "human life"; and because a concern with questions posed in terms of them seems to me constitutive of what we understand by the "morality" of a society. In saying this, I am of course disagreeing with those moral philosophers who have made attitudes of approval and disapproval, or something similar, fundamental in ethics, and who have held that the *objects* of such attitudes were conceptually irrelevant to the conception of morality. On that view, there might be a society where the sorts of attitude taken up in *our* society to questions about relations between the sexes were reserved, say, for questions about the length people wear their hair, and *vice versa*. This seems to me incoherent. In the first place, there would be a c confusion in *calling* a concern of that sort a "moral" concern, however passionately felt. The story of Samson in the Old Testament confirms rather than refutes this point, for the interdict on the cutting of Samson's hair is, of course, connected there with much else: and pre-eminently, it should be noted, with questions about sexual relations. But secondly, if that is thought to be merely verbal quibbling, I will say that it does not seem to me a merely conventional matter that T. S. Eliot's trinity of "birth, copulation and death" happen to be such deep objects of human concern. I do not mean just that they are made such by fundamental psychological and sociological forces, though that is no doubt true. But I want to say further that the very notion of human life is limited by these conceptions.

Unlike beasts, men do not merely live but also have a conception of life. This is not something that is simply added to their life; rather, it changes the very sense which the word "life" has, when applied to men. It is no longer equivalent to "animate existence." When we are speaking of the life of man, we can ask questions about what is the right way to live, what things are most important in life, whether life has any significance, and if so what.

To have a conception of life is also to have a conception of death. But just as the "life" that is here in question is not the same as animate existence, so the "death" that is here in question is not the same as the end of animate existence. My conception of the death of an animal is of an event that will take place in the world; perhaps I shall observe it—and my life will go on. But when I speak of "my death," I am not speaking of a future event in my life;[36] I am not even speaking of an event in anyone else's life. I am speaking of the cessation of my world. That is also a cessation of my ability to do good or evil. It is not just that *as a matter of fact* I shall no longer be able to do good or evil after I am dead; the point is that my very *concept* of what it is to be able to do good or evil is deeply bound up with my concept of my life as ending in death. If ethics is a concern with the right way to live, then clearly the nature of this concern must be deeply affected by the concept of life as ending in death. One's attitude to one's life is at the same time an attitude to one's death.

This point is very well illustrated in an anthropological datum which MacIntyre confesses himself unable to make any sense of.

> According to Spencer and Gillen some aborigines carry about a stick or stone which is treated *as if* it is or embodies the soul of the individual who carries it. If the stick or stone is lost, the individual anoints himself as the dead are anointed. Does the concept of "carrying one's soul about with one" make sense? Of course we can redescribe what the aborigines are doing and transform it into sense, and perhaps Spencer and Gillen (and Durkheim who follows them) misdescribe what occurs. But if their reports are not erroneous, we confront a blank wall here, so far as meaning is concerned, although it is easy to give the rules for the use of the concept.[37]

MacIntyre does not say why he regards the concept of carrying one's soul about with one in a stick "thoroughly incoherent." He is presumably influenced by the fact that it would be hard to make sense of an action like this if performed by a twentieth-century Englishman or American; and by the fact that the soul is not a material object like a piece of paper and cannot, therefore, be carried about in a stick as a piece of paper might be. But it does not seem to me so hard to see sense in the practice, even from the little we are told about it here. Consider that a lover in our society may carry about a picture or lock of hair of the beloved; that this may symbolize for him his relation to the beloved and may, indeed, change the relation in all sorts of ways: for example, strengthening it or perverting it. Suppose that when the lover loses the locket he feels guilty and asks his beloved for her forgiveness: there might be a parallel here to the aboriginal's practice of anointing himself when he "loses his soul." And is there necessarily anything irrational about either of these practices? Why should the lover not regard his carelessness in losing the locket as a sort of betrayal of the beloved? Remember how husbands and wives may feel about the loss of a wedding ring. The aborigine is clearly expressing a concern with his life as a whole in this practice; the anointing shows the close connection between such a concern and contemplation of death. Perhaps it is precisely this practice which makes such a concern possible for him, as religious sacraments make certain sorts of concern possible. The point is that a concern with one's life as a whole, involving as it does the limiting conception of one's death, if it is to be expressed *within* a person's life, can necessarily only be expressed quasi-sacramentally. The form of the concern shows itself in the form of the sacrament.

The sense in which I spoke also of sex as a "limiting concept" again has to do with the concept of a human life. The life of a man is a man's life and the life of a woman is a woman's life: the masculinity or the femininity are not just *components* in the life, they are its *mode*. Adapting Wittgenstein's remark about death, I might say that my masculinity is not an experience in the world, but my way of experiencing the world. Now the concepts of masculinity and femininity obviously require each other. A man is a man in relation to women; and a woman is a woman in relation to men.[38] Thus the form taken by man's relation to women is of quite fundamental importance for the significance he can attach to his own life. The vulgar identification of morality with sexual morality certainly *is* vulgar; but it is a vulgarization of an important truth.

The limiting character of the concept of birth is obviously related to the points I have sketched regarding death and sex. On the one hand, my birth is no more an event in my life than is my death; and through my birth ethical limits are set for my life quite independently of my will: I am, from the outset, in specific relations to other people, from which obligations spring which cannot but be ethically fundamental.[39] On the other hand, the concept of birth is fundamentally linked to that of relations between the sexes. This remains true, however much or little may be known in a society about the contribution of males and females to procreation; for it remains true that man is born of woman, not of man. This, then, adds a new dimension to the ethical institutions in which relations between the sexes are expressed.

I have tried to do no more, in these last brief remarks, than to focus attention in a certain direction. I have wanted to indicate that forms of these limiting concepts will necessarily be an important feature of any human society and that conceptions of good and evil in human life will necessarily be connected with such concepts. In any attempt to understand the life of another society, therefore, an investigation of the forms taken by such concepts—their role in the life of the society—must always take a central place and provide a basis on which understanding may be built.

> Now since the world of nations has been made by men, let us see in what institutions men agree and always have agreed. For these institutions will be able to give us the universal and eternal principles (such as every science must have) on which all nations were founded and still preserve themselves.
>
> We observe that all nations, barbarous as well as civilized, though separately founded because remote from each other in time and space, keep these three human customs: all have some religion, all contract solemn marriages, all bury their dead. And in no nation, however savage and crude, are any human actions performed with more elaborate ceremonies and more sacred solemnity than the rites of religion, marriage and burial. For by the axiom that "uniform ideas, born among peoples unknown to each other, must have a common ground of truth," it must

have been dictated to all nations that from these institutions humanity began among them all, and therefore they must be most devoutly guarded by them all, so that the world should not again become a bestial wilderness. For this reason we have taken these three eternal and universal customs as the first principles of this Science.[40]

NOTES

1. London and New York (Routledge & Kegan Paul; Humanities Press), 1958.

2. Oxford (Oxford University Press), 1937.

3. At this point the anthropologist is very likely to start speaking of the "social function" of the institution under examination. There are many important questions that should be raised about functional explanations and their relations to the issues discussed in this essay; but these questions cannot be pursued further here.

4. E. E. Evans-Pritchard, "Lévy-Bruhl's Theory of Primitive Mentality," *Bulletin of the Faculty of Arts,* University of Egypt, 1934.

5. "Science and Sentiment," *Bulletin of the Faculty of Arts, ibid.,* 1935.

6. Indeed, one way of expressing the point of the story of Job is to say that in it Job is shown as going astray by being induced to make the reality and goodness of God contingent on what happens.

7. R. G. Collingwood, *Principles of Art* (Oxford, Oxford University Press, Galaxy Books, 1958), p. 67.

8. *Witchcraft, Oracles and Magic among the Azande,* p. 64.

9. The italics are mine throughout this quotation.

10. *Op. cit.,* p. 12.

11. For further criticism of Pareto see Peter Winch, *The Idea of a Social Science,* pp. 95–111.

12. Evans-Pritchard's italics.

13. *Op. cit.,* p. 72.

14. *Ibid.,* p. 319.

15. Wittgenstein, *Tractatus Logico-Philosophicus,* paras. 5.6–5.61.

16. Evans-Pritchard, *op. cit.,* p. 194.

17. I shall discuss this point in a more general way in Part II.

18. *Ibid.,* p. 24.

19. *Ibid.,* p. 25.

20. L. Wittgenstein, *Remarks on the Foundations of Mathematics,* Pt. II, §77. Wittgenstein's whole discussion of "contradiction" in mathematics is directly relevant to the point I am discussing.

21. Notice that I have *not* said that Azande conceptions of witchcraft have nothing to do with understanding the world at all. The point is that a different form of the concept of understanding is involved here.

22. See *Faith and the Philosophers,* edited by John Hick (London, Macmillan, 1964).

23. Edited by Peter Laslett and W. G. Runciman (Oxford, Basil Blackwell, 1962).

24. *Ibid.,* p. 58.

25. *Ibid.*, p. 60.

26. *Ibid.*, p. 61.

27. Pp. 57–65; 91–94; 121–123.

28. I shall not discuss here what justifies us in saying *this* in the first place.

29. "Is Understanding Religion Compatible with Believing?" in *Faith and the Philosophers*, p. 123.

30. *Ibid.*, p. 121.

31. In what follows I have been helped indirectly, but greatly, by some unpublished notes made by Wittgenstein on Frazer, which Mr. Rush Rhees was kind enough to show me; and also by various scattered remarks on folklore in *The Notebooks* of Simone Weil (London, Routledge & Kegan Paul, 1963).

32. The point is beautifully developed by Simone Weil in her essay on "The Analysis of Oppression" in *Oppression and Liberty* (London, Routledge & Kegan Paul, 1958).

33. I have been helped to see this point by a hitherto unpublished essay on the concept of prayer by Mr. D. Z. Phillips.

34. Rush Rhees, "Wittgenstein's Builders," *Proceedings of the Aristotelian Society*, vol. 20 (1960), pp. 171–186.

35. Peter Winch, "Nature and Convention," *Proceedings of the Aristotelian Society*, vol. 20 (1960), pp. 231–252.

36. Cf. Wittgenstein, *Tractatus Logico-Philosophicus*, 6.431–6.4311.

37. "Is Understanding Religion Compatible with Believing?" in *Faith and the Philosophers*, pp. 122–123.

38. These relations, however, are not simple converses. See Georg Simmel, "Das Relative und das Absolute im Geschlechter-Problem" in *Philosophische Kultur* (Leipzig, Werner Klinkhardt, 1911).

39. For this reason, among others, I think A. I. Melden is wrong to say that parent-child obligations and rights have nothing directly to do with physical genealogy. Cf. Melden, *Rights and Right Conduct* (Oxford, Basil Blackwell, 1959).

40. Giambattista Vico, *The New Science*, §§332–333.

Understanding and Explanation in Sociology and Social Anthropology

I. C. JARVIE

I. Introduction

IT IS EASY TO CONFLATE PROBLEMS OF EXPLANATION AND OF UNDERstanding, perhaps because the ordinary words 'explanation' and 'understanding' are used almost interchangeably.[1] However, in the philosophy of science we can, by adopting a deductive explication of the former, serve clarity. Whatever understanding is, explanation is the process of deducing one statement from others in accordance with some formal and also some material requirements.[2] So, while what one man understands another can be puzzled by, it cannot be that what obeys the rules of valid deduction to one man does not to another. Understanding *might* seem amenable to analysis—or, rather, is it misunderstanding that is so amenable? Understanding or making sense of, like perceiving, would seem to be an interplay between expectation and feedback; the attempt to 'impose' a mental set and at the same time to correct that set. Our preconceptions are thus essentially involved in the process of understanding: and among these preconceptions are what appear to resemble standards: we find unsatisfactory those explanations of human behaviour which do not render it 'reasonable'; we are doubtful of theories attributing to atoms asymmetric properties. The analogy between rationality and symmetry in nature may not be close, but their roles as standards of understandability are: understanding a human being and understanding an atom are not different processes.

All this will seem like uncontroversial platitudes until it is put against the standard view that we should approach the study of alien societies without prejudice and preconception. It becomes my counter-contention that we *cannot*

I. C. Jarvie, "Understanding and Explanation in Sociology and Social Anthropology," in *Explanation in the Behavioral Sciences*, ed. Robert Borger and Frank Cioffi (Cambridge: At the University Press, 1970), pp. 231–48.

189

but attempt to translate alien societies into terms of ours, and only where there occur breakdowns and inconsistencies in our translation do we scrutinize our preconceptions and change them. The problem raised by my contention is how to study other societies objectively; that is, how to be critical of our preconceptions in order to test for their truth-values. In the heyday of intellectualist anthropology the scholar took it for granted that he and his society were models of rationality and understandability. He was thus led quickly into misunderstanding and misjudging alien societies simply because they were different. In the more liberal climate of this century it has been argued that we can avoid misjudgment by making no judgments at all—since moral value systems are incommensurable—and this will possibly help us to have fewer misunderstandings.

Like the liberal critics of intellectualism, I find myself against both misunderstandings and misjudgments. However, I do not regard relativism as either the only respectable or as a satisfactory alternative. Indeed my contention above leads me to conclude that *all* our efforts to understand will be misunderstandings, misjudgments and oversimplifications. All we can do about it is face the fact and be as critical as possible of our efforts.

Recently there has appeared a new and plausible doctrine which concedes many of the relativist points but seemingly avoids total commitment to it. Its author is Peter Winch, and he has published it in a paper, 'Understanding a Primitive Society' (Winch, 1964, pp. 307–24), which is a follow-up to his intriguing book *The Idea of a Social Science* (Winch, 1958). Winch argues that there are certain necessary conditions, social and moral, for there to be any social life at all, thus he is no relativist. He also argues, if I may indulge a crude first approximation to his position, that cross-cultural value-judgments will always be misjudgments—and therefore should be avoided—because there is no language game in which cross-cultural value-judgments could be legitimate moves. The conflict between his position and my previous contention about the whole nature of understanding itself is obvious. I therefore wish to argue that Winch yields too much to relativism, that there are language games in which cross-cultural value-judgments are legitimate moves, that these moves are played in all cultures as well as the sociologists' sub-culture. Indeed, such cross-cultural value-judgments, such use of one's own society as a measuring instrument or a sounding board, is the principal way sociological understanding of an alien society is reached.

2. Winch's Position in Outline

Winch's concern in 'Understanding a Primitive Society' is the broad problem of how we can understand the customs of an alien primitive society. He focusses his discussion not on understanding primitive customs in general, but on understanding those special cases of primitive customs which involve beliefs—like beliefs about how reproduction occurs—which conflict with beliefs taken for granted in our society. Thus we have a narrower problem of understanding and a broader one. The broader one is of understanding primitive customs in general; the narrower one is of understanding those customs involving ideas which conflict with our ideas. Winch apparently regards this narrower problem of understanding as crucial to the broader problem of understanding, and concentrates on it presumably in the belief that if we can understand the special cases, understanding primitive customs in general will be easy.[3]

Winch comes at his problem by discussing a remark in Evans-Pritchard's book on Azande magic (Evans-Pritchard, 1937) to the effect that Azande magical beliefs not only run counter to beliefs of ours, but do not themselves 'accord with objective reality'. In dealing with Azande witchcraft, Evans-Pritchard asserts that not only do some of its component beliefs contradict some of ours (which is not so serious, since both could be false), but also that ours are true and theirs false.

Winch's central argument is that in saying that the beliefs of primitives do not accord with objective reality we are talking in terms of reality seemingly conceived of outside language and culture. This, however, Winch believes we cannot legitimately do. Even if there is such a thing as objective reality outside language, to conceive it outside language and culture is impossible. In saying that primitive beliefs are false we are saying they do not accord with *our* conceptions of reality; with reality as *conceived* by us, if you prefer. But imposing our conceptions in this way is no way to come to understand primitive society. It is no way to understand it because magical beliefs, for example, may well be tied into a whole system of other beliefs, a veritable world-view in which the disputed beliefs play an essential social and theoretical role. This system constitutes an on-going way of life and it shows grave lack of understanding (in several senses) to single out elements of it and attempt to adjudge them not in accord with objective reality. They may not accord with reality as seen from the standpoint of our language and culture, but they can hardly be said not to accord with the same reality they themselves conceive—even the reality, linguistic and cultural, they themselves embody.

It would thus seem that in certain ways our society's beliefs and primitive beliefs are incommensurable, they cannot be compared. The road to understanding is nevertheless to seek out the universal problems of human life; but not to give them universal solutions, since these would be outside language and culture, which is impossible. Rather, we have to try to show how the primitive society solves them in its own way. Here Winch has skilfully pulled back from the relativist precipice by asserting that all societies do have something in common, the problem of human life in general and its general root in universal facts, i.e. birth, sex and death.[4] So if we begin social studies with these universal facts and their ensuing universal problems, we have some bases of comparison, some universals in terms of which we can begin to make sense of any society: namely, how each society handles the universal facts of birth, sex and death.

3. An Alternative to Winch

Before expanding and discussing what I take Winch's position to be,[5] I should like to contrast it with the admittedly not very sympathetic position from which my criticisms will come.[6]

I have no quarrel with the suggestion that in the social sciences we aim to understand other societies. But I would go further: social science also aims to *explain* and *appraise* societies, their institutions, and beliefs. Social science, like any other science, uses language in attempts to make true universal statements about the world, which will explain the world. We have these aims because of something like an innate curiosity which drives us to ask questions, formulate problems, seek answers which will improve our knowledge and understanding. The phylogenetic explanation of our curiosity and concern with problems sees it as an adaptive mechanism. The ontogenesis of problems seems to be something like disappointed expectations, i.e. refuted beliefs and theories.[7] The (conscious and unconscious) expectations and theories we hold are clearly deeply influenced by the upbringing and education—the culture, in fact—of which we are products.

It follows from all this that the entire activity of social science involves, and necessarily involves, bringing the ideas, standards and concepts of our language and culture to bear on those of other cultures, seeking to find correspondences and trying them out, then following through on the feedback and modifying both our concepts and the correspondences. What we find problematic will at first be a result of our culture and expectations (knowledge). What we find good and bad, true and false, will depend at first on our culture and knowledge. In trying to understand other peoples we resort to something rather resembling the act of translation from one language to another (see Gellner, 1965). We do our best to find equivalents in translating, but must also rely on analogy, similarity, metaphor and the occasional directly appropriated, then explicated, untranslatable concept—which litter the anthropological literature. This act of translation fails if it leaves us unable to appraise the truth of the beliefs of the other culture, or to discuss the values of that culture as we can our own. It would fail in the same way as a translation from a French or Russian science or religion or ethics text would fail if it left us in no position to appraise the finished product.

(One curious phenomenon which I will return to below in §6 is how constant acquaintance with alternative sets of concepts and ways of classifying the world tends to shatter a lot of one's own preconceptions. The bizarre ceases to be bizarre, and a degree of self-awareness about one's own culture and society is gained which only the greatest of imaginative leaps can otherwise obtain.)

4. Winch's Position Developed

Winch has produced a plausible, even a beguiling, argument. I am uneasy about more than I can coherently criticize; I can criticize more than I have space for. The general Wittgensteinian underlay has been discussed elsewhere.[8] My aim will be to come to a fuller understanding of how we understand alien societies, and I will proceed via a detour through Winch's pretty flower-bed of argument.

My entire account of understanding would seem to beg the questions Winch wants to raise. It seems that in his view whether a statement is true will depend upon what it means. What is means, in his view, will depend upon how it is used, how it functions as part of the form it belongs to. The notion, then, of translating one form of life into terms of another doesn't make much sense. The way beliefs operate in a form of life is peculiar to that form of life. In particular, there is no reason to suppose that a statement true-to-them is translatable into a statement true-to-us; but it if is translatable into a statement false-to-us that does not show that it is false-to-them or false *tout court*.

Winch would I think agree that anthropologists have always struggled to make beliefs we cannot share, held by others, e.g. magical beliefs, understandable. This involves giving an account of them which satisfies our 'scientific' culture's criteria of rationality[9] or intelligibility. In some cases we find ourselves studying beliefs that are not true, yet they are believed to be true by the culture we study. Winch would contend that the last sentence is illegitimate: that it cannot be uttered intelligibly because the words 'not true' and 'true' belong to two quite separate universes of discourse (ours and theirs), or they both belong to ours and are not found used, of the beliefs in question, in theirs. But our universe of discourse cannot appraise other universes of discourse, or appraise itself as the only true universe of discourse. Reality is built into a universe of discourse, and the outcome of a question about it in another cannot be appraised in the first. Winch gives an example from religion: 'What [God's] reality amounts to can only be seen from the religious tradition in which the concept of God is used . . . ' (p. 309). Winch is not here quite repeating the hoary old chestnut that only the religious can handle and discuss religious concepts. Unlike those religious people who claim this, Winch nowhere says there is anything to stop the non-believer coming fully to grasp and being able to play the religious language game. (It can hardly be a rule of the game that sincerity of belief is required, even though display of sincerity may be required in ritual fashion.) But the ability properly to play it, and only this, shows true understanding of it. 'Reality is not what gives language sense. What is real and what is unreal shows itself *in* the sense that language has' (p. 309).

There is then for Winch no external or objective reality against which to measure a universe of discourse; or, assuming that Winch thinks there is an external reality, discussion about it cannot take place within that universe of discourse. (The opacity of Winch's argument at this point may be a consequence of the classical difficulty of trying to express the ineffable (see Russell, 1922, p. 18).) This is true of the universe of discourse of science, apparently, as well as that of magic. Science exists in a cultural context outside of which the actions and statements which constitute it would not make sense. Those who do not play its game can hardly appraise, e.g. its theories or experiments; those who can play that game cannot use the game to appraise itself.

The question then about Azande magic is simply whether it is a coherent game, universe of discourse, world-view, form of life. Yet Winch denies that a 'yes' in answer to this question commits him to endorsing all magic. It only commits him to that which is 'one of the principal foundations of their whole social life' (p. 310). Magic in our culture is *not* foundational, it is parasitic as the black mass is on the mass. The former is not understandable without reference to the latter; but not vice versa. This aside, then, is the answer 'yes': are Azande beliefs a coherent system?

To begin with, not only do Azande beliefs lead to inconsistencies, but the Azande use *ad hoc* devices to evade these. Azande, however, do not themselves press their beliefs until they yield contradictions; and they showed no theoretical interest if these were pressed on them by the outsider. In their game so to speak they do not press; if we press them we are trying to force them to play our (scientific) culture's game. Azande do not regard the revelations of the oracle as hypotheses open to discussion and criticism: 'Oracular revelations are not treated as hypotheses and, since their sense derives from the way they are treated in their context, they therefore *are not* hypotheses' (p. 312). Indeed, 'to say of a society that it has a language is also to say that it has a concept of rationality' (or intelligibility? p. 318) and that standard may involve not bothering about *ad hoc*-ness, or about checking inconsistency; indeed, what is to *count* as consistency depends on the wider context of life (p. 318).

Are there then any universals on which the social sciences can get a purchase so that other forms of life can be understood without living them through? Winch isolates T. S. Eliot's trio of 'Birth, copulation, and death' as points every society has to be organized around. From motherhood, marriage and funerals, social science can start.

5. Critical Discussion of Winch

Many kinds of criticism have been levelled against Winch's ideas. One is that his conclusions fly in the face of what social scientists constantly and successfully do (cf. Gellner, 1968). Another is to show that his methodological conclusions do not follow from his philosophical premises (cf. Cohen, 1968). Convincing as these are, they by no means exhaust what is to be said. For my part, I shall criticize certain philosophical ideas Winch holds which seem to me to lead to totally mistaken views about what can and cannot be truly said about societies other than our own. Let me start where Winch is surely in the right: there is no point in defending Evans-Pritchard's statement that Azande magical beliefs do not accord with objective reality. On Evans-Pritchard's own evidence, Azande magic is irrefutable, quite metaphysical. It asserts that there is a presence in the world causing things to happen. Whatever happens can be made to fit this theory. For this reason it is a question whether we can claim that our (culture's) physiological explanation of a man's death is nearer to the truth than the Zande magical one. Certainly any conceivable crucial experiment could be interpreted to fit the magical theory.

What can be said—and surely Winch will agree (he even makes use of it)—is that whereas on the one hand, our explanation comes from an open and critical intellectual system in which ideas about the world are constantly scrutinized, criticized, and revised to meet these criticisms, on the other hand, Zande magic is part of a closed and unrevisable system of beliefs which may have been that way for a long time. The issue then is not whether magic or physiology truly explain the death, but whether the choice between an open and a closed world-view can be rationally argued. And here Winch's view seems to be, roughly, that the question cannot be rationally argued because there are different standards of rationality embedded in each position, and we could only decide the issue if one side was allowed to impose its standards on the other. If this happened it would indeed settle the argument before it started—as Winch himself tries to do by suggesting the outcome will be inconclusive.

It is at this point that my agreement with Winch stops. I would hold that there is something like a community of rationality shared by all men, but recognized or fostered by different societies in varying degrees (none being perfect). This rationality consists at the very least in learning from experience, and especially from mistakes. All the ethnography I have ever read turns up no people, however primitive, who do not in some matters learn from their mistakes. The minimum standard is thus ever present even though seldom acknowledged. Those unaware of having it could have it disclosed to them that they possessed it by outsiders, like white men. But self-discovery is also possible. This could come about in the following way. Their closed system of ideas comes into contact with another closed system of different ideas. Suddenly for the first time there is the shock of choice: another view of the world is possible. Once this is realized, to accept either becomes difficult, since what if there is a third, fourth, etc.? Of course I am idealizing and simplifying, but all I seek to establish is the possibility. It would not then be an unreasonable conclusion to decide that whatever world-view is chosen it had better be held tentatively in case something better comes along. The first culture we know to have broken through to this stage is that of Ionia and its intellectual heirs, including ourselves (Popper, 1963, Chap. 5). That it is something of a feat to get so far should not be forgotten, since other reactions to culture clash are possible, especially dogmatism (we just know we are right); mysticism (truth surpasses understanding); and scepticism (all world-views are equally doubtful and thus equally arbitrary).

Having suggested there is a community of rationality recognizing at least learning from mistakes; and having also shown how awareness of choice of world-views could lead to a more tentative attitude, a more rational attitude, one that recognizes and seeks to avoid the possibility of making mistakes; I shall now discuss certain *consequences* of Winch's view that different societies have different standards of rationality and that therefore there can be no mutual appraisal between those standards. I shall argue that, in contradiction to Winch's view that standards of rationality are incomparable, rational argument is possible between open and closed systems: indeed the way we discover intellectual problems and make intellectual progress (both ontogenetically and phylogenetically, so to speak) depends on such argument being carried out (not only between primitives and primitives, primitives and westerners, but even between Einsteins and Bohrs).[10] Winch's view seems to: (i) deny standards to other societies which they in fact possess; (ii) suggest that we are our own best interpreters, that a society's own view of itself is the best possible; (iii) postulate a metaphysical distinction between the core of a culture and what is parasitic on it; (iv) presuppose that societies are demarcatable and seamless; (v) deny empirical content to the beliefs of primitive peoples.

(i) If, when we say that there are inconsistencies within Azande ideas we are imposing our standards on them, then a curious situation is created. Do the Azande recognize this inconsistency as a problem? If they get contradictory advice from their oracles what do they do? They can't do both things; they must choose. How do Azande choose? They certainly do not allow that their oracles are in any way discredited by the contradictions. What they do is what we could call resorting to *ad hoc* reinterpretations which resolve the inconsistencies; they show no theoretical interest in exposing and extirpating these inconsistencies. But the problem confronting them—inconsistency of prescriptions—is there and cannot be evaded. In whatever way Azande reach decisions in such cases we can report truthfully that Azande ideas sometimes yield contradictions which they resolve by *ad hoc* measures. A contradiction exists whether or not someone faced with it fails to see it, refuses to see it, or is indifferent to whether he sees it or not. Its objectivity—if you like its reality—is affected by none of these attitudes. In fact with Azande it is not that they can't see any problem when they get contradictory advice, but that they adopt a poor strategy for dealing with it. Yet one should also acknowledge that *ad hoc* defence is common in our culture. This only goes to show that the standard which invokes consistency is by no means universally accepted in our society: but at least our culture has argued the issue.

Thus the Azande do possess some standard of rationality recognizable in the west as rational, though as rather poor. This contradicts Winch's claim that 'the context from which the suggestion about the contradiction is made, the context of our scientific culture, is not on the same level as the context in which the beliefs about witchcraft operate' (p. 315).

(ii) The above quotation from Winch already indicates what his probable reply would be: not that Zande have no standards, but that they have different and non-comparable standards. Even if I have shown that there is overlap between our standards and theirs, I have not shown that the non-overlap makes no decisive difference. Winch insists that it doesn't make sense to say that Azande magic is inconsistent, only: by our standards of consistency Azande magic is inconsistent. My claim is that overlap of standards is more important because in overlap may lie the seeds of appraisal and change. Winch's view somehow freezes them within their contemporary standards, unable to appraise and revise them. Most cultures will take their current beliefs as obviously true; in freezing current views Winch accepts the claim that they are (obviously) true. Assuming the alternative view for a moment, namely that a culture does not have to accept its own appraisal of itself, we would wonder why Winch thinks social anthropologists have to. Even in closed systems the *possibility* of rational discussion of current beliefs exists. Winch's view is based on a picture he seems to have of primitive society as clearly bordered, internally coherent and interlocking, all the parts reinforcing each other; he seems to think that Azande live by their magic and never sit around saying 'this is what we believe and it is true', for to say this they would have to have some conception of what it would mean if it were false. Winch claims their beliefs are not hypotheses and not, therefore, doubtable in this way. This amounts to the claim that a culture accepts its own appraisal of its own beliefs.[11] It is a false claim, and empirically refuted every time any society reappraises itself—whether from the inside or as the result of outside intrusions. To this Winch may say, from the inside never and from the outside only accompanied by violence of sorts which thus doesn't count. This answer, be it good or bad, cannot be seriously considered except on the view that societies are seamless and coherent, and especially that their systems of ideas are closed and cut off in some clear-cut sense. But consider the following argument.

An idealized model of Azande magic would be one of an isolated group of people bowling happily on their way in a social system heavily dependent on magic. Not being aware of alternative views they never consider the truth or falsity of their magical beliefs. They are just a part of their way of life and it makes no sense for us to declare some arbitrary part of that way of life false. But what then do they make of their own member who one day announces: it says in your book of laws . . . but verily I say unto you . . . ? Reforming kings and priests and prophets can change societies. They sometimes condemn previous beliefs not just as wicked, but as false, and previous deities and demons as false gods. So even within closed societies a monolithic world-view can come to be undermined.

Then, of course, if we look at culture clash we see other ways in which the Azande might come to doubt their own appraisal. Those Azande who have been educated abroad and have come back, what shall they believe? They can live as Azande half-believing in the old ways. Trying not to press the issue, under pressure they will usually hold to what their education has taught them. Consider the case of a member of a primitive society who has become a western doctor and returned to his society. He might turn a blind eye to local remedies for minor disorders; he will be more concerned to interfere in serious cases, or where the local remedy is harmful; when the case is hopeless he will again turn a blind eye to traditional practices.[12] What could be more reasonable? For minor matters and for hopeless matters it medically doesn't much matter what you do, so long as it is not positively harmful. Whereas in terms of public relations for when western medicine *can* do something, or culturally where the practices are intricately interlaced into the social system, it may matter a great deal not to interfere with custom. Yet there is a large class of serious but curable cases where traditional practices and modern medicine come into direct conflict and the former is to be rejected as false. It is a matter of empirical fact that in most parts of the world when this is put to practical test the population opts for the western magic (cf. Gellner, 1965). This may be because the westerners can often propose and then carry out crucial experiments. These have great power to impress—which also suggests that standards of rationality have universal components. Chinese in Hong Kong know that western medicine, given a chance, can cure most cases of TB: traditionally to catch it was to be doomed, as the folk-tradition and the many fictional characters who die of it testifies. Of course, viewing western medicine as magic is not in conflict with Winch's view. But the preference for western magic by local standards is a refutation of Winch's thesis that a culture accepts its own ideas as true; cannot but operate with them; would be 'utterly lost and bewildered' (p. 311) without them; and therefore can't judge them against others. Whenever a culture can adapt itself to new ideas, and implement them into its way of life, Winch's view doesn't hold.

(iii) In the light of Winch's assertion, quoted immediately above, and his citing with approval Wittgenstein's saying '*The limits of my language mean the limits of my world*', and his citing of Evans-Pritchard's view that, 'In this web of belief every strand depends on every other strand, and a Zande cannot get outside its meshes because this is the only world he knows. The web . . . is the texture of his thought and he cannot think that his thought is wrong' (both quotes in Winch at p. 313), it is not easy to reconstruct what Winch's reply to point (ii) would be. Perhaps, that culture clash is a special case unrelated to the case of widely separated societies trying to come to terms with one another. This raises the question of whether there is a Zande 'web' of thought in the required sense: whether there is a Zande culture utterly different from those it comes into contact with, and having at its core certain fundamental meanings or conventions in terms of which it organizes experience. Or whether it isn't rather typically the case that societies interact constantly both with their neighbours and so to speak with themselves, with their history, and that no demarcatable system of ideas or meanings ever is fixed and permanent.

Winch says he avoids relativism and is able to say magic in our society is false because it is parasitic on the main ideas of our society—i.e. religion—and therefore can rightly be judged false in terms of, and by the standards of, the dominant beliefs. This cannot be done with Azande magic because it is not parasitic but fundamental to their way of life. In other words, he is unwilling to separate Azande magic from Azande culture, but insists on separating Azande culture from English culture. Is this not arbitrary? Let us go slowly here. Not separating Azande magic from Azande culture involves not separating it from any other Azande aspect. Now the Azande have a 'scientific' (in our sense) technology as well: can they then judge the one in terms, and by the standards, of the other? If Zande technology is parasitic on Zande magic, then it should be judged in terms of Zande magic. If Zande magic is parasitic on Zande technology, then it should be judged by the standards of Zande technology. Should Zande technology be judged in terms of Zande magic or vice versa? Or both in terms of both?

What is parasitic exactly? Winch's claim that magic in our society is parasitic is based on his view that it is a parody: the black mass parodies and distorts the idea of the mass. The mass, however, is a parody of Jewish synagogue practices. These in their turn may be parodies of Egyptian, Babylonian and other ceremonies. Here internal reform makes Winch's idea of a parody a parody of the real situation. What goes on in present-day witches' covens probably antedates the mass (see Lethbridge, 1962; Hughes, 1952). What is parasitic on what? When does the parasitic parody become the mainstay? Moreover, our society contains science and religion, and these two clash constantly, or at least they did—rightly or wrongly—a few times in the past. That is, they did try to judge each other false, despite frequent attempts to avoid these clashes by *ad hoc* redefinitions of the scope and nature of religion (tending on the whole to make it ever more vacuous and metaphysical).[13] Which of these is parasitic? Or is neither? Is it not pure metaphysics to seek a core of a culture which makes it what it is?[14] Are not now most societies pluralistic, and does not that empirical fact refute Winch's attempt to escape relativism?

(iv) Winch's response to this might be that we are trying to impose our pluralistic standard of rationality on the Azande. My reply is the much more radical view that we and the Azande are all parts of one pluralistic world culture. Winch's whole view presupposes separate ways of life which enable their members to live untroubledly within their existing system of ideas and brush off all contact with the rest of the world. Once upon a time in small isolated Pacific island societies this might have been the case (although Kon Tiki and later investigations of Thor Heyerdahl and others showed that even that isolation was not complete) (see Heyerdahl, 1950, 1958). Now it is not. No culture really is a closed system, and any that fancies it is tends to get awakened rudely. In other words, Popper's model of the closed society probably never was actualized, and certainly is not now.[15] There are only different degrees of openness. And since they are not seamless the possibility for contrast and self-appraisal is always there. Azande differ from our society mainly in not having a tradition of self-reappraisal, and institutions to carry that tradition. They are *capable* of both things. And they certainly don't have our metatheory that self-appraisal and criticism is good. The differences between us are ones of empirical fact. But still there is a break-point. And that is when the conscious idea of critical appraisal and discussion is introduced.

This break-point may have much to do with the acquisition of literacy. For until there is literacy the past is in no way 'fixed' as a standard of comparison, the notion of learning is thus much less rich and definite. Indeed a very great strengthening of rationality in our sense of learning from experience seems to turn on literacy (see the important article by Goody & Watt, 1962, pp. 304–45). Moreover, our world-view seems more powerful because literacy enables us to incorporate and discuss other world-views.[16]

Winch's thesis that 'The concepts used by primitive peoples can only be interpreted in the context of the way of life of those peoples' (p. 315) founders because no such utterly cut-off and circumscribed 'way of life' exists.

(v) My last critical point is that Winch's curious view that primitive beliefs cannot be critically discussed along western lines empties them of empirical content. Western science is realistic. We believe it makes assertions about the world which are true or false. The reality of that world is extra-linguistic. Winch denies this last (p. 315) and thus denies realism. For Winch there is no linguistically external reality against which to match a dispute between our beliefs and primitive beliefs. However, this realism is presupposed by our science, to which Winch confesses no hostility. Science, in other words, sees itself as exploring reality, not *a* reality. Winch would presumably hold this is a misconception. Above I have argued that primitive peoples can come to appraise their own beliefs about why things happen against our competing suggestions. What is happening here? Are the primitives revising their conception of reality? How do they do that? For Winch reality is not what gives sense or meaning to language, but shows itself in the sense that language has. But how can one adopt another's conception of reality without judging it better, without claiming it is a truer conception of what is? If reality (or the world) shows itself *in the sense that language has* then there is no such thing as a truth independent of the ideas and wishes of man. Provided a culture is coherent, and one works within its well-entrenched beliefs, then there is no way of saying that these are false. They must be true. Only beliefs which run against the general grain of the culture, while accepting its terms of reference, can be false.

Does Winch want to deny that there exist primitive people who have beliefs, some of which make factual assertions about the world of existing things? Does he believe that factual assertions about the world can in any extra-linguistic sense be true or false? If he does not, then he is the sort of Protagorean relativist he strives to convince us he is not. A non-relativist would hold that the world is not altered by the language in which it is being discussed. Therefore it is in some sense extra-linguistic. Truth and consistency are qualities we attribute to statements *à propos* their relationship to this 'external world'. Inconsistent statements cannot possibly be true together of any world; true statements are true of this world; false statements are false of this world. That the Azande do not have explicit notions corresponding to these, show little interest in them, etc., is simply an empirical fact. These ideas are great discoveries in the history of mankind. They are accepted in a wide diversity of cultures, from Ancient Greek and Jewish, to modern European and American. They are not some special and weird peculiarity. They are at the core of what I earlier referred to as a universal standard of rationality. Diffusion isn't perfect and so they are not to be found everywhere yet. But, like industrialization, they will be.

This fact in itself must give Winch some discomfort. For how and why can two incommensurable belief-systems like that of the west and that of the Azande lead to one completely ousting and replacing the other? Did it just happen, or was there some rational discussion?

6. Sociological Problems and the Inescapability of Mutual and Self-Appraisal

Because of the existence of the universal standards of truth and consistency it seems to me that no two belief systems are incommensurable. My conviction is reinforced by Bartley's argument (Bartley, 1963, pp. 134–75) to the effect that there are no logical difficulties in maintaining that all elements of a belief system can be held tentatively, open to criticism. What he calls the checks of the problem, logic, and the facts are available, as well as the check of other components of the belief system. Since criticism is always possible, it cannot be dismissed as peculiar to one system and out of place in others. Those others may suppress it or ignore it, but it can erupt and since it can it 'belongs' there as much as anywhere. Thus it is my conclusion that there is nothing extraneous about our standards of truth and consistency and that provided they are manipulated with sympathy, and provided we do not make them the excuse for condescension, we are at liberty to discuss whether other people's beliefs have these properties.

However, I wish to claim more in this final section of the paper. It seems to me that if evaluative standards of different societies were incommensurable, there would be and could be no social science, indeed no history. After all, history is the attempt to explain the past in terms of the present—what we nowadays regard as satisfactory explanation is very much a product of current ideas. We have to explain historical events like why man did something apparently stupid. One explanation would be that he happened to hold a false belief. The falseness cannot be ignored, since from it may stem the consequences we are trying to explain. We cannot explain medieval plagues without reference to medieval ideas of disease and hygiene *and their falseness*. We no longer accept that race explains behaviour: few will get away with explaining wars by an aggressive instinct; theories that say societies degenerate are not much used. But in history we are in a way looking at, explaining, and evaluating the beliefs of, another society. As one explores further into the past of one's culture, or country, the gap becomes larger between them and us. Do we stop ourselves at some point and say we can't criticize, e.g. witch- and heretic-burning because 'what a witch's or a heretic's reality amounts to can be seen only from the (religious) tradition in which the concepts of witch and heretic are used . . . '? There is something absurd about this. We do it, and there is nothing wrong philosophically or otherwise with it. Similarly, in our contemporary society, we may not be able to explain actions without pointing out the falsity of the beliefs on which they were based. If we can appraise a past state of affairs of our own society, and segments of our own society today, then we can do it to others.

As to social science in general: my thesis would be that there is very unlikely to be any social science in a smoothly working closed society; that social science in fact is a product of other cultures' impact on one's own. What happens is that other possible ways of ordering social arrangements are seen, one's own ways come into question, if only in the sense that they have to be explained and defended to oneself. If our system of monogamy is better than say polygyny, what sociological and other arguments can we produce that it is?

First we question our own society. Then others raise puzzles. It is intriguing how many social scientists are themselves marginal to their society. They are refugees, foreigners, from minority groups, or otherwise 'loners'—perhaps they are trying to explain to themselves what others unthinkingly belong to. Thus my remark about ontogeny and phylogeny. Both curiosity about sociological questions as a matter of history, and its growth in individual men seems to me to be connected with contact, culture shock, disruption, which lead one into evaluative and comparative questions.

All this seems obvious enough, yet Winch flies in the face of it. He maintains in his book that understanding a society is a kind of conceptual empathy which imprisons you in a universe of discourse that cannot evaluate itself. He thus attacks Popper for saying that sociological concepts are explanatory models.[17] Since Winch holds sociological concepts play a role in the actions themselves, they somehow cannot explain it. There is some vacillation here in the use of 'understanding' and 'explanation' (cf. Rudner, 1966, pp. 81–3). True, participants in a war hold a concept or model of war. But this is purely conventional—it is *their* explanatory model of what they are doing. Whether it is a war or not is not decided by them or explained by their use of the concept. They may understand that they are in a war but be mistaken. War is a label that cannot be strictly applied and which is useful only if it satisfies someone asking for an explanation of what is going on.

Among the main problems of economics, sociology and social anthropology are the explanation of certain events, especially large-scales events like depressions, suicide of democracy, disintegration in circumstances of contact. Problems of this kind are not easy to handle. Unlike smaller-scale problems they cannot be put down to someone or some people aiming to bring them about (as can orderly traffic flow, or social security payments). On the contrary, these are events which everyone wants not to happen, they are unintended and unwanted. They are also inter-societal, not confined to one social system either in their occurrence or in the scope of the explanation. Social scientists can neither come face to face with them nor solve them without indulging in some evaluation of beliefs. However long an economy has been depressed (or underdeveloped), the economist can say that this needs explanation. He may find himself saying: 'the British have to learn that their twin desires to support an international reserve currency, and have a high growth rate, are inconsistent with each other'. Or that 'the Indians have to see that their desire for economic development is being vitiated partly by their religious love of cows'. Sociologists may in all conscience have to point out that 'total freedom for everyone and the *maintenance* of democratic systems are not simultaneously realizable in this unhappy world'. Anthropologists may say to missionaries: 'your declared love of this people and their way of life makes you blind to the fact that you will destroy it by your proselytizing and interference'. All these could be made logical inconsistencies by different formulations. But also, the British are being told their values are in conflict, so are the Indians, lovers of freedom, and missionaries. Such evaluations of evaluative systems are not somehow illegitimate straying by the social scientists, but what the social sciences are all about.

NOTES

1. Robert Brown (1963, p. 41) defines the one in terms of the other: 'Explaining away, then, is the removing of an impediment, an impediment either to someone's relationships with other people or to his intellectual understanding.'

2. For the requirements see Popper, 1959, pp. 59–62, and 1957, pp. 24 ff.; and Bartley, 1962, pp. 15–33.

3. Since Winch does not set out these relations between the problems explicitly I will not take up this latter contention. But that the solution of the general problem will flow from a solution of the narrower problem does not seem obviously true.

4. In another paper, Winch argues that there are also moral universals, especially truth-telling, integrity and justice. See Winch, 1959–60, pp. 231–52. Winch's universals bear comparison with Malinowski's theory of basic needs (see Ralph Piddington, 1957), which were mainly biological, and with Goldschmidt's recent theory that they are socio-cultural, see Goldschmidt, 1966.

5. Winch's ideas have already been discussed in the following: Brodbeck, 1963, pp. 309–24; Gellner, 1962, pp. 153–83; Louch, 1963, pp. 273–86; Winch, 1964, pp. 202–8; Louch, 1965, pp. 212–16; Saran, 1964–5, pp. 195–200; Martin, 1965, pp. 29–41. There are also three papers on Winch in the forthcoming volume *Problems in the Philosophy of Science, Proceedings of the International Colloquium, London, 1965*, vol. 3, eds. I. Lakatos & A. Musgrave (Amsterdam 1968). They are: 'The New Idealism' by Gellner, 'The Very Idea of a Social Science' by Cohen, and 'Anthropomorphism in Social Science', by Watkins.

6. There are some criticisms of Winch's book in my review in *Brit. J. Philos. of Sci.* **12**, 1961, 73–7. J. Agassi and I have developed our own view of how to understand magic in 'The Problem of the Rationality of Magic', *Brit. J. Sociol.* **18**, 1967, 55–74. The two extremely important papers of Gellner listed in the previous note have influenced me considerably, and a certain amount of overlap has been unavoidable.

7. This is the general tenor of the philosophy of K. R. Popper.

8. Criticism of the meaning/use thesis can be found in Gellner, 1959; and Wisdom, 1963, pp. 335–47.

9. Although, incidentally, it would be a mistake to think that our scientific culture admits as rational only those views which agree with current orthodoxy. No one calls Newton's optics, or Bohr's model of the atom irrational, though they are by now superseded.

10. I am referring to that part of the Einstein-Bohr debate which concerns standards of rational appraisal, see Niels Bohr, 'Discussion with Einstein on Epistemological Problems in Atomic Physics', in Schilpp (ed.), 1949.

11. Around this point the argument draws very heavily on Gellner, 'The New Idealism', see note 2.

12. I owe this rational reconstruction to a lecture given by Professor J. Agassi. He was discussing the uneasy coexistence of Chinese traditional medicine and western medicine in Hong Kong.

13. Clashes over policy are still frequent nowadays, e.g. birth control. Logically, ideas which lead on to absurd or false conclusions have doubt cast on them. It seems *false* to say the world will be a better place without birth control.

14. This kind of metaphysics is what Popper calls 'essentialism', see his *The Open Society and Its Enemies*, 1962, pp. 9–21.

15. Popper nowhere suggests that it ever was actualized, or even could be.

16. For actual demonstrations of how alien world-views can be handled see Lawrence, 1964; and Horton, 1964, pp. 85–103.

17. Martin's and Cohen's criticisms (see note 5 above) are especially pertinent here.

REFERENCES

Bartley, W. W. 1962. Achilles, the tortoise, and explanations in science and history. *Br. J. Phil. Sci.* **13.**

Bartley, W. W. 1963. *The Retreat to Commitment*. London.

Brodbeck, M. 1963. Meaning and action. *Philosophy of Sci.* **30.**

Brown, R. 1963. *Explanation and Social Science*. London.

Cohen, P. 1968. The very idea of a social science. *Problems in the Philosophy of Science, Proceedings of the International Colloquium, London, 1965*, vol. 3. Eds. I. Lakatos & A. Musgrave. Amsterdam.

Evans-Pritchard, E. E. 1937. *Witchcraft, Oracles and Magic Among the Azande*, London.

Gellner, E. 1959. *Words and Things.* London.

Gellner, E. 1962. Concepts and society. *Transactions of the 5th World Congress of Sociology*, vol. 1. Louvain.

Gellner, E. 1965. *Thought and Change*. London.

Gellner, E. 1968. The new idealism. *Problems in the Philosophy of Science, Proceedings of the International Colloquium, London, 1965*, vol. 3. Eds. I. Lakatos & A. Musgrave. Amsterdam.

Goldschmidt, W. 1966. *Comparative Functionalism*. Berkeley and Los Angeles.

Goody, J. & Watt, I. 1962. The consequences of literacy. *Comparative Studies in Society and History*, vol. 5.

Heyerdahl, T. 1950. *The Kon-Tiki Expedition*. London.

Heyerdahl, T. 1958. *Aku-Aku*. London.

Horton, W. R. G. 1964. Ritual man in Africa. *Africa* **34.**

Hughes, P. 1952. *Witchcraft*. London.

Lawrence, P. 1964. *Road Belong Cargo*. Manchester.

Lethbridge, T. C. 1962. *Witches*. London.

Louch, A. R. 1963. The very idea of a social science. *Inquiry* **6.**

Louch, A. R. 1965. On misunderstanding Mr. Winch. *Inquiry* **8.**

Martin, Michael. 1965. Winch on philosophy, social science and explanation. *Phil. Forum* **23.**

Piddington, R. 1957. Malinowski's theory of needs. *Man and Culture*. Ed. R. Firth. London.

Popper, K. R. 1957. The aim of science. *Ratio* **I.**

Popper, K. R. 1959. *The Logic of Scientific Discovery*. London.

Popper, K. R. (ed.) 1962. *The Open Society and Its Enemies,* vol. 2. London.

Popper, K. R. 1963. *Conjectures and Refutations*. London.

Rudner, R. 1966. *Philosophy of Social Science*. Englewood Cliffs.

Russell, B. 1922. 'Introduction' to L. Wittgenstein's *Tractatus Logico-Philosophicus*. London.

Saran, A. K. 1964. A Wittgensteinian sociology? *Ethics* **75.**

Schilpp, P. (ed.) 1949. *Albert Einstein: Philosopher-Scientist*. New York.

Watkins. J. W. N. 1968. Anthropomorphism in social science. *Problems in the Philosophy of Science, Proceedings of the International Colloquium, London, 1965,* vol. 3. Eds. I. Lakatos & A. Musgrave. Amsterdam.

Winch, P. 1958. *The Idea of a Social Science*. London.

Winch. P. 1959–60. Nature and convention. *Proc. Arist. Soc.* **60.**

Winch, P. 1964. Mr. Louch's idea of a social science. *Inquiry* **7.**

Winch, P. 1964. Understanding a primitive society. *Am. Phil. Qu.* **I.**

Wisdom, J. O. 1963. Metamorphoses of the verifiability theory of meaning. *Mind* **72.**

Comment

PETER WINCH

MR. JARVIE SAYS THAT 'A CRUDE FIRST APPROXIMATION' TO MY position is 'that cross-cultural value-judgments will always be misjudgments—and therefore should be avoided—because there is no language game in which cross-cultural value-judgments could be legitimate moves'. One relatively minor point to be made here is that, in the main body of the article to which Jarvie is chiefly referring (Winch, 1964; reprinted in *Religion and Understanding*, Ed. D. Z. Phillips, Blackwell, 1967) I had nothing much to say specifically about '*value*-judgments' at all. In the groping and tentative remarks which I made towards the end of that article (to the precise form of which it seems to me Jarvie pays insufficient attention in his references to them) I did, indeed, make reference to the importance which conceptions of good and evil have in our understanding of our own and other forms of social life. And in 'Nature and convention' (Winch, 1959) I was specifically concerned with questions of morality. It is remarkable, though, that in both these places I was explicitly arguing for a position contrary to the one Jarvie ascribes to me here. This makes it difficult for me to see how his formulation can appear to him to be even a 'crude approximation' to my position. It is true that, in these places and elsewhere, I was exercised to bring out some of the peculiar *difficulties* which face anyone who wishes to make moral judgments about actions belonging to a culture different from his own. But it does not seem to me from the way Jarvie writes that he would want to deny that such difficulties exist; and, as I have said, one of my main concerns was to see how some of those difficulties might be overcome. If I devoted a lot of attention to trying to make explicit precisely what the difficulties are, well this seems to me a not unreasonable preliminary to any serious attempt to overcome them.

On the wider question of cross-cultural comparisons involving conceptions

Peter Winch, "Comment" (in Jarvie's article, supra), in *Explanation in the Behavioral Sciences*, ed. Robert Borger and Frank Cioffi (Cambridge: At the University Press, 1970), pp. 249–54, 257–59.

of rationality, Jarvie repeatedly, in the body of his article, states it to be my view that 'standards of rationality are incomparable'. I do not quite understand what sense is to be attached to 'incomparable' here, but I have certainly never held any view of which I would be willing to accept this as a proper paraphrase. What, indeed, was I doing in the article about the Azande if not 'comparing' their conceptions of rationality with some of those with which we are familiar in our society? In the course of this article I criticized certain views expressed in Alasdair MacIntyre's 'Is Understanding Religion Compatible with Believing?' (MacIntyre, 1964). A point which I emphasized there, to which I think Jarvie gives insufficient attention, is that the very asking of the kind of question Jarvie is raising presupposes that we have already been able to identify certain features of the life of the society we are studying as involving something we are prepared to call 'an appeal to standards of rationality'. Our willingness to speak in such a way is obviously based on the way we already speak about such standards in our own social life; so in a sense a comparison between our society and theirs is already involved and we may speak, with Jarvie, of using our own society 'as a measuring instrument or a sounding board'. The question is not *whether* we can do this, but *what sort* of comparison is involved.

There is also the question of what we are comparing Zande (or whatever) standards with. Jarvie shares with MacIntyre a tendency which I criticized in the latter: to speak of the standards of 'our scientific culture' in this connection in a way which suggests that the only standards available to us against which to compare Zande standards are the standards involved in the practice of *scientific* work. Now it is of course true that the role played by such work in the culture of western industrialized societies is an enormously important one and that it has had a very far-reaching influence on what we are and what we are not prepared to call instances of 'rational thought'. But it was an essential part of my argument, both in *The Idea of a Social Science* and in 'Understanding a Primitive Society' (1964), to urge that our own conception of what it is to be rational is certainly not exhausted by the practices of science; and in the latter essay one of the main thrusts of my argument was an attempt to show (*a*) that misunderstandings of the sense and purport of an institutions like Zande magic arose from insisting on just *this* comparison; and (*b*) that an understanding of such an institution may be furthered by comparing it with quite other sectors of the kind of life we are familiar with. This is very far removed from the claim which Jarvie wishes to foster on me that we cannot make any comparisons at all between our institutions and theirs. I must also remark that Jarvie's holistic way of talking about 'our scientific culture' sits very ill together with his allegation (itself unfounded) that I think of the life of a culture as somehow 'seamless': this, I suggest, is precisely his way of looking at our own culture.

Jarvie says: 'Winch claims their (sc. the Azande's) beliefs are not hypotheses and are not therefore doubtàble in this way. This amounts to the claim that a culture accepts its own appraisal of its own beliefs.' Leaving aside the obscurity I find in the assertion that the first of these claims 'amounts to' the second, there are several comments I should like to make on what Mr. Jarvie says about 'appraisal' which are connected with the point I have just been making. I am confused—and I think Jarvie is too—by his way of talking about 'societies' and 'cultures' as having beliefs and appraising them. Beliefs may be more or less widely current amongst the members of a society and there may be stronger or weaker tendencies to criticize and discuss such beliefs amongst those members. Some societies have, to a greater or lesser degree than others, institutions and traditions of a predominantly critical nature. Where such traditions do exist, naturally individuals are more likely to be stimulated to think critically about the ideas and practices current in their society than where they do not. Jarvie quite rightly thinks it an important feature of Western culture that there are such critical traditions in it. He emphasizes the importance of science in this connection; I should be more inclined to emphasize the importance of philosophy and I did in fact so emphasize it in *The Idea of a Social Science* (*passim*; but cf. especially pp. 102–3, where special importance is attached to the recurrence within philosophy of discussions about the nature and possibility of philosophy itself). I do not know how Jarvie reconciles this passage with his claim that '[Winch] maintains in his book that understanding a society is a kind of conceptual empathy which imprisons you in a universe of discourse that cannot evaluate itself'.

However, even leaving aside the existence in a society of institutions of a self-consciously and explicity critical nature, it is a mistake to say that the view I developed about the relation between forms of social life and the standards according to which people act within these forms rules out the possibility of such standards being changed as a result of criticism. Indeed, one of my fundamental lines of argument was that the way in which characteristically human behaviour does involve the possibility of discussion and criticism itself shows the intimate connection between men's actions and the social context of rules and standards within which they perform those actions. This point is made most explicitly in Chapter 2 of *The Idea of a Social Science*; I draw Jarvie's attention especially to Section 5 of that chapter, where, in opposition to Michael Oakeshott, I argued that the concept of social life cannot be understood unless we give due prominence to what I there called 'reflectiveness'.

But more important than Jarvie's mis-statement of my position is the confusion which he himself betrays when he speaks of being 'imprisoned' in a universe of discourse. There are, of course, situations where we might quite properly speak of someone in this way. Consider, for example, a man, who, in the pursuit of business success, does something morally unjustifiable; and who, when we try to remonstrate with him on moral grounds, fails completely to respond to the moral categories involved in our arguments, but continues to think about his actions solely in terms of criteria of business efficiency. We might perhaps speak of such a man as being 'imprisoned' in the categories of the world of business. Now on my view, we, who oppose such a man on moral grounds, can think and argue as we do only in so far as we are masters of certain moral concepts which are intelligible to us because of the sort of life we lead. This does *not* mean, however, that we are 'imprisoned' in this life or by these concepts.

Why the difference? One important consideration is that, in the case of the man in my example, we can make clear sense of an *alternative* way of thinking about his situation to that which he in fact follows. His situation *has* an ethical dimension whether he recognizes it or not; it has this dimension because of its place in the life of the society in which it arises. In not seeing this his eyes are closed to a possibility which in fact exists for him—compare the sense in which the fly is 'imprisoned' in the fly-bottle. Someone who wanted to say that we are equally 'imprisoned' in the universe of the moral concepts with which we criticize this man would have to show that we, too, are being blind to a certain possibility. But then he must *specify* this possibility; and how is he to do this? It may be, of course, that in some particular circumstances he will be able to show further moral possibilities to which we are blind; or he may be able to argue that there are considerations—perhaps religious—which 'transcend morality'. But to do this he will, naturally, have to appeal to moral, or religious, considerations; and if we ask about the conditions under which it is possible for us to understand *these*, we are right back where we started.

There are two moves which might be made at this point towards specifying an alternative in terms which are not related as I have argued to the forms of life which our social environment makes available to us. On the one hand it might be argued that social anthropology, for example, presents us with forms of life very different from our own which we can come to understand; and that thereby we can both come to see possibilities to which our involvement in the life of our own society blinds us and also see more clearly certain features of that life to which for one reason or another we have been insensitive. On the other hand it might be held that our escape route lies through some direct confrontation with an 'objective, external reality'—'direct' in the sense that it is not mediated by concepts which are in any way culture-dependent.

Now the first of these moves is essentially the one I was making in 'Understanding a Primitive Society'. As I have argued, Jarvie does not see this because of his idea that I deny the possibility of ever understanding a form of social life very different from one's own. The second move is the one I was mainly opposing in my criticisms of Evans-Pritchard and MacIntyre in that article. Jarvie's position seems to be roughly as follows: We *are* able to understand forms of social life different from our own by something like a translation from one language into another. (There are some difficulties about this analogy which I will not pursue here.) Of course we are always liable to misinterpretations and 'mistranslations', but the critical apparatus provided by western science gives us the means of learning from our mistakes and so getting nearer the truth. I think probably the fundamental point of contention between Jarvie and myself concerns the relation between these methods of getting nearer the truth and the truth which we thus get nearer. He is not very explicit on this point, but I read him as thinking that the relation is an 'external' one in the sense that the methods of science are not essential to our understanding of the meaning of the truths which they enable us to discover; rather, it has just been found, by trial and error, that these methods do as a matter of fact constitute the best way of checking on the truth or falsity (the correspondence with some 'external', 'objective' reality) of thoughts which we can have quite apart from our participation in our 'scientific culture'. If something like this is not Jarvie's view, then I altogether fail to understand the nature of the disagreement between us. I think it is because he feels that the ultimate appeal is to this 'objective external reality', which is there and given quite independently of our methods of conceiving and discovering it, that he thinks, in opposition to me, that he has a way of comparing scientific modes of thinking with other modes of thinking and pronouncing it better; the point being that they are all, science, religion, magic or what have you, thought of as ultimately aiming at the same thing (perhaps 'understanding how things really are'), and science is plainly the best way of achieving this aim.

In opposition to this, I was arguing against the idea that all forms of human intellectual activity are comparable in *this* way. Even where we are dealing with modes of investigation, where it is appropriate to speak of 'understanding how things really are', it is a mistake to suppose that such modes of investigation are necessarily in competition with each other, or that their results, when different, are necessarily in conflict with each other. I do not, of course, rule out the possibility that there *may* sometimes be such conflict: whether this is really so or not in a given case will only be determinable by detailed examination of the particular case.

Thus, Jarvie discusses the Zande strategy for dealing with apparently conflicting oracular advice and comments that this shows that they 'do possess some standard of rationality recognizable in the west as rational, though as rather poor', claiming that this contradicts a remark of mine about the different levels on which witchcraft beliefs and the western scientific approach operate. Once again he here identifies 'western scientific culture' with 'the west' *tout court*. But, apart from that, I never of course denied that Zande witchcraft practices involve appeals to what we can understand as standards of rationality. Such appeals also involve behaviour which we can identify as 'the recognition of a contradiction'. What I was urging, though, was that we should be cautious in how *we* identify the contradiction, which may not be what it would appear to be if we approach it with 'scientific' preconceptions. Against the background of such preconceptions Zande standards might indeed seem 'rather poor', but whether they really are rather poor or not depends on the point of the activity within which the contradictions crop up. My claim was that this point is in fact very different from the point of scientific investigations. . . .

A western philosopher or anthropologist who says of Zande institutions: 'There are no witches' is not reporting the outcome of some empirical investigation he has conducted; he is expressing doubts he feels about the whole concept of a witch. He may continue to have these doubts even though he is perfectly well aware of the particular techniques by means of which Azande 'identify witches' and the kinds of thing they say about 'witches'. But he can see no sense in this whole complex of procedures; for him, witches have no reality.

When I, in 'Understanding a Primitive Society' (1964), objected to someone's saying, in this kind of context, 'there are no witches', I was not *contradicting* this claim. I was not saying 'Oh yes, there certainly are witches'. That is, I was not, as Jarvie puts it, 'endorsing' Zande beliefs, or saying that they are 'obviously true'. That is something I should find as hard to understand as I should someone's saying that they are 'obviously false'. The heightless stranger who says 'There is no height' is not, whatever he may think he is doing, denying the truth of certain propositions which we affirm. He is betraying his lack of comprehension of the institution in the context of which we do affirm those propositions.

Confusion on this matter is encouraged by talk about Zande 'beliefs'. If we think about the Zande institution of witchcraft in terms of what the Azande 'believe', we seem to invite the question: 'Well, is what they believe true or false?' I say we 'seem' to invite this question, because I should as a matter of fact be willing to argue that it is *not* always possible to ask this question with regard to what it is perfectly proper to call 'beliefs' (cf. the 'belief in other minds'). But it might be better in this context to say that the subject of discussion is not Zande beliefs but Zande *concepts*. Zande concepts are, of course, exercised or applied in the beliefs which Azande hold; and we can learn what Zande concepts are by studying the various beliefs they hold in particular contexts and by enquiring into what those beliefs mean to them in those contexts, into the importance those beliefs have for them in the lives they lead.

There is a passage in Wittgenstein's *Philosophical Investigations* which is fundamental here:

> 241 'So you are saying that human agreement decides what is true and what is false?'—It is what human beings *say* that is true and false; and they agree in the *language* they use. That is not agreement in opinions but in form of life.
> 242 If language is to be a form of communication there must be agreement not only in definitions but also (queer as this may sound) in

judgements. This seems to abolish logic, but does not do so.—It is one thing to describe methods of measurement, and another to obtain and state results of measurement. But what we call 'measuring' is partly determined by a certain constancy in results of measurement.

Let us apply this to the way Azande think about witches. The Azande 'agree in the language they use' about witches. It is a feature of this agreement that, in certain circumstances, certain procedures having been carried out with due precautions, there would be overwhelming agreement to the effect that such and such a person is a witch. This does *not* mean that anyone is made into a witch simply by being thought (even unanimously thought) to be a witch. But to suppose that the judgment of the totality is wrong on a particular occasion is to invoke the standards appropriate for judging such matters and the existence of such standards does depend on the fact that in general, when certain criteria are applied, agreement is usually reached.

Of course, what I have just said applies to cases where we take the institution of witchcraft for granted and ask about the position of particular judgments made within the context of that institution; somebody may want to raise doubts about the whole institution; but these will have to be of quite a different sort. Such a person would not be straightforwardly contradicting any particular claim but would be arguing against a whole way of speaking.

Now I do *not* deny the possibility of ever mounting such an argument. I have criticized a certain way of trying to mount it, i.e. by appealing to western 'scientific' conceptions, in order to show Zande beliefs false. But this of course is not the only possibility. And I agree with Jarvie here about the importance of the fact that an institution like that of Zande witchcraft does not exist in a vacuum, but that Zande life contains other important elements which may develop in such a way as to make witchcraft practices lose their foothold. This process will involve the making of certain sorts of criticism, but here it is of the utmost importance to be clear about what kinds of criticism they are. It may be that Azande come to think of certain new ways of living (perhaps introduced from the West) as 'better' than their traditional ways. I certainly do not wish to argue that they must inevitably be mistaken if they take such a view and it is easy to point out, as Jarvie does, obvious advantages in tackling, e.g. disease by the methods of western medicine rather than by the methods of Zande magic. It is also easy to overlook the good things that may be lost in such a transition; though again, of course, I do not claim that the losses must outweigh the gains. Such questions can only be settled, if at all, by patient and sensitive attention to particular cases. I do, however, want to protest very strongly against the sort of claim that creeps into Jarvie's paper towards the end to the effect that the almost universal success of western ways of life in ousting other 'more primitive' ways shows anything about the superior rationality (or superior anything else, except persuasiveness) of western institutions. In this connection I should like to remind Mr. Jarvie both of Plato's remarks about the difference between persuasion and instruction in his *Gorgias* (as well as what he says about 'The Great Beast' in *The Republic*) and also of Sir Karl Popper's criticisms of moral and other forms of historicism.

REFERENCES

MacIntyre, A. 1964. *Faith and the Philosophers*. Ed. J. Hick.
Winch, P. 1959. Nature and convention. *Proc. Arist. Soc.* **60**.
Winch, P. 1964. Understanding a primitive society. *Am. Phil. Qu.* **I.**
Wittgenstein, L. 1954. *Philosophical Investigations*. Blackwell.

Suggested Readings

ANSCOMBE, G. E. M. *Intention*. Oxford: Basil Blackwell, 1957.

APEL, Karl-Otto. *Analytic Philosophy of Language and the Geisteswissenschaften*. Dordrecht, Holland: Reidel, 1967.

CONNOLLY, William E. *The Terms of Political Discourse*. Lexington, Mass.: D. C. Heath & Co., 1974.

CRITTENDEN, Charles. "Wittgenstein on Philosophical Therapy and Understanding." *International Philosophical Quarterly* 10 (1970):20–43.

GELLNER, Ernest. "Concepts and Society." In *Rationality*, edited by Bryan R. Wilson, pp. 18–49. New York: Harper & Row, 1970.

_____. "The New Idealism—Cause and Meaning in the Social Sciences." In *Problems in the Philosophy of Science*, edited by Imre Lakatos and Alan Musgrave, pp. 377–406. Amsterdam: North Holland Publishing Co., 1968.

_____. *Words and Things: A Critical Account of Linguistic Philosophy and a Study in Ideology*. London: Gollancz, 1963.

GOLDSTEIN, Leon J. "The Idea of a Social Science and Its Relation to Philosophy" (review of Winch). *The Philosophical Review* 49 (1960):411–14.

GUNNELL, John G. "Reduction, Explanation, and Social Scientific Inquiry." *American Political Science Review* 63 (1969):1233–46.

HAMPSHIRE, Stuart. *Thought and Action*. London: Chatto and Windus, 1959.

LEVISON, Arnold. "Knowledge and Society." *Inquiry* 9 (1966):132–46; with discussion, *Inquiry* 10 (1967):96–100.

LOUCH, A. R. *Explanation and Human Action*. Oxford: Basil Blackwell, 1966.

_____. "On Misunderstanding Mr. Winch." *Inquiry* 8 (1965):212–16.

_____. "The Very Idea of a Social Science." *Inquiry* 6 (1963):273–86.

McCARTHY, Thomas A. "The Problem of Rationality in Social Anthropology." *Stony Brook Studies in Philosophy* 1 (1974):1–21.

MacINTYRE, Alasdair. *Against the Self-Images of the Age*. New York: Schocken, 1971.

_____. "The Idea of a Social Science." In *Proceedings of the Aris-*

215

totelian Society Supplement 61 (1967); reprinted in *Rationality*, edited by Bryan R. Wilson, pp. 112–30. New York: Harper & Row, 1970.

_____. "Is Understanding Religion Compatible with Believing?" In *Faith and the Philosophers*, edited by John Hick, pp. 115–33. London: Macmillan, 1964; reprinted in *Rationality,* edited by Bryan R. Wilson, pp. 62–77. New York: Harper & Row, 1970.

_____. "A Mistake about Causality in Social Science." In *Philosophy, Politics, and Society,* edited by Peter Laslett and W. G. Runciman, pp. 48–70. Second series. Oxford: Basil Blackwell, 1964.

MEHTONEN, Lauri. "Some Reflections on Theory and Practice in Peter Winch's Idea of Science." *Ajatus* 33 (1971):274–79.

MEYNELL, Hugo. "Truth, Witchcraft, and Professor Winch." *Heythrop Journal* 3 (1972):162–72.

PETERS, Richard S. *The Concept of Motivation.* London: Routledge and Kegan Paul, 1958.

PITCHER, George, ed. *Wittgenstein: The Philosophical Investigations.* Garden City, N.Y.: Anchor Books, 1966.

POLE, David. "Breadth and Depth of Understanding." *Philosophy* 46 (1971):109–20.

RYAN, Alan. *The Philosophy of the Social Sciences.* London: Oxford University Press, 1970.

TAYLOR, R. *Action and Purpose.* Englewood Cliffs, N.J.: Prentice Hall, 1966.

VON WRIGHT, G. H. *Explanation and Understanding.* Ithaca, N.Y.: Cornell University Press, 1971.

WILSON, Bryan, R., ed. *Rationality.* New York: Harper & Row, 1970.

WINCH, Peter. "Mr. Louch's Idea of a Social Science." *Inquiry* 7 (1964):202–8.

PART FOUR

Phenomenology and Ethnomethodology

Introduction

PHENOMENOLOGY, IN THE CONTEMPORARY MEANING OF THE TERM, AROSE as part of a broad-scale intellectual counteroffensive against the progressive sway of positivism and empiricism at the turn of the century. At the same time when Dilthey formulated the notion of *Geisteswissenschaften* and Rickert defined "cultural sciences" by the "value-relation" of their data, Edmund Husserl inaugurated the rigorous but nonempiricist study of phenomena of all kinds. The initial impulse for Husserl's inquiries derived from the claim of the nascent discipline of experimental psychology to be able to account for cognition and all types of intellectual insights in terms of empirical psychic processes. Countering this claim, his *Logical Investigations* (published in 1900–1901) tried to demonstrate that "psychologism" was at odds with the universal status of logical and mathematical propositions, that is, with the universal recognition of such propositions as valid irrespective of contingent psychic stimuli. Pursuing this line of argument, Husserl explored the possibility of noncausal cognition or knowledge on a broad scale and especially with reference to perceived phenomena. As access route to this knowledge, subsequent writings stipulated complex epistemological procedures, including the method of *epoché*, or "bracketing," or "reduction," designed to suspend concern with empirical proof or causal conditions. Harking back to the Platonic distinction between "intelligible" ideas and sense data, a major thrust of Husserlian phenomenology aimed at the intuitive understanding of the *eidos*, or essence, of perceptions and cognitive experiences. In line with modern idealist teachings, the foundation for such intuition was located in a purified layer of awareness construed as "transcendental" ego consciousness.

In application to concrete social and historical inquiry, Husserl's transcendental or "pure eidetic" approach conjured up a host of quandaries. The focus on invariant essences or meaning structures tended to shortchange the uniqueness and variability of social situations and historical contexts. More importantly, the insistence on "egological" premises threatened to confine phenomenology in a solipsistic straitjacket, blocking access to intersubjective meanings and experiences. To alleviate the first quandary, Husserl juxtaposed to eidetic analysis a more "mundane" type of inquiry—labeled "descriptive psychology"—designed to explore individual motivations and intentions operative on the level of the "natural attitude." With regard to the second issue, the focus on the "life-world" (*Lebenswelt*) evident in his later work reflected the desire to bridge the gulf between ego consciousness and social context. Despite strenuous efforts, however, the goal of integration remained elusive: Husserl's opus left unresolved both the relationship between eidetic and mundane approaches and their pertinence to the investigation of the life-world. The strengths as well as the quandaries of this legacy are manifest in the writings of Alfred Schutz, the principal pioneer and architect of phenomenological sociology. Schutz's first major study, *The Phenomenology of the Social World* (1932), was an attempt to provide a phenomenological grounding or foundation to Weberian sociology and especially to Weber's core notion of meaningful social action. Relying on the method of bracketing, he argued that the source of meaning had to be found in lived experience or internal time-consciousness and more specifically in the reflective glance of the ego upon such experience. When turning to the domain of "social action," however, the study bypassed bracketing and egological derivation in favor of a "mundane" perspective, treating intersubjectivity as a "common-sense" assumption taken for granted in the "natural attitude."

In his subsequent writings, Schutz moved progressively away from transcendental-egological concerns in the direction of a sociology of the life-world—but without relinquishing the accent on subjective intentionality and motivation. The essay "Concept and Theory Formation in the Social Sciences" (1954), reprinted below, offers in capsule form some of Schutz's mature thoughts on interpretive sociology. Countering arguments advanced by logical positivists, the essay insists that intersubjective understanding involves neither mere observation of external behavior, nor private introspection, nor a process of psychic identification. Borrowing at least in part from Heidegger's analysis of human existence (*Dasein*), Schutz presents *Verstehen* not merely as a cognitive tool but as a prereflective faculty: as "the particular experiential form in which common-sense thinking takes cognizance of the social cultural world." Other dimensions of *Verstehen*, especially its epistemological and methodological connotations, in his view are subsidiary and superimposed on this primordial faculty. Rooted in commonsense thinking, *Verstehen* according to Schutz is enmeshed from the beginning in the fabric of a shared life-world. "From the outset," he writes, "we, the actors on the social scene, experience the world we live in as a world both of nature and of culture, not as a private one but as an intersubjective one, that is, as a world common to all of us." This stress on shared or common experiences, however, does not prevent Schutz from construing social action as subjectively motivated and the life-world as an environment or grid of typified behavior patterns centered around the "biographically determined situation" of individual actors: "It is this insight of the actor into the dependencies of the motives and goals of his actions upon his biographically determined situation which social scientists have in view when speaking of the subjective meaning which the actor 'bestows upon' or 'connects with' his action. . . . The postulate of subjective interpretation has to be understood in the sense that all scientific explanations of the social world *can*, and for certain purposes *must*, refer to the subjective meaning of the actions of human beings from which social reality originates."

Schutz's presentation raises a number of questions which the reader may wish to ponder. Foremost among these questions is the philosophical and epistemological status of the life-world and the respective weight of subjective intention and social context. Schutz recognizes that, to his knowledge, the issue of intersubjectivity has not been satisfactorily resolved—a circumstance that he terms a "scandal of philosophy." This scandal, however, is bound to affect the project of mundane phenomenology concentrating on the life-world. Does the social world "originate" from the subjective intentions of individual actors (as the above citation claims) or is it an environment conditioning or constraining such intentions? Some statements of the essay seem to point in the latter direction—as when the "common-sense knowledge of everyday life" is said to be the result of structural, genetic, and cognitive socialization. In this case, does phenomenology succumb to historical contingency or else to an environmental determinism familiar from empiricist versions of the sociology of knowledge? If this alternative is rejected, the significance and implications of subjective action require clarification. Since the essay steers clear of transcendental-egological "constitution," such action presumably occurs on the mundane level of everyday life. In this case, however, does subjective motivation and intention not become amenable to psychological analysis, with the result that phenomenology is in danger of lapsing into "psychologism"? Related questions concern the role of the social scientist in mundane inquiry. Is the social scientist enmeshed in his own particular life-world, or does he have privileged access to any and all social contexts? According to Schutz, social science properly speaking involves the formulation and testing of "second level constructs," patterned on the commonsense meanings of the life-world, and thus a switch from the "biographical situation" of the participant to the "scientific situation" of the neutral observer. But (one may ask) what is the relationship between participation and observation? More specifically: how can scientific constructs be "founded upon" commonsense experiences if the latter, as participatory events, cannot objectively be known independently of the former?

Among the offshoots of phenomenological sociology, ethnomethodology enjoys the widest attention today. The central aim of this type of inquiry is to elucidate the arena of commonsense experience and to "understand" life-world situations as perceived by concrete social actors or participants. Stimulated by Schutz's distinction between "first level" and "second level" constructs, Aaron Cicourel has tried to obviate the abstract and arbitrary character of social-scientific theories through recourse to mundane phenomenology; as he argued in *Method and Measurement in Sociology* (1964), only a concrete "theory of culture" incorporating the rules and meaning-structures of ordinary life can provide a solid basis for social-scientific analysis. Harold Garfinkel —probably the leading spokesman of the approach—has delineated its chief ambitions in the chapter reproduced below. In his usage, ethnomethodology is an exercise in "practical sociological reasoning" and refers to "the investigation of the rational properties of indexical expressions and other practical actions as contingent ongoing accomplishments of organized artful practices of everyday life." In this statement, the term "rational" is a synonym for "meaningful" or "understandable," while "indexical" stands for "contextual" or "context-bound," and "artful" stands for "deliberate" or "purposive." Despite strenuous efforts on the part of professional sociology, Garfinkel argues, the substitution of objective, scientific propositions for indexical expressions remains "unrealizably programmatic." Sociologists, he adds, are commonly disinterested in, and unaware of, the "essential reflexivity" of their own practices, that is, of the preunderstanding permeating the fabric of everyday life. The chapter offers examples of concrete ethnomethodological inquiry. One example shows the importance of "ad hoc" considerations in coding practices, illustrating the inability of coding instructions to exhaust the richness of everyday activities. Focusing on commonsense understanding, the second example indicates that conversations or communicative exchanges should be seen not as reflections of empirical data or externally imposed logical rules, but (in Wittgenstein's sense) as "language games" manifesting particular forms of life—forms that are virtually self-contained and guided by their own "inner" logic: "Not *a* method of understanding, but immensely various methods of understanding are the professional sociologist's proper and hitherto unstudied and critical phenomena. Their multitude is indicated in the endless list of ways that persons speak."

Phenomenological sociology and ethnomethodology have been challenged from diverse quarters, only one of these being "mainstream" (positivist) sociology wedded to rigid standards of verification. Concentrating his attention exclusively on Husserl's legacy, Jürgen Habermas criticizes the "phenomenological approach" for clinging to the perspective of a transcendental spectator, a perspective still operative in Schutz's accent on neutral scientific observation (but hardly in Garfinkel's multiplicity of life-worlds).[1] Pursuing this line of argument, James Heap and Phillip Roth observe that "without explicating intersubjectivity, it is difficult to understand how, from within the reduction, we are to study and explain observed social action as phenomenon. . . . Any attempt to graft phenomenological concepts onto a sociology which has not been fundamentally reconstituted can only lead to a distortion, if not perversion, of both phenomenology and sociology." According to the authors, ethnomethodology can be seen as major type of a "reconstituted" phenomenology, a type untroubled by the dilemmas of pure eidetic analysis: "The domain of phenomenological inquiry . . . consists solely of the recognizable structures of immediate consciousness; while the domain of ethnomethodological inquiry consists solely of members' situated practices which produce for themselves and for observers the *sense* of objective social structures."

William Mayrl's paper on ethnomethodology raises troublesome queries about phenomenological inquiry, whether "reconstituted" or not. Mayrl stresses the linkage between mundane and eidetic versions of phenomenology; both, in his view, tend to treat social life as derivative from processes of individual or subjective consciousness. Ethnomethodology, he notes, "shares with all phenomenological philosophy a fundamental ambivalence on the question of reality external to the solitary ego. The world, in this case society, is said to exist but not in any meaningful sense independent of individual consciousness." Although perhaps avoiding the problems of transcendental "constitution," mundane research relies on contingent subjectivity, thus courting the danger of "psychologism." In response to a critic, Mayrl subsequently has refined his argument, especially by acknowledging differences of accent between Husserl's pure eidetic and Schutz's mundane approach. As he insists, however, the difference cannot be erected into a radical break: "The prime focus of *both* levels of analysis is on the activities of intentional consciousness." Even a completely mundane ethnomethodology, in his view, is exposed to the pitfalls of subjective idealism and ideological obfuscation: "The only thing that can be established with any certainty on the basis of descriptions from the participants' point of view is the participants' point of view. Any attempt to use members' interpretations as descriptions of social reality runs the risk of being caught up in the members' illusions." The reply makes it clear, incidentally, that Mayrl's argument is predicated not on "mainstream" empiricism, but rather on a dialectical Marxist outlook: "The theoretical penetration of reified social structures has been, at the very least, the implicit goal of all genuinely Marxist social analysis. And insofar as Schutz's work alerts us to the rootedness of such structures in conscious human activity, there is a point of convergence between the two perspectives. However it is clear more is claimed by the postulate of subjective interpretation than the dissolution of reified structures. Purported to be the necessary foundation of any science which seriously attempts to understand social reality, this postulate must be taken to maintain that society can be understood *only* from the point of view of the individuals who experience it."

NOTES

1. For the appropriate references, see the list of suggested readings.

Concept and Theory Formation
in the Social Sciences[1]

ALFRED SCHUTZ

THE TITLE OF MY PAPER REFERS INTENTIONALLY TO THAT OF A
Symposium held in December, 1952, at the annual meeting of the American
Philosophical Association.[2] Ernest Nagel and Carl G. Hempel contributed
highly stimulating comments on the problem involved, formulated in the
careful and lucid way so characteristic of these scholars. Their topic is a
controversy which for more than half a century has split not only logicians and
methodologists but also social scientists into two schools of thought. One of
these holds that the methods of the natural sciences which have brought about
such magnificent results are the only scientific ones and that they alone,
therefore, have to be applied in their entirety to the study of human affairs.
Failure to do so, it has been maintained, prevented the social sciences from
developing systems of explanatory theory comparable in precision to those
offered by the natural sciences and makes debatable the empirical work of
theories developed in restricted domains such as economics.

The other school of thought feels that there is a basic difference in the
structure of the social world and the world of nature. This feeling led to the
other extreme, namely the conclusion that the methods of the social sciences are
toto coelo different from those of the natural sciences. In order to support this
position a variety of arguments was proffered. It has been maintained that the
social sciences are idiographic, characterized by individualizing conceptualization and seeking singular assertory propositions, whereas the natural sciences
are nomothetic, characterized by generalizing conceptualization and seeking
general apodictic propositions. The latter have to deal with constant relations of
magnitude which can be measured and can perform experiments, whereas

Alfred Schutz, "Concept and Theory Formation in the Social Sciences," in *Collected
Papers*, ed. Maurice Natanson (The Hague: Martinus Nijhoff, 1967), vol. 1, *The
Problem of Social Reality*, pp. 48–66.

neither measurement nor experiment is practicable in the social sciences. In general, it is held that the natural sciences have to deal with material objects and processes, the social sciences, however, with psychological and intellectual ones and that, therefore, the method of the former consists in explaining, that of the latter in understanding.

Admittedly, most of these highly generalized statements are untenable under closer examination, and this for several reasons. Some proponents of the characterized arguments had a rather erroneous concept of the methods of the natural sciences. Others were inclined to identify the methodological situation in one particular social science with the method of the social sciences in general. Because history has to deal with unique and nonrecurrent events, it was contended that all social sciences are restricted to singular assertory propositions. Because experiments are hardly possible in cultural anthropology, the fact was ignored that social psychologists can successfully use laboratory experiments at least to a certain extent. Finally, and this is the most important point, these arguments disregard the fact that a set of rules for scientific procedure is equally valid for all empirical sciences whether they deal with objects of nature or with human affairs. Here and there, the principles of controlled inference and verification by fellow scientists and the theoretical ideals of unity, simplicity, universality, and precision prevail.

This unsatisfactory state of affairs results chiefly from the fact that the development of the modern social sciences occurred during a period in which the science of logic was mostly concerned with the logic of the natural sciences. In a kind of monopolistic imperialism the methods of the latter were frequently declared to be the only scientific ones and the particular problems which social scientists encountered in their work were disregarded. Left without help and guidance in their revolt against this dogmatism, the students of human affairs had to develop their own conceptions of what they believed to be the methodology of the social sciences. They did it without sufficient philosophical knowledge and stopped their effort when they reached a level of generalization which seemed to justify their deeply felt conviction that the goal of their inquiry could not be reached by adopting the methods of the natural sciences without modification or implementation. No wonder that their arguments are frequently ill-founded, their formulations insufficient, and that many misunderstandings obfuscate the controversy. Not what social scientists *said* but what they *meant* is therefore our main concern in the following.

The writings of the late Felix Kaufmann[3] and the more recent contributions of Nagel[4] and Hempel[5] have criticized many fallacies in the arguments proposed by social scientists and prepared the ground for another approach to the problem. I shall here concentrate on Professor Nagel's criticism of the claim made by Max Weber and his school that the social sciences seek to "understand" social phenomena in terms of "meaningful" categories of human experience and that, therefore, the "causal functional" approach of the natural sciences is not applicable in social inquiry. This school, as Dr. Nagel sees it, maintains that all socially significant human behavior is an expression of motivated psychic states, that in consequence the social scientist cannot be satisfied with viewing social processes simply as concatenations of "externally related" events, and that the establishment of correlations or even of universal relations of concomitance cannot be his ultimate goal. On the contrary, he must construct "ideal types" or "models of motivations" in terms of which he seeks to "understand" overt social behavior by imputing springs of action to the actors involved in it. If I understand Professor Nagel's criticism correctly, he maintains:

1) That these springs of action are not accessible to sensory observation. It follows and has frequently been stated that the social scientist must imaginatively identify himself with the participants and view the situation which they face as the actors themselves view it. Surely, however, we need not undergo other men's psychic experiences in order to know that they have them or in order to predict their overt behavior.

2) That the imputation of emotions, attitudes, and purposes as an explanation of overt behavior is a twofold hypothesis: it assumes that the agents participating in some social phenomenon are in certain psychological states; and it assumes also definite relations of concomitance between such states, and between such states and overt behavior. Yet none of the psychological states which we imagine the subjects of our study to possess may in reality be theirs, and even if our imputations should be correct none of the overt actions which allegedly issue from those states may appear to us understandable or reasonable.

3) That we do not "understand" the nature and operations of human motives and their issuance in overt behavior more adequately than the "external" causal relations. If by meaningful explanation we assert merely that a particular action is an instance of a pattern of behavior which human beings exhibit under a variety of circumstances and that, since some of the relevant circumstances are realized in the given situation, a person can be expected to manifest a certain form of that pattern, then there is no sharp gulf separating such explanations from those involving merely "external" knowledge of causal connections. It is possible to gain knowledge of the actions of men on the evidence supplied by their overt behavior just as it is possible to discover and know the atomic constitution of water on the evidence supplied by the physical and chemical behavior of that substance. Hence the rejection of a purely "objective" or "behavioristic" social science by the proponents of "meaningful connections" as the goal of social sciences is unwarranted.

Since I shall have to disagree with Nagel's and Hempel's findings on several questions of a fundamental nature, I might be permitted to start with a brief summary of the no less important points on which I find myself happily in full agreement with them. I agree with Professor Nagel that all empirical knowledge involves discovery through processes of controlled inference, and that it must be statable in propositional form and capable of being verified by anyone who is prepared to make the effort to do so through observation[6]—although I do not believe, as Professor Nagel does, that this observation has to be sensory in the precise meaning of this term. Moreover, I agree with him that "theory" means in all empirical sciences the explicit formulation of determinate relations between a set of variables in terms of which a fairly extensive class of empirically ascertainable regularities can be explained.[7] Furthermore, I agree whole-heartedly with his statement that neither the fact that these regularities have in the social sciences a rather narrowly restricted universality, nor the fact that they permit prediction only to a rather limited extent, constitutes a basic difference between the social and the natural sciences, since many branches of the latter show the same features.[8] As I shall try to show later on, it seems to me that Professor Nagel misunderstands Max Weber's postulate of subjective interpretation. Nevertheless, he is right in stating that a method which would require that the individual scientific observer identify himself with the social agent observed in order to understand the motives of the latter, or a method which would refer the selection of the facts observed and their interpretation to the private value system of the particular observer, would merely lead to an uncontrollable private and subjective image in the mind of this particular student of human affairs, but never to a scientific theory.[9] But I do not know of any social scientist of stature who ever advocated such a concept of subjectivity as that criticized by Professor Nagel. Most certainly this was not the position of Max Weber.

I also think that our authors are prevented from grasping the point of vital concern to social scientists by their basic philosophy of sensationalistic empiricism or logical positivism, which identifies experience with sensory observation and which assumes that the only alternative to controllable and, therefore, objective sensory observation is that of subjective and, therefore, uncontrollable and unverifiable introspection. This is certainly not the place to renew the age old controversy relating to the hidden presuppositions and implied metaphysical assumptions of this basic philosophy. On the other hand, in order to account for my own position, I should have to treat at length certain principles of phenomenology. Instead of doing so, I propose to defend a few rather simple propositions:

1) The primary goal of the social sciences is to obtain organized knowledge of social reality. By the term "social reality" I wish to be understood the sum total of objects and occurrences within the social cultural world as experienced by the common-sense thinking of men living their daily lives among their fellow-men, connected with them in manifold relations of interaction. It is the

world of cultural objects and social institutions into which we all are born, within which we have to find our bearings, and with which we have to come to terms. From the outset, we, the actors on the social scene, experience the world we live in as a world both of nature and of culture, not as a private but as an intersubjective one, that is, as a world common to all of us, either actually given or potentially accessible to everyone; and this involves intercommunication and language.

2) All forms of naturalism and logical empiricism simply take for granted this social reality, which is the proper object of the social sciences. Intersubjectivity, interaction, intercommunication, and language are simply presupposed as the unclarified foundation of these theories. They assume, as it were, that the social scientist has already solved his fundamental problem, before scientific inquiry starts. To be sure, Dewey emphasized, with a clarity worthy of this eminent philosopher, that all inquiry starts and ends within the social cultural matrix; to be sure, Professor Nagel is fully aware of the fact that science and its self-correcting process is a social enterprise.[10] But the postulate of describing and explaining human behavior in terms of controllable sensory observation stops short before the description and explanation of the process by which scientist B controls and verifies the observational findings of scientist A and the conclusions drawn by him. In order to do so, B has to know what A has observed, what the goal of his inquiry is, why he thought the observed fact worthy of being observed, *i.e.*, relevant to the scientific problem at hand, etc. This knowledge is commonly called understanding. The explanation of how such a mutual understanding of human beings might occur is apparently left to the social scientist. But whatever his explanation might be, one thing is sure, namely, that such an intersubjective understanding between scientist B and scientist A occurs neither by scientist B's observations of scientist A's overt behavior, nor by introspection performed by B, nor by identification of B with A. To translate this argument into the language dear to logical positivism, this means, as Felix Kaufmann[11] has shown, that so-called protocol propositions about the physical world are of an entirely different kind than protocol propositions about the psycho-physical world.

3) The identification of experience with sensory observation in general and of the experience of overt action in particular (and that is what Nagel proposes) excludes several dimensions of social reality from all possible inquiry.

a) Even an ideally refined behaviorism can, as has been pointed out for instance by George H. Mead,[12] merely explain the behavior of the observed, not of the observing behaviorist.

b) The same overt behavior (say a tribal pageant as it can be captured by the movie camera) may have an entirely different meaning to the performers. What interests the social scientist is merely whether it is a war dance, a barter trade, the reception of a friendly ambassador, or something else of this sort.

c) Moreover, the concept of human action in terms of common-sense think-ing and of the social sciences includes what may be called "negative actions," *i.e.*, intentional refraining from acting,[13] which, of course, escapes sensory observation. Not to sell certain merchandise at a given price is doubtless as economic an action as to sell it.

d) Furthermore, as W. I. Thomas has shown,[14] social reality contains elements of beliefs and convictions which are real because they are so defined by the participants and which escape sensory observation. To the inhabitants of Salem in the seventeenth century, witchcraft was not a delusion but an element of their social reality and is as such open to investigation by the social scientist.

e) Finally, and this is the most important point, the postulate of sensory observation of overt human behavior takes as a model a particular and relatively small sector of the social world, namely, situations in which the acting individ-ual is given to the observer in what is commonly called a face-to-face relation-ship. But there are many other dimensions of the social world in which situations of this kind do not prevail. If we put a letter in the mailbox we assume that anonymous fellow-men, called postmen, will perform a series of manipula-tions, unknown and unobservable to us, with the effect that the addressee, possibly also unknown to us, will receive the message and react in a way which also escapes our sensory observation; and the result of all this is that we receive the book we have ordered. Or if I read an editorial stating that France fears the re-armament of Germany, I know perfectly well what this statement means without knowing the editorialist and even without knowing a Frenchman or a German, let alone without observing their overt behavior.

In terms of common-sense thinking in everyday life men have knowledge of these various dimensions of the social world in which they live. To be sure, this knowledge is not only fragmentary since it is restricted principally to certain sectors of this world, it is also frequently inconsistent in itself and shows all degrees of clarity and distinctness from full insight or "knowledge-about," as James[15] called it, through "knowledge of acquaintance" or mere familiarity, to blind belief in things just taken for granted. In this respect there are consider-able differences from individual to individual and from social group to social group. Yet, in spite of all these inadequacies, common-sense knowledge of everyday life is sufficient for coming to terms with fellow-men, cultural objects, social institutions—in brief, with social reality. This is so, because the world (the natural and the social one) is from the outset an intersubjective world and because, as shall be pointed out later on, our knowledge of it is in various ways socialized. Moreover, the social world is experienced from the outset as a meaningful one. The Other's body is not experienced as an organism but as a fellow-man, its overt behavior not as an occurrence in the space-time of the outer world, but as our fellow-man's action. We normally "know" what the Other does, for what reason he does it, why he does it at this particular time and in these particular circumstances. That means that we experience our fellow-man's action in terms of his motives and goals. And in the same way, we experience cultural objects in terms of the human action of which they are the result. A tool, for example, is not experienced as a thing in the outer world (which of course it is also) but in terms of the purpose for which it was designed by more or less anonymous fellow-men and its possible use by others.

The fact that in common-sense thinking we take for granted our actual or potential knowledge of the meaning of human actions and their products, is, I suggest, precisely what social scientists want to express if they speak of understanding or *Verstehen* as a technique of dealing with human affairs. *Verstehen* is, thus, primarily not a method used by the social scientist, but the particular experiential form in which common-sense thinking takes cognizance of the social cultural world. It has nothing to do with introspection; it is a result of processes of learning or acculturation in the same way as the common-sense experience of the so-called natural world. *Verstehen* is, moreover, by no means a private affair of the observer which cannot be controlled by the experiences of other observers. It is controllable at least to the same extent to which the private sensory perceptions of an individual are controllable by any other individual under certain conditions. You have just to think of the discussion by a trial jury of whether the defendant has shown "pre-meditated malice" or "intent" in killing a person, whether he was capable of knowing the consequences of his deed, etc. Here we even have certain "rules of procedure" furnished by the "rules of evidence" in the juridical sense and a kind of verification of the findings resulting from processes of *Verstehen* by the Appellate Court, etc. Moreover, predictions based on *Verstehen* are continuously made in common-sense thinking with high success. There is more than a fair chance that a duly stamped and addressed letter put in a New York mailbox will reach the addressee in Chicago.

Nevertheless, both defenders and critics of the process of *Verstehen* maintain, and with good reason, that *Verstehen* is "subjective." Unfortunately, however, this term is used by each party in a different sense. The critics of understanding call it subjective, because they hold that understanding the motives of another man's action depends upon the private, uncontrollable, and unverifiable intuition of the observer or refers to his private value system. The social scientists, such as Max Weber, however, call *Verstehen* subjective because its goal is to find out what the actor "means" in his action, in contrast to the meaning which this action has for the actor's partner or a neutral observer. This is the origin of Max Weber's famous postulate of subjective interpretation, of which more will have to be said in what follows. The whole discussion suffers from the failure to distinguish clearly between *Verstehen* 1) as the experiential form of common-sense knowledge of human affairs, 2) as an epistemological problem, and 3) as a method peculiar to the social sciences.

So far we have concentrated on *Verstehen* as the way in which common-sense thinking finds its bearing within the social world and comes to terms with it. As to the epistemological question: "How is such understanding or *Verstehen* possible?" Alluding to a statement Kant made in another context, I suggest that it is a "scandal of philosophy" that so far a satisfactory solution to the problem of our knowledge of other minds and, in connection therewith, of the intersubjectivity of our experience of the natural as well as the socio-cultural world has not been found and that, until rather recent times, this problem has even escaped the attention of philosophers. But the solution of this most difficult problem of philosophical interpretation is one of the first things taken for granted in our common-sense thinking and practically solved without any difficulty in each of our everyday actions. And since human beings are born of mothers and not concocted in retorts, the experience of the existence of other human beings and of the meaning of their actions is certainly the first and most original empirical observation man makes.

On the other hand, philosophers as different as James, Bergson, Dewey, Husserl, and Whitehead agree that the common-sense knowledge of everyday life is the unquestioned but always questionable background within which inquiry starts and within which alone it can be carried out. It is this *Lebenswelt*, as Husserl calls it, within which, according to him, all scientific and even logical concepts originate; it is the social matrix within which, according to Dewey, unclarified situations emerge, which have to be transformed by the process of inquiry into warranted assertibility; and Whitehead has pointed out that it is the aim of science to produce a theory which agrees with experience by explaining the thought-objects constructed by common sense through the mental constructs or thought objects of science.[16] For all these thinkers agree that any knowledge of the world, in common-sense thinking as well as in science, involves mental constructs, syntheses, generalizations, formalizations, idealizations specific to the respective level of thought organization. The concept of Nature, for instance, with which the natural sciences have to deal is, as Husserl has shown, an idealizing abstraction from the *Lebenswelt*, an abstraction which, on principle and of course legitimately, excludes persons with their personal life and all objects of culture which originate as such in practical human activity. Exactly this layer of the *Lebenswelt,* however, from which the natural sciences have to abstract, is the social reality which the social sciences have to investigate.

This insight sheds a light on certain methodological problems peculiar to the social sciences. To begin with, it appears that the assumption that the strict adoption of the principles of concept and theory formation prevailing in the natural sciences will lead to reliable knowledge of social reality is inconsistent in itself. If a theory can be developed on such principles, say in the form of an ideally refined behaviorism—and it is certainly possible to imagine this—then it will not tell us anything about social reality as experienced by men in everyday life. As Professor Nagel himself admits,[17] it will be highly abstract, and its concepts will apparently be remote from the obvious and familiar traits found in any society. On the other hand, a theory which aims at explaining social reality has to develop particular devices foreign to the natural sciences in order to agree with the common-sense experience of the social world. This is indeed what all theoretical sciences of human affairs—economics, sociology, the sciences of law, linguistics, cultural anthropology, etc.—have done.

This state of affairs is founded on the fact that there is an essential difference in the structure of the thought objects or mental constructs formed by the social sciences and those formed by the natural sciences.[18] It is up to the natural scientist and to him alone to define, in accordance with the procedural rules of his science, his observational field, and to determine the facts, data, and events within it which are relevant for his problem or scientific purpose at hand. Neither are those facts and events pre-selected, nor is the observational field pre-interpreted. The world of nature, as explored by the natural scientist, does not "mean" anything to molecules, atoms, and electrons. But the observational field of the social scientist—social reality—has a specific meaning and relevance structure for the human beings living, acting, and thinking within it. By a series of common-sense constructs they have pre-selected and pre-interpreted this world which they experience as the reality of their daily lives. It is these thought objects of theirs which determine their behavior by motivating it. The thought objects constructed by the social scientist, in order to grasp this social reality, have to be founded upon the thought objects constructed by the common-sense thinking of men, living their daily life within their social world. Thus, the constructs of the social sciences are, so to speak, constructs of the second degree, that is, constructs of the constructs made by the actors on the social scene, whose behavior the social scientist has to observe and to explain in accordance with the procedural rules of his science.

Thus, the exploration of the general principles according to which man in daily life organizes his experiences, and especially those of the social world, is the first task of the methodology of the social sciences. This is not the place to outline the procedures of a phenomenological analysis of the so-called natural attitude by which this can be done. We shall briefly mention only a few problems involved.

The world, as has been shown by Husserl, is from the outset experienced in the pre-scientific thinking of everyday life in the mode of typicality. The unique objects and events given to us in a unique aspect are unique within a horizon of typical familiarity and pre-acquaintanceship. There are mountains, trees, animals, dogs—in particular Irish setters and among them my Irish setter, Rover. Now I may look at Rover either as this unique individual, my irreplaceable friend and comrade, or just as a typical example of "Irish setter," "dog," "mammal," "animal," "organism," or "object of the outer world." Starting from here, it can be shown that whether I do one or the other, and also which traits or qualities of a given object or event I consider as individually unique and which as typical, depends upon my actual interest and the system of relevances involved—briefly, upon my practical or theoretical "problem at hand." This "problem at hand," in turn, originates in the circumstances within which I find myself at any moment of my daily life and which I propose to call my biographically determined situation. Thus, typification depends upon my problem at hand for the definition and solution of which the type has been formed. It can be further shown that at least one aspect of the biographically and situationally determined systems of interests and relevances is subjectively experienced in the thinking of everyday life as systems of motives for action, of choices to be made, of projects to be carried out, of goals to be reached. It is this insight of the actor into the dependencies of the motives and goals of his actions upon his biographically determined situation which social scientists have in view when speaking of the subjective meaning which the actor "bestows upon" or "connects with" his action. This implies that, strictly speaking, the actor and he alone knows what he does, why he does it, and when and where his action starts and ends.

But the world of everyday life is from the outset also a social cultural world in which I am interrelated in manifold ways of interaction with fellow-men known to me in varying degrees of intimacy and anonymity. To a certain extent, sufficient for many practical purposes, I understand their behavior, if I understand their motives, goals, choices, and plans originating in *their* biographically determined circumstances. Yet only in particular situations, and then only fragmentarily, can I experience the Others' motives, goals, etc.—briefly, the subjective meanings they bestow upon their actions, in their uniqueness. I can, however, experience them in their typicality. In order to do so I construct typical patterns of the actors' motives and ends, even of their attitudes and personalities, of which their actual conduct is just an instance or example. These typified patterns of the Others' behavior become in turn motives of my own actions, and this leads to the phenomenon of self-typification well known to social scientists under various names.

Here, I submit, in the common-sense thinking of everyday life, is the origin of the so-called constructive or ideal types, a concept which as a tool of the social sciences has been analyzed by Professor Hempel in such a lucid way. But at least at the common-sense level the formation of these types involves neither intuition nor a theory, if we understand these terms in the sense of Hempel's statements.[19] As we shall see, there are also other kinds of ideal or constructive types, those formed by the social scientist, which are of a quite different structure and indeed involve theory. But Hempel has not distinguished between the two.

Next we have to consider that the common-sense knowledge of everyday life is from the outset socialized in many respects.

It is, first, structurally socialized, since it is based on the fundamental idealization that if I were to change places with my fellow-man I would experience the same sector of the world in substantially the same perspectives as he does, our particular biographical circumstances becoming for all practical purposes at hand irrelevant. I propose to call this idealization that of the reciprocity of perspectives.[20]

It is, second, genetically socialized, because the greater part of our knowledge, as to its content and the particular forms of typification under which it is organized, is socially derived, and this in socially approved terms.

It is, third, socialized in the sense of social distribution of knowledge, each individual knowing merely a sector of the world and common knowledge of the same sector varying individually as to its degree of distinctness, clarity, acquaintanceship, or mere belief.

These principles of socialization of common-sense knowledge, and especially that of the social distribution of knowledge, explain at least partially what the social scientist has in mind in speaking of the functional structural approach to studies of human affairs. The concept of functionalism—at least in the modern social sciences—is not derived from the biological concept of the functioning of an organism, as Nagel holds. It refers to the socially distributed constructs of patterns of typical motives, goals, attitudes, personalities, which are supposed to be invariant and are then interpreted as the function or structure of the social system itself. The more these interlocked behavior patterns are standardized and institutionalized, that is, the more their typicality is socially approved by laws, folkways, mores, and habits, the greater is their usefulness in common-sense and scientific thinking as a scheme of interpretation of human behavior.

These are, very roughly, the outlines of a few major features of the constructs involved in common-sense experience of the intersubjective world in daily life, which is called *Verstehen*. As explained before, they are the first level constructs upon which the second level constructs of the social sciences have to be erected. But here a major problem emerges. On the one hand, it has been shown that the constructs on the first level, the common-sense constructs, refer to subjective elements, namely the *Verstehen* of the actor's action from his, the actor's, point of view. Consequently, if the social sciences aim indeed at explaining social reality, then the scientific constructs on the second level, too, must include a reference to the subjective meaning an action has for the actor. This is, I think, what Max Weber understood by his famous postulate of subjective interpretation, which has, indeed, been observed so far in the theory formation of all social sciences. The postulate of subjective interpretation has to be understood in the sense that all scientific explanations of the social world *can*, and for certain purposes *must*, refer to the subjective meaning of the actions of human beings from which social reality originates.

On the other hand, I agreed with Professor Nagel's statement that the social sciences, like all empirical sciences, have to be objective in the sense that their propositions are subjected to controlled verification and must not refer to private uncontrollable experience.

How is it possible to reconcile these seemingly contradictory principles? Indeed, the most serious question which the methodology of the social sciences has to answer is: How is it possible to form objective concepts and an objectively verifiable theory of subjective meaning-structures? The basic insight that the concepts formed by the social scientist are constructs of the constructs formed in common-sense thinking by the actors on the social scene offers an answer. The scientific constructs formed on the second level, in accordance with the procedural rules valid for all empirical sciences, are objective ideal typical constructs and, as such, of a different kind from those developed on the first level of common-sense thinking which they have to supersede. They are theoretical systems embodying testable general hypotheses in the sense of Professor Hempel's definition.[21] This device has been used by social scientists concerned with theory long before this concept was formulated by Max Weber and developed by his school.

Before describing a few features of these scientific constructs, let us briefly consider the particular attitude of the theoretical social scientist to the social world, in contradistinction to that of the actor on the social scene. The theoretical scientist—qua scientist, not qua human being (which he is, too)—is not involved in the observed situation, which is to him not of practical but merely of cognitive interest. The system of relevances governing common-sense interpretation in daily life originates in the biographical situation of the observer. By making up his mind to become a scientist, the social scientist has replaced his personal biographical situation by what I shall call, following Felix Kaufmann,[22] a scientific situation. The problems with which he has to deal might be quite unproblematic for the human being within the world and vice versa. Any scientific problem is determined by the actual state of the respective science, and its solution has to be achieved in accordance with the procedural rules governing this science, which among other things warrant the control and verification of the solution offered. The scientific problem, once established, alone determines what is relevant for the scientist as well as the conceptual frame of reference to be used by him. This and nothing else, it seems to me, is what Max Weber means when he postulates the objectivity of the social sciences, their detachment from value patterns which govern or might govern the behavior of the actors on the social scene.

How does the social scientist proceed? He observes certain facts and events within social reality which refer to human action and he constructs typical behavior or course-of-action patterns from what he has observed. Thereupon he co-ordinates to these typical course-of-action patterns models of an ideal actor or actors, whom he imagines as being gifted with consciousness. Yet it is a consciousness restricted so as to contain nothing but the elements relevant to the performing of the course-of-action patterns observed. He thus ascribes to this fictitious consciousness a set of typical notions, purposes, goals, which are assumed to be invariant in the specious consciousness of the imaginary actor-model. This homunculus or puppet is supposed to be interrelated in interaction patterns to other homunculi or puppets constructed in a similar way. Among these homunculi with which the social scientist populates his model of the social world of everyday life, sets of motives, goals, roles—in general, systems of relevances—are distributed in such a way as the scientific problems under scrutiny require. Yet—and this is the main point—these constructs are by no means arbitrary. They are subject to the postulate of logical consistency and to the postulate of adequacy. The latter means that each term in such a scientific model of human action must be constructed in such a way that a human act performed within the real world by an individual actor as indicated by the typical construct would be understandable to the actor himself as well as to his fellow-men in terms of common-sense interpretation of everyday life. Compliance with the postulate of logical consistency warrants the objective validity of the thought objects constructed by the social scientist; compliance with the postulate of adequacy warrants their compatibility with the constructs of everyday life.[23]

As the next step, the circumstances within which such a model operates may be varied, that is, the situation which the homunculi have to meet may be imagined as changed, but not the set of motives and relevances assumed to be the sole content of their consciousness. I may, for example, construct a model of a producer acting under conditions of unregulated competition, and another of a producer acting under cartel restrictions, and then compare the output of the same commodity of the same firm in the two models.[24] In this way, it is possible to predict how such a puppet or system of puppets might behave under certain conditions and to discover certain "determinate relations between a set of variables, in terms of which . . . empirically ascertainable regularities . . . can be explained." This, however, is Professor Nagel's definition of a theory.[25] It can easily be seen that each step involved in the construction and use of the scientific model can be verified by empirical observation, provided that we do not restrict this term to sensory perceptions of objects and events in the outer world but include the experiential form, by which common-sense thinking in everyday life understands human actions and their outcome in terms of their underlying motives and goals.

Two brief concluding remarks may be permitted. First, a key concept of the basic philosophic position of naturalism is the so-called principle of continuity, although it is under discussion whether this principle means continuity of existence, or of analysis, or of an intellectual criterion of pertinent checks upon the methods employed.[26] It seems to me that this principle of continuity in each of these various interpretations is fulfilled by the characterized device of the social sciences, which even establishes continuity between the practice of everyday life and the conceptualization of the social sciences.

Second, a word on the problem of the methodological unity of the empirical sciences. It seems to me that the social scientist can agree with the statement that the principal differences between the social and the natural sciences do not have to be looked for in a different logic governing each branch of knowledge. But this does not involve the admission that the social sciences have to abandon the particular devices they use for exploring social reality for the sake of an ideal unity of methods which is founded on the entirely unwarranted assumption that only methods used by the natural sciences, and especially by physics, are scientific ones. So far as I know, no serious attempt has ever been made by the proponents of the "unity of science" movement to answer or even to ask the question whether the methodological problem of the natural sciences in their present state is not merely a special case of the more general, still unexplored, problem how scientific knowledge is possible at all and what its logical and methodological presuppositions are. It is my personal conviction that phenomenological philosophy has prepared the ground for such an investigation. Its outcome might quite possibly show that the particular methodological devices developed by the social sciences in order to grasp social reality are better suited than those of the natural sciences to lead to the discovery of the general principles which govern all human knowledge.

NOTES

1. Paper presented at the 33rd Semi-Annual Meeting of the Conference on Methods in Philosophy and the Sciences, New York, May 3, 1953.

2. Published in the volume *Science, Language and Human Rights* (American Philosophical Association, Eastern Division, Vol. I), Philadelphia, 1952, pp. 43–86 (referred to as SLH).

3. Especially his *Methodology of the Social Sciences,* New York, 1941.

4. *SLH*, pp. 43–64.

5. *SLH*, pp. 65–86.

6. *SLH*, p. 56.

7. *SLH*, p. 46.

8. *SLH*, pp. 60 ff.

9. *SLH*, pp. 55–57.

10. *SLH*, p. 53.

11. *Op. cit.*, p. 126.

12. *Mind, Self and Society*, Chicago, 1937.

13. See Max Weber, *The Theory of Social and Economic Organization*, translated by A. M. Henderson and Talcott Parsons, New York, 1947, p. 88.

14. See W. I. Thomas, *Social Behavior and Personality*, edited by E. H. Volkart, New York, 1951, p. 81.

15. *Principles of Psychology*, Vol. I, pp. 221f.

16. See Schutz in *Collected Papers*, "Common-Sense and Scientific Interpretation of Human Action," edited by Maurice Natanson, The Hague, 1967, vol. I, pp 3–47.

17. *SLH*, p. 63.

18. Some of the points dealt with in the following are presented more elaborately in "Common-Sense and Scientific Interpretation of Human Action".

19. *SLH*, pp. 76ff. and 81.

20. See "Common-Sense and Scientific Interpretation of Human Action," p. 11f.

21. *SLH*, pp. 77ff.

22. *Op. cit.*, pp. 52 and 251.

23. See "Common-Sense and Scientific Interpretation of Human Action," p. 43f.

24. See Fritz Machlup, *The Economics of Seller's Competition: Model Analysis of Seller's Conduct*, Baltimore, 1952, pp. 9 ff.

25. *SLH*, p. 46

26. See Thelma Z. Lavine, "Note to Naturalists on the Human Spirit," *Journal of Philosophy*, Vol. L, 1953, pp. 145–154, and Ernest Nagel's answer, *ibid.*, pp. 154–157.

What Is Ethnomethodology?

HAROLD GARFINKEL

THE FOLLOWING STUDIES SEEK TO TREAT PRACTICAL ACTIVITIES, practical circumstances, and practical sociological reasoning as topics of empirical study, and by paying to the most commonplace activities of daily life the attention usually accorded extraordinary events, seek to learn about them as phenomena in their own right. Their central recommendation is that the activities whereby members produce and manage settings of organized everyday affairs are identical with members' procedures for making those settings "account-able." The "reflexive," or "incarnate" character of accounting practices and accounts makes up the crux of that recommendation. When I speak of accountable my interests are directed to such matters as the following. I mean observable-and-reportable, *i.e.* available to members as situated practices of looking-and-telling. I mean, too, that such practices consist of an endless, on-going, contingent accomplishment; that they are carried on under the auspices of, and are made to happen as events in, the same ordinary affairs that in organizing they describe; that the practices are done by parties to those settings whose skill with, knowledge of, and entitlement to the detailed work of that accomplishment—whose competence—they obstinately depend upon, recognize, use, and take for granted; and *that* they take their competence for granted itself furnishes parties with a setting's distinguishing and particular features, and of course it furnishes them as well as resources, troubles, projects, and the rest.

Some structurally equivocal features of the methods and results by persons doing sociology, lay and professional, of making practical activities observable were epitomized by Helmer and Rescher.[1] When members' accounts of everyday activities are used as prescriptions with which to locate, to identify, to analyze, to classify, to make recognizable, or to find one's way around in

Harold Garfinkel, "What is Ethnomethodology?" in *Studies in Ethnomethodology* © 1967, pp. 1–11, 18–34. Reprinted by permission of Prentice-Hall, Inc., Englewood Cliffs, New Jersey.

comparable occasions, the prescriptions, they observe, are law-like, spatiotemporally restricted, and "loose." By "loose" is meant that though they are intendedly conditional in their logical form, "the nature of the conditions is such that they can often not be spelled out completely or fully." The authors cite as an example a statement about sailing fleet tactics in the 18th century. They point out the statement carries as a test condition reference to the state of naval ordnance.

> In elaborating conditions (under which such a statement would hold) the historian delineates what is typical of the place and period. The full implications of such reference may be vast and inexhaustible; for instance . . . ordnance soon ramifies *via* metal working technology into metallurgy, mining, etc. Thus, the conditions which are operative in the formulation of an historical law may only be indicated in a general way, and are not necessarily, indeed, in most cases cannot be expected to be exhaustively articulated. This characteristic of such laws is here designed as *looseness*. . . .
>
> A consequence of the looseness of historical laws is that they are not universal, but merely quasi-general is that they admit of exceptions. Since the conditions delimiting the area of application of the law are often not exhaustively articulated, a supposed violation of the law may be explicable by showing that a legitimate, but as yet unformulated, precondition of the law's applicability is not fulfilled in the case under consideration.

Consider that this holds in every *particular* case, and holds not by reason of the meaning of "quasi-law," but because of investigators' actual, particular practices.

Further, Helmer and Rescher point out,

> The laws may be taken to contain a tacit caveat of the "usually" or "other things being equal" type. An historical law is thus not strictly universal in that it must be taken as applicable to all cases falling within the scope of its explicitly formulated or formulable conditions; rather, it may be thought to formulate relationships which obtain generally, or better, which obtain "as a rule."
>
> Such a "law" we will term *quasi-law*. In order for the law to be valid it is not necessary that no apparent exceptions occur. It is only necessary that, if an apparent exception should occur, an adequate explanation be forthcoming, an explanation demonstrating the exception characteristic of the case in hand by establishing the violation of an appropriate, if hitherto unformulated, condition of the law's applicability.

These and other features can be cited for the cogency with which they describe members' accounting practices. Thus: (1) Whenever a member is required to demonstrate that an account analyzes an actual situation, he invariably makes use of the practices of "et cetera," "unless," and "let it pass" to demonstrate the rationality of his achievement. (2) The definite and sensible character of the matter that is being reported is settled by an assignment that reporter and auditor make to each other that each will have furnished whatever unstated understandings are required. Much therefore of what is actually reported is not mentioned. (3) Over the time for their delivery accounts are apt to require that "auditors" be willing to wait for what will have been said in order that the present significance of what has been said will have become clear. (4) Like conversations, reputations, and careers, the particulars of accounts are built up step by step over the actual uses of and references to them. (5) An account's materials are apt to depend heavily for sense upon their serial placement, upon their relevance to the auditor's projects, or upon the developing course of the organizational occasions of their use.

In short, *recognizable* sense, or fact, or methodic character, or impersonality, or objectivity of accounts are not independent of the socially organized occasions of their use. Their rational features *consist* of what members do with, what they "make of" the accounts in the socially organized actual occasions of their use. Members' accounts are reflexively and essentially tied for their rational features to the socially organized occasions of their use for they are *features* of the socially organized occasions of their use.

That tie establishes the central topic of our studies: the rational accountability of practical actions as an ongoing, practical accomplishment. I want to specify the topic by reviewing three of its constituent, problematic phenomena. Wherever studies of practical action and practical reasoning are concerned, these consist of the following: (1) the unsatisfied programmatic distinction between and substitutability of objective (context free) for indexical expressions; (2) the "uninteresting" essential reflexivity of accounts of practical actions; and (3) the analyzability of actions-in-context as a practical accomplishment.

The Unsatisfied Programmatic Distinction between and Substitutability of Objective for Indexical Expressions

Properties that are exhibited by accounts (by reason of their being features of the socially organized occasions of their use) are available from studies by logicians as the properties of indexical expressions and indexical sentences. Husserl[2] spoke of expressions whose sense cannot be decided by an auditor without his necessarily knowing or assuming something about the biography and the purposes of the user of the expression, the circumstances of the utterance, the previous course of the conversation, or the particular relationship of actual or potential interaction that exists between the expressor and the auditor. Russell[3] observed that descriptions involving them apply on each occasion of use to only one thing, but to different things on different occasions. Such expressions, wrote Goodman,[4] are used to make unequivocal statements that nevertheless seem to change in truth value. Each of their utterances, "tokens," constitutes a word and refers to a certain person, time, or place, but names something not named by some replica of the word. Their denotation is relative to the speaker. Their use depends upon the relation of the user to the object with which the word is concerned. Time for a temporal indexical expression is relevant to what it names. Similarly, just what region a spatial indexical expression names depends upon the location of its utterance. Indexical expressions and statements containing them are not freely repeatable; in a given discourse, not all their replicas therein are also translations of them. The list can be extended indefinitely.

Virtually unanimous agreement exists among students of practical sociological reasoning, laymen and professionals, about the properties of indexical expressions and indexical actions. Impressive agreement exists as well (1) that although indexical expressions "are of enormous utility" they are "awkward for formal discourse"; (2) that a distinction between objective expressions and indexical expressions is not only procedurally proper but unavoidable for whosoever would do science; (3) that without the distinction between objective and indexical expressions, and without the preferred use of objective expressions the victories of generalizing, rigorous, scientific inquiries—logic, mathematics, some of the physical sciences—are unintelligible, the victories would fail, and the inexact sciences would have to abandon their hopes; (4) that the exact sciences are distinguishable from the inexact sciences by the fact that in the case of the exact sciences the distinction between and substitution of objective for indexical expressions for problem formulation, methods, findings, adequate demonstration, adequate evidence and the rest is both an actual task and an actual achievement, whereas in the case of the inexact sciences the availability of the distinction and substitutability to actual tasks, practices, and results remains unrealizably programmatic; (5) that the distinction between objective and indexical expressions, insofar as the distinction consists of inquirers' tasks, ideals, norms, resources, achievements, and the rest describes the difference between sciences and arts—*e.g.*, between biochemistry and documentary filming; (6) that terms and sentences can be distinguished as one or the other in accordance with an assessment procedure that makes decidable their character as indexical or objective expressions; and (7) that in any particular case only practical difficulties prevent the substitution by an objective expression for an indexical expression.

Features of indexical expressions motivate endless methodological studies directed to their remedy. Indeed, attempts to rid the practices of a science of these nuisances lends to each science its distinctive character of preoccupation and productivity with methodological issues. Research practitioners' studies of practical activities of a science, whatever their science, afford them endless occasions to deal rigorously with indexical expressions.

Areas in the social sciences where the promised distinction and promised substitutability occur are countless. The promised distinction and substitutability are supported by and themselves support immense resources directed to developing methods for the strong analysis of practical actions and practical reasoning. Promised applications and benefits are immense.

Nevertheless, *wherever practical actions are topics of study* the promised distinction and substitutability of objective for indexical expressions remains programmatic in every *particular* case and in every *actual* occasion in which the distinction or substitutability must be demonstrated. In every actual case without exception, conditions will be cited that a competent investigator will be required to recognize, such that in *that* particular case the terms of the demonstration can be relaxed and nevertheless the demonstration be counted an adequate one.

We learn from logicians and linguists, who are in virtually unanimous agreement about them, what some of these conditions are. For "long" texts, or "long" courses of action, for events where members' actions are features of the events their actions are accomplishing, or wherever tokens are not used or are not suitable as proxies for indexical expressions, the program's claimed demonstrations are satisfied as matters of practical social management.

Under such conditions indexical expressions, by reason of their prevalence and other properties, present immense, obstinate, and irremediable nuisances to the tasks of dealing rigorously with the phenomena of structure and relevance in theories of consistency proofs and computability, and in attempts to recover actual as compared with supposed common conduct and common talk with full structural particulars. Drawing upon their experience in the uses of sample surveys, and the design and application of measurements of practical actions, statistical analyses, mathematical models, and computer simulations of social processes, professional sociologists are able to document endlessly the ways in which the programmatic distinction and substitutability is satisfied in, and depends upon, professional practices of socially managed demonstration.

In short, wherever studies of practical actions are involved, the distinction and substitutability is always accomplished *only* for all practical purposes. Thereby, the first problematic phenomenon is recommended to consist of the reflexivity of the practices and attainments of sciences in and of the organized activities of everyday life, which is an essential reflexivity.

The "Uninteresting" Essential Reflexivity of Accounts

For members engaged in practical sociological reasoning—as we shall see in later studies, for staff personnel at the Los Angeles Suicide Prevention Center, for staff users of psychiatric clinic folders at U.C.L.A., for graduate student coders of psychiatric records, for jurors, for an intersexed person managing a sex change, for professional sociological researchers—their concerns are for what is decidable "for practical purposes," "in light of this situation," "given the nature of actual circumstances," and the like. Practical circumstances and practical actions refer for them to many organizationally important and serious matters; to resources, aims, excuses, opportunities, tasks, and of course to grounds for arguing or foretelling the adequacy of procedures and of the findings they yield. One matter, however, is excluded from their interests: practical actions and practical circumstances are not in themselves *a* topic, let alone a sole topic of their inquiries; nor are their inquiries, addressed to the tasks of sociological theorizing, undertaken to formulate what these tasks consist of as practical actions. In no case is the investigation of practical actions undertaken in order that personnel might be able to recognize and describe what they are doing in the first place. Least of all are practical actions investigated in order to explain to practitioners their own talk about what they are doing. For example personnel at the Los Angeles Suicide Prevention Center found it altogether incongruous to consider seriously that they be so engaged in the work of certifying mode of death of a person seeking to commit suicide, and they could concert their efforts to assure the unequivocal recognition of "what really happened."

To say they are "not interested" in the study of practical actions is not to complain, nor to point to an opportunity they miss, nor is it a disclosure of error, nor is it an ironic comment. Neither is it the case that because members are "not interested" that they are "precluded" from sociological theorizing. Nor do their inquiries preclude the use of the rule of doubt, nor are they precluded from making the organized activities of everyday life scientifically problematical, nor does the comment insinuate a difference between "basic" and "applied" interests in research and theorizing.

What does it mean then to say that they are "not interested" in studying practical actions and practical sociological reasoning? And what is the import of such a statement?

There is a feature of members' accounts that for them is of such singular and prevailing relevance that it controls other features in their specific character as recognizable, rational features of practical sociological inquiries. The feature is this. With respect to the problematic character of practical actions and to the practical adequacy of their inquiries, members take for granted that a member must at the outset "know" the settings in which he is to operate if his practices are to serve as measures to bring particular, located features of these settings to recognizable account. They treat as the most passing matter of fact that members' accounts, of every sort, in all their logical modes, with all of their uses, and for every method for their assembly are constituent features of the settings they make observable. Members know, require, count on, and make use of this reflexivity to produce, accomplish, recognize, or demonstrate rational-adequacy-for-all-practical-purposes of their procedures and findings.

Not only do members—the jurors and the others—take that reflexivity for granted, but they recognize, demonstrate, and make observable for each other the rational character of their actual, and that means their occasional, practices while respecting that reflexivity as an unalterable and unavoidable condition of their inquiries.

When I propose that members are "not interested" in studying practical actions, I do not mean that members will have none, a little, or a lot of it. That they are "not interested" has to do with reasonable practices, with plausible argument, and with reasonable findings. It has to do with treating "account-able-for-all-practical-purposes" as a discoverable matter, exclusively, only, and entirely. For members to be "interested" would consist of their undertaking to make the "reflexive" character of practical activities observable; to examine the artful practices of rational inquiry as organizational phenomena without thought for correctives or irony. Members of the Los Angeles Suicide Prevention Center are like members wherever they engage in practical sociological inquiries: though they would, they *can* have none of it.

The Analyzability of Actions-in-Context as a Practical Accomplishment

In indefinitely many ways members' inquiries are constituent features of the settings they analyze. In the same ways, their inquiries are made recognizable to members as adequate-for-all-practical-purposes. For example, at the Los Angeles Suicide Prevention Center, that deaths are made accountable-for-all-practical-purposes are practical organizational accomplishments. Organizationally, the Suicide Prevention Center consists of practical procedures for accomplishing the rational accountability of suicidal deaths as recognizable features of the settings in which that accountability occurs.

In the actual occasions of interaction that accomplishment is for members omnipresent, unproblematic, and commonplace. For members doing sociology, to make that accomplishment a topic of practical sociological inquiry seems unavoidably to require that they treat the rational properties of practical activities as "anthropologically strange." By this I mean to call attention to "reflexive" practices such as the following: that by his accounting practices the member makes familiar, commonplace activities of everyday life recognizable *as* familiar, commonplace activities; that on each occasion that an account of common activities is used, that they be recognized for "another first time"; that the member treat the processes and attainments of "imagination" as continuous with the *other* observable features of the settings in which they occur; and of proceeding in such a way that at the same time that the member "in the midst" of witnessed actual settings recognizes that witnessed settings have an *accomplished* sense, an accomplished facticity, an accomplished objectivity, an accomplished familiarity, an accomplished accountability, for the member the organizational hows of these accomplishments are unproblematic, are known vaguely, and are known only in the doing which is done skillfully, reliably, uniformly, with enormous standardization and as an unaccountable matter.

That accomplishment consists of members doing, recognizing, and using ethnographies. In unknown ways that accomplishment is for members a commonplace phenomenon. And in the unknown ways that the accomplishment is commonplace it is for our interests an awesome phenomenon, for in its unknown ways it consists (1) of members' uses of concerted everyday activities as methods with which to recognize and demonstrate the isolatable, typical, uniform, potential repetition, connected appearance, consistency, equivalence, substitutability, directionality, anonymously describable, planful—in short, the rational properties of indexical expressions and indexical actions. (2) The phenomenon consists, too, of the analyzability of actions-in-context given that not only does no concept of context-in-general exist, but every use of "context" without exception is itself essentially indexical.

The *recognizedly* rational properties of their common sense inquiries—their recognizedly consistent, or methodic, or uniform, or planful, etc. character —are *somehow* attainments of members' concerted activities. For Suicide Prevention Center staff, for coders, for jurors the rational properties of their practical inquiries *somehow* consist in the concerted work of making evident from fragments, from proverbs, from passing remarks, from rumors, from partial descriptions, from "codified" but essentially vague catalogues of experience and the like how a person died in society, or by what criteria patients were selected for psychiatric treatment, or which among the alternative verdicts was correct. *Somehow* is the problematic crux of the matter.

What Is Ethnomethodology?

The earmark of practical sociological reasoning, whereever it occurs, is that it seeks to remedy the indexical properties of members' talk and conduct. Endless methodological studies are directed to the tasks of providing members a remedy for indexical expressions in members' abiding attempts, with rigorous uses of ideals to demonstrate the observability of organized activities in actual occasions with situated particulars of talk and conduct.

The properties of indexical expressions and indexical actions are ordered properties. These consist of organizationally demonstrable sense, or facticity, or methodic use, or agreement among "cultural colleagues." Their ordered properties consist of organizationally demonstrable rational properties of indexical expressions and indexical actions. Those ordered properties are ongoing achievements of the concerted commonplace activities of investigators. The demonstrable rationality of indexical expressions and indexical actions retains over the course of its managed production by members the character of ordinary, familiar, routinized practical circumstances. As process and attainment the produced rationality of indexical expressions consists of practical tasks subject to every exigency of organizationally situated conduct.

I use the term "ethnomethodology" to refer to the investigation of the rational properties of indexical expressions and other practical actions as contingent ongoing accomplishments of organized artful practices of everyday life. The papers of this volume treat that accomplishment as the phenomenon of interest. They seek to specify its problematic features, to recommend methods for its study, but above all to consider what we might learn definitely about it. My purpose in the remainder of this chapter is to characterize ethnomethodology, which I have done by presenting three [two given here] studies of the work of that accomplishment together with a concluding recitation of study policies. . . .

Practical Sociological Reasoning: Following Coding Instructions

Several years ago my co-workers and I undertook to analyze the experience of the U.C.L.A. Outpatient Clinic in order to answer the questions "By what criteria are its applicants selected for treatment?" To formulate and to answer this question we used a version of a method of cohort analysis that Kramer and his associates[5] had used to describe load and flow characteristics of patients in mental hospitals. Successive activities of "first contact," "intake interview," "psychological testing," "intake conference," "in-treatment," and "termination" were conceived with the use of the tree diagram of Figure I. Any path from first contact to termination was called a "career."

We wished to know what characteristics of patients, of clinical personnel, of their interactions, and of the tree were associated with which careers. Clinic records were our sources of information, the most important of which were intake application forms and case folder contents. In order to obtain a continuing record of patient-clinic case transactions from the time of a patient's initial

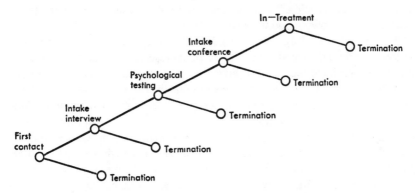

Figure 1. Career paths of patients of a psychiatric clinic

contact until he terminated a "Clinic Career Form" was designed and inserted into case folders. Because clinic folders contain records that clinic personnel provide of their own activities, almost all of these sources of data were the results of self-reporting procedures.

Two graduate students in Sociology at UCLA examined 1,582 clinic folders for the information to complete the items of a Coding Sheet. A conventional reliability procedure was designed and conducted with the aim of determining the amount of agreement between coders and between successive trials of their coding. According to conventional reasoning, the amount of agreement furnishes one set of grounds for lending credence to coded events as actual clinic events. A critical feature of conventional reliability assessments is that the agreement between coders consists of agreement on the end results.

To no one's surprise, preliminary work showed that in order to accomplish the coding, coders were assuming knowledge of the very organized ways of the clinic that their coding procedures were intended to produce descriptions of. More interestingly, such presupposed knowledge seemed necessary and was most deliberately consulted whenever, for whatever reasons, the coders needed to be satisfied that they had coded "what really happened." *This was so regardless of whether or not they had encountered "ambiguous" folder contents.* Such a procedure undermined any claim that actuarial methods for interrogating the folder contents had been used, no matter how apparently clear the coding instructions were. Agreement in coding results was being produced by a contrasting procedure with unknown characteristics.

To find out more about the procedure that our students used, the reliability procedure was treated as a problematic activity in its own right. The "reliability" of coded results was addressed by asking how the coders had actually brought folder contents under the jurisdiction of the Coding Sheet's item. Via what practices had actual folder contents been assigned the status of answers to the researcher's questions? What actual activities made up those coders' practices called "following coding instruction"?

A procedure was designed that yielded conventional reliability information so that the original interests of the study were preserved. At the same time the procedure permitted the study of how any amount of agreement or disagreement had been produced by the actual ways that the two coders had gone about treating folder contents as answers to the questions formulated by the Coding Sheet. But, instead of assuming that coders, proceeding in whatever ways they did, might have been in error, in greater or lesser amount, the assumption was made that *whatever* they did could be counted correct procedure in *some* coding "game." The question was, what were these "games"? How *ever* coders did it, it was sufficient to produce whatever they got. How did they do it to get what they got?

We soon found the essential relevance to the coders, in their work of interrogating folder contents for answers to their questions, of such considerations as "et cetera," "unless," "let it pass," and "factum valet" (*i.e.*, an action that is otherwise prohibited by a rule is counted correct once it is done). For convenience let me call these "*ad hoc*" considerations, and call their practice "*ad hocing*." Coders used the same *ad hoc* considerations in order to recognize the relevance of the coding instructions to the organized activities of the clinic. Only when this relevance was clear were the coders satisfied that the coding instructions analyzed actually encountered folder contents so as to permit the coders to treat folder contents as reports of "real events." Finally, *ad hoc* considerations were invariant features of the practices of "following coding instructions." Attempts to suppress them while retaining an unequivocal sense to the instructions produced bewilderment on their part.

Various facets of the "new" reliability study were then developed, at first in order to see if these results could be firmly established, and after it was clear, to my satisfaction, that they could, to exploit their consequences for the general sociological character of the coders' methods of interrogation (as well as contrasting methods) as well as for the work that is involved in recognizing or claiming that something had been done by rule—that an action had followed or had been "governed" by instructions.

Ad hoc considerations are invariably relevant considerations in deciding the fit between what could be read from the clinic folders and what the coder inserted into the coding sheet. No matter how definitely and elaborately instructions had been written, and despite the fact that strict actuarial coding rules[6] *could* be formulated for every item, and with which folder contents *could* be mapped into the coding sheet, insofar as the claim had to be advanced that Coding Sheet entries reported real events of the clinic's activities, then in every instance, and for every item, "et cetera," "unless," "let it pass" and "factum valet" accompanied the coder's grasp of the coding instructions as ways of analyzing actual folder contents. Their use made it possible, as well, for the coder to read a folder's contents as a report about the events that the Coding Sheet provided and formulated as events of the processing tree.

Ordinarily researchers treat such *ad hoc* procedures as flawed ways of writing, recognizing, or following coding instructions. The prevailing view holds that good work requires researchers, by extending the number and explicitness of their coding rules, to minimize or even eliminate the occasions in which "et cetera" and other such *ad hocing* practices would be used.

To treat instructions as though *ad hoc* features in their use were a nuisance, or to treat their presence as grounds for complaint about the incompleteness of instructions, is very much like complaining that if the walls of a building were only gotten out of the way one could see better what was keeping the roof up. Our studies showed that *ad hoc* considerations are essential features of coding procedures. *Ad hocing* is required if the researcher is to grasp the relevance of the instructions to the particular and actual situation they are intended to analyze. For every particular and actual occasion of search, detection, and assignment of folder contents to a "proper" category—which is to say, over the course of actually coding—such *ad hoc* considerations have irremediable priority over the usually talked about "necessary and sufficient" criteria. It is not the case that the "necessary and sufficient" criteria are procedurally defined by coding instructions. Nor is it the case that *ad hoc* practices such as "et cetera" or "let it pass" are controlled or eliminated in their presence, use, number, or occasions of use by making coding instructions as definite as possible. Instead *ad hoc* considerations are consulted by coders and *ad hocing* practices are *used in order to recognize what the instructions are definitely talking about*. *Ad hoc* considerations are consulted by coders in order to recognize coding instructions as "operational definitions" of coding categories. They operate as the grounds for and as methods to advance and secure researchers' claims to have coded in accordance with "necessary and sufficient" criteria.

Ad hocing occurs (without, I believe, any possibility of remedy), whenever the coder assumes the position of a socially competent member of the arrangement that he seeks to assemble an account of and, when from this "position," he treats actual folder contents as standing in a relationship of trusted signification to the "system" in the clinic activities. Because the coder assumes the "position" of a competent member to the arrangements that he seeks to give an account of, he can "see the system" in the actual content of the folder. This he accomplishes in something like the way that one must know the orderly ways of English usage in order to recognize an utterance as a word-in-English or know the rules of a game to make out a move-in-a-game, given that alternative ways of making out an utterance or a board play are always imaginable. Thereby, the coder recognizes the folder content for "what it actually is," or can "see what a note in the folder 'is really talking about.' "

Given this, if the coder has to be satisfied that he has detected a real clinic occurrence, he must treat actual folder contents as standing proxy for the social-order-in-and-of-clinic-activities. Actual folder contents stand to the socially ordered ways of clinic activities as *representations* of them; they do not describe the order, nor are they evidences of the order. It is the coder's use of folder documents as *sign-functions* to which I mean to be pointing in saying that the coder must know the order of the clinic's activities that he is looking at in order to recognize the actual content as an appearance-of-the-order. Once the coder can "see the system" in the content, it is possible for the coder to extend and to otherwise interpret the coding instructions—to *ad hoc* them—so as to maintain the relevance of the coding instructions to the actual contents, and in this way to formulate the sense of actual content so that its meaning, even though it is transformed by the coding, is preserved in the coder's eyes as a real event of the clinic's actual activities.

There are several important consequences:

(1) Characteristically, coded results would be treated as if they were disinterested descriptions of clinic events, and coding rules are presumed to back up the claim of disinterested description. But if the work of *ad hocing* is required to make such claims intelligible, it can always be argued—and so far I do not see a defensible reply—that the coded results consist of a persuasive version of the socially organized character of the clinic's operations, regardless of what the actual order is, perhaps independently of what the actual order is, and even without the investigator having detected the actual order. Instead of our study of patients' clinic careers (as well as the multitude of studies of various social arrangements that have been carried out in similarly conventional ways) having described the order of the clinic's operations, the account may be argued to consist of a socially invented, persuasive, and proper way of talking about the clinic as an orderly enterprise, since "after all" the account was produced by "scientific procedures." The account would be itself part of the actual order of the clinic's operations, in much the same way that one might treat a person's report on his own activities as a feature of his activities. *The actual order would remain to be described.*

(2) Another consequence arises when we ask what is to be made of the care that nevertheless is so assiduously exercised in the design and use of coding instructions for interrogating actual contents and transforming them into the language of the coding sheet? If the resulting account is itself a feature of the clinic's activities, then perhaps one ought not read the coding instructions as a way of obtaining a scientific description of the clinic's activities, since this assumes that the coding language, in what it is talking *about*, is independent of

the interests of the members that are being served in using it. Coding instructions ought to be read instead as consisting of a grammar of rhetoric; they furnish a "social science" way of talking so as to persuade consensus and action within the practical circumstances of the clinic's organized daily activities, a grasp of which members are expected to have as a matter of course. By referring to an account of the clinic that was obtained by following coding instructions, it is possible for members with different interests to persuade each other and to reconcile their talk about clinic affairs in an impersonal way, while the matters that are really being talked *about* retain their sense, for the "discussants," as a legitimate, or illegitimate, a desirable or undesirable, an advantaged or disadvantaged state of affairs for the "discussants" in their occupational lives. It furnishes an impersonal way of characterizing their affairs without the members relinquishing important organizationally determined interests in what the account, in their eyes, is "after all" all about. What it is all about is the clinic order whose real features, as any member knows that Anyone Knows, are always none of somebody-else-in-that-organization's business.

Practical Sociological Reasoning: Common Understanding

Sociologists distinguish the "product" from the "process" meanings of a common understanding. As "product," a common understanding is thought to consist of a shared agreement on substantive matters; as "process," it consists of various methods whereby something that a person says or does is recognized to accord with a rule. With his concepts of *Begreifen* and *Verstehen*, each with its distinct character as method and knowledge, Weber provided sociologists an authority for this distinction.

An analysis of students' experiences in reporting commonplace conversation suggests that for either case, for "product" or "process," a common understanding consists of an inner-temporal course of interpretive work. Their experiences suggest some strange consequences of the facts that *in either case* a common understanding has necessarily an operational structure.

In Chapter Two research is reported in which students were asked to report common conversations by writing on the left side of a sheet what the parties actually said, and on the right side what they and their partners understood they were talking about. The following colloquy is reported there:

| HUSBAND: | Dana succeeded in putting a penny in a parking meter today without being picked up. | This afternoon as I was bringing Dana, our four-year-old son, home from the nursery school, he succeeded in reaching high enough to put a penny in a parking meter when |

		we parked in a meter zone, whereas before he had always had to be picked up to reach that high.
WIFE:	Did you take him to the record store?	Since he put a penny in a meter that means that you stopped while he was with you. I know that you stopped at the record store either on the way to get him or on the way back. Was it on the way back, so that he was with you or did you stop there on the way to get him and somewhere else on the way back back?
HUSBAND:	No, to the shoe repair shop.	No, I stopped at the record store on the way to get him and stopped at the shoe repair shop on the way home when he was with me.
WIFE:	What for?	I know of one reason why you might have stopped at the shoe repair shop. Why did you in fact?
HUSBAND:	I got some new shoe laces for my shoes.	As you will remember I broke a shoe lace on one of my brown oxfords the other day so I stopped to get some new laces.
WIFE:	Your loafers need new heels badly.	Something else you could have gotten that I was thinking of. You could have taken in your black loafers which need heels badly. You'd better get them taken care of pretty soon.

Students filled out the left side of the sheet quickly and easily, but found the right side incomparably more difficult. When the assignment was made, many asked how much I wanted them to write. As I progressively imposed accuracy, clarity, and distinctness, the task became increasingly laborious. Finally, when I required that they assume I would know what they had actually talked about only from reading literally what they wrote literally, they gave up with the complaint that the task was impossible.

Although their complaints were concerned with the laboriousness of having to write "more," the frustrating "more" was not made up of the large labor of having to reduce a mountain with buckets. It was not their complaint that what was talked about consisted of bounded contents made so vast by pedantry that they lacked sufficient time, stamina, paper, drive, or good reason to write "all of it." Instead, the complaint and its circumstances seemed to consist of this: *if,* for whatever a student wrote, I was able to persuade him that it was not yet accurate, distinct, or clear enough, and *if* he remained willing to repair the ambiguity, then he returned to the task with the complaint that the writing itself developed the conversation as a branching texture of relevant matters. The very *way* of accomplishing the task multiplied its features.

What task had I set them such that it required that they write "more"; such that the progressive imposition of accuracy, clarity, and literalness made it increasingly difficult and finally impossible; and such that the way of accomplishing the task multiplied its features? If a common understanding consisted of shared agreement on substantive matters, their task would have been identical with one that professional sociologists supposedly address. The task would have been solved as professional sociologists are apt to propose its solution, as follows:

Students would first distinguish *what* was said from *what* was talked about, and set the two contents into a correspondence of sign and referent. *What the parties said* would be treated as a sketchy, partial, incomplete, masked, elliptical, concealed, ambiguous, or misleading version of *what the parties talked about.* The task would consist of filling out the sketchiness of what was said. What was talked about would consist of elaborated and corresponding contents of what the parties said. Thus the format of left and right hand columns would accord with the "fact" that the contents of what was said were recordable by writing what a tape recorder would pick up. The right hand column would require that something "more" be "added." Because the sketchiness of what was said was its defect, it would be necessary for students to look elsewhere than to what was said in order (a) to find the corresponding contents, and (b) to find the grounds to argue—because they would need to argue—for the correctness of the correspondence. Because they were reporting the actual conversation of particular persons, they would look for these further contents in what the conversationalists had "in mind," or what they were "thinking," or what they "believed," or what they "intended." Furthermore, they would need to be assured that they had detected what the conversationalists actually, and not supposedly, hypothetically, imaginably, or possibly had in mind. That is to say, they would need to cite observed actions—observed ways that the parties conducted themselves—in order to furnish grounds for the claim of "actually." This assurance would be obtained by seeking to establish the presence, in the conversationalists' relationship, of warranting virtues such as their having spoken honestly, openly, candidly, sincerely, and the like. All of which is to say that students would invoke their knowledge of the community of understandings, and their knowledge of shared agreements to recommend the adequacy of their accounts of what the parties had been talking about, *i.e.,* what the parties understood in common. Then, for anything the students wrote, they could assume that I, as a competent co-member of the same community (the conversations were after all commonplace) should be able to see the correspondence and its grounds. If I did not see the correspondence or if I made out the contents differently than they did, then as long as they could continue to assume my competence—*i.e.*, as long as my alternative interpretations did not undermine my right to claim that such alternatives needed to be taken seriously by them and by me—I could be made out by the students as insisting that they furnish me with finer detailing than practical considerations required. In such a case, they should have charged me with blind pedantry and should have complained that because "anyone can see" when, for all practical purposes, enough is enough, none are so blind as those who *will* not see.

This version of their task accounts for their complaints of having to write "more." It also accounts for the task's increasing laboriousness when clarity and the like were progressively imposed. But it does not account very well for the final impossibility, for it explains one facet of the task's "impossibility" as students' unwillingness to go any further, but it does not explain an accompanying sense, namely, that students somehow saw that the task was, in principle, unaccomplishable. Finally, this version of their task does not explain at all their complaint that the way of accomplishing the task multiplied its features.

An alternative conception of the task may do better. Although it may at first appear strange to do so, suppose we drop the assumption that in order to describe a usage as a feature of a community of understandings we must at the outset know what the substantive common understandings consist of. With it, drop the assumption's accompanying theory of signs, according to which a "sign" and "referent" are respectively properties of something said and something talked about, and which in this fashion proposes sign and referent to be related as corresponding contents. By dropping such a theory of signs we drop as well, thereby, the possibility that an invoked shared agreement on substantive matters explains a usage.

If these notions are dropped, then what the parties talked about could not be distinguished from *how* the parties were speaking. An explanation of what the parties were talking about would then consist entirely of describing how the parties had been speaking; of furnishing a method for saying whatever is to be said, like talking synonymously, talking ironically, talking metaphorically, talking cryptically, talking narratively, talking in a questioning or answering way, lying, glossing, double-talking, and the rest.

In the place of and in contrast to a concern for a difference between *what* was said and *what* was talked about, the appropriate difference is between a language-community member's recognition that a person is saying something, *i.e.*, that he was *speaking*, on the one hand, and *how* he was speaking on the other. Then the recognized sense of what a person said consists only and entirely in recognizing the method of his speaking, of *seeing how he spoke*.

I suggest that one not read the right hand column as corresponding contents of the left, and that the students' task of explaining what the conversationalists talked about did not involve them in elaborating the contents of what the conversationalists said. I suggest, instead, that their written explanations consisted of their attempts to instruct me in how to use what the parties said as a method for seeing what the conversationalists said. I suggest that I had asked the students to furnish me with instructions for recognizing what the parties were actually and certainly saying. By persuading them of alternative "interpretations," by insisting that ambiguity still remained, I had persuaded them that they had demonstrated to me only what the parties were supposedly, or probably, or imaginably, or hypothetically saying. *They took this to mean that their instructions were incomplete: that their demonstrations failed by the extent to which their instructions were incomplete; and that the difference between claims of "actually" and "supposedly" depended on the completeness of the instructions.*

We now see what the task was that required them to write "more," that they found increasingly difficult and finally impossible, and that became elaborated in its features by the very procedures for doing it. I had set them the task of formulating these instructions so as to make them "increasingly" accurate, clear, distinct, and finally literal where the meanings of "increasingly" and of clarity, accuracy, distinctness, and literalness were supposedly explained in terms of the properties of the instructions themselves and the instructions alone. I had required them to take on the impossible task of "repairing" the essential incompleteness of *any* set of instructions no matter how carefully or elaborately written they might be. I had required them to formulate the method that the parties had used in speaking as rules of procedure to follow in order to say what the parties said, rules that would withstand every exigency of situation, imagination, and development. I had asked them to describe the parties' methods of speaking as if these methods were isomorphic with actions in strict compliance with a rule of procedure that formulated the method as an instructable matter. To recognize *what* is said *means* to recognize how a person is speaking, *e.g.*, to recognize that the wife in saying "your shoes need heels badly" was speaking narratively, or metaphorically, or euphemistically, or double-talking.

They stumbled over the fact that the question of how a person is speaking, the task of describing a person's method of speaking, is not satisfied by, and is not the same as showing that what he said accords with a rule for demonstrating consistency, compatibility, and coherence of meanings.

For the conduct of their everyday affairs, persons take for granted that what is said will be made out according to methods that the parties use to make out what they are saying for its clear, consistent, coherent, understandable, or planful character, *i.e.*, as subject to some rule's jurisdiction—in a word, as rational. To see the "sense" of what is said is to accord to what was said its character "as a rule." *"Shared agreement" refers to various social methods for accomplishing the member's recognition that something was said-according-to-a-rule and not the demonstrable matching of substantive matters. The appropriate image of a common understanding is therefore an operation rather than a common intersection of overlapping sets.*

A person doing sociology, be it lay or professional sociology, can treat a common understanding as a shared agreement on substantive matters by taking for granted that what is said will be made out in accordance with methods that need not be specified, which is to say that need only be specified on "special" occasions.

Given the discovering character of what the husband and wife were talking about, its recognizable character for both entailed the use by each and the attribution by each to the other of work whereby what was said is or will have been understood to have accorded with their relationship of interaction as an invokable rule of their agreement, as an intersubjectively used grammatical scheme for analyzing each other's talk whose use provided that they *would* understand each other in ways that they *would* be understood. It provides that neither one was entitled to call upon the other to specify how it was being done; neither one was entitled to claim that the other needed to "explain" himself.

In short, a common understanding, entailing as it does an "inner" temporal course of interpretive work, necessarily has an operational structure. For the analyst to disregard its operational structure, is to use common sense knowledge of the society in exactly the ways that members use it when they must decide what persons are really doing or really "talking about," *i.e.*, to use common sense knowledge of social structures as *both* a topic and a resource of inquiry. An alternative would be to assign exclusive priority to the study of the methods of concerted actions and methods of common understanding. Not *a* method of understanding, but immensely various methods of understanding are the professional sociologist's proper and hitherto unstudied and critical phenomena. Their multitude is indicated in the endless list of ways that persons speak. Some indication of their character and their differences occurs in the socially available glosses of a multitude of sign functions as when we take note of marking, labeling, symbolizing, emblemizing, cryptograms, analogies, anagrams, indicating, miniaturizing, imitating, mocking-up, simulating—in short, in recognizing, using, and producing the orderly ways of cultural settings from "within" those settings.[7]

Policies

That practical actions are problematic in ways not so far seen; how they are problematical; how to make them accessible to study; what we might learn about them—these are proposed tasks. I use the term "ethnomethodology" to refer to the study of practical actions according to policies such as the following, and to the phenomena, issues, findings, and methods that accompany their use.

(1) An indefinitely large domain of appropriate settings can be located if one uses a search policy that *any occasion whatsoever* be examined for the feature that "choice" among alternatives of sense, of facticity, of objectivity, of cause, of explanation, of communality of *practical actions* is a project of members' actions. Such a policy provides that inquiries of every imaginable kind, from divination to theoretical physics, claim our interest as socially organized artful practices. That the social structures of everyday activities furnish contexts, objects, resources, justifications, problematic topics, etc. to practices and products of inquiries establishes the eligibility for our interest of every way of doing inquiries without exception.

No inquiries can be excluded no matter where or when they occur, no matter how vast or trivial their scope, organization, cost, duration, consequences, whatever their successes, whatever their repute, their practitioners, their claims, their philosophies or philosophers. Procedures and results of water witching, divination, mathematics, sociology—whether done by lay persons or professionals—are addressed according to the policy that every feature of sense, of fact, of method, for every particular case of inquiry without exception, is the managed accomplishment of organized settings of practical actions, and that particular determinations in members' practices of consistency, planfulness, relevance, or reproducibility of their practices and results—from witchcraft to topology—are acquired and assured only through particular, located organizations of artful practices.

(2) Members to an organized arrangement are continually engaged in having to decide, recognize, persuade, or make evident the rational, *i.e.*, the coherent, or consistent, or chosen, or planful, or effective, or methodical, or knowledgeable character of such activities of their inquiries as counting, graphing, interrogation, sampling, recording, reporting, planning, decision-making, and the rest. It is not satisfactory to describe how actual investigative procedures, as constituent features of members' ordinary and organized affairs, are accomplished by members as recognizedly rational actions *in actual occasions* of organizational circumstances by saying that members invoke some rule with which to define the coherent or consistent or planful, *i.e.*, rational, character of their actual activities. Nor is it satisfactory to propose that the rational properties of members' inquiries are produced by members' compliance to rules of

inquiry. Instead, "adequate demonstration," "adequate reporting," "sufficient evidence," "plain talk," "making too much of the record," "necessary inference," "frame of restricted alternatives," in short, every topic of "logic" and "methodology," including these two titles as well, are glosses for organizational phenomena. These phenomena are contingent achievements of organizations of common practices, and as contingent achievements they are variously available to members as norms, tasks, troubles. Only in these ways rather than as invariant categories or as general principles do they define "adequate inquiry and discourse."

(3) Thus, a leading policy is to refuse serious consideration to the prevailing proposal that efficiency, efficacy, effectiveness, intelligibility, consistency, planfulness, typicality, uniformity, reproducibility of activities—*i.e.*, that rational properties of practical activities—be assessed, recognized, categorized, described by using a rule or a standard obtained outside actual settings within which such properties are recognized, used, produced, and talked about by settings' members. All procedures whereby logical and methodological properties of the practices and results of inquiries are assessed in their general characteristics by rule are of interest as *phenomena* for ethnomethodological study but not otherwise. Structurally differing organized practical activities of everyday life are to be sought out and examined for the production, origins, recognition, and representations of rational practices. All "logical" and "methodological" properties of action, every feature of an activity's sense, facticity, objectivity, accountability, communality is to be treated as a contingent accomplishment of socially organized common practices.

(4) The policy is recommended that any social setting be viewed as self-organizing with respect to the intelligible character of its own appearances as either representations of or as evidences-of-a-social-order. Any setting organizes its activities to make its properties as an organized environment of practical activities detectable, countable, recordable, reportable, tell-a-story-aboutable, analyzable—in short, *accountable*.

Organized social arrangements consist of various methods for accomplishing the accountability of a settings' organizational ways as a concerted undertaking. Every claim by practitioners of effectiveness, clarity, consistency, planfulness, or efficiency, and every consideration for adequate evidence, demonstration, description, or relevance obtains its character as a *phenomenon* from the corporate pursuit of this undertaking and from the ways in which various organizational environments, by reason of their characteristics as organizations of activities, "sustain," "facilitate," "resist," etc. these methods for making their affairs accountable-matters-for-all-practical-purposes.

In exactly the ways that a setting is organized, it *consists* of members' methods for making evident that settings' ways as clear, coherent, planful, consistent, chosen, knowable, uniform, reproducible connections,—*i.e.*, rational connections. In exactly the way that persons are members to organized affairs, they are engaged in serious and practical work of detecting, demonstrating, persuading through displays in the ordinary occasions of their interactions the appearances of consistent, coherent, clear, chosen, planful arrangements. In exactly the ways in which a setting is organized, it *consists* of methods whereby its members are provided with accounts of the setting as countable, storyable, proverbial, comparable, picturable, representable—*i.e.*, accountable events.

(5) Every kind of inquiry without exception consists of organized artful practices whereby the rational properties of proverbs, partially formulated advice, partial description, elliptical expressions, passing remarks, fables, cautionary tales, and the like are made evident, are demonstrated.

The demonstrably rational properties of indexical expressions and indexical actions are an ongoing achievement of the organized activities of everyday life. Here is the heart of the matter. The managed production of this phenomenon in every aspect, from every perspective, and in every stage retains the character for members of serious, practical tasks, subject to every exigency of organizationally situated conduct. Each of the papers in this volume, in one way or another, recommends that phenomenon for professional sociological analysis.

NOTES

1. Olaf Helmer and Nicholas Rescher, *On the Epistemology of the Inexact Sciences,* P-1513 (Santa Monica, California: RAND Corporation, October 13, 1958), pp. 8–14.

2. In Marvin Farber, *The Foundation of Phenomenology* (Cambridge, Massachusetts: Harvard University Press, 1943), pp. 237–238.

3. Bertrand Russell, *Inquiry into Meaning and Truth* (New York: W. W. Norton & Company, Inc., 1940), pp. 134–143.

4. Nelson Goodman, *The Structure of Appearance* (Cambridge, Massachusetts: Harvard University Press, 1951), pp. 287–298.

5. M. Kramer, H. Goldstein, R. H. Israel, and N. A. Johnson, "Applications of Life Table Methodology to the Study of Mental Hospital Populations," *Psychiatric Research Reports of the American Psychiatric Association*, June, 1956, pp. 49–76.

6. David Harrah's model of an information-matching game was taken to define the meaning of "strict actuarial method for interrogating." See David Harrah, "A Logic of Questions and Answers," *Philosophy of Science,* **28**, No. 1 (January, 1961), 40–46.

7. This note was touched off by Monroe Beardsley's remark in "The Metaphorical Twist," *Philosophy and Phenomenological Research*, March, 1962, to the effect that we do not decide that a word is used metaphorically because we know what a person is thinking; rather we know what he is thinking because we see that a word is used metaphorically. Taking poetry for his case, Beardsley points out that "the clues of this fact must somehow be in the poem itself, or we should seldom be able to read poetry."

Ethnomethodology:
Sociology without Society?

WILLIAM W. MAYRL

THE ATTEMPT TO DEVELOP A SOCIOLOGY OF THE LEBENSWELT DEMON-strates again that an intellectual system cannot get beyond its starting point. Phenomenological sociology suffers from the same affliction which plagues its philosophical forebearer. By commencing with the structure of individual consciousness, it is forced to bypass any exterior and therefore social reality. To anyone who thinks that the above is exclusively the problem of philosophers, that scientific methods have a way of obviating such metaphysical considerations, is recommended a reading of ethnomethodological research.

Ethnomethodology represents an attempt to develop a systematic program of research based upon phenomenological premises. Its program has been successful. In fact, this paper will attempt to demonstrate that *it is the success* of ethnomethodology which exposes the inability of phenomenology to come to grips with social reality. We will commence with a brief consideration of the essential elements of phenomenological methodology especially Husserl's critique of empirical science. Some understanding of this approach in its "pure" form should enable us to evaluate the stated objectives of ethnomethodology and the extent to which these are truly phenomenological. We will then be in a position to consider recent ethnomethodological research.

The Phenomenological Method

There is a distinction in Husserl between the sciences of existence (empirical) and those of essence (eidetic).[1] The latter are more fundamental. Eidetic investigations are based upon description. But unlike positivistic descriptions,

William W. Mayrl, "Ethnomethodology: Sociology Without Society?" *Catalyst*, no. 7 (Winter 1973): 15–28.

for example, which are based upon an examination of what is actually given in experience, Husserl's investigations deal with "imagined objects."[2] Now the ideal objects of eidetic science are not found in Plato's world of ideas nor do they appear to the investigator in the form of mystical presentation. They are rather the result of his "re-enacting and re-activating experiences such as remembrances, conceptual abstractions and recognitions."[3] Objects which are actually experienced may be the points of departure for these investigations but they are clearly secondary to them. Schutz comments:

> The phenomenologist, we may say, does not have to do with the objects themselves; he is interested in their meaning *as it is constituted by the activities of our mind.*[4]

The eidos, in other words, are characteristics *for us*. Schutz is quite right when he suggests that this method "leads to an entirely new theory of induction and association."[5] Eidetic analyses not only involve *interpretive* rather than *enumerative* induction, they force a refocusing of attention from problems which are strictly methodological to those hitherto thought of as strictly epistemological. Crucial to the phenomenologist at this point is the genesis and development of meaning.

For Husserl "the basis of meaning . . . in every science is the prescientific lifeworld (*Lebenswelt*)."[6] Our insights and impressions, or intuitions concerning relationships among phenomena in the world, our procedures for the handling of data and the assumptions which underlie even our most sophisticated techniques are rooted in the natural attitude of everyday life. Phenomenology "claims to be a philosophy of man in his lifeworld and to be able to explain the meaning of this lifeworld in a rigorously scientific manner."[7] The world of everyday life has been characterized by the phenomenologist as "immediate," "commonsensical," and "taken-for-granted." Above all, however, it is a subjective, i.e. a psychic world. By devoting its major attention to a study of the *process* of investigation (i.e. the bestowal of meaning) phenomenology hopes to cast a new light on the *objects* of investigation. The connection between these two takes on critical importance in the area of the human sciences. For in this realm, the *process* and *object* of study, in so far as they are both meaningful human activity, are basically the same.

Ethnomethodology

In his inimitable language, Harold Garfinkel defines the major objectives of ethnomethodology as " . . . the investigation of the rational properties of indexical expressions and other practical actions as contingent ongoing accomplishments of organized artful practices of everyday life."[8] By indexical expressions Garfinkel, following Husserl, refers to those statements " . . . whose sense cannot be decided by an auditor without his necessarily knowing or assuming something about the biography and the pusposes of the user, . . . [and] the circumstance, . . . that exists between the expressor and the auditor."[9] Their communicative value, in other words, is relative to their *user* and the *occasion* of their use.

The value of indexical expressions for sociological inquiry lies in their characterization first as members' reports or accounts as to what's happening in everyday situations and second as contingent upon the situated activities whereby members produce and manage settings of organized everyday affairs that are identical with their procedures for making these settings "accountable."[10]

By "rational properties" Garfinkel seems to refer to those which make an action or expression understandable to a "cultural colleague,"[11] i.e. a fellow participant in the situation in question. He is *not* refering to properties conforming with a previously operationalized or standardized notion of rationality.

> Instead of the properties of rationality being treated as a methodological principle for interpreting activities, they are to be treated only as empirically problematical material. They would have the status only of data and would have to be accounted for in the same way that the more familiar properties of conduct are accounted for.[12]

Garfinkel thus sets himself at odds with the mainstream of the Weberian position. "Rationality" is rationality within or relative to, a particular situation. Thus, "as process and attainment the produced rationality of indexical expressions consists of practical tasks *subject to every exigency of organizationally situated conduct.*"[13]

Garfinkel presents several "policies" which recommend themselves to, and in some sense, clarify the objectives of ethnomethodology. In the first place, "any occasion whatsoever" is of interest to the student of practical activity. "Such a policy provides that inquiries of every imaginable kind, from divination to theoretical physics" claim the ethnomethodologist's interest, "as socially artful practices."[14] The second and third policies remind the researcher that since the rational properties of ordinary activities, i.e. those properties which make the activities workable and communicable for those involved, are "contingent achievements" of the activities themselves, he must " . . . refuse serious consideration to the prevailing proposal that . . . these properties be assessed . . . by using a rule or standard obtained outside actual settings."[15] Policies four and five repeat two, three and one albeit in slightly different words. Number four recommends that the social setting "be viewed as self-organizing with respect to the intelligible (i.e. rationa)l character of its own appearances . . . "[16] Five reminds us again that "every kind of inquiry without exception consists of organized artful practices whereby the rational properties of proverbs, partially formulated advice, partial description, elliptical expressions . . . etc. are made evident, are demonstrated."[17]

Taken on its own, Garfinkel's presentation of the objectives of ethnomethodology is virtually indecipherable. However it can be clarified somewhat through consideration of the works of Cicourel, McHugh and Sacks. These authors contend that Garfinkel's concern with members' accounts of familiar, everyday activities gets at something very basic to sociology: the foundations of the normative order. In brief, it is argued, accounts of mundane activities probably provide the key to the rules which seem to govern social behavior. "How can norms be described or imputed to an environment of objects," asks Cicourel, "unless we make the actor's differential perception and interpretation of them, and his general definition of the situation, the *basic* properties of the concept"?[18] A major objective of ethnomethodology for Cicourel thus becomes the discovery of "basic or interpretative" rules which underlie the normative order and, in some sense, make it viable. Similarly McHugh suggests that sociologists should commence with an analysis of an actor's definition of the situation rather than with "grand matters" such as normative structures.[19] For it is "the prosaic details of everyday life upon which any cosmos (i.e. normative or moral structure) logically depends."[20] It should be noted that, at least, with Cicourel and McHugh, this position does not imply the denial of "objective," formal structures of rules. It merely asserts that mundane experiences and definitions (accounts) are prior to such structures. It is the "informal," "unstated" understanding between people which makes for the binding character of such rules.[21] Thus McHugh grants the pre-existence of society "as an abstraction." The fundamental question and directive for research is "how does this abstraction enter into the daily lives of individuals whose definitions are continually being made and remade?"[22]

There are both similarities and differences between Garfinkel's "rational properties," Cicourel's "basic rules," and McHugh's "definition of the situation." In the first place, all of them are involved with the problem which constitutes a focal concern of classical phenomenology: the production and communication of meaning. We saw that for Garfinkel the crucial problem is the discovery of those factors (methods, techniques, artful practices) whereby participants in on-going everyday activity are able to justify to each other what they are doing. These were aptly called "accounting practices."[23] Now although Garfinkel has on occasion disclaimed an interest in problems of meaning, wishing instead to focus upon the "features" of organized settings,[24] it would seem that every accounting practice must, of necessity, include a process whereby the basic meaning of a situation is produced by a participant along with a process whereby this meaning is communicated to "cultural colleagues." Quite obviously, Garfinkel's remarks on the unimportance of meaning to ethnomethodology cannot be taken seriously. Clearly his own work gives the lie to them. For without a consideration of meaning, analysis of "settings features" would amount to little more than exercises in the most crassly positivistic sort of ethnography.

Cicourel and McHugh are by no means vague when it comes to the role of meaning in their analyses. This is evidenced in the emphasis which McHugh places upon "the definition of the situation" and which Cicourel puts on the notion of "basic" or "interpretive rules." Indeed, for both writers, these processes constitute, in McHugh's words, the "bedrock" of social order.[25] For Cicourel, interpretive rules are constantly developing categories of meaning which provide the actor with "a sense of social structure."[26] "Surface rules" (what most sociologists refer to as norms), on the other hand, "enable the actor to line his view of the world to that of others in concerted social action."[27] Thus "while the two orders are always in interaction and it would be absurd to speak of one without the other," Cicourel leaves little doubt that the basic rules are "fundamental for the normative order."[28] In like manner, for McHugh, the "definition of the situation" which might be understood as "interpretive rules" in operation, is considered to be so elemental it cannot be explained by rules or standards outside itself.[29] It can only be *described* because as a bedrock element of social order it "requires no further justification."[30]

It should be apparent that an important objective of ethnomethodology lies in the area of sociological description. At first glance it would seem that this should not be classified as an objective but rather as a strategy or even a procedure. However, owing to its phenomenological roots, ethnomethodological description clearly becomes more of a process to be achieved than an instrument of research. Description, in other words, becomes a problem intricately involved with the nature of social reality.

We saw that for Husserl, phenomenological description is a description of essences. It was further seen that essences do not inhere in nature itself but become apparent through a dialogue, as it were, between nature and consciousness. They are constituted by the activities of our mind. As Farber[31] and Molina[32] among others have pointed out this position leads almost inevitably to absolute idealism. In any event it has certain interesting implications for social science. In the first place whether one is seeking a description of "accounting practices" or, on a more primitive level, members' "definitions," the researcher's perspective becomes a major consideration. There is little scientific value, the phenomenologist would argue, in merely affixing one's own artificial categories of essence upon social events. The fact this is done with respect to the world of nature is not withstanding. Social accounts and definitions are not rocks and chemicals. (Even the study of rocks and chemicals would be greatly improved, according to Husserl, if we were able to understand how they are constituted through experience in consciousness). The social scientist must make every attempt to render his categories of meaning congruent with those of his subjects or, at least, to understand the relationship between the two kinds of perspective (i.e. that of participant and that of observer). Thus Cicourel suggests that one of the first objectives of social inquiry must be "the formation of a general model which permits the researcher to recognize the possible differences between how the scientist goes about assigning meanings to events and objects he studies and how the actor being studied accomplishes the same objectives."[33] To use phenomenological terminology, we might say that Cicourel seems to be calling for a conversion chart for eidetic description. We might take this matter one step further by suggesting that ethnomethodological description of definitions and accounts is a description of descriptions!

It should now be evident that McHugh's notion of the description of definitions "because they require no further justification" is more complicated than it first appeared. It is not the description of the positivist who in attempting to get at his ultimate referent must finally resort to pointing at the object in question. Rather it is an eidetic description of eidetic descriptions. Sacks makes this point rather directly. " . . . if it can be said that persons produce descriptions of the social world, the task of sociology is not to clarify these, or to 'get them on the record' or to criticise them, but to describe them."[34] We would call the readers attention to Sacks' distinction between "getting them on the record" and "describing" them. For the positivist those two would be virtually the same. Sacks further develops this point by arguing that "it is not in its descriptions that sociology differs from commonsense talk of society."[35] The difference between the two lies only in their purpose at hand, not in the nature of their descriptions. Thus there is no essential difference between the procedures of the professional sociologist and that of the ordinary man engaged in his everyday activities. Following Schutz, the ethnomethodologist agrees that " . . . the whole methodological problem of the social sciences and their categories has already been posed in the prescientific sphere, i.e. in the midst of life in the social world."[36]

It seems apparent that the objectives and procedures of phenomenological philosophy and ethnomethodology are essentially the same. While the latter has introduced, according to its purpose, new terminology such as "culture," "social structure," "normative order," etc. these are clearly, in phenomenological terms, second order conceptions. They have no referent in reality. They are abstractions which serve as " . . . a kind of intellectual shorthand [in which] the underlying subjective elements of human actions are either taken for granted or deemed to be irrelevant to the scientific purpose at hand."[37] Thus the phenomenological sociologist (and the ethnomethodologist who is true to phenomenological principles) hastens to admit that the reality of these "sociological" concepts must be sought in the world of everyday life, in the "bedrock" experiences of the *Lebenswelt*. The imputation of a reality to such second order abstractions has misled many sociologists and even some ethnomethodologists into thinking that ethnomethodology is really not much different from most other schools of sociology. Tiryakian goes so far to suggest that it is a part of the dominant thrust of mainstream sociology.[38] And Denzin argues that very little stands between a synthesis of ethnomethodology and symbolic interactionism.[39] However, research based upon phenomenological assumptions goes far in clearing this confusion. For empirical investigations, if done well, will always clarify the premises of the philosophical system in which they are rooted.

Ethnomethodological Research

Regardless of their particular research strategy or their subject matter in any given study, ethnomethodological analyses tend to focus upon two basic themes: decision-making in common sense situations of choice and the process of reality maintenance. Each of these involves the description of subjective processes. And each contains, by its very nature, an attempt to render "sociological" considerations irrelevant to any account of human behavior. In this respect ethnomethodological research shows itself to be the true heir of phenomenological philosophy.

Decision-Making in Common Sense Situations of Choice

Earlier it was noted the rational properties of indexical statements of activities are determined not by some outside, objective standard of rationality (e.g. Weber's typology of motives) but rather by the participants in the activities themselves. For this reason such statements or activities must be examined in terms of their own context. In other words, the "rules" governing what ethnomethodologists often refer to as social games are so flexible and easily amendable that a shift in what Garfinkel calls a constitutive accent i.e. that which defines the character of an ongoing game, can produce an entirely new game. The problem with most non-phenomenological sociology, according to the ethnomethodologist, is that it tends to confuse what are merely features of a setting with "rules" which determine behavior. Garfinkel's study of decision-making procedures among graduate student coders[40] provides an illuminating analysis of this.

Normally, in professional sociological research, the reliability of coders is determined by developing tests which measure the amount of agreement between coders during various sample stages of their coding. This conventional procedure, according to Garfinkel, is based on the assumption that "the amount of agreement furnishes one set of grounds for lending credence to coded events as actual clinic [the coding was part of a study of the practical workings of a psychiatric outpatient clinic] events."[41] The result of such a procedure is normally an error factor which provides an "objective" measure of coding reliability. Now Garfinkel was interested in this test of reliability with regard to the psychiatric clinic study. However the analysis of decision-making among the coders had an entirely different goal.

> . . . instead of assuming that coders, proceeding in whatever ways they did, might have been in error, in greater or lesser amount, the assumption was made that *whatever* they did could be counted as correct *procedure* in *some* coding "game." The question was what were these "games"? How *ever* coders did it, it was sufficient to produce whatever they got. How did they get what they got?[42]

The process of decision-making on the part of the coders was characterized by Garfinkel as *ad hocing*. The rules which made up the coding instructions served, in effect, merely as a point of orientation rather than a rigid objective standard by which items were classified. They were mitigated by the coder's ad hoc considerations and interpretations. The important decisions did not necessarily involve the direct application of the rules but rather the coders' highly situational interpretations of them. This process was characterized by such considerations as "et cetera,"[43] "unless," "let it pass" and "factum valet" (i.e. an action that is otherwise prohibited by a rule is counted correct once it is done).[44] A similar process was found working among specialists employed by the Los Angeles Coroner's Office to decide which sudden and unnatural deaths were suicides[45] and among jurors making decisions of culpability in negligence cases.[46] In all of these cases individuals were involved in common sense situations of choice. In each there existed external more or less formal rules which set the criteria for the decisions of choice. And in each the "real" rationality was to be found not so much in the adherence to the rules but in informal subjective processes rooted in everyday life. Thus in his discussion of the techniques which jurors use in their deliberations, Garfinkel remarks "a person is 95 per cent juror before he comes near the court."[47]

This theme has been developed in research other than Garfinkel's. Arlene Daniels, for instance, has examined the process whereby diagnostic decisions were made in several military mental hospitals. Following Durkheim, the traditional sociological definition of deviance specifies behavior which is in violation of social norms. Through the efforts of scholars like Barbara Wooton in England and Thomas Szasz in the U.S. this definition has come to include behaviors defined as mentally ill. Now the ethnomethodologist reacts to this in much the same way he reacts to any decisions made in terms of objective criteria whether these be social norms, coding instructions or legal definitions of right and wrong. He wants to know the manner in which interpretive rules,

rules of definition as well as the resulting practices of accounting, operate in relation to the objective standards. On a theoretical level, for example, McHugh proposes a modification of the objective standards approach to deviance which bears a striking resemblance to Flectcher's "modification" of traditional ethical theory. "In its conventional aspect," he comments, "deviance is not merely not following a rule, but whether the rule can be conceived to have been follow*able* and followable in the situation in which it was not followed."[48] Once this consideration is termed "conventional"—critics of Flectcher and the ethnomethodologists might suggest that their illustrations tend to focus on extreme or rare cases—then the door is open for a phenomenological analysis of all decision-making processes. In considering normal as well as pathological behaviors, stated or objective rules are merely points of orientation or departure. The real decisions are made on the basis of common sense understandings and interpretations. This is the thrust of Daniels' analysis. "The world which the psychiatrist constructs through his diagnoses," she suggests, "bears many resemblances to the world of everyday life with its commonsense value judgements."[49] Of course, this assessment stands in contrast to the official "line" of organized psychiatry. Ethnomethodologist Emanuel Schegloff had concluded in an early study of psychiatric literature, that its theory "provides the rules by which psychiatrically understood behaviors may be related to one another."[50] "Psychiatric theory, as written in books and articles, with attendant case materials [official accounts?], can be read as a normative and credential-conferring theory, in that it may provide and legitimate sets of proper meanings and responses to patient behavior."[51] Daniels argues that in the light of "military expectations," psychiatric evidences and the rules which govern them are often thrown to the wind. Military psychiatrists, for example, often have to make diagnostic choices between such categories as psychoses, "character and behavior" disorder, and "situational stress." In the process of deciding among these alternatives, "official" psychiatric theory is greatly tempered by commonsense values and military expedience. Thus a soldier who displays behavior easily diagnosable as psychoses may be classified as "situational stress" depending upon such exigencies as his military record, his rank, length of time in the service, pressure from the CO, etc.[52] In this sense the psychiatrist seems to be involved in Garfinkel's "common sense situation of choice."

The Process of Reality Maintenance

Earlier it was seen that every social encounter analyzable in game terms is characterized by a particular accent or definition of the situation. A shift in accent, insofar as it alters the constitutive expectancies, can result in the development of a new game. Everyday life is full of examples of such shifts in accent or definition. A man conversing with a woman on politics or philosophy, for instance, may, upon finding she has more knowledge on the topic than himself, shift the accent by commenting on her pretty dress. His intention of course is the development of a new game which accentuates culturally sanctioned male superiority. Since the world for the phenomenologist is constituted primarily of meanings, attempts to shift or maintain the meanings in any situation involve questions of reality. In order to learn more about the techniques of definition and redefinition, Joan Emerson examined an extreme situation in which the participants were likely to have a vested interest in the maintenance of a particular accent.

The participants in a gynecological examination must constantly straddle the lines between what might be called medical and sexual games.[53] Emerson was interested in the methods used by both doctor and patient to insure a continued accentuation upon the former. Some of these methods, she found, were built into the settings' physical features, e.g. the presence of a nurse in the examining room. Others involved the mode of communication between the examiner and examinee, e.g. the use of objective medical terms when referring to the genital region, etc. While most of the 75 examinations observed by Emerson "proceeded smoothly" i.e. remained characterized by the medical accent, there were a few where the patient displayed embarrassment or sexual excitement thus threatening to cross the line between the two types of game. Several techniques were used by doctors in these precarious situations. They might "recharge" the medical accent by defining a sexual response as "fear of pain" or "ticklishness." On some occasions humor was used to neutralize the threat. In all cases, smooth or threatening, certain elements of the settings' features were continually and consciously emphasized, e.g. the sterile and detached professional aspects, whereas others were constantly played down, e.g. contact with genitalia, intimacy, etc.

While realizing that the gynecological examination is an extreme situation Emerson argues that it is by no means an anomaly. "It merely exaggerates the internally contradictory nature of definitions of reality found in most situations."[54] The composite definitions of work and pleasure in business entertaining, the undertaker's dealings with a bereaved family, and a boss's attempt to "butter up" his secretary are cited as examples of situations where conflicting definitions or accents are encountered and must be handled.[55]

On several occasions, ethnomethodologists have developed their own extreme situations in order to observe the process of reality maintenance. Apparently following Freud's and Durkheim's suggestion that a good way to study the normal is to examine the pathological, the ethnomethodologists have hit upon the strategy of disruption or altering the routine progress of everyday activities. The reasoning behind this move can be clarified as follows.

In giving the individual a "sense of social structure," Cicourel's interpretive rules also provide him with a sense of reality. Schutz has referred to this as "the paramount reality of the lifeworld." The subjective lifeworld is characterized by schemes of meaningful experience. Insofar as these schemes provide the individual with a stable orientation towards the physical and social world, i.e. insofar as they adequately account for events in these worlds, they are the basès for interpretive rules. Normally, the interpretive rules retain their validity (i.e. applicability), and one's sense of reality is taken for granted. However it is possible for a novel experience through "failure to connect," to throw either part or all of one's schemes into question and thereby to dissolve their taken for granted status. Theoretically, it would seem, once open to question, schemes and their "rules" should be open to inspection. Therefore, by carefully setting up situations which challenge an individual's schemes of experience, the researcher should be in a position to observe the intensity of the victim's defensive responses at various points and thus obtain readings on the dimensions of his interpretive rules.

As early as 1952, in his doctoral dissertation, Garfinkel was altering "perceivedly normal events" in an attempt to experimentally test Schutz's constitutive phenomenology of the natural attitude. In one experiment pre-medical students were asked to listen to a recording of what was proportedly an actual interview between a medical school admissions officer and an applicant to the school.[56] The "applicant" responded to the "interviewer" in a manner which seemed to defy the usual expectations for such an occasion. He was arrogant and insulting and came off to be such a boor that all of the subjects were quite convinced that he could not have passed the interview. Their agreement on this indicated the existence of commonly held interpretive rules, characterized by a particular set of constitutive expectancies, which applied to professional interviews. The experimenter then radically shifted the accent or definition of the situation by announcing that the "applicant" had passed the interview with flying colors and had been accepted into the school. The subjects were then asked to re-listen to the tape and further comment on it. Garfinkel was interested in the level of confusion and anxiety in these comments as a measure of the subjects' commitment to their prior notions of reality with respect to interview situations. He found that while all of the subjects manifested a marked increase in measured anxiety, most of them were able to normalize the situation by somehow redefining the "boor" as a successful candidate.

Other, less rigidly controlled, disruptions of expected routines resulted in similar findings. Subjects' reactions ranged from anger to mild annoyance and in many instances attempts were made to shift the accent in order to understand the situation in terms of a different but also familiar game. For example, Garfinkel asked his students to act as strangers in their own homes. They were instructed to behave and respond to members of their families with the politeness and reserve one would expect to find among unrelated individuals in a boarding house. In several of the cases the families refused to go along with the act immediately interpreting it as a joke. In the majority of cases, however, family members were stupefied. They responded to the student experimenters with "astonishment, bewilderment, shock, anxiety, embarrassment, and anger, and with charges . . . that the student was mean, inconsiderate, selfish, nasty or impolite."[57] Like the pre-medical students, victimized family members attempted to normalize the situation or at least to maintain a sense of reality by seeking explanations for the experimenter's behavior "in previous, understandable motives . . . e.g. the student was working too hard in school, he was ill, there had been another fight with a fiancee."[58]

It would be possible to mention other ethnomethodological studies which have utilized a number of settings and strategies. However, this would only amount to a continued elaboration of the two basic themes we have already discussed. At this point we are able to specify the way in which ethnomethodological research clarifies phenomenological principles.

Sociology without Society

In the course of his recent reflections on the state of sociology, Blau comments on ethnomethodology.

> [It] presents no clear conceptual framework and no specific procedures for research, and its practitioners neither engage in systematic research nor try to construct systematic theories but comment in quite obscure language on some random observations of human behavior they have made.[59]

For these reasons Blau concludes, this school impedes the development of sociology. Clearly Blau does not understand ethnomethodology. For it impedes sociology not because of haphazard research or even because it lacks systematic theory. In most cases ethnomethodological research has been systematic; their observations have been carefully selected with respect to the processes to be interpretively described and their analyses have been organized and consistent. The major problem of ethnomethodology is its subject matter. It is not that it collects facts improperly, rather it collects the wrong facts.

In a sense, it would seem difficult to level a sociological criticism at specific research done by ethnomethodologists because the questions they deal with are only marginally relevant to sociology. However the problem with ethnomethodology goes well beyond the asking of un-sociological questions. Close examination of the research of this "branch of sociology" reveals an attempt to systematically eliminate sociological considerations.

While ethnomethodology ignores sociological questions, its research does make use of social facts. These facts—roles, norms, institutions, and even interaction—are abstracted from any social context and are used as situational conditions. Thus the activity of doctors and patients, students and parents, jurors and lawyers, etc. are studied in order to achieve an understanding of the techniques which *individuals* develop and use in various game situations. In fact, ethnomethodological research is considered successful in the measure to which these social factors can be shown to be irrelevant to the interpretation of observed behavior. The manifest goal of Garfinkel's research on workers in the Los Angeles Suicide Prevention Center, student coders, and jurors deliberating in accident cases, for example, was to demonstrate that differences in expectations which characterize the medical, professional-academic and legal roles were unimportant to an understanding of what was really happening in these three *apparently* diverse situations.

The same anti-sociological thrust can be found in research which focuses on the theme of processes and techniques of reality maintenance. The major goal seems to be the demonstration of the way in which individuals manipulate "settings' features" in the maintenance or alteration of a given accent or reality. Thus, for example, Emerson does not propose to tell us anything about the gynecological examination which does not equally apply to an undertaker with a bereaved family, a boss and his secretary or, for that matter, any number of other settings. In brief, settings' features including social facts are things to be "seen through" rather than to be considered as determinants of behavior. It is interesting to note that Daniels' research is unique among the others reported. For although her study appears in a volume devoted to ethnomethodology, the factors she utilizes in her interpretations are not always consistent with phenomenological premises. The notion of "military expectations," for instance, is clearly of a different order than "common sense values." In lumping the two together, Daniels commits what for the phenomenologist is the unpardonable sin of confusing two levels of reality: the concrete with the abstract. For once this confusion takes place and the latter level is reified, it begins to assume a determining character in interpretive descriptions of behavior. This is precisely what the ethnomethodologist wants to avoid.

Perhaps one of the most surprising revelations of ethnomethodological research concerns the place of interaction. There is a common belief, which has been bolstered by the analyses of Denzin and Tiryakian, among others along with a misunderstanding of several of Schutz's remarks on Cooley and Mead, that ethnomethodology is very similar to symbolic interactionism. If a reading of phenomenological literature does not destroy this belief then a brief perusal of ethnomethodological research will. The two schools, it has been suggested, are the same insofar as they both take as a major problem the production, maintenance and change of meaning. However close examination of the literature and the research of these schools reveals two entirely different conceptions of meaning. For Mead and the symbolic interactionists meaning, in its most reduced sense, is a product of a hypothetical dyad. It has no existence without the Other. Thus in Mead's classic formulation, the meaning of A's activities are found in B's responses.[60] For Schutz, following Husserl, on the other hand, meaning originates in the stream of experiences of the solitary ego. Specifically, for the phenomenologist, meaning can be understood as being contained in a process whereby the ego assumes a reflective attitude towards a moment of its elapsed duration.[61] Based upon Bergson's notion of subjective inner time (*la durée*), and utilized by Husserl as "inner time consciousness," the duration refers to the internal flow of experience; the temporal sedimentation of experiences (both past and future) within ego's consciousness. While all experiences constitute the *durée* only those which are grasped reflectively are meaningful.[62] While Others enter into one's schemes of meaningful experience they do not constitute it. In fact, the existence of the Other—without which, for Mead, there can be no consciousness—is something which is "arrived at" as the result of phenomenological reflection.

This position is carried into ethnomethodological research. For while few of its practitioners would deny that members' definitions or accounts are social, their research is true to its phenomenological heritage in that it treats interaction as incidental to the real problems of the creation, maintenance and justification of meaning. Whether the subjects are student coders, jurors or gynecologists, they are essentially solitary individuals coping with definitions in a world wherein Others are relegated to the status of settings' features. Thus the relationship with Others, when reported on, is primarily a process of manipulation. In most cases interaction *per se* is not even mentioned much less considered a relevant factor. For example, in Garfinkel's research on medical students, as it was reported on as a study in ethnomethodology, the question of possible variations in the subjects' anxiety depending upon such factors as Others' redefinitions is never raised. In fact we are never even told whether they knew each other.

Perhaps the best way to typify the subject matter of ethnomethodological research is found in Lyman and Scott's recent work on phenomenological-existentialist sociology.

> The sociology of the absurd [phenomenology] assumes a model of man in conflict with others, with society, with nature and even with himself.[63]

The authors go on explicitly to deny the "sociological conception" of man as an interdependent being and to accept, as closer to their own position, Freud's model of man in society. Lyman and Scott notwithstanding, most phenomenologists take serious issue with Freud's notion of consciousness. However, the Freudian perspective is certainly more acceptable to them than objectivist positions such as sociological realism or symbolic interactionism because like their own it is essentially a psychologism.

The ground we have covered might be summed up as follows. Ethnomethodology is a phenomenology. Its overall theoretical thrust is entirely consistent with Schutz's postulate of subjective interpretation and its use of meaning in no way contradicts the conception of that phenomenon as a quality of individual subjectivity. It further shares with all phenomenological philosophy a fundamental ambivalence on the question of reality external to the solitary ego. The world, in this case society, is said to exist but not in any meaningful sense independent of individual consciousness. Therefore its role as a determinant of human activity becomes confused. The resolution of this confusion is found in the relegation of social facts to the status of abstractions built out of members' definitions. One ethnomethodologist even supports this notion metaphorically by referring to these definitions as the "bedrock elements" out of which society is constructed. In this light, the major goal of ethnomethodological research is to demonstrate that what appear to be objective realities such as norms, relationships and institutions are not really determinants of behavior. They are the features of various settings which are themselves meaningful only through definitions. Ultimately then, society exists in the individual mind as a factor which is constructed by, yet at the same time enters into, mental activity.

It might be worth further noting that the relationship which exists between ethnomethodology and more or less objective approaches to social reality finds an analogy in the distinction between James and Cooley on the one hand, and G. H. Mead. James, and Cooley, like the phenomenologists,[64] held an essentially individualistic theory of the self and the genesis of meaning wherein, in the final analysis, interaction was imaginary. In this respect, Mead observes of Cooley's conception of society

> It is an affair of consciousness, and a consciousness that is necessarily social. One's consciousness of himself is directly a reflection of the ideas about himself which he attributes to the others. Others exist in his imagination of them, and only there do they affect him, and only in the imaginations which others have of him does he affect them.[65]

Mead was entirely correct when he pointed out that ultimately Cooley's position led to solipsism.[66] This criticism can be applied even more forcefully to the social phenomenologists. For them, we saw earlier, while the content of consciousness is social its nature is individual. Thus from the perspective of the objectivist-naturalist,[67] the idealist Cooley in a sense represents an advance over the phenomenologist.

Conclusions

I think many ethnomethodologists would be angered if they were told their methodological stance leads quite logically to idealism and ultimately to solipsism. They do not claim to be philosophers after all and by ignoring the basic implications of their position, they do seem to have a good deal of elbow room for grappling with what seems to be the most direct and immediate of empirical realities. Certainly the appeal of social phenomenology does not lie in its idealism but rather in its apparent ability to get at something which seems lacking in objectivist analyses with their deductive systems or their historical dialectics. Social phenomenology claims to be able to get at the blood and guts of human existence. Whereas objectivist analyses, it might argue in the words of Sartre, tends to "dissolve man in a bath of sulphuric acid," social phenomenology in its perspective and ethnomethodology in its research seem to deal with factors which are relevant to our everyday lives. Insights derived from their works seem directly applicable to the people we know and even to ourselves. The major appeal of this school is that it seems immediately and concretely human.

However what is immediately human is not *fully* human. In fact, it is almost ironic that while all social research must deal with abstractions, the ethnomethodologists, by focusing upon the consciousness of the solitary individual have picked the one abstraction which is not justifiable. Unlike economic, political, religious and familial processes it cannot be concretized by being put back into a larger structural context of which it is a part. As Marx, Mead, and more recently, Goldmann among many others have forcefully demonstrated, social relationships are derivable (and explainable) from social relationships and not individual consciousness. The only thing that can be derived from the solitary ego is the solitary ego.

Social phenomenology, like all idealism, is an exercise in avoidance. The assumption of the priority of individual consciousness over history and the division of labor represents the feeble attempt to control these perplexing realities by substituting for them something which seems more manageable. Dreitzel is correct in pointing to fundamental similarities between the hippie movement and ethnomethodology. The former's response to crises in society is quite analogous to the latter's solution to problems in sociology.

NOTES

1. Alfred Schutz, "Some Leading Concepts of Phenomenology," *Collected Papers*, ed. Maurice Natanson (The Hague: Martinus Nijhoff, 1967), vol. I, p. 113.
2. *Ibid.*, p. 114.

3. Marvin Farber, *Naturalism and Subjectivism* (Springfield, Ill.: Charles C. Thomas, 1959), p. 60.

4. Schutz, *op. cit.*, p. 115.

5. *Ibid.*

6. Schutz, "Phenomenology and the Social Sciences", *Collected Papers I*, p. 120.

7. *Ibid.*

8. Harold Garfinkel, *Studies in Ethnomethodology* (Englewood Cliffs: Prentice-Hall, 1967), p. 11.

9. *Ibid.*, p. 4.

10. *Ibid.*, p. 1.

11. *Ibid.*, p. 11.

12. *Ibid.*, p. 282.

13. *Ibid.*, p. 11.

14. *Ibid.*

15. *Ibid.*, p. 33.

16. *Ibid.*

17. *Ibid.*, p. 34.

18. Aaron Cicourel, *Method and Measurement in Sociology* (New York: The Free Press, 1964), p. 202.

19. Peter McHugh, *Defining the Situation* (New York: Bobbs-Merrill, 1968), p. 11.

20. *Ibid.*

21. Cicourel, *op. cit.* p. 203.

22. McHugh, *op. cit.* p. 12.

23. Garfinkel, p. 3.

24. Cf. Richard J. Hill and Kathleen S. Crittenden, eds., *Proceedings of the Purdue Symposium on Ethnomethodology* (Purdue University: Institute for the Study of Social Change, Monograph 1, 1968), p. 113.

25. McHugh, *op. cit.*, p. 18.

26. Aaron Cicourel, "Basic and Normative Rules in the Negotiation of Status and Role," in *Recent Sociology 2*, ed. Hans Peter Dreitzel (London: Macmillan, 1970), p. 29.

27. *Ibid.*

28. *Ibid.*, p. 30.

29. McHugh, *op. cit.*

30. *Ibid.*, p. 19.

31. Farber, *op. cit.*, pp. 57ff.

32. Fernando Molina, "The Husserlian Ideal of a Pure Phenomenology," in *An Invitation to Phenomenology*, ed. James M. Edie (Chicago: Quadrangle Books, 1965), p. 164.

33. Cicourel, *Method and Measurement in Sociology*, p. 199.

34. Harvey Sacks, "Sociological Description," *Berkeley Journal of Sociology*, vol. 8 (1963), p. 7.

35. *Ibid.*, p. 12.

36. Alfred Schutz, *The Phenomenology of the Social World* (Evanston: Northwestern University Press, 1967), p. 141.

37. Schutz, "Common-Sense and Scientific Interpretations of Human Action". *Collected Papers I*, p. 35.

38. Edward A. Tiryakian, "Existential Phenomenology and the Sociological Tradition," *American Sociological Review*, vol. 30 (October 1965), pp. 674–688.

39. Norman K. Denzin, "Symbolic Interactionism and Ethnomethodology: A Pro-

posed Synthesis," *American Sociological Review,* vol. 34 (December 1969), pp. 922–934.

40. Garfinkel, *op. cit.,* pp. 18–24. The study for which the coding was done appears as Chapter 6, pp. 187–207.

41. *Ibid.,* p. 19.

42. *Ibid.,* p. 20. (Emphasis in original).

43. The notion of "et cetera" has been analyzed by Sacks in the previously mentioned article. It refers to the process whereby a report is brought to a close in spite of the fact that it is not (and never can be for all purposes) complete. The "et cetera" decision indicates that for the purpose at hand the report is considered finished.

44. Garfinkel, *op. cit.,* pp. 20–21.

45. *Ibid.,* pp. 11–18.

46. *Ibid.,* pp. 104–115.

47. *Ibid.,* p. 110.

48. Peter McHugh, "A Common-Sense Perception of Deviance," in Dreitzel, *op. cit.,* p. 157.

49. Arlene Daniels, "The Social Construction of Military Psychiatric Diagnoses," in Dreitzel, *op. cit.,* p. 194.

50. Emanuel A. Schegloff, "Toward a Reading of Psychiatric Theory," *Berkeley Journal of Sociology,* vol. VIII, (1963), p. 74.

51. *Ibid.*

52. Daniels, *op. cit.,* pp. 188–197.

53. Joan Emerson, "Behavior in Private Places: Sustaining Definitions of Reality in Gynecological Examinations," in Dreitzel, *op. cit.,* p. 76.

54. *Ibid.,* p. 91.

55. *Ibid.*

56. Garfinkel, *op. cit.,* pp. 58–62. Cf. Cicourel, *Method and Measurement in Sociology,* pp. 165–166.

57. Garfinkel, *op. cit.,* p. 47.

58. *Ibid.,* p. 48.

59. Peter Blau, "Sociological Analysis: Current Trends and Personal Practice." *Sociological Inquiry,* vol. 39, No. 2 (Spring 1969), pp. 119–130.

60. Anselm Strauss, ed., *G. H. Mead on Social Psychology* (Chicago: University of Chicago Press, 1964), especially pp. 163–169.

61. Schutz, *The Phenomenology of the Social World,* pp. 69–70.

62. Schutz, "Symbol, Reality and Society," *Collected Papers* I, p. 269.

63. Stanford Lyman and Marvin Scott, *A Sociology of the Absurd* (New York: Appleton-Century-Crofts, 1970), p. 6.

64. While Schutz mentions all three scholars as possible avenues through which phenomenology can be brought to an American public, he quite obviously sees James as the most important in this respect. Cf. A. Schutz, *Collected Papers* I, p. 183.

65. Strauss, *op. cit.,* p. 295.

66. *Ibid.,* p. 244 n.

67. Mead, for example, considers his work to be of this variety. Cf. A. Strauss, *op. cit.,* p. 244n.

Suggested Readings

BERGER, Peter, and Luckmann, Thomas. *The Social Construction of Reality*. New York: Doubleday, 1966.

CHUA, Beng-Huat. "Comment" (on Mayrl). *Catalyst,* no. 8 (Winter 1974):76–85.

CICOUREL, Aaron. *Method and Measurement in Sociology*. New York: Free Press, 1964.

CICOUREL, Aaron, ed. *Cognitive Sociology: Language and Meaning in Social Interaction*. New York: Free Press, 1974.

COULTER, Jeff. "The Ethnomethodological Programme in Contemporary Sociology." *Human Context* 6 (1974):103–22.

DALLMAYR, Fred R. "Phenomenology and Social Science: An Overview and Appraisal." In *Explorations in Phenomenology*, edited by David Carr and Edward S. Casey, pp. 133–66. The Hague: Martinus Nijhoff, 1974.

DOUGLAS, Jack D. *American Social Order*. New York: Free Press, 1971.

DOUGLAS, Jack D., ed. *Understanding Social Life*. Chicago: Aldine Publishing Co., 1970.

DREITZEL, Hans Peter, ed. *Recent Sociology No. 2*. London: Macmillan, 1970.

FILMER, Paul, et al. *New Directions in Sociological Theory*. London: Collier-Macmillan, 1972.

GELLNER, Ernest. "Ethnomethodology: The Re-Enactment Industry or the Californian Way of Subjectivity." *Philosophy of the Social Sciences* 5 (1975):431–50.

GIDLOW, Robert. "Ethnomethodology—A New Name for Old Practices." *British Journal of Sociology* 23 (1972):395–405.

GORMAN, Robert A. *The Dual Vision: Alfred Schutz and the Myth of Phenomenological Social Science*. London: Routledge & Kegan Paul, 1976.

HABERMAS, Jürgen. *Zur Logik der Sozialwissenschaften: Materialien*. Frankfurt: Suhrkamp Verlag, 1970, pp. 188–220.

HEAP, James, and Roth, Philip. "Phenomenological Sociology." *American Sociological Review* 38 (1973):354–67.

HILL, Richard J., and Crittenden, Kathleen S., eds. *Proceedings of the Purdue Symposium on Ethnomethodology*. Lafayette, Ind.: Purdue University Press, 1968.

HOLZNER, Burkhart. *Reality Construction in Society.* Cambridge: Schenkman, 1968.

KOCKELMANS, Joseph. *A First Introduction to Husserl's Phenomenology.* Pittsburgh: Duquesne University Press, 1967.

LAURER, Quentin. *Phenomenology: Its Genesis and Prospect.* New York: Harper & Row, 1965.

McCALL, George J., and Simmons, J. L., eds. *Issues in Participant Observation: A Text and a Reader.* Reading, Mass.: Addison-Wesley Publishing Co., 1969.

McHUGH, Peter. *Defining the Situation: The Organization of Meaning in Social Interaction.* Indianapolis: Bobbs-Merrill, 1968.

McHUGH, Peter, et al. *On the Beginning of Social Inquiry.* London: Routledge and Kegan Paul, 1974.

MAYRL, William W. "Reply." *Catalyst,* no. 8 (Winter 1974):85–95.

MEHAN, Hugh, and Wood, Houston. "An Image of Man for Ethnomethodology." *Philosophy of the Social Sciences* 5 (1975):365–76.

――――――. *The Reality of Ethnomethodology.* New York: Wiley and Sons, 1975.

NATANSON, Maurice. "Phenomenology and Typification: A Study in the Philosophy of Alfred Schutz." *Social Research* 37 (1970):1–22.

NATANSON, Maurice, ed. *Phenomenology and the Social Sciences.* 2 vols. Evanston, Ill.: Northwestern University Press, 1973.

O'NEILL, John. *Sociology as a Skin Trade: Essays towards a Reflexive Sociology.* New York: Harper & Row, 1972.

PIVĆEVIĆ, Edo. "Can There Be a Phenomenological Sociology?" *Sociology* 6 (September 1972):335–49.

PIVĆEVIĆ, Edo, ed. *Phenomenology and Philosophical Understanding.* Cambridge: Cambridge University Press, 1975.

PSATHAS, George. "Ethnomethods and Phenomenology." *Social Research* 35 (1968):500–520.

PSATHAS, George, ed. *Phenomenological Sociology.* New York: Wiley, 1973.

REVIEW SYMPOSIUM. "Studies in Ethnomethodology." *American Sociological Review* 33 (1968):122–30.

SCHUTZ, Alfred. *The Phenomenology of a Social World.* Evanston, Ill.: Northwestern University Press, 1967.

――――――. *Reflections on the Problem of Relevance.* New Haven, Conn.: Yale University Press, 1970.

SCHUTZ, Alfred, and Luckmann, Thomas. *The Structures of the Life-World.* Evanston, Ill.: Northwestern University Press, 1973.

SMART, Barry. *Sociology, Phenomenology, and Marxian Analysis*. London: Routledge & Kegan Paul, 1976.

TURNER, Roy, ed. *Ethnomethodology: Selected Readings*. London: Penguin Books, 1974.

ZANER, Richard M. "A Certain Rush of Wind: Misunderstanding Understanding in the Social Sciences." *Cultural Hermeneutics* 1 (1973):383–402.

_____. *The Way of Phenomenology*. New York: Pegasus, 1970.

PART FIVE

Hermeneutics and Critical Theory

Introduction

IN THE ENGLISH-SPEAKING WORLD THE SOCIAL SCIENCES HAVE BEEN viewed largely against the background of the natural sciences. The problems that are typically discussed—the existence of general laws of history and society, the structure of explanation of social phenomena, the possibilities and limitations of social prediction and control, the objectivity of sociological data—reflect this orientation. With few exceptions, philosophers and methodologists of social science have not devoted much attention to analyzing the distinctive research procedures and forms of argumentation that obtain in the human sciences or "humanities." This neglect can draw support from a long-standing cultural tradition—after all, the humanities are not "sciences," but "arts." Apart from periodic reminders of the undesirable consequences that are likely to result from the mutual isolation of the "two cultures," we have by and large been contented with their peaceful coexistence. This tenuous arrangement, however, can persist only so long as there are no fundamental disagreements about respective spheres of influence. The extension of hermeneutic procedures to the domain of social inquiry, in particular, would require a rethinking of accepted boundaries.

Hermeneutics, the art of textual interpretation, developed in intimate connection with theology and jurisprudence.[1] The gradual disintegration of the medieval world fostered a growing awareness of the problems involved in correctly interpreting canonical texts. Biblical exegesis in particular was forced to become more self-conscious in response to the palpable "distance" from the original. A similar consciousness of distance, and the problems it implies for correct understanding, exercised the Renaissance humanists in their encounter with classical texts. From its beginnings as an auxiliary to theology and jurisprudence, hermeneutics eventually expanded to include the whole range of text-interpreting philologies. With the awakening of historical consciousness in late eighteenth and early nineteenth century Germany (Herder, romanticism, Hegel), the importance of interpretive procedures for deciphering the meaning and significance of historical phenomena became apparent. At the very latest,

Dilthey's investigation of the conditions of possibility and validity of *Verstehen* marked the generalization of hermeneutic procedures to the whole of the human world.

But in this process of expansion, the original self-understanding of hermeneutics became problematic. In the interpretation of canonical texts (religious or legal), the text's claim to meaning and truth provided the standard of adequate understanding. Interpretation was "normative-dogmatic" in the sense that it took its orientation from the authority of the text and inquired after its normative meaning for the present. Its aim, that is, was the transmission—not the criticism, not the disinterested presentation—of traditional beliefs and norms that were to be mediated with or applied to present circumstances. This respect for the normative validity of tradition was also a component of the humanists' orientation to the classical texts of the "golden age of man." Although there were certainly instances of critical hermeneutics before the nineteenth century (for example, Spinoza's critical interpretation of the Bible), the traditional connection of hermeneutics with normatively binding transmission was seriously undermined only with the rise of historicism. The view that cultural phenomena could be understood and assessed only in relation to the historical context in which they were rooted tended to lead to moral and intellectual scepticism. Dilthey's psychologistic approach to *Verstehen* as a self-transposition into the life of the author or agent eliminated its practical relation to life in favor of a contemplative model of scientific objectivity. Rather than a source of transhistorically valid truths and values, history became a repository of the wealth and variety of human life. Historical consciousness was no longer the shepherd of tradition, but the *musée imaginaire* of the past.

More recently, Heidegger's existential ontology has provided the point of departure for a hermeneutics of language that attempts to steer between the dogmatic traditional views of interpretation on the one hand and the relativistic historicist views on the other. In the selections of Part 5, this approach is advanced, elaborated, and criticized. Apel takes up once again the neopositivist logic of unified science and opposes to it a "thesis of complementarity": interpretive understanding is complementary to (that is, supplements and excludes) objectifying explanation. In maintaining the universal applicability of objectifying science (and consequently the "reducibility" of the intentional to the nonintentional), logical positivism implicitly presupposes "methodical solipsism," that is, the notion that objective knowledge is possible without intersubjective understanding—"that one solitary subject of knowledge could objectify the whole world, including his fellow men." Against this Apel argues that empirical science itself is possible only on the basis of communication among the members of the scientific community. In his view, the norms, standards, conventions, rules, goals, concepts, methods, and so forth that constitute scientific activity presuppose intersubjective understanding within this community as well as procedures for maintaining and improving it. In this sense, the rationality of science is predicated on the "metascientific rationality of intersubjective discourse." The partners in this discourse cannot be reduced to objects of description and explanation without breaking off communication. Thus science, as a form of social or communicative activity, presupposes modes of experience and cognition that cannot be consistently rendered in a universal "thing language."

According to Apel, this "a priori of communication" is the foundation of the humanities. It points to a type of knowledge that, in comparison with natural science, pursues different goals and has a different (that is, nontechnological) relation to practice. The failure to appreciate that there are *fundamental interests of knowledge* other than explanation, prediction and technical control is at the root of the neopositivist misunderstanding of *Verstehen*. It is not a "shortcut to explanation," but seeks to improve communication "in its own dimension of intersubjectivity." The aims and intentions, beliefs and values, reasons and motives that pervade human life are not simple "hypostasized" causes of behavior, but "possibilities of life" that can be understood, discussed, and perhaps realized in our own lives. Hermeneutics expands the possibilities of communication across the boundaries of space and time and thus contributes to the "shaping and reshaping of an educated public," which is no less fundamental a human interest than that in the technical control of our natural environment.

Of course, this argument for the legitimacy and irreducibility of interpretive procedures in general does not itself constitute a justification of the particular approach of hermeneutics. In the essay reprinted below, Paul Ricoeur attempts to detail the respects in which the object of social inquiry—meaningful action—may be viewed as analogous to the traditional object of hermeneutics—the text. On the basis of this analogy, he argues that many of the problems and methods of hermeneutics turn up in the human sciences and that to this extent "the human sciences may be said to be hermeneutical." In this respect, his argument is similar to Taylor's (Part 2) and can be instructively compared with it.

The most extensive contemporary discussion of the relevance of hermeneutics to social inquiry is to be found in the debate between Hans-Georg Gadamer and Jürgen Habermas. Gadamer's main work, *Wahrheit und Methode* (1960), was markedly influenced by Heidegger's ontology of language. In it he was not so much concerned to work out methodological procedures for the cultural sciences or to elucidate their theoretical foundations; he wanted instead to disclose "linguisticality" (*Sprachlichkeit*) as the basic mode of human existence. This he did in exploring the structure of understanding in the traditional hermeneutic domains of aesthetics, philology, and history. Largely through the efforts of Apel and Habermas, Gadamer's work has since been introduced into discussions of the theory and methodology of the social sciences. And the ensuing debate between hermeneutics and critical theory has become a staple of contemporary German intellectual life. Habermas's review of *Truth and Method* is perhaps the central document in this controversy.[2]

Gadamer's hermeneutical reflections can be methodologically situated by way of a confrontation with the work of Wittgenstein and Winch. As the contributions in Part 3 make evident, the view that beliefs and actions must always be understood in the context of the language game or form of life in which they are located has strongly relativistic implications (reminiscent of historicism). To this "monadology of language games" closed off from one another, Habermas opposes the hermeneutical starting point of the inter-translatability of different languages. As he tries to show, we are not locked within the grammatical boundaries of our respective life-worlds; rather, "every ordinary language grammar itself furnishes the possibility to transcend the language it determines." Gadamer also differs from Wittgenstein and Winch in stressing the historicity of understanding. Language and tradition are inextricably bound together: language is the "mode of being of tradition," and tradition is the medium in which language continues and develops. From this perspective, the process of socialization in a language community (which serves as Winch's model for understanding) is regarded as a component part of an ongoing process in which language is interpreted, changed, and developed. The learning of a primary language is not a paradigm for reflective understanding, but an "accomplishment of life." A more appropriate model for reflective understanding can be gained from cases in which it is particularly difficult to achieve and where the conditions of success are more likely to become explicit—for example, in cases involving two different languages. For this reason Gadamer adopts translation as a model from which to develop his analysis of *Verstehen*.

This model excludes from the start an analysis of understanding in psychological terms; understanding is inseparable from interpretation, from linguistic articulation of the meanings grasped. According to Gadamer, the interpreter does not approach his subject as a *tabula rasa*; he brings with him a certain horizon of expectations—of beliefs and practices, concepts and norms—that comprise his own life-world. Thus he must capture the sense of his material in and through articulating it in a conceptual framework different from that in which it is originally constituted as meaningful. And he must do so in such a way that while its foreignness is preserved, it is nevertheless brought into intelligible relation with his own form of life. In Gadamer's terms, a successful interpretation involves a "fusion of horizons." From this point of view it becomes clear that there is no such thing as *the* correct interpretation, "in itself" as it were. If interpretation is always a hermeneutic mediation of different languages, the notion of a final, once-and-for-all valid interpretation makes no sense: "Each time will have to understand the written tradition in its way . . . one understands otherwise if one understands at all."

The process of interpretation itself has a hypothetical and circular character. From the perspectives available to him in his horizon, the interpreter makes a preliminary projection of the sense of the text as a whole. With further penetration into the more detailed aspects of his material, this preliminary projection is revised, alternative proposals are considered, and new projections are tested. This hypothetico-circular movement of understanding the parts in terms of a projected sense of the whole and revising the latter in the light of a closer investigation of the parts, has as its goal the achievement of a unity of sense, that is, an interpretation of the whole in which our detailed knowledge of the parts can be integrated without violence. Arbitrary preconceptions derived from the interpreter's own cultural context show themselves to be arbitrary only in collision with his material. There can be no question of the interpreter ridding himself of *all* preconceptions and prejudgments. This is a logical impossibility—the idea of an interpreter without a language. Nor is it possible to bring to consciousness all-at-once and once-and-for-all one's preconceptions and prejudgments. It is, rather, in the interpretive process itself that one's own structure of prejudices gradually becomes clearer.

According to Gadamer, the usual description of the "hermeneutic circle" is purely formal and, as such, inadequate as an analysis of historical understanding. The interpretive appropriation of one's own tradition has, to be sure, a circular structure, but it is of a material nature. The anticipation or projection of meaning that guides the interpreter's work is, in this case, itself a product of the tradition he is trying to understand. That is, the interpretive understanding of one's own tradition departs from a structure of prejudices, from preconceptualizations and prejudgments, which themselves belong to this tradition. This is especially true of classical texts, since these, by definition, have had a particularly important *Wirkungsgeschichte*—their interpretive appropriation has played a major role in the development of the tradition that is the object of the interpretation. And this interpretation is itself a reappropriation, a moment of their *Wirkungsgeschichte*, a building forth of the very tradition being studied. But this circle has a positive significance; for it implies that there is some common ground between the preconceptions of the interpreter and the material that he is investigating, that his points of reference for understanding the tradition have a foundation in that tradition itself.

In Habermas's view, the most significant achievement of Gadamer's hermeneutics is the demonstration against historicism that "understanding is linked with transcendental necessity to the articulation of action-orienting self-understanding," that hermeneutic knowledge has an irreducible practical dimension. In a certain sense this is a rehabilitation of the prehistoricist view of interpretation as being realized only in the application of a normatively binding meaning to present circumstances. But Gadamer does not want to restrict this connection to the interpretation of canonical or institutionally sanctioned texts; nor does he wish to base it on a merely dogmatic attitude toward tradition. He attempts instead to show that the applicative moment of *Verstehen* is universal and necessary: "there always takes place something like an application of the text to be understood to the present situation of the interpreter." The interpreter "must relate the text to his situation if he wants to understand at all." Unless we return to the view that the task of the historian or social scientist is to transfer himself imaginatively into the situation of the subject under investigation, to see things exactly as he saw them, grasping the meaning of a system of beliefs and practices requires making it intelligible to oneself and one's culture. But this means finding points of reference in one's own culture from which the beliefs and practices can be said to have a point: "Traditional meanings are understood only when we have arrived at a consensus about their significance."[3]

Although Habermas accepts the argument that "some form of application" is essential to understanding, he rejects the conservative implications that Gadamer draws from it. The fact that "the moment of historical influence is and remains effective in all understanding of tradition" is itself no justification of the legitimacy and authority of tradition. To identify hermeneutic inquiry simply with the continuation of tradition is to underestimate the reflective and critical dimensions of understanding: "From the fact that understanding is structurally a part of the traditions that it further develops, it does not follow that the medium of tradition is not profoundly altered by scientific reflection." In critical reflection we can reject as well as accept the validity claims of tradition. In either case, "the element of authority that was simply domination can be stripped away and dissolved in the less violent force of insight and rational decision."

Reflection of this sort, however, requires a point of reference that goes beyond tradition, a point from which tradition can be criticized. Tradition must somehow be relativized in a more comprehensive system of reference. At the close of his essay, Habermas suggests how this might be done. He proposes deabsolutizing tradition by systematically taking into account the constraints of nature—inner and outer—that are incorporated in the structure of communication. The symbolic framework of society is dependent on processes of social labor and institutionalized relations of power. These aspects of society are not only objects of interpretation; they are empirical conditions under which worldviews and systems of norms arise, develop and change: "Hermeneutic experience that encounters this dependency of the symbolic framework on actual conditions changes into the critique of ideology." Sociology cannot be reduced to interpretive sociology; what is needed is an empirically grounded "philosophy of history with practical intent."

NOTES

1. See the suggested readings by Apel (1955), Palmer, and Radnitzky for background on the history of hermeneutics.

2. For other important contributions see the volume *Hermeneutik und Ideologiekritik* listed in the suggested readings; some aspects of the controversy appeared in English in *Continuum* 8 (1970).

3. For a development of this point see Ricoeur's "Ethics and Culture," listed under suggested.

The A Priori of Communication
and the Foundation of the Humanities

KARL-OTTO APEL

(What sort of relation between science and the humanities should be postulated within the context of contemporary society?)

I. Exposition

I DO NOT BELIEVE THAT THE QUESTION CONCERNING THE RELATION between science and the humanities is any more settled, or more clearly established, today than when it was brought to the fore in the days of Dilthey and Neo-Kantianism. It is true that, from time to time, speakers at congresses affirm that the old controversy between understanding and explanation has been overcome and rendered obsolete. And their audience may applaud their appeal not to split the unity of science, not to re-establish "two cultures," as Snow uses the term. But I think that appeasements and quasi-moral appeals of this kind should not intervene in, or worse, prevent, a serious meta-scientific analysis of the relations between science and the humanities. In my opinion, the chief question still is: whether it does or does not make a difference for the philosophy of science that in the human sciences the *object* of science is also the *subject* of science, namely human society as a communication community. From this substantive question a methodological question arises: Should the humanities imitate the methods that have been so successful in the natural sciences in order thus to arrive at the status of genuine science, also? Or should they perhaps develop methods which are complementary to those used in the natural sciences, methods that flow from their own leading knowledge inter-

Karl-Otto Apel, "The A Priori of Communication and the Foundation of the Humanities," *Man and World* 5 (1972): 3–12, 14–16, 22–37.

ests? In the latter case it could very well be that the knowledge interest guiding the humanities is equally complementary to that found in the natural sciences.

This question, or so it seems to me, if for us more significant than ever before, because we have learned—or must soon learn—to consider the methodological problems of science and the humanities in connection with their relations to social *praxis*. Dilthey's old question as to whether the goal of the humanities is or is not the same as that of natural science—namely, explanations according to laws as a basis for predictions—is today exemplified by the question as to whether, in the humanities, the relation to social *praxis* is or is not the same as in the case of natural science: that is, is it a social technology or not? This question is, in fact, answered in the affirmative by the prevailing philosophy of science, and the practical significance of this answer itself [shows] in the fact that, from this perspective, pedagogy, for example, is considered to be applied psychology, primarily in the sense of conditioning technology. Since, however, the human object in this conditioning technology is also a co-subject of the educator, the question arises as to whether there must be a complementary method of critical-humanistic education to prevent splitting society into the manipulated and the manipulators. Such a split society would, of course, be the ideal presupposition of an objectifying social science and social technology. It could perform repeatable experiments without being disturbed by a feedback that turns controllable predictions into self-fulfilling or self-destroying prophecies. But the question remains as to whether the humanities, by their very method, should not presuppose a relation to social *praxis* that is complementary to the ideal objectification of human behavior, namely, unrestricted communication by way of intersubjective "understanding."

It is against this concrete and current background that I wish once again to raise the question of the relation between science and the humanities.[1] And I will do so by way of a critical examination of the neo-positivistic "logic of unified science."

I think that the clear-cut model of scientistic reductionism developed by this representative school of meta-science is even today a paradigm that dominates the tacit preconceptions even of those scientists and philosophers who would not wish to be understood to be neo-positivists. The most deeply rooted of these preconceptions, it seems, is the idea of knowledge as description and explanation of objectified data, conceived—a priori—as cases of instances of possible laws. Apparently even the understanding and the interpretation of symbolic meaning is to be subsumed under this conception of knowledge, if it is to be regarded as a topic of methodological relevance. In this context, my question is whether there are, perhaps, ultimate metaphysical presuppositions in the modern "logic of science" which imply conceptions of this kind, presuppositions that prevent the possibility of even imagining a "leading interest of knowledge" outside or beyond scientism. I would, indeed, reply to this question by way of a heuristic suspicion that a modern "logic of science" that does not reflect upon ultimate a priori presuppositions has just by this very fact inherited a tacit presupposition of traditional epistemology: namely, that one solitary subject of knowledge could objectify the whole world, including his fellowmen. To put it another way, it inherits the presupposition that the knowing subject can, in principle, win objective knowledge about the world without at the same time presupposing knowledge by sign-interpretation or intersubjective understanding, which cannot have the character of objectivity, and nevertheless may be improved upon in a methodical way. Let me explain—or better, explicate —this, by some remarks about the metaphysical background of the modern, analytical philosophy of science.

If one were to ask about the a priori presuppositions of modern neo-positivistic logic of science, several answers could be given. The first might be: the only a priori presupposition here implied is logic itself, which in science has to be combined in some way with the observation of facts. This might, perhaps, fit the original self-understanding of the logical positivists. But after some reflection, it becomes clear that, even in logical positivism, a few more a priori presuppositions are actually involved. Thus, it is not simply a matter of fact that there are facts; rather, it has to be presupposed, a priori, in the logic of science that there exist facts that are independent of human thinking about them, and that those facts can be recognized, intersubjectively, *as* facts. Now, what we have stated as presuppositions of logical positivism are, in fact, two of the metaphysical principles of Leibniz, namely, that there are "truths of reason" (*vérités de raison*) based on logic and "truths of fact" (*vérités de fait*) based on experience.[2] And here, immediately, a further a priori presupposition comes to light which the logical positivists originally also shared with Leibniz: the presupposition of an ideal language of science which can bring together mathematical logic and experienced facts in an unequivocal manner (as Leibniz puts it: in a *lingua philosophica sive calculus ratiocinator*, which puts an end to misunderstandings in philosophical communication by providing recourse to a "calculemus"[3]). I might add that the logical positivists had at their disposal a theoretical basis for their semantical critique of metaphysics, only as long as the neo-Leibnizian metaphysics that they inherited from Russell and the young Wittgenstein remained hidden. Obviously, they lost this theoretical basis once they were forced to question these metaphysical presuppositions. And this happened once it became clear that the following ideal postulates simply could not be realized in the logic of science: first, the idea of one syntactico-semantical framework which could be presupposed as the universal language of science as a whole; second, the idea of observational sentences which could be considered as copies of facts (protocol sentences) independent of theoretical contexts already implied in the formulation of the observational sentences.

Since the language applicable in science always presupposes some reference to particular facts, while the observational statements always presuppose some orientation with respect to theoretical frameworks, a further a priori presupposition of the logic of science comes to light: "convention." Conventions are needed to construct "semantical frameworks" as possible languages of science and to interpret these frameworks as applicable to languages of science with the help of a metalanguage, which is, in practice, the non-formalized language of the science already being used. Conventions are also needed to establish observational statements which could function as basic propositions for confirmation and falsification of hypotheses or theories. But what are "conventions"? If one reads the literature of logical positivism one might think that a convention is some absolutely irrational factor that precedes all reasonable discourse, because it is already presupposed by the rules of a semantical framework. A convention seems to be the same thing as a solitary and arbitrary decision, such as, for instance, the decision of a sovereign ruler who, according to Hobbes, establishes and interprets the law by the authority of his will, or still earlier in the history of nominalism, the fiat of God's will which, according to the Franciscan theologians, precedes all reasoning.

While it is true that a convention precedes all rational operations which are conceivable according to the neo-positivistic idea of reason—for conventions cannot be deduced from first principles within a calculus—neither can they be derived from empirical observation or by induction from such observation. (In fact, the neo-positivists seriously tried to reduce the so-called pragmatic dimension of the language of science, which includes the ultimate conventions about the rules of semantical frameworks and their interpretations, to an object of empirical observation by way of another, behavioral science. But this enterprise was, of course, doomed to failure, for even if it were possible to describe conventions by means of a behavioral science, this would in turn presuppose conventions embedded in the observational sentences of this description, and so on, *ad infinitum*.)

Thus, for the neo-positivistic logic of science conventions are, indeed, ultimate presuppositions which have to be acknowledged as prior to all scientific rationality. But here the question arises as to whether scientific rationality, in the sense of the logic of science (i.e., logical inferences plus observation), in fact exhausts the whole of human rationality, so that beyond its limits only the irrationality of arbitrary decisions can exist. Such a limited view of rationality could, in my opinion, be justified only if one man, alone, could at least in principle practice science. For, in this case, the conventions which, so to speak, intervene in the rational operations of cognition would indeed have to be conceived of as completely irrational personal decisions. But the very word "con-vention" (in German *Überein-kunft*) speaks against this interpretation. Indeed, the later Wittgenstein even explained his conventionalism by pointing out that one person alone cannot be said to follow a rule. Thus he has shown that conventions presuppose language games. However, language games cannot be founded by conventions in the same way that artificial semantic frameworks can. Instead, they must on their own provide the foundations for rule conventions in a communication community. Now, is it possible to point out the pre-scientific rationality of meaning conventions in a communication community? Even tacit conventions about the use of words—not to mention explicit conventions about definitions, theoretical frameworks or statements of facts in empirical science—imply an intersubjective consensus about situational meanings and the aims of practical life which can only be achieved by a mutual understanding of intentions and motivations as the very sense of the conventions. While it is true that conventions cannot be deduced from their motives, and thus cannot be justified by the logic of an axiomatic system, they must nevertheless not be conceived of as arbitrary acts of a solitary will or—what amounts to the same thing in the context of justification—as events which can only be described and explained from the outside, as determined by extra-rational motives as causes. For it is by their *intelligibility* that meaning conventions must fulfill the condition of being presupposed by a communication community as a *common* basis of interaction and world interpretation, at the same time being improved in the course of improving such interaction and world interpretation. And it is by such improvements of meaning conventions, implicit in public language games, that explicit conventions, for instance the definitions of concepts, come about.

Now the question arises whether there should not exist an intrinsic connection between the prescientific rationality of meaning conventions and the methodical *ratio* of the humanities. So far as I know, only the nearly forgotten American philosopher Josiah Royce realized this possibility of a nonscientistic and nonobjectivistic foundation of the humanities in his philosophy of "interpretation."[4] [As] Royce made it clear, indispensable conventions about the meanings of concepts needed in science presuppose that there are not only cognitive operations, such as perceptions and conceptions, which rest on an exchange between man and nature, but also cognitive operations, such as interpretation of signs, which rest on an exchange between men in a "community of interpretation."[5] This conception of Royce's which is, so to speak, a hermeneutical elaboration of the semiotical ideas of C. S. Peirce, in my opinion, provides the decisive suggestion as to the context in which conventions have their dimension of possible rationality. Conventions—so it seems to me—may be mediated by a rationality of a peculiar kind: it is not the scientific rationality of operations on objects which could be performed in a repeatable way by exchangeable human subjects, but rather the pre- and *meta-scientific rationality* of intersubjective discourse mediated by *explication of concepts* and interpretation of intentions. This dimension of reasonable discourse is inaccessible to those philosophies which proceed from methodical solipsism, that is, from the a priori presupposition that "one person alone could follow a rule," for example, that one person alone could perform scientific research, etc. Therefore, I call the presupposition that makes the dimension of the rationality of conventions accessible the *A Priori of Communication*, or rather, the *A Priori of Language Communication,* because no other communication provides the possibility of rational conventions.

My first claim in this paper is that the *logic of science*, as it was developed by the logical positivists, has not, up to now, reflected upon the fact that, after the exposure of the hidden metaphysics of its early days, it moved to the new ground of the *A Priori of Communication*. Instead of reflecting upon this new presupposition of its *conventionalist* phase, it has tacitly held on to its former presuppositions (inherited from *logical atomism* which implied methodical solipsism).[6] I will then illustrate my first thesis by displaying the consequences of methodical solipsism in the logic of science. My exposition of these consequences amounts to the assertion that methodical solipsism is one of the main reasons why the neo-positivistic logic of science has not, up to now, been able to cope with the peculiar interests and problems of the humanities, but has had to cling to the program of a scientistic reduction of the methods of the humanities to those of the natural sciences, or at least to those of the social sciences styled natural sciences. This assertion will make up the second thesis of my paper. Finally, the basis of this critique of reductive scientism as a consequence of methodological solipsism will be made explicit by my third thesis: that the *A Priori of Language Communication* provides an adequate presupposition for understanding the social function and the methodological approach of the humanities.

II. Methodical Solipsism as Metaphysical Presupposition of Logical Positivism

It might perhaps seem curious, at first sight, that modern analytical logic of science, based on semantical reconstruction of the language of science, should have *methodical solipsism* as its tacit presupposition. At first sight, the neo-Leibnizian postulate of a universal language of science lying at the ground of the Russell-Wittgenstein-Carnap program seems to be equivalent to an acknowledgement of the quasi-transcendental function of language communication as a condition of the possibility and validity of human knowledge. In particular, Carnap's transition from the language of private experience (in *Der logische Aufbau der Welt*, 1928) to the intersubjective "thing language" of "physicalism" (cf. "Die physikalische Sprache als Universalsprache der Wissenschaft," *Erkenntnis 3*, 1932) seems in principle to surmount the tradition of the *methodical solipsism* that is involved in the very foundations of traditional empiricism and positivism (and, by the way, also in that tradition of rationalistic philosophy which, from Descartes to Husserl, conceives of truths as evidence for consciousness). This view, however, is, it seems to me, unjustified. Indeed, I wish to maintain the thesis that a philosophy which postulates a physicalistic-behavioristic language for objectifying the phenomena of human intersubjectivity involves methodical solipsism to no less an extent than a philosophy that starts from the assumption that meaning and truth are matters of introspective evidence of private experiences of consciousness. The common bias of both philosophies lies in the tacit assumption that *objective* knowledge should be possible without *intersubjective* understanding by communication being presupposed. The traditional subjectivistic form of empiricism tries to realize this idea of knowledge without presupposing language as a condition of intersubjectivity at all. Modern logical (semantical) empiricism also leapfrogs the communicative function of language by postulating a language which would be a priori intersubjective by being simply objective and universal. It is, however, just this idea of intersubjectivity as warranted by objectivity that makes the neo-Leibnizian conception of a universal "thing-language" a new expression of the epistemological idea of methodical solipsism.

In order to elucidate this point let me first make some remarks about the peculiarities of formalized languages as possible realizations of the neo-positivistic idea of a universal language of science.

At the outset let us note that the formalized languages of the logic of science, in principle, cannot be used for *intersubjective communication* in the full sense of that word. It is only *sentences* about *states of affairs* (not even *statements* about *facts*!) and *logical connections* between sentences that can be formulated in these languages, but not "utterances"[7] or "speech acts"[8] because these units of ordinary language do not get their meaning exclusively from the syntactical and semantical rules of a formal system, but [also] from the context of the pragmatical use of language in concrete situations of life. Now, among those parts of speech which cannot be expressed are, above all, personal identifiers such as "I," "you," "we," etc., which immediately express the situation of intersubjective communication, and the reflection upon this situation. Such utterances, which attest the human "competence of communication" by language can, in the logic of formalized "thing-languages," only be the object of descriptions of "verbal behavior" by an observer who does not himself participate in the communication. Now, strictly speaking, a description of verbal behavior in a formalized language cannot express an *understanding* of the intentions of the persons speaking, because this always implies that these persons and the "descriptor" participate in a common language game taking regard of the communicative competence of both sides.[9] The language of science as conceived by the neo-positivistic logic of science excludes—in principle—the existence of a language game common to the subjects and to the objects of science. It has to exclude this because the very point of constructing formalized languages for scientific use is to get rid of the *hermeneutic* problems of communication, that is, of interpreting one another's intentions, by establishing a framework of language which is *a priori* an *intersubjective* one and so provides the conditions of the possibility of objective knowledge. In short, the logically reconstructed language of science is destined for describing and explaining a world of pure objects; it is not suited to express communication which is the intersubjective dimension of language.

However, one could perhaps still ask what all this should have to do with methodical solipsism as an ultimate presupposition of thinking. I have to concede that the logic of science would not, in fact, imply methodical solipsism if it were to reflect upon two things: first, that even the constructor, let alone the user, of a formalized language of science already presupposes communication, in the full sense of understanding human intentions, for bringing about those conventions that are needed for introducing and testing the formalized languages; second, that human beings, so long as they are considered as possible partners of communication, and so of interaction, cannot be reduced to objects of description and/or explanation of their behavior by means of formalized languages, but have to be dealt with in the context of a language game which is, in principle, common to the subjects and to the objects of science (i.e., the humanities).

The logical positivists would presumably not deny the first of these two points. Particularly in the school's recent stages, when the basic need for conventions could no longer be overlooked, it has begun to move in this direction. But still there are intrinsic reasons that prevent it from taking all the consequences of the *A Priori of Communication* into account. The main such reason is the idea of a unified science, originally connected with the idea of the universal language. It is this reason that prevents logical positivism from methodically reflecting upon the intersubjective communication presupposed by constructive semantics in the manner of a transcendental pragmatics that does not reduce the intersubjective dimension of communication to "verbal behavior." And it is this same reason that prevents logical positivism from acknowledging as genuine the methods of understanding in the humanities, and so prevents it from acknowledging that human beings cannot be reduced to objects of description and/or explanation of their behavior by means of formalized languages.

If one really hopes to objectify the whole world, including the dimension of communication, by a language of a unified science, then one must, strictly speaking, cling to the a priori of methodical solipsism, for the totalization of the idea of scientific objectivity implies that the subject of the objectifying science could, in principle, practice science without being a member of a communication community. He should, on this view, be able to follow the rules of the universal "thing-language" as if they were rules of a "private language"—to speak as the later Wittgenstein does. It is well known that the later Wittgenstein denied this possibility; and, in my opinion, he has, indeed, refuted "methodical solipsism" with his notion of public "language games" as presuppositions of all intentionality of actions and cognitions. But the neo-positivistic "logic of unified science," as it is represented for instance by Hempel, Nagel, and Stegmüller, has not, up to now, drawn epistemological consequences from Wittgenstein's refutation of "methodical solipsism." Rather it clings to the idea of a universal "thing-language" as developed in the *Tractatus Logico-Philosophicus* of the younger Wittgenstein. . . .

III. Methodical Solipsism as Presupposition of the Neo-Positivist Idea of "Understanding"

I will now go on to illustrate my first thesis by giving a critical sketch of the neo-positivist treatment of the humanities, especially of the old question about the relationship between nomological explanations and the understanding of meaning-intentions. Strictly speaking, it is not quite correct to speak of a neo-positivistic treatment of the humanities because the very heart of the humanities, *philology* in a broad sense, was not treated but simply ignored in the "logic of unified science." As has still to be shown, this exclusion is rather characteristic, and instructive with regard to the neo-positivists' strategy of argument. Nevertheless, there remains the fact that the "social sciences," and within their context also history, had to be dealt with by the logical positivists. In this context, they had also to discuss "understanding" which was claimed by Droysen, Dilthey, Croce, Collingwood and other philosophers to be the very method of the "Geisteswissenschaften."[10] Now, how did they proceed in dealing with "understanding"? Let us at this point take a closer look at their *strategy of argument.*

The first thing which strikes one upon reading the discussions by, say, O. Neurath, C. G. Hempel, P. Oppenheim, E. Nagel, Th. Abel, and W. Stegmüller,[11] is the fact that they do not at all discuss the *understanding of language-signs*, of statements, or whole texts of science, philosophy or literature. This is curious if one remembers the fact that the modern *logic of science* is, according to their own method, essentially an *analysis of language* which, for instance, transforms the older positivistic logic of explanation[12] into the *formal mode*, according to which it is no longer events that are explained by laws and causes, but sentences making up the *explanandum* that are deduced from sentences making up the *explanans*. Thus, the first thing analytic philosophers themselves do is always to *explicate* the concepts of traditional philosophy by reconstructing their semantical framework. But shouldn't this enterprise stand in close connection with the activity of those sciences that *interpret* texts, for instance, the history of science? That is what one might ask as an outsider; but one gets no answer to this question, for, as I have already mentioned, the neo-positivist logic of science does not deal with the philological, or, to use another term, with the hermeeutical, sciences. (I will return to this later on, with a conjecture as to the reasons why the neo-positivists' analyses of language overlook their most congenial relatives among the sciences, in a broad sense.)

But what about *understanding of actions* in history and sociology? As an outsider, again, one might think that this kind of understanding should itself stand in close connection with an *understanding of signs and texts* because ultimately the operation of understanding is directed to meaning as it is expressed by texts, works or actions, more or less according to the meaning-intentions of their authors.[13] One could here, perhaps, follow the later Wittgenstein and take it as a heuristic horizon that speech, actions and interpretations as meaning-intentions are always "interwoven" in *language-games* as "forms of life." One might thus be led to think that the historians and sociologists had to inquire into actions, institutions, etc., in a way similar to that in which philologists inquire into texts, in order to understand forms of life by interpreting the meaning of the goal-setting and the value-systems expressed by actions and institutions. Elaborated understanding of this kind is, indeed, needed not only for answering the question *why* certain actions or institutions came about but for answering the earlier question as to *what* is given: that is, as to what those actions (especially collective ones) and institutions are that are to be identified and described within a context of an historical situation and a socio-cultural form of life. Thus answering "what?" questions and answering teleological "why?" questions seems to be interwoven in historico-sociological descriptions with the so-called "hermeneutic circle" which also makes up the methodical rule of text interpretation. Sometimes the historian might even be interested in actions as supplements of texts; thus for instance, he could inquire into the political actions of Martin Luther as being elucidations or, perhaps also, contradictions of his theological writings. All these possibilities of methodical interpretation—which have nothing to do with *causal explanation*—have already been explored in a rich literature extending from Schleiermacher, Boeckh, Droysen to Dilthey, Weber, Croce, Collingwood, Rothacker, Gadamer, Betti and others.[14] And, as I have already mentioned, the later Wittgenstein has also given an important hint as to the possibility of a hermeneutic approach in sociology, as P. Winch, for instance has shown.[15] But if one hopes to find the neo-positivists dealing with this kind of understanding in history and sociology, one is once again disappointed. True, they do speak about the "so-called theoreticians of *understanding* or *Verstehen* in the *Geisteswissenschaften*" and they try to come to terms with these people, but just at the beginning of the hoped-for discussion they introduce a rather cunning presupposition, namely: that the "theoreticians of the *Geisteswissenschaften*" conceive of understanding (*Verstehen*) as a method that competes with "covering law explanation" by appealing instead to higher, intuitive insights.[16] Thereby they assume that *understanding*, if it were a *method* of cognition, would answer the same kinds of questions as *explanation*, the only difference between the two operations being that understanding would have the additional ambition of reaching the same goal as explanation by a shortcut, so to speak. Having introduced these presuppositions—which, by the way, show that they are unable to conceive of any other leading interest of knowing[17] than that of the natural sciences—they start elaborating their own theory of "the operation called 'Verstehen'. . . ."[18]

. . . I do not, of course, wish to deny that empathy ("*Einfühlung*" as Herder said; or "*Nacherleben*" as Dilthey said) is an important ingredient of understanding, but, as even Dilthey maintained, it has to be integrated into, and checked by, the proper methods and contexts of understanding, which have been distinguished and diligently described in hermeneutics, particularly since Schleiermacher and Boeckh.[19] These canonical methods, as for instance, grammatical interpretation, interpretation in the light of literary genre or topic, interpretation of single utterances of a work by the whole of it, and vice versa, historical interpretation, psychological-biographical interpretation, in themselves already provide contexts in which the "divinations of understanding" (Hamann, Schleiermacher) are continually elaborated and corrected by way of a fruitful counterchecking of a priori and a posteriori, subjective and objective, universal and empirical, presuppositions of understanding. These traditional canons of interpretation may, today, be supplemented by sophisticated methods of, for instance, semiotical analysis, but this does not mean that understanding should be reduced to a heuristic device in the context of covering-law explanation, in order to become controllable, and thus respectable, as a rational method of cognition. How misleading this claim of the logic of unified science is may be shown by two further arguments.

1. Hempel and Oppenheim take it for granted that, in the case of intentionally goal-directed actions, one has only two alternative ways of analyzing these phenomena.[20] Either one has to start a teleological analysis, presupposing the goal as a *causa finalis* which can determine people's actions from the future, *or* one must replace goals by *causal motives*, supposing for every single intended goal a corresponding wish or will to reach just this goal, thus providing antecedent conditions for a covering-law explanation. Hempel and Oppenheim, of course, decide in favor of the second alternative, but what is interesting in our context is the reason they give for this decision: if the motive were to be conceived as a goal lying in the future, they argue, we could not deal with cases where the goal was not attained at all.

Now, this argument, from my point of view, again shows that the neo-positivists are unable a priori to conceive of a *leading interest of cognition* other than *causal explanation*. For, the teleological alternative to their own approach, as they conceive of it, is only another type of causal explanation. If they could imagine a genuine interest in understanding goals as motives they would see that, even in the case where goals have not been reached, historians may, nevertheless, be concerned with understanding the goals as such, and not just the causes of what really happened. Human goals, for example social or political programs, even if not realized, may be the topic of detailed interpretation as possibilities of life to be discussed and eventually realized by later generations. From this one may realize that it is, indeed, possible and necessary for hermeneutical sciences to separate human motives *qua* goals from factual actions and to treat them like meaning-intentions in texts. But even if, as in history and sociology, one is primarily interested in *explaining why* certain actions (or forbearances!) take place, it is far from being self-evident that hermeneutical methods could be dispensed with and understanding of reasons be reduced to *explanation by causal motives*. The problem here is whether those volitional cognitive complexes which may be formed out of wishes to reach some goals and beliefs such that, in a certain situation, certain actions become necessary and sufficient means for reaching those goals, may be considered as antecedent conditions in the sense of the Hempel-Oppenheim scheme. The difficulty here lies in the fact that the wishes and beliefs can only be defined with reference to their intentional objects. Thus they are internally (conceptually) connected with the "explanandum," whereas in genuine causal explanation an external (contingent) relation between the antecedent conditions and the explanandum is presupposed, and therefore an *empirical law*, instead of a *practical inference of understanding*, is required in order to bridge the gulf between the explanandum and the antecedent conditions. It may be objected that, within the context of an explanation, it is not the internal relation between wishes or beliefs and their intentional objects that is relevant, but the external relation between the occurrences of wishes and beliefs on the one hand and the explanandum on the other. But this objection overlooks the fact [that]—in contradistinction to natural causes—the relevant occurrences of wishes and beliefs cannot be identified (or verified) without presupposing the internal relation to the explanandum as intentional object. And the explanandum, in turn, cannot be identified (verified) as a certain action without already presupposing the intentions by which the "antecedent conditions" are defined.[21] If one takes into consideration that, in any case, goal-directed action presupposes for its realization a genuine causal connection, one may wonder whether the search for such connections and thus for genuine natural laws is not obscured by claiming that all possible human intentions are possible causes within the context of covering-law explanations. But even if this would be allowable, it would by no means prove that *hermeneutical* methods could be dispensed with, for in order to delineate the *volitional-cognitive complex* which is said to function as cause within the context of an explanation one has first to understand the corresponding human intentions, and for this one has to reconstruct the whole context of the corresponding forms of life, including value systems, world views, and so on. The unintended irony of Hempel's and Oppenheim's conception of causal motives lies in the fact that precisely as many different wishes and beliefs must be available as causes as were previously discovered by methodical efforts of understanding.

2. Our last hint, as to the reconstruction of whole forms of life including world views, may lead us to a further criticism of the whole conception of understanding as empathy, as it is presupposed in neo-positivism. The tacit presupposition of applying empathy as a paradigm for understanding is the idea of *empirical data* as results of a description which would precede all *understanding* as well as *explaining*. Among all the empirical data provided by description—so they would have us think—there are simply some kinds which may be internalized by empathy and thus connected by so-called understanding. This positivistic idea of experience, stemming from Hume, J. S. Mill and Mach, completely overlooks the fact that understanding must be presupposed in order to describe the experienced data of the world *as something*, that is, for answering the question *what* a thing is. This primary understanding of the data of the world is internally connected with understanding human language and forms of life. This circumstance may be neglected in the case of natural science because here the fundamental world-interpretation which precedes all single explanations (as answers to the question of why this or that is the case) is generally not called into question except, perhaps, in a so-called fundamental crisis of normal science.[22] In the case of the humanities, however, such a fundamental crisis is, in a sense, the normal situation, for here one has always to understand human utterances, works, and actions in the light of their world-interpretation. On the other hand, one also has to interpret the data of the world as those of a historical "*Lebenswelt*" (E. Husserl) in the light of human language games and forms of life. It is just in this fruitful *circle of a transcendental hermeneutic* that, in my opinion, the point of convergence between Dilthey, Heidegger, and the later Wittgenstein is to be sought. One thus sees that the concept of empathy does not throw much light upon the operation called "Verstehen." Taken in psychologistic isolation, as is presupposed by the neo-positivists, it rather leads to overlooking the elementary faculty of *sign-understanding* or *communicative experience* which is at the center of all interpretation in the humanities. It is much more useful for hermeneutics to start from "pragmatical understanding" of signs, actions and circumstances of a situation within the context of a "common sphere" of life, as the later Dilthey did.[23] If one does so, one has however to take into account that Dilthey's

"pragmatical understanding," which comes near to Wittgenstein's idea of understanding within a language game, is not yet understanding in the sense of the humanities, as hermeneutic sciences. Only if the "pragmatical understanding" within the "common sphere" of life becomes doubtful, for example when a crisis in understanding religious or legal traditions comes about, does *methodical understanding* in the sense of hermeneutics arise, according to Dilthey.[24] And now, when the problem is no longer understanding within the framework of an established language game or "common sphere," but rather finding the access to a foreign language game as a foreign form of life, empathy (*Einfühlung*), as a key to the phenomena of *sense-expression*, also fulfills its heuristic function within the context of hermeneutic methods, as already suggested.[25]

It is now time to close this criticism by asking the question: why, after all, are the neo-positivists prevented from coping with the humanities by those shortcomings which I have tried to reveal? This question may, as a function of my criticism, be divided into three parts.

1) Why do the neo-positivists ignore, in their "logic of science," *philology* in the broadest sense as the heart of the humanities considered as hermeneutic sciences? Why, in particular, do they overlook the fact that these empirico-hermeneutic sciences stand in a close connection to their own meta-scientific business of reconstructing the language of science?

2) Why do the neo-positivists, in the historical and in the social sciences, from the outset overlook the genuine *interest in understanding goals and reasons* as being different from the interest in causal explanation? In other words: why do they beg the question in their discussion with the "theoreticians of understanding" by presupposing that explanation is the aim of understanding, and thus bring about the cup-of-coffee theory of understanding.

3) Why, finally, do the logical positivists overlook the fact that the function of understanding lies not only in answering *why*-questions but, more fundamentally, in answering *what*-questions, and that answering these questions is "interwoven" with answering questions as to the meaning of language-signs?

I think that these three questions point to three fundamental shortcomings of neo-positivism that have this in common: they spring from a lack of reflection upon the fact that all cognition of objects presupposes understanding as a means of intersubjective communication. The most curious aspect of this lack of reflection lies in the fact that even the idea of constructing semantical frameworks (as a means of fixing, a priori, the ontological categories implied in a language of science), that even this method of language analysis has not prevented logical positivists from excluding all genuine interest of understanding from their methodology of possible sciences. They, so to speak, try to anticipate the results of intersubjective understanding once and for all in their semantic frameworks, leaving to science only the description and explanation of objective data within the framework they have established. But even this practice would be all right if they were to reflect upon the fact that constructing semantical frameworks has to be conceived as only an indirect way[26] of improving intersubjective communication—a way that always remains dependent upon, and indebted to, understanding and interpreting meaning within the context of communication in natural languages. If they did reflect upon this thoroughly, they would have to acknowledge that behind the construction of semantical frameworks there stand not just irrational *ad hoc* conventions, but long chains of rational discourse mediated by interpretation and criticism of the tradition of philosophy and science. And by reflecting upon this fact they would, furthermore, have to acknowledge that there are "sciences" in a broader sense of the word which make up a continuum with their own meta-scientific language analysis by understanding and interpreting the form and the context of traditional languages. They would thus not try to reduce understanding to an auxiliary function of scientific explanation, as they do in the cup-of-coffee theory, but would rather see the meta-scientific function of understanding already presupposed in all description and explanation of science.

By a consideration of these criticisms, in my opinion, an answer is suggested to our question regarding the shortcomings of the logic of unified science with respect to the humanities: the answer was already anticipated by our first thesis and is only to be illustrated in this paragraph. Methodical solipsism is, so far as I can see, the ultimate, tacit presupposition of the positivists' idea of cognition. It is for this reason that they can only deal with cognition by inference and observation; that is, with cognition as an exchange between man and the world of objects, but not with cognition as understanding and interpretation, that is, primarily with cognition as an exchange between men in a communication-community.

IV. The A Priori of Communication and the Foundation of the Humanities

I think that by the preceding explication of my two initial theses concerning methodical solipsism and its consequences in the philosophy of science, I have already sufficiently suggested my own position to the point where I can now be brief in the exposition of my third thesis: that the *A Priori of Language Communication* is, in fact, the adequate basis for understanding the social function and the methodology of the humanities. I will try to divide this thesis into two partial theses, or figures of argument, the first dealing with intersubjective communication as the ideal frame of the humanities, the second one introducing a methodological restriction on pure hermeneutics, and so perhaps on the humanities themselves, in favor of critical social science.

My first partial thesis starts from the fact that natural science itself, that is, describing and explaining objective spatio-temporal events, presupposes understanding and interpretation in a communication-community, because one man alone cannot follow a rule and thus cannot practice science. From this it follows that understanding and interpretation as means of communication fulfil a complementary function to description and explanation. This means, taking "complementarity" in the sense of N. Bohr, that cognition by objectifying and cognition as intersubjective understanding supplement and exclude one another at the same time. You can test this phenomenon of *complementarity* in every discussion by trying to "reduce" your partner's utterances to mere verbal behavior (say, in the sense of Skinner). If you succeed in objectifying them in this way, you will lose your partner as a communication-partner and you will need other partners (not yet objectified) to whom to tell the results of your behavioral science. From this I conclude that philosophy of science in a broad sense, including the humanities, has to take into account two quite different, but complementary, leading interests of cognition. Only one of them is that of science in the narrow sense of the modern logic of science, that is, the leading interest of describing and explaining objectified data of the world. I would assume a close connection between this interest of cognition and instrumental labor, that is, operating upon nature as an environment to be adapted to by experimental behavior, learning by trial and error, and so on. In any event, the relation of scientific cognition in this sense to the practice of life is, nowadays, a *technological* one. Now, the other leading interest of cognition, complementary to the interest of an objectifying science, is, in my opinion, the *interest in improving communication in its own dimension of intersubjectivity.*

One has to stress this last remark in our age of science because most people may perhaps be disposed to think that the rational improvement of communication can also be brought about only by objectifying communication itself and by explaining its functions, as is done partly by information theory and, in a sense, also by linguistics.[27] But I do not think that these narrowly scientific means are the only ways of improving intersubjective communication. In any case, these methods are not the way in which the humanities improve communication. They do so not by objectifying and explaining instruments and functions of communication but by elaborating the very understanding of meaning by methods of interpretation. That there is a decisive difference between this kind of hermeneutic rationalizing of communication and scientific objectifying becomes clear by reflection on the fact that all the objectifying sciences themselves, including linguistics, already presuppose the result of rationalized intersubjective conventions about the meanings of their language and about the aims of their practice. Thus, the hermeneutic preliminaries to meaning-conventions are conditions of the possibility and validity of scientific objectivity and, for this reason, cannot themselves be objective in the same sense that the results of science have to be. Explication of conceptual meanings, for instance, is a precondition for scientific objectivity and therefore cannot presuppose that exchangeability and repeatability of subjective operations of cognition which it is predestined to make possible. Instead, it must engage in creative interpretation of ordinary language and of those contexts—mostly of philosophical character—in which the relevant conceptual meanings are already articulated. If one conceives of hermeneutics from this meta-scientific point of view, it becomes clear that the conjectures of understanding cannot be tested in the same way as explanatory hypotheses can. They cannot themselves presuppose fixed meaning-conventions and standards of significance, but in the long run the pragmatic criterion of their validity may be found in their contribution to the formation of meaning-conventions in the interpretation-community.

This leads us to the question of the practical significance of the humanities. If the relation between the objectifying sciences and the practice of life is a technological one, then the relation between the humanities and the practice of life must also, in my opinion, provide a complementary orientation with regard to technology. This may be performed by the humanities in a twofold manner: first, in a narrower sense, by way of hermeneutics, simply ensuring the understanding of meaning-intentions among people, and not least between scientists and technicians, and between these experts and society as a whole (here, it seems to me, the need for a comprehensive philosophy and history of science as a new, and even paradigmatic, branch of the humanities actually arises); second, in a broader sense, by suggesting world-views and ways of life, that is, ultimate values and possible aims of practice which could provide criteria for discussions and conventions about the requirements of a good life, including the very application of science and technology. And at this point, I would think, all our historical research, all our study of past ages and foreign cultures ought to contribute its results to the shaping and reshaping of an educated public opinion. I cannot imagine that this function of the humanities could be replaced at any time by reducing understanding and interpretation to the method of objectifying science, as is suggested by positivism. On the contrary, I am inclined to think that the need for *intersubjective understanding* in the narrow sense, as well as in the broad sense of goal-orientation, will grow in direct proportion to the growth of science and technology as primary productive forces of modern industrial society.

So much for the first part of my thesis about the *A Priori of Communication* as the basis and frame for understanding the function of the humanities. I will call this first part, for the sake of brevity, the *thesis of complementarity*, and I explicitly state my claim that this thesis refutes every kind of *scientific reductionism*. Nevertheless, I have still to restrict this approach to the humanities by setting forth another thesis, or figure of argument.

It is not literally true that the humanities should never objectify human behavior, that they should, so to speak, deal with men only as co-subjects of communication. Perhaps the closest approximation to this idea which I have summarized in the complementarity thesis, is text-interpretation as the heart of the hermeneutic sciences.

Texts, as so-called "objects" of interpretation, are, in the last analysis, only objectified manifestations of the meaning-intentions of their authors and thus of a communication between human beings which surmounts, so to speak, space and time as the very realm of objectification. But this function of texts in the humanistic dialogue of the great spirits of all ages (to speak with Petrarch and P. Bembo) is already essentially modified if texts are only taken as *documents* ("sources" or "remains") by which historians get information about spatio-temporal events. For history must objectify men and their actions in a spatio-temporal frame, and so must a fortiori the generalizing social sciences. It also has to be conceded that history and the social sciences ask not only for the meaning and the reasons of actions and institutions, but also ask for causes of what, in fact, happened or generally happens with men. Now the question arises as to how to deal with these phenomena from the point of view of a philosophy of the humanities.

To prepare for an appropriate answer to this question I will first exclude one type of social science which I would really not consider as an example for the concept of humanities. I mean those behavioral sciences which, in fact, are only interested in causal of statistical explanations and thus have become the basis for social engineering. I am not so much of a romantic as to think that these sciences could be dispensed with in a modern industrial society. Men have to calculate and even technically to manipulate their social behavior in order to survive as members of social systems. But this very concession has to be supplemented, in my opinion, by the urgent demand that all social technology has to be counterchecked by an improvement of intersubjective understanding, complementary to objectifying and manipulating men. Thus the narrowly scientific and technological type of social sciences has itself to be supplemented by another type of *humanistic social science* in order to prevent the very present danger of a technocracy.[28] I might add that, fortunately, in most cases, the human objects of science and social technology show that they are not mere natural objects in their relations to science. If they are able to understand the very theories by which their behavior is objectified and explained, they are able to join, at least in principle, the communication-community of the scientists and social engineers and thus they may emancipate themselves from the status of mere objects of science and technology. I shall come back to this later.

Nevertheless, even a critical and emancipatory type of social science,[29] including history, has to make use not only of understanding meaning-intentions but also of quasi-naturalistic causal explanation within the framework of a historical objectification of human life. The reason for this lies simply in the fact that men are still natural beings, and do not (yet!) really make or shape their own history as a result of their conscious and responsible decisions, but rather undergo history as a result of causally determined processes which evade the control of consciousness. So, in many aspects of their personal lives, and even more so of their social and historical lives, they themselves—or their behavior—lend themselves to being objectified and explained in a quasi-naturalistic way. What, however, does this mean? I now have to introduce the second half of my own conception of an adequate foundation of the humanities, that is, a figure of argument, or of thought, which may supplement and, in a sense, restrict, the thesis of the complementarity of explanation and understanding. (But it has to be noticed that the following restriction of the complementarity thesis presupposes the complementarity of understanding and explanation as an ideal model of what, in fact, must be anticipated in every genuine communication. Only a philosophy which starts out from that idealized distinction may win an adequate idea of what it means to treat human beings as quasi-natural objects of description and quasi-explanation, as is, in fact, possible and necessary; whereas a scientistic philosophy which derives from a naive totalization of our interest in causal explanation does not even *see* a problem in the transition from understanding to quasi-explanation, as may be concluded from Hempel's treatment of pathological behavior explaining as a paradigm for human science.)

We all know by experience that one sometimes can—and even must—unmask hidden motives of human beings, motives hidden to the agents themselves. This can take place in the middle of a conversation, and when that happens, we cannot help suspending the actual intersubjective communication to some extent or for some time, and reduce our partner to an object of description and of quasi-causal explanation. Nevertheless, this need not be the beginning of a natural science of human behavior in the service of social technology, although it, doubtless, may be (for instance in the case of a conditioning psychology which is apt to reduce education to mere drill). There exists, however, quite another possibility—the possibility, so to speak, of the application of quasi-*explanation* in the service of *emancipation*. In order to illustrate this I shall try to give a rough sketch of my conception of the methodology of psychoanalysis, the controversial details of the doctrine being of minor interest in this context.

S. Freud himself, as a physician, tried to understand his method as a new branch of natural science, later to be worked out completely in terms of physiology. And, in fact, there is a good deal of causal explanation according to presupposed drive-mechanisms in his theory, not to speak of the fact that the analyst always has to suspend, in a sense, the normal situation of intersubjective communication with respect to the patient, by objectifying his behavior, especially his neurotic symptoms. Nevertheless, there are, besides this, quite different features of the method which may be characterized as pre-eminently hermeneutic ones. Thus the analyst may never completely break off communication with the analysand, and, in a sense, he even tries to understand and interpret phenomena which a normal hermeneutician would never consider as understandable at all: for instance, the symbolic language of dreams and the purposeful strategy of evading conflicts by taking refuge in illness and, generally, the subconscious processing of experiences reaching back to the earliest days of childhood. So it is not surprising that many reflective psychoanalysts and philosophers, especially of the phenomenological stripe, claimed psychoanalysis to be a hermeneutical method, more precisely a method going beyond normal hermeneutics in the sense of a "depth hermeneutic" (*Tiefenhermeneutik*).

Now, I myself have come to the conclusion that psychoanalysis is neither a natural science nor a purely hermeneutical science. Rather, it incorporates a peculiar methodological model which constitutes the very heart of a branch of humanistic social science which I would call *critical-emancipatory* social science. The point of the model is, in my opinion, the *dialectical mediation of communicative understanding*—especially human self-understanding—by the quasi-naturalistic objectification and explanation of human behavior and human history.[30] It is true that the analyst has to objectify the behavior and the life story of the analysand as a quasi-determined section of nature, and he is, so to speak, entitled to this suspending of intersubjective communication by the fact that the patient is not able to communicate about his illness because he is undergoing a partial splitting off or estrangement of his true motives. He himself has, so to speak, objectified these contents of a "virtual communication" by repressing them into the reified pseudo-language of neurotical symptoms. Precisely to the extent that the patient undergoes, for instance, neurotic compulsion in his behavior, he presents himself as an object for causal explanation. But notwithstanding this quasi-naturalistic approach, the analyst, at the same time, tries to *understand* the reactions and the life-story of the patient as—in a way—meaningful, and even as resting on good reasons. He not only does so for himself, but he provokes self-reflection and, so to speak, reorganization of self-understanding in his patient. To that extent he is not concerned with objectifying a human being but, quite on the contrary, with rebuilding his autonomy as a subject of social interaction and intersubjective communication. The proper aim of psychoanalysis as a method—this is the crucial point, in my opinion—does not lie in the nomological deduction of predictions which could be tested by observation, but in the restitution of communication between the analyst and the analysand on a higher level. Thus the object of the analysis should himself confirm the hypotheses of the analyst and even supplement them by his self-understanding. Of course, the verification of the diagnosis would also lie in the elimination of the neurotic symptoms, but this means that the very object of causal explanation would be replaced by a new behavior, no longer compulsive, and therefore *understandable*.

I think that this methodological pattern of *dialectically mediating communicative understanding by methods of causal explanation* is, in fact, the model for a philosophical understanding of all those types of *critical social science* which have their relation to the practice of life, not in the realm of social engineering, but in provoking public self-reflection and in the emancipation of men as subjects. In the light of this idea, I would see, especially, the critique of ideology founded by Marx. By changing over from personal life to the life of the society, of course, a host of new problems arise;[31] nevertheless, the methodological analogies are striking. Within the frame of this paper I can mention only one point, which Habermas has stressed in his "Erkenntnis und Interesse."[32] *Psychoanalysis* as well as *critique* in the sense of Marx pre-suppose as their theoretical basis not a universal deductive-nomological model, such as natural science since Newton has sought to realize as its ideal of knowledge. Rather, they presuppose the construction of a story of self-estrangement and possible emancipation, be it of personal life, be it of human history, and these stories must not be conceived as independent of one another, but rather as dialectically mediated by one another. Perhaps it is not unnecessary to point out that the postulated construction of a story as the basis of a *narrative explanation*[33] and understanding of human self-estrangement and liberation, needs not have the character of an objectivist dogma in the sense of Popper's *historicism*. It should rather be a hypothetical sketch which remains within the criticism frame of intersubjective communication and, so far as emancipatory practice is concerned, has the character of a proposal. From this one can conclude, I think, that the *A Priori of Language Communication*—and of the indefinitive community of interpretation—is, in fact, the basis not only for the *thesis of complementarity* of understanding and explanation but also for the *thesis of dialectic mediation* of understanding. And thus it provides, I believe, the very foundation of the humanities.

NOTES

1. Cf. the following of my papers: 'Die Entfaltung der 'sprachanalytischen' Philosophie und das Problem der 'Geisteswissenschaften',' in *Philos. Jahrbuch*, 72. Jg. (1965), pp. 239-89 (English trans.: 'Analytic Philosophy of Language and the 'Geisteswissenschaften',' in *Foundations of Language*, Suppl. series, vol. 5, Dordrecht-Holland, 1967); 'Wittgenstein und das Problem des hermeneutischen Verstehens,' in *Zeitschrift für Thelogie und Kirche*, 63. Jg. (1966), pp. 49–87; 'Szientistik, Her-

meneutik, Ideologiekritik: Entwurf einer Wissenschaftslehre in erkenntnisanthro-pologischer Sicht,' in *Wiener Jahrbuch f. Philosophie*, Bd. I (1968), pp. 15–45 (shortened version in *Man and World*, 1968); 'Die erkenntnisanthropologische Funktion der Kommunikationsgemeinschaft und die Grundlagen der Hermeneutik,' in S. Moser (ed.), *Information und Kommunikation*, München/Wien (1968); 'Szientismus oder transzendentale Hermeneutik ? Zur Frage nach dem Subjekt der Zeicheninterpretation in der Semiotik des Pragmatismus,' in *Hermeneutik und Dialektik*, Festschrift f. H. G. Gadamer, Tübingen (1970), Bd. I, pp. 105–44; 'Die Kommunikationsgemeinschaft als transzendentale Voraussetzung der Sozialwissenschaften,' in *Neue Hefte für Philosophie*, H. 2/3 (1972), pp. 1–40. Cf. further G. Radnitzky, *Contemporary Schools of Metascience*, 2nd vol.: 'Continental Schools,' 2nd Göteborg (1970).

2. The difference between Leibniz and the Neo-Leibnizianism of the founders of neo-positivism essentially lies in the fact that the latter do not take over Leibniz' idea that in the light of God's mind also the contingent truths may be demonstrated a priori. Nevertheless Carnap's Logicism and Syntacticism comes often close to the point of a model-Platonism which loses all empirical content.

3. Cf. L. Couturat, *La Logique de Leibniz*, Paris (1901); L. Couturat (ed.), *Opuscules et fragments inédits de Leibniz*, Paris (1903).

4. See L. Wittgenstein, *Philosophical Investigations*, I, par. 199.

5. See J. Royce, *The Problem of Christianity*, New York (1913), vol. 2, pp. 146 ff. Cf. K. O. Apel, 'Szientismus oder transzendentale Hermeneutik?' *loc. cit.* (note 1).

6. For an interpretation of the internal connection of methodical solipsism with the thesis of extensionality within logical atomism, see K. O. Apel, *Analytic Philosophy of Language* (s. note 1).

7. Cf. Y. Bar-Hillel, *Aspects of Language*, Jerusalem (1970), p. 364 ff.

8. Cf. J. R. Searle, *Speech Acts*, Cambridge, Mass. (1969).

9. I am here indebted to the ideas of P. Winch, *The Idea of a Social Science and Its Relation to Philosophy*, London (1958), and to papers of J. Habermas concerning the idea of communication competence (e.g., J. Habermas and N. Luhmann, *Theorie der Gesellschaft oder Sozialtechnologie?* Frankfurt (1971), pp. 101–141). Cf. also my booklet, *Analytic Philosophy of Language and the 'Geisteswissenschaften,'* *loc. cit.* (note 1).

10. Cf. K. O. Apel, 'Das Verstehen. Eine Problemgeschichte als Begriffsgeschichte,' in *Archiv f. Begriffsgeschichte*, Bd. I, Bonn (1955), pp. 142–199; cf. further my article, 'Verstehen,' in J. Ritter (ed.), *Historisches Wörterbuch der Philosophie* (forthcoming).

11. W. Stegmüller has summarized these discussions in his book *Resultate und Probleme der analytischen Philosophie und Wissenschaftstheorie*, Bd. I: 'Erklärung und Begründung,' München-Wien-New York (1969).

12. See, for instance, the following definition of A. Comte: 'L'explication des faits . . . n'est plus désormais que la liaison établie entre les divers phénomènes particuliers et quelques faits généraux, dont les progrès de la science tendent de plus à diminuer le nombre' (*Cours de Philosophie positive*, tom. I, 1ère lec.). J. S. Mill defines: 'An individual fact is said to be explained, by pointing out its cause, that is, by stating the law or laws of causation, of which its production is an instance' (*A System of Logic* (1943), Bk. III, Ch. 11, sect. 1).

13. The difference between the meaning-intentions of the author and the expressed meaning of texts, works, or actions constitutes one of the main problems of hermeneutics.

14. See note 10.

15. See note 9.

16. So does, for instance, W. Stegmüller (*l.c.*, p. 300 ff.) following Th. Abel and C. G. Hempel. The standard presupposition of these authors is formulated by Stegmüller as follows (trans. by K. O. Apel): 'The method in question, if it is not to be dismissed as something a priori completely unclear, therefore must be characterized as a procedure for acquiring appropriate explanations, i.e. for acquiring the hypotheses required by those explanations or non-hypothetical insights' (*l.c.*, p. 362).

17. This term ('Erkenntnisinteresse') was introduced by J. Habermas and myself in order to designate a transcendental condition of the possibility and validity of knowledge within the framework of 'Wissenschaftstheorie in erkenntnisanthropologischer Sicht.' So far the 'leading interest of knowing' is not an *external* motivation which would be only psychologically interesting but an *internal* motivation which constitutes the meaning of different questions and so of different possible answers in explanatory and hermeneutic science respectively. See J. Habermas' 'Erkenntnis und Interesse' in *Wissenschaft und Technik als Ideologie*, Frankfurt a/M. (1968), and his elaboration upon this in his book *Erkenntnis und Interesse*, Frankfurt a/M. (1968). Cf. K. O. Apel, *Analytic Philosophy of Language and the 'Geisteswissenschaften,'* *loc. cit.*, and 'Szientistik, Hermeneutik, Ideologiekritik: Entwurf einer Wissenschaftslehre in erkenntnisanthropologischer Sicht,' *loc. cit.* (note 1). Cf. also G. Radnitzky, *loc. cit.* (note 1).

18. Cf. Th. Abel, 'The Operation called 'Verstehen',' in H. Feigl and M. Brodbeck (eds.), *Readings in the Philosophy of Science*, New York (1953).

19. For a comprehensive historical account of hermeneutics, see J. Wach, *Das Verstehen*, 3 vols. Tübingen (1926–33). See further the classical account by W. Dilthey, 'Die Entstehung der Hermeneutik' in *Gesammelte Schriften*, Bd. V, pp. 233 ff.

20. See C. G. Hempel and P. Oppenheim, 'Theory of Scientific Explanation,' in *Philosophy of Science*, vol. 15 (1948), reprinted in H. Feigl and M. Brodbeck (eds.), *loc. cit.*; cf. Stegmüller, *loc. cit.*, pp. 329 ff. and 530 ff.

21. Cf. G. H. Von Wright, *Explanation and Understanding*, Ithaca, N.Y. (1971) Ch. III.

22. Cf. Th. Kuhn, *The Structure of Scientific Revolutions*, Chicago (1962). In the context of a confrontation of K. Popper's and his own view of science, Th. S. Kuhn sets the following provocative thesis: 'In a sense, to turn Sir Karl's view on its head, it is precisely the abandonment of critical discourse that marks the transition to a science. Once a field has made that transition, critical discourse recurs only at moments of crisis when the bases of the field are again in jeopardy. Only when they must choose between competing theories do scientists behave like philosophers' (in I. Lacatos and A. Musgrave (eds.), *Criticism and the Growth of Knowledge*, Cambridge (1970), p. 6f.) It is precisely this transition to 'normal science' that is, in my opinion, impossible for the humanities because innovative understanding of the world of human affairs in the light of critical discussion belongs to their very method of cognition.

23. See W. Dilthey, *Gesammelte Schriften*, Bd. VII ('Aufbau der geschichtlichen Welt in den Geisteswissenschaften'), 3rd ed. (1961), pp. 146 f.: 'Every single human expression represents something that is common to many and therefore part of the realm of the objective mind. Every work, or sentence, every gesture or form of politeness, every work of art and every historical deed is only understandable, because the person expressing himself and the one understanding him are connected through something they have in common; the individual always thinks, experiences and acts as well as understands in this 'common sphere'.' (Translation by K. O. Apel.)

24. Cf. Dilthey, *loc. cit.*, p. 210 f. Something similar to a genuine crisis of 'prag-

matical understanding' may be intentionally provoked by an author by means of alienation (*Verfremdung* in the sense of B. Brecht). Thus, already on the level of grammar the ordinary understanding within the framework of a language game may be intentionally impeded by grammatically deviant (for instance, ironic) utterances which compel the reader to impose an *interpretation* on them by reflection on the very rules of the ordinary language games. These hints may suggest that hermeneutic understanding cannot be understood on the basis of Wittgenstein's closed (finite) language games but rather presupposes a reflective transcending of these games according to the regulative principles of the *transcendental* language game of the indefinite Community of Interpretation. Cf. my paper 'Die Kommunikationsgemeinschaft als transzendentale Voraussetzung der Sozialwissenschaften,' *loc. cit.* (see note 1).

25. Cf. K. O. Apel, 'Wittgenstein und das Problem des hermeneutischen Verstehens,' *loc. cit.* (see note 1).

26. Yehoshua Bar-Hillel, 'Argumentation in Pragmatic Languages,' *Aspects of Language, loc. cit.*, pp. 206–21.

27. Cf. K. O. Apel, 'Noam Chomsky's Sprachtheorie und die Philosophie der Gegenwart,' in *Jahrbuch des Instituts für Deutsche Sprache,* Mannheim (1972). Linguistics is here interpreted as a boundary case between natural science and hermeneutics.

28. Cf. K. O. Apel, 'Wissenschaft als Emanzipation?' in *Zeitschrift f. allg. Wissenschaftstheorie*, Bd. I, Heft 2 (1970). All technocracy, of course, presupposes a split society, that is, labor division between the manipulators and the manipulated. This is overlooked by those naive totalizations of behavioral technology as B. F. Skinner's *Beyond Freedom and Dignity,* which cannot answer to the famous question of the young Marx: who educates the educators? (Cf. the second thesis on Feuerbach.)

29. I refer here in particular to what J. Habermas conceives of as 'critique' in a neo-Marxist sense and what he associates with a third type of leading interest of knowing—besides technological objectifying and communicative understanding—which he calls "emancipatory.' (Cf. note 17).

30. Cf. K. O. Apel, *Analytic Philosophy and the 'Geisteswissenschaften'*, *loc. cit.*, pp. 25 ff. and 55 ff.; K. O. Apel, 'Szientistik, Hermeneutik, Ideologiekritik,' *loc. cit.* Cf. also the works of Habermas (see note 17); Alfred Lorenzer, *Sprachzerstörung und Rekonstruktion, Vorabeiten zu einer Metatheorie der Psychoanalyse,* Frankfurt (1970), and Paul Ricoeur, *De l'Interprétation, Essai sur Freud,* Paris (1965).

31. For discussion of these problems cf. Apel/Bormann/Bubner/Gadamer/ Giegel/Habermas, *Hermeneutik und Ideologiekritik,* Frankfurt (1971).

32. Cf. J. Habermas, *Erkenntnis und Interesse, loc. cit.*, pp. 315 ff.

33. Cf. also A. C. Danto, *Analytical Philosophy of History*, Cambridge (1955).

The Model of the Text:
Meaningful Action Considered as a Text

PAUL RICOEUR

MY AIM IN THIS PAPER IS TO TEST AN HYPOTHESIS WHICH I WILL expound briefly.

I assume that the primary sense of the word "hermeneutics" concerns the rules required for the interpretation of the written documents of our culture. In assuming this starting point I am remaining faithful to the concept of *Auslegung* as it was stated by Wilhelm Dilthey; whereas *Verstehen* (understanding, comprehension) relies on the recognition of what a foreign subject means or intends on the basis of all kinds of signs in which psychic life expresses itself (*Lebensäusserungen*), *Auslegung* (interpretation, exegesis) implies something more specific: it covers only a limited category of signs, those which are fixed by writing, including all the sorts of documents and monuments which entail a fixation similar to writing.

Now my hypothesis is this: if there are specific problems which are raised by the interpretation of texts because they are texts and not spoken language, and if these problems are the ones which constitute hermeneutics as such, then the human sciences may be said to be hermeneutical (1) inasmuch as their *object* displays some of the features constitutive of a text as text, and (2) inasmuch as their *methodology* develops the same kind of procedures as those of *Auslegung* or text-interpretation.

Hence the two questions to which my paper will be devoted are: (1) To what extent may we consider the notion of text as a good paradigm for the so-called object of the social sciences? (2) To what extent may we use the methodology of text-interpretation as a paradigm for interpretation in general in the field of the human sciences?

Paul Ricoeur, "The Model of the Text," *Social Research* 38 (1971):529–55.

I. The Paradigm of Text

In order to justify the distinction between spoken and written language, I want to introduce a preliminary concept, that of *discourse*. It is as discourse that language is either spoken or written.

Now what is discourse?

We shall not seek the answer from the logicians, not even from the exponents of linguistic analysis, but from the linguists themselves. Discourse is the counterpart of what linguists call language-systems or linguistic codes. Discourse is language-event or linguistic usage. This pair of correlative terms—system/event, code/message—has played a basic role in linguistics since it was introduced by Ferdinand de Saussure and Louis Hjelmslev. The first spoke of language (*lange*)—speech (*parole*), the second of schema —usage. We can also add competence—"performance," in Chomsky's language. It is necessary to draw all the epistemological consequences of such a duality, namely, that the linguistics of discourse has different rules than does the linguistics of language. It is the French linguist Emile Benvéniste who has gone the furthest in distinguishing two linguistics. For him, these two linguistics are not constructed upon the same units. If the sign (phonological or lexical) is the basic unit of language, the sentence is the basic unit of discourse. Therefore it is the linguistics of the sentence which supports the theory of speech as an event. I will retain four traits from this linguistics of the sentence which will help me to elaborate the hermeneutic of the event and of discourse.

First trait: Discourse is always realized temporally and in a present, whereas the language system is virtual and outside of time. Emile Benvéniste calls this the "instance of discourse."

Second trait: Whereas language lacks a subject—in the sense that the question "Who is speaking?" does not apply at its level—discourse refers back to its speaker by means of a complex set of indicators such as the personal pronouns. We will say that the "instance of discourse" is self-referential.

Third trait: Whereas the signs in language only refer to other signs within the same system, and whereas language therefore lacks a world just as it lacks temporality and subjectivity, discourse is always about something. It refers to a world which it claims to describe, to express, or to represent. It is in discourse that the symbolic function of language is actualized.

Fourth trait: Whereas language is only the condition for communication for which it provides the codes, it is in discourse that all messages are exchanged. In this sense, discourse alone has not only a world, but an other, another person, an interlocutor to whom it is addressed.

These four traits taken together constitute speech as an event.

It is remarkable that these four traits only appear in the movement of effectuation from language to discourse. Every apology for speech as an event therefore is significant if, and only if, it makes visible the process of effectuation through which our linguistic competence actualizes itself in performance. But the same apology becomes abusive as soon as this event character is extended from the problematic of effectuation, where it is valid, to another problematic, that of understanding.

In effect, what is it to understand a discourse?

Let us see how differently these four traits are actualized in spoken and written language.

1. Discourse, as we said, only exists as a temporal and present instance of discourse. This first trait is realized differently in living speech and in writing. In living speech, the instance of discourse has the character of a fleeting event. The event appears and disappears. This is why there is a problem of fixation, of inscription. What we want to fix is what disappears. If, by extension, we can say that one fixes language—inscription of the alphabet, lexical inscription, syntactical inscription—it is for the sake of that which alone has to be fixed, discourse. Only discourse is to be fixed, because discourse disappears. The atemporal system neither appears nor disappears; it does not happen. Here is the place to recall the myth in Plato's *Phaedo*. Writing was given to men to "come to the rescue" of the "weakness of discourse," a weakness which was that of the event. The gift of the *grammata*—of that "external" thing, of those "external marks," of that materializing alienation—was just that of a "remedy" brought to our memory. The Egyptian king of Thebes could well respond to the god Theuth that writing was a false remedy in that it replaced true reminiscence by material conservation, and real wisdom by the semblance of knowing. This inscription, in spite of its perils, is discourse's destination. What in effect does writing fix? Not the event of speaking, but the "said" of speaking, where we understand by the "said" of speaking that intentional exteriorization constitutive of the aim of discourse thanks to which the *sagen*—the saying—wants to become *Aus-sage*—the enunciation, the enunciated. In short, what we write, what we inscribe, is the *noema* of the speaking. It is the meaning of the speech event, not the event as event.

What, in effect, does writing fix? If it is not the speech *event*, it is speech itself in so far as it is *said*. But what is said?

Here I would like to propose that hermeneutics has to appeal not only to linguistics (linguistics of discourse versus linguistics of language) as it does above, but also to the theory of the speech-act such as we find it in Austin and Searle. The act of speaking, according to these authors, is constituted by a hierarchy of subordinate acts which are distributed on three levels: (1) the level of the locutionary or propositional act, the act *of* saying; (2) the level of the illocutionary act or force, that which we do *in* saying; and (3) the level of the perlocutionary act, that which we do *by* saying. In the case of an order, when I tell you to close the door, for example, "Close the door!" is the act of speaking.

But when I tell you this with the force of an order and not of a request, this is the illocutionary act. Finally, I can stir up certain effects like fear by the fact that I give you an order. These effects make my discourse act like a stimulus producing certain results. This is the perlocutionary act.

What is the implication of these distinctions for our problem of the intentional exteriorization by which the event surpasses itself in the meaning and lends itself to material fixation? The locutionary act exteriorizes itself in the sentence. The sentence can in effect be identified and re-identified as being the same sentence. A sentence becomes an e-nunciation (*Aus-sage*) and thus is transfered to others as being such-and-such a sentence with such-and-such a meaning. But the illocutionary act can also be exteriorized through grammatical paradigms (indicative, imperative, and subjunctive modes, and other procedures expressive of the illocutionary force) which permit its identification and re-identification. Certainly, in spoken discourse, the illocutionary force leans upon mimicry and gestural elements and upon the non-articulated aspects of discourse, what we call prosody. In this sense, the illocutionary force is less completely inscribed in grammar than is the propositional meaning. In every case, its inscription in a syntactic articulation is itself gathered up in specific paradigms which in principle make possible fixation by writing. Without a doubt we must concede that the perlocutionary act is the least inscribable aspect of discourse and that by preference it characterizes spoken language. But the perlocutionary action is precisely what is the least discourse in discourse. It is the discourse as stimulus. It acts, not by my interlocutor's recognition of my intention, but sort of energetically, by direct influence upon the emotions and the affective dispositions. Thus the propositional act, the illocutionary force, and the perlocutionary action are apt, in a decreasing order, for the intentional exteriorization which makes inscription in writing possible.

Therefore it is necessary to understand by the meaning of the speech-act, or by the *noema* of the saying, not only the sentence, in the narrow sense of the propositional act, but also the illocutionary force and even the perlocutionary action in the measure that these three aspects of the speech-act are codified, gathered into paradigms, and where, consequently, they can be identified and re-identified as having the same meaning. Therefore I am here giving the word "meaning" a very large acceptation which covers all the aspects and levels of the intentional exteriorization that makes the inscription of discourse possible.

The destiny of the other three traits of discourse in passing from discourse to writing will permit us to make more precise the meaning of this elevation of saying to what is said.

2. In discourse, we said—and this was the second differential trait of discourse in relation to language—the sentence designates its speaker by diverse indicators of subjectivity and personality. In spoken discourse, this reference by discourse to the speaking subject presents a character of immedi-

acy that we can explain in the following way. The subjective intention of the speaking subject and the meaning of the discourse overlap each other in such a way that it is the same thing to understand what the speaker means and what his discourse means. The ambiguity of the French expression *vouloir-dire,* the German *meinen*, and the English "to mean," attests to this overlapping. It is almost the same thing to ask "What do you mean?" and "What does that mean?" With written discourse, the author's intention and the meaning of the text cease to coincide. This dissociation of the verbal meaning of the text and the mental intention is what is really at stake in the inscription of discourse. Not that we can conceive of a text without an author; the tie between the speaker and the discourse is not abolished, but distended and complicated. The dissociation of the meaning and the intention is still an adventure of the reference of discourse to the speaking subject. But the text's career escapes the finite horizon lived by its author. What the text says now matters more than what the author meant to say, and every exegesis unfolds its procedures within the circumference of a meaning that has broken its moorings to the psychology of its author. Using Plato's expression again, written discourse cannot be "rescued" by all the processes by which spoken discourse supports itself in order to be understood—intonation, delivery, mimicry, gestures. In this sense, the inscription in "external marks," which first appeared to alienate discourse, marks the actual spirituality of discourse. Henceforth, only the meaning "rescues" the meaning, without the contribution of the physical and psychological presence of the author. But to say that the meaning rescues the meaning is to say that only interpretation is the "remedy" for the weakness of discourse which its author can no longer "save."

　　3. The event is surpassed by the meaning a third time. Discourse, we said, is what refers to the world, to *a* world. In spoken discourse this means that what the dialogue ultimately refers to is the *situation* common to the interlocutors. This situation in a way surrounds the dialogue, and its landmarks can all be shown by a gesture, or by pointing a finger, or designated in an ostensive manner by the discourse itself through the oblique reference of those other indicators which are the demonstratives, the adverbs of time and place, and the tense of the verb. In oral discourse, we are saying, reference is *ostensive*. What happens to it in written discourse? Are we saying that the text no longer has a reference? This would be to confound reference and monstration, world and situation. Discourse cannot fail to be about something. In saying this, I am separating myself from any ideology of an absolute text. Only a few sophisticated texts satisfy this ideal of a text without reference. They are texts where the play of the signifier breaks away from the signified. But this new form is only valuable as an exception and cannot give the key to all other texts which in one manner or another speak about the world. But what then is the subject of texts when nothing can be shown? Far from saying that the text is then without a

world, I will now say without paradox that only man *has a world* and not just a situation. In the same manner that the text frees its meaning from the tutelage of the mental intention, it frees its reference from the limits of ostensive reference. For us, the world is the ensemble of references opened up by the texts. Thus we speak about the "world" of Greece, not to designate any more what were the situations for those who lived them, but to designate the non-situational references which outlive the effacement of the first and which henceforth are offered as possible modes of being, as symbolic dimensions of our being-in-the-world. For me, this is the referent of all literature; no longer the *Umwelt* of the ostensive references of dialogue, but the *Welt* projected by the non-ostensive references of every text that we have read, understood, and loved. To understand a text is at the same time to light up our own situation, or, if you will, to interpolate among the predicates of our own situation all the significances which make a *Welt* of our *Umwelt*. It is this enlarging of the *Umwelt* into the *World* which permits us to speak of the references *opened up* by the text—it would be better to say that the references *open up* the world. Here again the spirituality of discourse manifests itself through writing, which frees us from the visibility and limitation of situations by opening up a world for us, that is, new dimensions of our being-in-the-world.

In this sense, Heidegger rightly says—in his analysis of *verstehen* in *Being and Time*—that what we understand first in a discourse is not another person, but a project, that is, the outline of a new being-in-the-world. Only writing, in freeing itself, not only from its author, but from the narrowness of the dialogical situation, reveals this destination of discourse as projecting a world.

In thus tieing reference to the projection of a world, it is not only Heidegger whom we rediscover, but Wilhelm von Humboldt for whom the great justification of language is to establish the relation of man to the world. If you suppress this referential function, only an absurd game of errant signifiers remains.

4. But it is perhaps with the fourth trait that the accomplishment of discourse in writing is most exemplary. Only discourse, not language, is addressed to someone. This is the foundation of communication. But it is one thing for discourse to be addressed to an interlocutor equally present to the discourse situation, and another to be addressed, as is the case in virtually every piece of writing, to whoever knows how to read. The narrowness of the dialogical relation explodes. Instead of being addressed just to you, the second person, what is written is addressed to the audience that it creates itself. This, again, marks the spirituality of writing, the counterpart of its materiality and of the alienation which it imposes upon discourse. The *vis-à-vis* of the written is just whoever knows how to read. The co-presence of dialoguing subjects ceases to be the model for every "understanding." The relation writing—reading ceases to be a particular case of the relation speaking—hearing. But at the same time, discourse is revealed as discourse in the universality of its address. In escaping

the momentary character of the event, the bounds lived by the author, and the narrowness of ostensive reference, discourse escapes the limits of being face to face. It no longer has a visible auditor. An unknown, invisible reader has become the unprivileged addressee of the discourse.

To what extent may we say that the object of the human sciences conforms to the paradigm of the text? Max Weber defines this object as *sinnhaft orientiertes Verhalten*, as meaningfully oriented behavior. To what extent may we replace the predicate "meaningfully oriented" by what I would like to call *readability-characters* derived from the preceding theory of the text?

Let us try to apply our four criteria of what a text is to the concept of meaningful action.

A. The Fixation of Action

Meaningful action is an object for science only under the condition of a kind of objectification which is equivalent to the fixation of a discourse by writing. This trait presupposes a simple way to help us at this stage of our analysis. In the same way that interlocution is overcome in writing, interaction is overcome in numerous situations in which we treat action as a fixed text. These situations are overlooked in a theory of action for which the discourse of action is itself a part of the situation of transaction which flows from one agent to another, exactly as spoken language is caught in the process of interlocution, or, if we may use the term, of translocution. This is why the understanding of action at the prescientific level is only "knowledge without observation," or as E. Anscombe says, "practical knowledge" in the sense of "knowing how" as opposed to "knowing that." But this understanding is not yet an *interpretation* in the strong sense which deserves to be called scientific interpretation.

My claim is that action itself, action as meaningful, may become an object of science, without losing its character of meaningfulness, through a kind of objectification similar to the fixation which occurs in writing. By this objec-tification, action is no longer a transaction to which the discourse of action would still belong. It constitutes a delineated pattern which has to be interpreted according to its inner connections.

This objectification is made *possible* by some inner traits of the action which are similar to the structure of the speech-act and which make doing a kind of utterance. In the same way as the fixation by writing is made possible by a dialectic of intentional exteriorization immanent to the speech-act itself, a similar dialectic within the process of transaction prepares the detachment of the *meaning* of the action from the *event* of the action.

First an action has the structure of a locutionary act. It has a *propositional* content which can be identified and re-identified as the same. This "propositional" structure of the action has been clearly and demonstratively expounded by Antony Kenny in *Action, Emotion and Will*.[1] The verbs of action constitute a specific class of predicates which are similar to relations and which, like relations, are irreducible to all the kinds of predicates which may follow the copula "is." The class of action predicates, in its turn, is irreducible to the relations and constitutes a specific set of predicates. Among other traits, the verbs of action allow a plurality of "arguments" capable of complementing the verb, ranging from no argument (Plato taught) to an indeterminate number of arguments (Brutus killed Caesar in the Curia, on the Ides of March, with a. . . , with the help of . . .). This variable polydicity of the predicative structure of the action-sentences is typical of the propositional structure of action. Another trait which is important for the transposition of the concept of fixation from the sphere of discourse to the sphere of action concerns the ontological status of the "complements" of the verbs of action. Whereas relations hold between terms equally existing (or non-existing), certain verbs of action have a topical subject which is identified as existing and to which the sentence refers, and complements which do not exist. Such is the case with the "mental acts" (to believe, to think, to will, to imagine, etc.).

Antony Kenny describes some other traits of the propositional structure of actions derived from the description of the functioning of the verbs of action. For example, the distinction between states, activities, and performances can be stated according to the behavior of the tenses of the verbs of action which fix some specific temporal traits of the action itself. The distinction between the formal and the material object of an action (let us say the difference between the notion of all inflammable things and this letter which I am now burning) belongs to the logic of action as mirrored in the grammar of the verbs of action. Such, roughly described, is the propositional content of action which gives a basis to a dialectic of *event* and *meaning* similar to that of the speech-act. I should like to speak here of the noematic structure of action. It is this noematic structure which may be fixed and detached from the process of interaction and become an object to interpret.

Moreover, this *noema* has not only a propositional content, but also presents "illocutionary" traits very similar to those of the complete speech-act. The different classes of performative acts of discourse described by Austin at the end of *How to Do Things with Words* may be taken as paradigms not only for the speech-acts themselves, but for the actions which fulfill the corresponding speech-acts.[2] A typology of action, following the model of illocutionary acts, is therefore possible. Not only a typology, but a criteriology, inasmuch as each type implies *rules*, more precisely "constitutive rules" which, according to Searle in *Speech Acts*, allow the construction of "ideal models" similar to the *Idealtypen* of Max Weber.[3] For example, to understand what a promise is, we have to understand what the "essential condition" is according to which a given action "counts as" a promise. Searle's "essential condition" is not far from what Husserl called *Sinngehalt*, which covers both the "matter" (propositional content) and the "quality" (the illocutionary force).

We may now say that an action, like a speech-act, may be identified not only according to its propositional content, but also according to its illocutionary force. Both constitute its "sense-content." Like the speech-act, the action-event (if we may coin this analogical expression) develops a similar dialectic between its temporal status as an appearing and disappearing event, and its logical status as having such-and-such identifiable meaning or "sense-content." But if the "sense-content" is what makes possible the "inscription" of the action-event, what makes it real? In other words, what corresponds to writing in the field of action?

Let us return to the paradigm of the speech-act. What is fixed by writing, we said, is the *noema* of the speaking, the saying as *said*. To what extent may we say that what is *done* is inscribed? Certain metaphors may be helpful at this point. We say that such-and-such event *left its mark* on its time. We speak of marking events. Are not there "marks" on time, the kind of thing which calls for a reading, rather than for a hearing? But what is meant by this metaphor of the printed mark?

The three other criteria of the text will help us to make the nature of this fixation more precise.

B. The Autonomization of Action

In the same way that a text is detached from its author, an action is detached from its agent and develops consequences of its own. This autonomization of human action constitutes the *social* dimension of action. An action is a social phenomenon not only because it is done by several agents in such a way that the role of each of them cannot be distinguished from the role of the others, but also because our deeds escape us and have effects which we did not intend. One of the meanings of the notion of "inscription" appears here. The kind of distance which we found between the intention of the speaker and the verbal meaning of a text occurs also between the agent and its action. It is this distance which makes the ascription of responsibility a specific problem. We do not ask, who smiled? who raised his hand? The doer is present to his doing in the same way as the speaker is present to his speech. With simple actions like those which require no previous action in order to be done, the meaning (*noema*) and the intention (*noesis*) coincide or overlap. With complex actions some segments are so remote from the initial simple segments, which can be said to express the intention of the doer, that the ascription of these actions or action-segments constitutes a problem as difficult to solve as that of authorship in some cases of literary criticism. The assignation of an author becomes a mediate inference well known to the historian who tries to isolate the role of an historical character in the course of events.

We just used the expression "the course of events." Could we not say that what we call the course of events plays the role of the material thing which "rescues" the vanishing discourse when it is written? As we said in a metaphorical way, some actions are events which imprint their mark on their time. But on what did they imprint their mark? Is it not in something spatial that discourse is inscribed? How could an event be printed on something temporal? Social time, however, is not only something which flees; it is also the place of durable effects, of persisting patterns. An action leaves a "trace," it makes its "mark" when it contributes to the emergence of such patterns which become the *documents* of human action.

Another metaphor may help us to delineate this phenomenon of the social "imprint": the metaphor of the "record" or of the "registration." Joel Feinberg, in *Reason and Responsibility*, introduces this metaphor in another context, that of responsibility, in order to show how an action may be submitted to blame. Only actions, he says, which can be "registered" for further notice, placed as an entry on somebody's "record," can be blamed.[4] And when there are no formal records (such as those which are kept by institutions like employment offices, schools, banks, and the police), there is still an informal analogue of these formal records which we call reputation and which constitutes a basis for blaming. I would like to apply this interesting metaphor of a record and reputation to something other than the quasi-judicial situations of blaming, charging, crediting, or punishing. Could we not say that history is itself the record of human action? History is this quasi-"thing" *on* which human action leaves a "trace," puts its mark. Hence the possibility of "archives." Before the archives which are intentionally written down by the memorialists, there is this continuous process of "recording" human action which is history itself as the sum of "marks," the fate of which escapes the control of individual actors. Henceforth history may appear as an autonomous entity, as a play with players who do not know the plot. This hypostasis of history may be denounced as a fallacy, but this fallacy is well entrenched in the process by which human action becomes social action when written down in the archives of history. Thanks to this sedimentation in social time, human deeds become "institutions," in the sense that their meaning no longer coincides with the logical intentions of the actors. The meaning may be "depsychologized" to the point where the *meaning* resides in the work itself. In the words of P. Winch, in *The Idea of a Social Science*, the object of the social sciences is a "rule-governed behavior."[5] But this rule is not superimposed; it is the meaning as articulated from within these sedimented or instituted works.

Such is the kind of "objectivity" which proceeds from the "social fixation" of meaningful behavior.

C. Relevance and Importance

According to our third criterion of what a text is, we could say that a meaningful action is an action the *importance* of which goes "beyond" its *relevance* to its initial situation. This new trait is very similar to the way in which a text breaks the ties of discourse to all the ostensive references. As a result of this emancipation from the situational context, discourse can develop non-ostensive references which we called a "world," in the sense in which we speak of the Greek "world," not in the cosmological sense of the word, but as an ontological dimension.

What would correspond in the field of action to the non-ostensive references of a text?

We opposed, in introducing the present analysis, the *importance* of an action to its *relevance* as regards the situation to which it wanted to respond. An important action, we could say, develops meanings which can be actualized or fulfilled in situations other than the one in which this action occurred. To say the same thing in different words, the meaning of an important event exceeds, overcomes, transcends, the social conditions of its production and may be reenacted in new social contexts. Its importance is its durable relevance and, in some cases, its omnitemporal relevance.

This third trait has important implications as regards the relation between cultural phenomena and their social conditions. Is it not a fundamental trait of the great works of culture to overcome the conditions of their social production, in the same way as a text develops new references and constitutes new "worlds"? It is in this sense that Hegel spoke, in *The Philosophy of Right,* of the institutions (in the largest sense of the word) which "actualize" freedom as a *second nature* in accordance with freedom. This "realm of actual freedom" is constituted by the deeds and works capable of receiving relevance in new historical situations. If this is true, this way of overcoming one's own conditions of production is the key to the puzzling problem raised by Marxism concerning the status of the "superstructures." The autonomy of superstructures as regards their relation to their own infrastructures has its paradigm in the non-ostensive references of a text. A work does not only mirror its time, but it opens up a world which it bears within itself.

D. Human Action as an "Open Work"

Finally, according to our fourth criterion of the text as text, the meaning of human action is also something which is *addressed* to an indefinite range of possible "readers." The judges are not the contemporaries, but, as Hegel said, history itself. *Weltgeschichte ist Weltgericht.* That means that, like a text, human action is an open work, the meaning of which is "in suspense." It is because it "opens up" new references and receives fresh relevance from them, that human deeds are also waiting for fresh interpretations which decide their meaning. All significant events and deeds are, in this way, opened to this kind of practical interpretation through present *praxis.* Human action, too, is opened to anybody who *can read.* In the same way that the meaning of an event is the sense of its forthcoming interpretations, the interpretation by the contemporaries has no particular privilege in this process.

This dialectic between the work and its interpretations will be the topic of the *methodology* of interpretation that we shall now consider.

A. The Paradigm of Text-Interpretation

I want now to show the fruitfulness of this analogy of the text at the level of methodology.

The main implication of our paradigm, as concerns the methods of the social sciences, is that it offers a fresh approach to the question of the relation between *erklären* (explanation) and *verstehen* (understanding, comprehension) in the human sciences. As is well known, Dilthey gave this relation the meaning of a dichotomy. For him, any model of explanation is borrowed from a different region of knowledge, that of the natural sciences with their inductive logic. Thereafter, the autonomy of the so-called *Geisteswissenschaften* is preserved only by recognizing the irreducible factor of understanding a foreign psychic life on the basis of the signs in which this life is immediately exteriorized. But, if *verstehen* is separated from *erklären* by this logical gap, how can the human sciences be scientific at all? Dilthey kept wrestling with this paradox. He discovered more and more clearly, mainly after having read Husserl's *Logical Investigations,* that the *Geisteswissenschaften* are sciences inasmuch as the expressions of life undergo a kind of objectification which makes possible a scientific approach somewhat similar to that of the natural sciences, in spite of the logical gap between *Natur* and *Geist,* factual knowledge and knowledge by signs. In this way the mediation offered by these objectifications appeared to be more important, for a scientific purpose, than the immediate meaningfulness of the expressions of life for everyday transactions.

My own interrogation starts from this last perplexity in Dilthey's thought. And my hypothesis is that the kind of objectification implied in the status of discourse as text provides a better answer to the problem raised by Dilthey. This answer relies on the dialectical character of the relation between *erklären* and *verstehen* as it is displayed in reading.

Our task therefore will be to show to what extent the paradigm of reading, which is the counterpart of the paradigm of writing, provides a solution for the methodological paradox of the human sciences.

The dialectic involved in reading expresses the originality of the relation between writing and reading and its irreducibility to the dialogical situation based on the immediate reciprocity between speaking and hearing. There is a dialectic between explaining and comprehending *because* the writing/reading situation develops a problematic of its own which is not merely an extension of the speaking/hearing situation constitutive of dialogue.

It is here, therefore, that our hermeneutic is most critical as regards the Romanticist tradition in hermeneutics which took the dialogical situation as the standard for the hermeneutical operation applied to the text. My contention is that it is this operation, on the contrary, which reveals the meaning of what is already hermeneutical in dialogical understanding. Then, if the dialogical relation does not provide us with the paradigm of reading, we have to build it as an original paradigm, as a paradigm of its own.

This paradigm draws its main features from the status of the text itself as characterized by (1) the fixation of the meaning, (2) its dissociation from the mental intention of the author, (3) the display of non-ostensive references, and (4) the universal range of its addresses. These four traits taken together constitute the "objectivity" of the text. From this "objectivity" derives a possibility of *explaining* which is not derived in any way from another field, that of natural events, but which is congenial to this kind of objectivity. Therefore there is no transfer from one region of reality to another—let us say, from the sphere of facts to the sphere of signs. It is within the same sphere of signs that the process of objectification takes place and gives rise to explanatory procedures. And it is within the same sphere of signs that explanation and comprehension are confronted.

I propose that we consider this dialectic in two different ways: (1) as proceeding from comprehension to explanation, and (2) as proceeding from explanation to comprehension. The exchange and the reciprocity between both procedures will provide us with a good approximation of the dialectical character of the relation.

At the end of each half of this demonstration I shall try to indicate briefly the possible extension of the paradigm of reading to the whole sphere of the human sciences.

A. From Understanding to Explanation

This first dialectic—or rather this first figure of a unique dialectic—may be conveniently introduced by our contention that to understand a text is not to rejoin the author. The disjunction of the meaning and the intention creates an absolutely original situation which engenders the dialectic of *erklären* and *verstehen*. If the objective meaning is something other than the subjective intention of the author, it may be construed in various ways. The problem of the right understanding can no longer be solved by a simple return to the alleged intention of the author.

This construction necessarily takes the form of a process. As Hirsch says in his book *Validity in Interpretation,* there are no rules for making good guesses. But there are methods for validating guesses.[6] This dialectic between guessing and validating constitutes one figure of our dialectic between comprehension and explanation.

In this dialectic both terms are decisive. Guessing corresponds to what Schleiermacher called the "divinatory," validation to what he called the "grammatical." My contribution to the theory of this dialectic will be to link it more tightly to the theory of the text and text-reading.

Why do we need an art of guessing? Why do we have to "construe" the meaning?

Not only—as I tried to say a few years ago—because language is metaphorical and because the double meaning of metaphorical language requires an art of deciphering which tends to unfold the several layers of meaning. The case of the metaphor is only a particular case for a general theory of hermeneutics. In more general terms, a text has to be construed because it is not a mere sequence of sentences, all on an equal footing and separately understandable. A text is a whole, a totality. The relation between whole and parts—as in a work of art or in an animal—requires a specific kind of "judgment" for which Kant gave the theory in the Third Critique. Correctly, the whole appears as a hierarchy of topics, or primary and subordinate topics. The reconstruction of the text as a whole necessarily has a circular character, in the sense that the presupposition of a certain kind of whole is implied in the recognition of the parts. And reciprocally, it is in construing the details that we construe the whole. There is no necessity and no evidence concerning what is important and what is unimportant, what is essential and what is unessential. The judgment of importance is a guess.

To put the difficulty in other terms, if a text is a whole, it is once more an individual like an animal or a work of art. As an individual it can only be reached by a process of narrowing the scope of generic concepts concerning the liiterary genre, the class of text to which this text belongs, the structures of different kinds which intersect in this text. The localization and the individualization of this unique text is still a guess.

Still another way of expressing the same enigma is that as an individual the text may be reached from different sides. Like a cube, or a volume in space, the text presents a "relief." Its different topics are not at the same altitude.

Therefore the reconstruction of the whole has a perspectivist aspect similar to that of perception. It is always possible to relate the same sentence in different ways to this or that sentence considered as the cornerstone of the text. A specific kind of onesidedness is implied in the act of reading. This onesidedness confirms the guess character of interpretation.

For all these reasons there is a problem of interpretation not so much because of the incommunicability of the psychic experience of the author, but because of the very nature of the verbal intention of the text. This intention is something other than the sum of the individual meanings of the individual sentences. A text is more than a linear succession of sentences. It is a cumulative, holistic process. This specific structure of the text cannot be derived from that of the sentence. Therefore the kind of plurivocity which belongs to texts as texts is something other than the polysemy of individual words in ordinary language and the ambiguity of individual sentences. This plurivocity is typical of the text considered as a whole, open to several readings and to several constructions.

As concerns the procedures of validation by which we test our guesses, I agree with Hirsch that they are closer to a logic of probability than to a logic of empirical verification. To show that an interpretation is more probable in the light of what is known is something other than showing that a conclusion is true. In this sense, validation is not verification. Validation is an argumentative discipline comparable to the juridical procedures of legal interpretation. It is a logic of uncertainty and of qualitative probability. In this sense we may give an acceptable sense to the opposition between *Geisteswissenschaften* and *Naturwissenschaften* without conceding anything to the alleged dogma of the ineffability of the individual. The method of conveyance of indices, typical of the logic of subjective probability, gives a firm basis for a science of the individual deserving the name of science. A text is a quasi-individual, and the validation of an interpretation applied to it may be said, with complete legitimacy, to give a scientific knowledge of the text.

Such is the balance between the genius of guessing and the scientific character of validation which constitutes the modern complement of the dialectic between *verstehen* and *erklären*.

At the same time, we are prepared to give an acceptable meaning to the famous concept of a *hermeneutical circle*. Guess and validation are in a sense circularly related as subjective and objective approaches to the text. But this circle is not a vicious circularity. It would be a cage if we were unable to escape the kind of "self-confirmability" which, according to Hirsch (p. 164ff.), threatens this relation between guess and validation. To the procedures of validation also belong procedures of invalidation similar to the criteria of falsifiability emphasized by Karl Popper in his *Logic of Scientific Discovery*.[7] The role of falsification is played here by the conflict between competing interpretations. An interpretation must not only be probable, but more probable than another. There are criteria of relative superiority which may easily be derived from the logic of subjective probability.

In conclusion, if it is true that there is always more than one way of construing a text, it is not true that all interpretations are equal and may be assimilated to so-called "rules of thumb." The text is a limited field of possible constructions. The logic of validation allows us to move between the two limits of dogmatism and skepticism. It is always possible to argue for or against an interpretation, to confront interpretations, to arbitrate between them and to seek for an agreement, even if this agreement remains beyond our reach.

To what extent is this dialectic between guessing and validating paradigmatic for the whole field of the human sciences?

That the meaning of human actions, of historical events, and of social phenomena may be *construed* in several different ways is well known by all experts in the human sciences. What is less known and understood is that this methodological perplexity is founded in the nature of the object itself and, moreover, that it does not condemn the scientist to oscillate between dogmatism and skepticism. As the logic of text-interpretation suggests, there is a *specific plurivocity* belonging to the meaning of human action. Human action, too, is a limited field of possible constructions.

A trait of human action which has not yet been emphasized in the preceding analysis may provide an interesting link between the specific plurivocity of the text and the analogical plurivocity of human action. This trait concerns the relation between the purposive and the motivational dimensions of action. As many philosophers in the new field of Action Theory have shown, the purposive character of an action is fully recognized when the answer to the question "what" is explained in terms of an answer to the question "why." I *understand* what you intended to do, if you are able to *explain* to me why you did such-and-such an action. Now, what kinds of answer to the question "why" make sense? Only those answers which afford a motive understood as a reason for _____ and not as a cause. And what is a reason for _____ which is not a cause? It is, in the terms of E. Anscombe and A. I. Meldon, an expression, or a phrase, which allows us to consider the action *as* this or that. If you tell me that you did this or that because of jealousy or in a spirit of revenge, you are asking me to put your action in the light of this category of feelings or dispositions. By the same token, you claim to make sense with your action. You claim to make it understandable for others and for yourself. This attempt is particularly helpful when applied to what E. Anscombe calls the "desirability-character" of wanting. Wants and beliefs have the character not only of being *forces* which make people act in such-and-such ways, but of making sense as a result of the apparent good which is the correlate of their desirability-character. I may have to answer the question, *as* what do you want this? On the basis of these desirability-characters and the apparent good which corresponds to them, it is possible to *argue* about the meaning of an action, to argue for or against this or that interpretation. In this way the account of motives already foreshadows a logic of argumentation procedures. Could we not say that what can be (and must be) *construed* in human action is the motivational basis of this action, i.e., the set of desirability-characters which may explain it? And could we not say that the process of *arguing* linked to the explanation of action by its motives unfolds a kind of plurivocity which makes action similar to a text?

What seems to legitimate this extension from guessing the meaning of a text to guessing the meaning of an action is that in arguing about the meaning of an action I put my wants and my beliefs at a distance and submit them to a concrete dialectic of confrontation with opposite points of view. This way of putting my action at a distance in order to make sense of my own motives paves the way for the kind of distanciation which occurs with what we called the social *inscription* of human action and to which we applied the metaphor of the "record." The same actions which may be put into "records" and henceforth "recorded" may also be *explained* in different ways according to the multivocity of the arguments applied to their motivational background.

If we are correct in extending to action the concept of "guess" which we took as a synonym for *verstehen*, we may also extend to the field of action the concept of "validation" in which we saw an equivalent of *erklären*.

Here, too, the modern theory of action provides us with an intermediary link between the procedures of literary criticism and those of the social sciences. Some thinkers have tried to elucidate the way in which we *impute* actions to agents in the light of the juridical procedures by which a judge or a tribunal validates a decision concerning a contract or a crime. In a famous article, "The Ascription of Responsibility and Rights," H. L. A. Hart shows in a very convincing way that juridical reasoning does not at all consist in applying general laws to particular cases, but each time in construing uniquely referring decisions.[8] These decisions terminate a careful refutation of the excuses and defenses which could "defeat" the claim or the accusation. In saying that human actions are fundamentally "defeatible" and that juridical reasoning is an argumentative process which comes to grips with the different ways of "defeating" a claim or an accusation, Hart has paved the way for a general theory of validation in which juridical reasoning would be the fundamental link between validation in literary criticism and validation in the social sciences. The intermediary function of juridical reasoning clearly shows that the procedures of validation have a polemical character. In front of the court, the plurivocity common to texts and to actions is exhibited in the form of a conflict of interpretations, and the final interpretation appears as a verdict to which it is possible to make appeal. Like legal utterances, all interpretations in the field of literary criticism and in the social sciences may be challenged, and the question "what can defeat a claim" is common to all argumentative situations. Only in the tribunal is there a moment when the procedures of appeal are exhausted. But it is because the decision of the judge is implemented by the force of public power. Neither in literary criticism, nor in the social sciences, is there such a last word. Or, if there is any, we call that violence.

B. From Explanation to Understanding

The same dialectic between comprehension and understanding may receive a new meaning if taken in the reverse way, from explanation to understanding. This new *Gestalt* of the dialectic proceeds from the nature of the referential function of the text. This referential function, as we said, exceeds the mere ostensive designation of the situation common to both speaker and hearer in the dialogical situation. This abstraction from the surrounding world gives rise to two opposite attitudes. As readers, we may either remain in a kind of state of suspense as regards any kind of referred-to world, or we may actualize the potential non-ostensive references of the text in a new situation, that of the reader. In the first case, we treat the text as a worldless entity; in the second, we create a new ostensive reference through the kind of "execution" which the art of reading implies. These two possibilities are equally entailed by the act of reading, conceived as their dialectical interplay.

The first way of reading is exemplified today by the different *structural* schools of literary criticism. Their approach is not only possible, but legitimate. It proceeds from the suspension, the *epoché*, of the ostensive reference. To read, in this way, means to prolong this suspension of the ostensive reference to the world and to transfer oneself into the "place" where the text stands, within the "enclosure" of this worldless place. According to this choice, the text no longer has an outside, it has only an inside. Once more, the very constitution of the text as text and of the system of texts as literature justifies this conversion of the literary thing into a closed system of signs, analogous to the kind of closed system which phonology discovered at the root of all discourse, and which de Saussure called "*la langue*." Literature, according to this working hypothesis, becomes an *analogon* of "*la langue*."

On the basis of this abstraction, a new kind of explanatory attitude may be extended to the literary object, which, contrary to the expectation of Dilthey, is no longer borrowed from the natural sciences, i.e., from an area of knowledge alien to language itself. The opposition between *Natur* and *Geist* is no longer operative here. If some model is borrowed, it comes from the same field, from the semiological field. It is henceforth possible to treat texts according to the elementary rules which linguistics successfully applied to the elementary systems of signs that underlie the use of language. We have learned from the Geneva school, the Prague school, and the Danish school, that it is always possible to abstract *systems* from *processes* and to relate these systems —whether phonological, lexical, or syntactical—to units which are merely defined by their opposition to other units of the same system. This interplay of merely distinctive entities within finite sets of such units defines the notion of structure in linguistics. . . .

NOTES

1. Antony Kenny, *Action, Emotion and Will* (London: Routledge, 1963).

2. John Austin, *How to Do Things with Words* (Cambridge, Mass.: Harvard University Press, 1962).

3. John Searle, *Speech Acts* (London: Cambridge University Press, 1969), p. 56.

4. J. Feinberg, *Reason and Responsibility* (Belmont, Calif.: Dickenson Pub. Co., 1965).

5. Peter Winch, *The Idea of a Social Science* (London: Routledge, 1958).

6. Eric D. Hirsch, Jr., *Validity in Interpretation* (New Haven, Conn.: Yale University Press, 1967), p. 25.

"The act of understanding is at first a genial (or a mistaken) guess and there are no methods for making guesses, no rules for generating insights; the methodological activity of interpretation commences when we begin to test and criticize our guesses." And further: "A mute symbolism may be construed in several ways."

7. Karl Popper, *The Logic of Scientific Discovery* (New York: Basic Books, 1959).

8. H. L. A. Hart, "The Ascription of Responsibility and Rights," *Proceedings of the Aristotelian Society*, 49 (1948):171–194.

A Review of Gadamer's
*Truth and Method**

JÜRGEN HABERMAS

I

GENERAL LINGUISTICS IS NOT THE ONLY ALTERNATIVE TO A HISTOR-
ically oriented language analysis that immerses itself in the pluralism of
language games without being able to justify the language of analysis itself. To
break through the grammatical barriers of individual linguistic totalities we do
not need to follow Chomsky in leaving the dimension of ordinary language.
Not only the distance of a theoretical language from the primary languages
secures the unity of analytical reason in the pluralism of language games.
Apparently every ordinary language grammar itself furnishes the possibility to
transcend the language it determines, that is, to translate from and into other
languages. To be sure, the anguish of translation brings to consciousness in a
particularly clear manner the objective connection of linguistic structure and
world-conception, the unity of word and thing. To procure a hearing for a text
in a foreign language requires often enough a new text rather than a translation
in the ordinary sense. Since Humboldt the sciences of language have been
informed with the intention of demonstrating the close correlation of linguistic
form and world view. But even this demonstration of the individuality of
linguistic structure, leading to resignation in the face of the "untranslatability"
of traditional formulations, is based on the daily experience that we are never
locked within a single grammar. Rather, the first grammar that we learn to
master already puts us in a position to step out of it and to interpret what is
foreign, to make comprehensible what initially is incomprehensible, to assimilate in our own words what at first escapes them. The relativism of linguistic

world views and the monadology of language games are equally illusory. For we become aware of the boundaries drawn for us by the grammar of ordinary language by means of the same grammar—Hegel's dialectic of the limit formulates the experience of the translator. The concept of translation is itself dialectical; only where we lack transformation rules permitting the establishment of a deductive relation between languages through substitution and where an exact "translation" is excluded do we need that kind of interpretation that we commonly call translation. It expresses in one language a state of affairs that cannot be literally expressed in it, but can nevertheless be rendered "in other words." H. G. Gadamer calls this experience, which is at the basis of hermeneutics, the hermeneutic experience.

> Hermeneutic experience is the corrective through which thinking reason escapes the spell of language; and it is itself linguistically constituted . . . To be sure, the multiplicity of languages with which linguistics is concerned also poses a question for us. But this is merely the single question: how is every language, in spite of its differences from other languages, supposed to be in a position to say everything it wants? Linguistics teaches us that every language does this in its own way. For our part, we pose the question: how does the same unity of thought and speech assert itself everywhere in the multiplicity of these ways of saying, in such a way that every written tradition can be understood?[1]

Hermeneutics defines its task as a countermove to the linguistic descriptions of different grammars. However, to preserve the unity of reason in the pluralism of languages, it does not rely on a metatheory of ordinary language grammars, as does the program of general linguistics. Hermeneutics mistrusts any mediatizing of ordinary languages and refuses to step out of their dimension; instead it makes use of the tendency to self-transcendence embedded in linguistic practice. Languages themselves possess the potential of a reason that, while expressing itself in the particularity of a specific grammar, simultaneously reflects on its limits and negates them as particular. Although always bound up in language, reason always transcends particular languages; it lives in language only by destroying the particularities of languages through which alone it is incarnated. Of course, it can cleanse itself of the dross of one particularity only in passing over into another. This intermittent generality is certified in the act of translation. It is reflected formally in a characteristic that is common to all traditional languages and guarantees their transcendental unity, namely, in the fact that they are in principle intertranslatable.

Wittgenstein, the logician, interpreted "translation" as a transformation according to general rules. Since the grammar of language games cannot be reconstructed according to general rules, he conceived linguistic understanding [Sprachverstehen] from the point of view of socialization, as training in a cultural form of life. It makes sense to conceive of the learning of "language in general" according to this model. But we can study the problem of linguistic understanding by focusing initially on the less fundamental process of learning a foreign language. To learn a language is not identical with learning to speak; it already presupposes the mastery of at least one language. With this primary language we have learned the rules that make it possible not only to achieve understanding within the framework of this one grammar but also to make foreign languages understandable. In learning a specific language, we have at the same time learned how one learns languages in general. We assimilate foreign languages through translation. Of course, as soon as we have mastered them, we no longer need translation. Translations are necessary only when understanding is disturbed. On the other hand, difficulties in achieving understanding arise even in conversations within our own language. Communication takes place according to rules that are shared by the partners in discussion. But these rules not only make consensus possible; they also include the possibility of putting an end to situations of disturbed understanding. To converse means both: to understand one another in principle and to be able to make oneself understood when necessary. The role of the discussion partner includes virtually the role of the interpreter, that is, of someone who can not only converse in one language but can bring about an understanding between different languages. The role of the interpreter is not different in principle from that of the translator. Translation is only the extreme variant of an achievement upon which every normal conversation must depend.

> Thus the case of translation makes us conscious of linguisticality [*Sprachlichkeit*] as the medium in which understanding is achieved; for in translation understanding must first be artfully produced through an explicit contrivance. [It] is certainly not the normal case of conversation. Translation is also not the normal case of our behavior toward a foreign language. . . . When one really masters a language, there is no longer a need for translation; indeed translation seems impossible. To understand a language is thus not yet at all a real understanding and does not include any interpretative process; it is rather an accomplishment of life [*Lebensvollzug*]. For one understands a language in living in it—a proposition that holds true not only for living languages but, as is well known, for dead languages as well. The hermeneutic problem is thus not a problem of the correct mastery of language but one of correctly coming to an understanding about what happens in the medium of language. . . . Only where it is possible to come to an understanding in language, through talking to one another, can understanding and coming to an understanding be at all a problem. Being dependent on the translation of an interpreter is an extreme case that doubles the hermeneutic process, the conversation: It involves a conversation of the interpreter with one's discussion partner and one's own conversation with the interpreter.[2]

The hermeneutic border-line case of translation, which at the same time provides the model for scientific interpretation, discloses a form of reflection that we implicitly carry out in every linguistic communication. It remains, to be sure, concealed in naive conversation; for understanding in reliably institutionalized language games rests on an unproblematic foundation of mutual understanding [*Verständigtseins*]—it is "not an interpretive process, but an accomplishment of life."

Wittgenstein analyzed only this dimension of the language game as a form of life. For him understanding was limited to the virtual repetition of the training through which "native" speakers are socialized into their form of life. For Gadamer this understanding of language is not yet at all a "real understanding" [*Verstehen*] because the accompanying reflection on the application of linguistic rules emerges only when a language game becomes problematic. Only when the intersubjectivity of the validity of linguistic rules is disturbed is an interpretive process set in motion that reestablishes consensus. Wittgenstein conflated this hermeneutic understanding with the primary process of learning to speak. Correspondingly, he was convinced that learning a foreign language has the same structure as growing up in one's mother tongue. This identification was necessary for him because he lacked a dialectical concept of translation. For translation is not a transformation that permits the reduction of statements in one language system to statements in another. Rather, the act of translation highlights a productive achievement to which language always empowers those who have mastered its grammatical rules: to assimilate what is foreign and thereby to further develop one's own linguistic system. This happens daily in situations in which discussion partners must first find a "common language." This language is the result of coming to an understanding [*Verständigung*], the structure of which is similar to translation.

> Coming to an understanding in conversation involves a readiness on the part of the participants and an attempt by them to make room for what is foreign and contrary. When this is mutually the case, and each partner weighs the counterarguments while simultaneously holding fast to his own, then we can finally come to a common language and a common judgment in an imperceptible and spontaneous reciprocal transference of points of view. (We call this an exchange of opinions.) In just the same way, the translator must hold fast to the rights of his mother tongue into which he translates and yet allow its own worth to what is foreign, even contrary, in the text and its mode of expression. But this description of the activity of the translator is perhaps already too abbreviated. Even in such extreme situations of translating from one language into another, the matter under discussion [*Sache*] can scarcely be separated from the language. Only that translator will translate in a truly genuine sense who gives voice to the subject matter disclosed in the text; but this means: who finds a language that is not his own but one adequate to the original.[3]

Gadamer sees in grammatical rules not only institutionalized forms of life but delimitations of horizons. Horizons are open, and they shift; we enter into them and they in turn move with us. This Husserlian concept presents itself as a way of accentuating the assimilative and generative power of language vis-à-vis its structural accomplishments. The life-worlds that determine the grammar of language games are not closed forms of life, as Wittgenstein's monadological conception suggests.

Wittgenstein showed how the rules of linguistic communication imply the conditions of possibility of their own application. They are at the same time rules for the instructional practice through which they can be internalized. But Wittgenstein failed to appreciate that the same rules also include the conditions of possibility of their interpretation. It is proper to the grammar of a language game not only that it defines a form of life but that it defines a form of life as one's own over against others that are foreign. Because every world that is articulated in a language is a totality, the horizon of a language also encompasses that which it is not—it discloses itself as particular among particulars. For this reason, the limits of the world that it defines are not irrevocable; the dialectical confrontation of what is one's own with what is foreign leads, for the most part imperceptibly, to revisions. Translation is the medium in which these revisions take place, and language is continuously developed further. The inflexible reproduction of language and form of life at the level of the immature is only a boundary case of the flexible renewal to which a transmitted language is continually exposed, in that those who have already mastered it bridge disturbances of communication, respond to new situations, assimilate what is foreign, and find a common language for divergent tongues.

Translation is necessary not only at the horizontal level, between competing linguistic communities, but between generations and epochs as well. Tradition [*Überlieferung*], as the medium in which languages propagate themselves, takes place as translation, namely, as the bridging of distances between generations.[4] The process of socialization, through which the individual grows into his language, is the smallest unity of the process of tradition. Against this background we can see the foreshortening of perspective to which Wittgenstein succumbed; the language games of the young do not simply reproduce the practice of the aged. With the first fundamental rules of language the child learns not only the conditions of possible consensus but at the same time the conditions of a possible interpretation of these rules, which permit him to overcome, *and thereby also to express*, distance. Linguistic understanding [*Sprachverstehen*] is based not only upon a primary mutual understanding [*Verständigtsein*] but also upon a hermeneutic understanding [*Verstehen*] that is only articulated when there are disturbances in communication.

Hermeneutic self-reflection goes beyond the socio-linguistic stage of language analysis marked by the later Wittgenstein. When the transcendental construction of a pure language was shattered, language gained a new dimension through the pluralism of language games. The grammar of a language game no longer regulated only the connection of symbols but at the same time their institutionalized application in interaction. But Wittgenstein still conceived this dimension of application too narrowly. He saw only invariant linkages of symbols and activities and failed to appreciate that the application of rules includes their interpretation and further development. To be sure, Wittgenstein first made us aware—in opposition to the positivist bias—that the application of grammatical rules cannot in turn be defined at the symbolic level according to general rules; it can only be inculcated as a complex of language and practice and internalized as part of a form of life. But he remained enough of a positivist to conceive of this practice as the reproduction of fixed patterns—as if socialized individuals were subsumed under a total system composed of language and activities. In his hands the language game congeals to an opaque unity.

Actually, language spheres are not monadically sealed off but are inwardly as well as outwardly porous. The grammar of a language cannot contain a rigid design for its application. Whoever has learned to apply its rules has not only learned to express himself but also to interpret expressions in this language. Both translation (outwardly) and tradition (inwardly) must be possible in principle. Along with their possible application, grammatical rules simultaneously imply the necessity of interpretation. Wittgenstein failed to see this; as a consequence he conceived the practice of language games unhistorically. With Gadamer language gains a third dimension—grammar governs an application of rules, which, for its part, further develops the system of rules historically. The unity of language, submerged in the pluralism of language games, is reestablished dialectically in the context of tradition. Language exists only as transmitted [*tradierte*]. For tradition mirrors on a large scale the life-long socialization of individuals in their language.

Despite the abandonment of an ideal language, the concept of a language game remains bound to the unacknowledged model of formalized languages. Wittgenstein tied the intersubjectivity of ordinary language communication to the intersubjective validity of grammatical rules. To follow a rule means to apply it in the same way. The ambiguity of ordinary language and the imprecision of its rules are, for Wittgenstein, only apparent; every language game is completely ordered. The language analyst can rely on this order as a standard for his critique. Even though ordinary language cannot be reconstructed in formal language without being destroyed as such, its grammar is still no less precise and unequivocal than that of a calculus. This assumption is plausible only for someone who—contrary to Wittgenstein's own intention—has a prior commitment to the standard of formalized language. For one who ties linguistic analysis to the self-reflection of ordinary language the opposite is plainly the case. The unequivocal character of calculi is purchased with their monadological structure, that is, with a construction that excludes conversations. Strictly deductive systems permit implications, not communications. Dialogue is replaced, at best, with the transfer of information. Only dialogue-free languages have a complete order. Ordinary languages are incomplete and provide no guarantee for the absence of ambiguity. Consequently, the intersubjectivity of ordinary language communication is always "broken." It exists because consensus [*Einverständnis*] is in principle possible; and it does not exist because it is in principle necessary to achieve effective communication [*Verständigung*]. Hermeneutic understanding (*Verstehen*) is applied to the points of rupture; it compensates for the brokenness of intersubjectivity.

Whoever starts from the normal case of conversation—and not from the model of a precision language—immediately grasps the open structure of ordinary language. An "unbroken" intersubjectivity of the grammar in force would certainly make possible identity of meaning, and thereby constant relations of understanding; but it would at the same time destroy the identity of the self in communication with others. Klaus Heinrich has examined ordinary language from this perspective of the dangers of a complete integration of individuals.[5] Languages that are no longer inwardly porous and have hardened into rigid systems remove the breaks in intersubjectivity and, simultaneously, the hermeneutic distance of individuals from one another. They no longer permit the vulnerable balance between separation and union in which the identify of every ego has to develop. The problem of an ego-identity that can be established only through identifications—and this means through alienations [*Entäusserungen*] of identity—is at the same time the problem of a linguistic communication that permits the saving balance between speechless union and speechless alienation [*Entfremdung*], between the sacrifice of individuality and the isolation of the individualized. Experiences of imminent loss of identity refer to experiences of the reification of linguistic communication. In the sustained nonidentity of a successful communication the individual can develop a precarious ego-identity and preserve it against the risks of reification or formlessness. Heinrich analyzes primarily one side: the conditions of protest against the self-destruction of a society sinking back into indifference, a society that obliterates through forced integration the distance of individuals from one another. This is the situation of dictated language regulation and unbroken intersubjectivity that cancels out the subjective range of application. Wittgenstein's conception of a language game would be realized in this way. For a strictly regulated language, that inwardly closes all gaps, must be monadically sealed off outwardly. The speech of protest is, thus, the other side of hermeneutic understanding; the latter bridges a sustained distance and prevents the breaking off of communication. The power of reconciliation is intrinsic to translation. It marshals the unifying power of language against its disintegration into a number of dispersed languages, which, as isolated systems, would exact the penalty of immediate unity.[6]

II

Gadamer uses the image of a horizon to capture the basic hermeneutic character of every concrete language—far from having a closed boundary, each concrete language can in principle incorporate what is linguistically foreign and at first incomprehensible. Each of the partners among whom communication must be brought about lives in a horizon. For this reason Gadamer represents effective hermeneutic communication [*Verständigung*] with the image of a fusion [*Verschmelzung*] of horizons. This holds true for the vertical plane in which we overcome historical distance through understanding as well as for the horizontal plane in which understanding mediates geographical or cultural-linguistic distance. The appropriation [*Aneignung*] of a tradition through understanding follows the pattern of translation. The horizon of the present is not, so to speak, extinguished but fused with the horizon from which the tradition comes.

> To understand a tradition requires, to be sure, a historical horizon. But there can be no question of gaining this horizon by transposing oneself [*sich versetzen*] into a historical situation. It is, rather, necessary to have a horizon already if one is to be able to transpose oneself in this way. For what does it mean to "transpose oneself"? Certainly not simply to disregard oneself. Of course, this is necessary insofar as one must really keep the other situation before one's eyes. But one must bring *oneself* into this other situation. Only that consummates the meaning of "transposing oneself." If one transposes oneself, for instance, into the situation of another, one will understand him, i.e., become conscious of the otherness, indeed the inextinguishable individuality of the other, precisely through transposing oneself into his situation. Such self-transposition is neither the empathetic projection of one individuality into another nor the subjection of the other to one's own standards; it means, rather, rising to a higher level of generality on which not only one's own particularity but that of the other is overcome. The concept of horizon presents itself here because it expresses the superior farsightedness that the one who is understanding must possess. To acquire a horizon means that one learns to see beyond the near and the all-too-near not in order to overlook it but in order better to see it in a larger whole and with a more accurate sense of its proportions. Nietzsche's account of the many changing horizons into which one needs to transpose oneself is not a correct description of historical consciousness. Whoever overlooks himself in this way has

precisely no historical horizon. . . . To acquire a historical horizon certainly demands effort on one's part. We are always preoccupied, hopefully and fearfully, with what is closest to us; and we always approach the testimony of the past with this bias. Thus we have continually to curb the precipitous assimilation of the past to our own expectations of meaning. Only then will one hear the tradition as it makes itself audible in its own, distinct meaning. . . . Actually, the horizon of the present is constantly being developed to the extent that we must continually put our prejudices to the test. Not the least of these tests is the encounter with the past and the understanding of the tradition out of which we come. Thus the horizon of the present is not formed without the past. There is no more a separate horizon of the present than there are historical horizons that have to be acquired. Rather, understanding is always the process of fusing such supposedly self-sufficient horizons.[7]

This interlacing of horizons cannot be methodologically eliminated; it belongs to the very conditions of hermeneutic work. This becomes evident in the circular relation of prior understanding [*Vorverständnis*] to the explication of what is understood. We can decipher the parts of a text only if we anticipate an understanding—however diffuse—of the whole; and conversely, we can correct this anticipation [*Vorgriff*] only to the extent to which we explicate individual parts.

Thus the circle is not a formal circle. It is neither subjective nor objective but describes understanding as the interplay between the movement of tradition and that of the interpreter. The anticipation of meaning that guides our understanding of a text is not an action of subjectivity; it is determined instead by the common bond that links us with the tradition. This common bond, however, is constantly being developed in our relationships to tradition.[8]

The interpreter is a moment of the same fabric of tradition as his object. He appropriates a tradition from a horizon of expectations that is already informed by this tradition. For this reason we have, in a certain way, already understood the tradition with which we are confronted. And only for this reason is the horizon opened up by the language of the interpreter not merely something subjective that distorts our interpretation. In opposition to theoretically oriented language analysis, hermeneutics insists that we learn to understand a language from the horizon of the language we already know. In a way, we repeat virtually those learning processes through which the native was socialized into his language. However, we are not drawn into these learning processes immediately [*unvermittelt*] but through the mediation of the rules that we internalized in our own socialization processes. Hermeneutics comprehends the mediation of what the interpreter brings with him, with what he appropriates, as a further development of the same tradition which the interpreter seeks to appropriate. Hermeneutics avoids the embarassment of a language analysis that cannot justify its own language game; for it starts with the idea that learning language games can never succeed abstractly but only from the basis of the language games that the interpreter has already mastered. Hermeneutic understanding is the interpretation of texts in the knowledge of already understood texts. It leads to new learning processes [*Bildungsprozesse*] out of the horizon of already completed learning processes. It is a new step of socialization that takes previous socialization as its point of departure. In appropriating tradition, it continues tradition. Because hermeneutic understanding itself belongs to the objective context that is reflected in it, the overcoming of temporal distance cannot be interpreted as a construction of the knowing subject. The continuity of tradition already bridges the distance of the interpreter from his object.

From the perspective of hermeneutic self-reflection, the phenomenological and linguistic foundations of interpretive [*verstehenden*] sociology move to the side of historicism. Like the latter, they succumb to objectivism, since they claim for the phenomenological observer and the language analyst a purely theoretical attitude. But both are connected with their object domain through communication experience alone and cannot, therefore, lay claim to the role of uninvolved spectators. Impartiality is guaranteed only through reflected participation, that is, by monitoring the initial situation [*Ausgangssituation*] of the interpreter—the sounding-board from which hermeneutic understanding cannot be detached. At the level of communication, the possible objectivity of experience is endangered precisely to the degree that the interpreter is seduced by the illusion of objectivism into concealing from himself the methodologically indissoluble bond to the hermeneutic initial situation. Gadamer's first-rate critique of the objectivistic self-understanding of the cultural sciences [*Geisteswissenschaften*] hits not only historicism but also the false consciousness of the phenomenological and linguistic executors of its legacy. The pluralism of life-worlds and language games is only a distant echo of the world views and cultures projected by Dilthey onto a fictive plane of simultaneity.

In the second part of his work. Gadamer discusses the romantic empathy theory of hermeneutics and its application to history (Scheiermacher and Droysen). Using Dilthey, he demonstrates the paradoxical consequences of a historical consciousness that—while transcending the psychological approach to understanding expressions in favor of an analysis of constellations of meaning—remains dependent on the deceptive capacity for an all-understanding reproduction of any objectivated meaning-content whatever. Against Schleiermacher's and Dilthey's aestheticizing of history and against their anaesthetizing of historical reflection, Gadamer brings to bear, subtly and relentlessly, Hegel's insight that the restitution of past life is possible only to the extent that it is a reconstruction of the present out of its past. In the place of an illusory reproduction of the past, we have its reflective mediation with present life.

Subsequent understanding is in principle superior to the original production and can, therefore, be formulated as a "better understanding." This is not so much due to a subsequent bringing-to-consciousness that places us on a par with the author (as Schleiermacher thought). On the contrary, it describes the ineradicable difference between the author and the interpreter that is given with historical distance. Each time will have to understand a transmitted text in its own way; for the text belongs in the whole of the tradition that is of substantive interest to the age and in which it tries to understand itself. The actual meaning of a text, as it speaks to the interpreter, is not dependent on the occasion represented by the author and his original public. At least it is not exhausted by it; for the meaning is also determined by the historical situation of the interpreter and thus by the whole of the objective course of history. An author like Chladenius, who has not yet submerged understanding in past history, takes this naively and artlessly into account when he suggests that an author need not himself recognize the true meaning of his text and, therefore, that the interpreter often can and must understand more than he. But this is of fundamental significance. The meaning of a text goes beyond its author, not only occasionally, but always. Understanding is therefore not merely reproductive but also productive.[9]

Objectivism conceals the complex of historical influences [*den wirkungsgeschichtlichen Zusammenhang*] in which historical consciousness itself is located. The principle of the historical influence [*Wirkungsgeschichte*] of a text becomes for Gadamer a basic methodological axiom for the interpretation of the text itself. This is not a question of an auxiliary discipline that supplies additional information but of research fundamental to the interpretation itself. For "historical influence" refers to the chain of past interpretations through which the prior understanding of the interpreter is objectively mediated with his object, even if behind his back. Transmitted [*überlieferte*] documents and historical events do not acquire their meaning—which hermeneutic understanding endeavors to grasp descriptively—independently of the events and interpretations that follow them. Meaning [*Sinn*] is an aggregate of sedimented significations [*Bedeutungen*] that continuously emerge from new retrospectives. Thus a transmitted meaning [*tradierter Sinn*] is in principle incomplete, that is, open for sedimentations from future perspectives. Historians and philologists who reflect on historical influences take into account the openness of the horizon of meaning. They anticipate that the progress of events will bring out new aspects of their object. This is the rational core of the philologist's experience that the content of transmitted texts is "inexhaustible."[10] Corresponding to this is the historian's experience that he cannot in principle give a conclusive description of any event.

Completely to describe an event is to locate it in all the right stories, and this we cannot do. We cannot because we are temporally provincial with regard to the future.[11]

A. C. Danto corroborates Gadamer's principle of historical influence through an analysis of the form of historical statements. Historical accounts make use of narrative statements. They are called narrative because they present events as elements of stories [*Geschichten*]. Stories have a beginning and an end; they are held together by an action. Historical events are reconstructed within the reference system of a story. They cannot be presented without relation to other, later events. Narrative statements are in general characterized by the fact that they refer to at least two events with different temporal indices, the earlier of these being the theme of the description. Narrative statements describe an event with the aid of categories under which it could not have been observed. The sentence, "The Thirty Years War began in 1618," presupposes that at least those events have elapsed which are relevant for the history of the war up to the Peace of Westphalia, events that could not have been narrated by any observer at the outbreak of the war. According to the context, the expression "Thirty Years War" signifies not only a military happening that extended through three decades but the political collapse of the German Empire, the postponement of capitalist development, the end of the Counter-Reformation, the motif for a Wallenstein drama, etc., etc. The predicates with which an event is narratively presented require the appearance of later events in the light of which the event in question appears as an historical event. Consequently, the historical description of events becomes in the course of time richer than empirical observation at the moment of their happening permits.

In the reference system of theories of empirical science events are described only with categories that could be used to record an observation of these events. A scientifically predicted event can only be identified in an observation language that is neutral with respect to the time of its happening. A historical account of the same event—a solar eclipse, let us say—has to relate to the languages of interpretation of all those for whom it has acquired historical significance, i.e., relevance in the framework of a story. If the historian wanted to proceed like the astronomer or physicist in describing an event and to use a temporally neutral observation language, he would have to assume the role of an ideal chronicler. Danto introduces this fiction; he places at the disposal of the historian a machine that records all events at each moment, stores them, and retrieves them. This ideal eyewitness notes down in an observation language everything that historically happens and how it happens. Notwithstanding, this fabulous machine would be almost worthless for our historian; for the perfect eyewitness reports would be meaningless if they were not constructions of at least one single living eyewitness who could make use of narrative statements. The ideal chronicler is not in a position to describe intentional actions, for that would presuppose anticipating events beyond the time of observation. Such a machine is unable to establish causal relationships, for this would require that an event could be described retrospectively—the observation of a temporally later event is the necessary condition for identifying a previous event as its cause. The mechanical chronicler cannot tell a single story because relations between events with different temporal indices escape its observation; it cannot see the beginning, crisis, and end of an action complex because it lacks a point of view for possible interpretation.

Of course, the descriptions of the ideal eyewitness would also have to be interpretations. But a temporally neutral observation language excludes that mode of interpretation that alone makes it possible to comprehend an observed event as an historical event. Two successive historical events can be understood as the relation of a past-present to a past-future only by retrospectively applying the reference system of acting subjects who assess present conditions with a view to anticipated future conditions. When we speak of the outbreak of the Thirty Years War, we grasp the events of 1618 from the retrospective of a war ended thirty years later. For a contemporary of 1618 this expression could have had only a prospective significance. Thus we describe the event in categories that would have been relevant for a contemporary not as an observer but as an actor who could anticipate something of the future. To comprehend events historically, i.e., to present them in the form of narrative statements, means that we comprehend them in the schema of possible action.

In doing this, the historian limits himself of course to the actual intentions of the actor. As someone who has been born later, he has already transcended the horizon of history as it presented itself to the actor. But even the unintended components and consequences of intentional complexes are grasped from the point of view of possible intentionality as soon as they enter the historical horizon of one who has come later. Gadamer demonstrates the transition from the psychological to the hermeneutic foundation of the cultural sciences with this point: "The problem of history is not how relationships are in general experienciable and knowable but how relationships that no one has experienced as such should be knowable."[12] Danto discusses this relation of subjectively intended meaning to objective meaning through the example of the romantic traits subsequently discovered in the works of classicism.

> It is a discovery for which we require the concept of romanticism and criteria for identifying the romantic. But a concept of romanticism would naturally not have been available in the heyday of classicism. . . . Whatever in classical writings turns out to fall under the concept of romanticism was doubtless put in those works intentionally. But they were not intentional under the description "putting in romantic ele-

ments," for the authors lacked that concept. This is an important limitation on the use of *Verstehen*. It was not an intention of Aristarchus to
anticipate Copernicus, nor of Petrarch to open the Renaissance. To give
such descriptions requires concepts which were only available at a later
time. From this it follows that even having access to the minds of the men
whose action he describes will not enable the Ideal Chronicler to appreciate the significance of those actions.[13]

The historian does not observe from the perspective of the actor but describes
events and actions out of the experiential horizon of a history that goes beyond
the actor's horizons of expectations. But the meaning that retrospectively
accrues to events in this way emerges only in the schema of possible action, that
is, only if the events are viewed as if this meaning had—with the knowledge of
those who were born later—been intended. Thus the language in which the
historian presents events does not primarily express observations but the
interrelations of a series of interpretations. The interpretation of contemporary
observers is the last rung on a ladder of interpretations. Its first rung is the
reference system of the historian, which, insofar as he is himself an acting
subject, cannot be independent of his horizon of expectations. The ladder itself
is the relationship of tradition that connects the historian with his object. It is
constructed from the retrojections of those coming later who, knowing better,
have reconstructed what happened in the schema of possible action. The
historian is no chronicler restricted to observation; he is engaged in communicative experiences. Instead of the uninvolved recording of events, we have the
task of hermeneutic understanding. At the level of historical presentation it
proves to be meaningless to want to separate something like a pure description
of the chronicler from interpretation. Danto criticizes such a conception

> that, in a way, accepts the ideal of imitation of the past but wants to insist
> that there is something beyond giving accounts, even perfect accounts, of
> the past or parts of the past, which is also the aim of history to do. For in
> addition to making true statements about the past, it is held, historians are
> interested in giving interpretations of the past. And even if we had a
> perfect account, the task of interpretation would remain to be done. The
> problem of just giving descriptions belongs to a humbler level of histor-
> ical work; it is, indeed, the work of chroniclers. That is a distinction I am
> unable to accept. For I wish to maintain that history is all of a piece. It is
> all of a piece in the sense that there is nothing one might call a pure
> description in contrast with something else to be called an interpretation.
> Just to do history at all is to employ some overarching conception that
> goes beyond what is given. And to see that this is so is to see that history
> as an imitation or duplication of the past is an impossible ideal.[14]

A series of events acquires the unity of a story only from a point of view that
cannot be taken from those events themselves. The actors are caught in their

histories; even for them—if they tell their own stories—the point of view from which the events can take on the coherence of a story arises only subsequently. The story has a meaning, of course, only for someone who is in general capable of acting. As long as new points of view arise, the same events can enter into other stories and acquire new significations. We could give a definitive and complete description of a historical event only if we could be certain that new points of view would no longer appear, that is, that we could anticipate all the relevant points of view that would emerge in the future. In this sense, philosophy of history anticipates the point of view that could guide the last historian at the close of history as a whole. Since we are unable to anticipate the future course of events, we are also unable to anticipate, with good grounds, the point of view of the last historian. But without philosophy of history no historical event can be completely represented.

> Any account of the past is essentially incomplete. It is essentially incomplete, that is, if its completion would require the fulfillment of a condition that simply cannot be fulfilled. And my thesis will be that a complete account of the past would presuppose a complete account of the future so that one could not achieve a complete historical account without also achieving a philosophy of history. So that if there cannot be a legitimate philosophy of history, there cannot be a legitimate and complete historical account. Paraphrasing a famous result in logic, we cannot, in brief, consistently have a complete historical account. Our knowledge of the past, in other words, is limited by our knowledge (or ignorance) of the future. And this is the deeper connection between substantive philosophy of history and ordinary history.[15]

As long as the choice of descriptive expressions is determined by a theoretical system of reference, incompleteness of descriptions is no defect. Because, however, historians do not have at their disposal theories like those in the empirical sciences, their incomplete descriptions are in principle also arbitrary.

> Completely to describe an event is to locate it in all the right stories, and this we cannot do. We cannot because we are temporally provincial with regard to the future. We cannot for the same reasons that we cannot achieve a speculative philosophy of history. The complete description then presupposes a narrative organization, and narrative organization is something that we do. Not merely that, but the imposition of a narrative organization logically involves us with an inexpungeable subjective factor. There is an element of sheer arbitrariness in it. We organize events relative to some events which we find significant in a sense not touched upon here. It is a sense of significance common, however, to all narratives and is determined by the topical interests of this human being or that.[16]

These implications are plausible, however, only if we accept the ideal of complete description as a meaningful historiographical ideal. Danto develops the *idea of all possible histories* through the hypothetical role of the last historian. But for the last historian, as for every historian before him, the series of past events can take the shape of a story only from a point of view that he does not acquire from these events themselves. Only if he himself acts in a horizon of expectations can he delineate the last of all possible reference systems for the presentation of historical events. But as soon as the historian acts at all, he produces new relationships that combine into a further story from a new retrospective. The definitive and complete description would thereby be subjected to a revision. Consequently, the historical presentation of history as a whole would require a qualification that is per se incompatible with the end of history. The ideal of complete description cannot be consistently formulated; it ascribes to history a claim to contemplation that it not only cannot redeem but that is illegitimate as a claim.

Every historian is in the role of the last historian. Hermeneutic deliberations about the inexhaustibility of the horizon of meaning and the new interpretations of future generations remain empty; they have no consequences for what the historian has to do. For he does not at all organize his knowledge according to standards of pure theory. He cannot grasp anything that he can know historically independently of the framework of his own life-practice [*Lebenspraxis*]. In this context the future exists only as a horizon of expectations. And these expectations fuse hypothetically the fragments of previous traditions into an intuitively grasped totality of universal history, in the light of which every relevant event can in principle be described as completely as is possible for the practically effective self-understanding of a social life-world. Implicitly every historian proceeds in the way that Danto wishes to forbid to the philosopher of history. From the viewpoints of practice he anticipates end-states from which the multiplicity of events coalesces smoothly into action-orienting stories. Precisely the openness of history, that is, the situation of the actor, permits the hypothetical anticipation of history as a whole, without which the retrospective significance of the parts would not emerge. Dilthey already saw this.

> We grasp the significance of a moment of the past. It is significant insofar as a linkage to the future was achieved in it, through action or through an external event. . . . The individual moment [has] significance through its connection with the whole, through the relation of past and future, of individual being and mankind. But what constitutes the peculiar nature of this relation of part to whole within life? It is a relation that is never entirely completed. One would have to await the end of one's life and could only in the hour of death survey the whole from which the relation of the parts could be determined. One would have to await the end of history to possess all the material needed for determining its significance. On the other hand, the whole is only there for us to the extent that it

becomes comprehensible from the parts. Understanding moves constantly between these two modes of consideration. Our interpretation of the meaning of life changes constantly. Every plan of life is an expression of a comprehension of the significance of life. What we set as the goal of our future conditions the determination of the past's significance.[17]

Of course these goal-settings, i.e., the hermeneutic anticipations rooted in the interests of life-practice, are not arbitrary. For they can hold good only to the degree that reality does not escape their grasp. Moreover, it is the peculiar achievement of hermeneutic understanding that—in relation to the successful appropriation of traditions—the prejudices that are attached to the initial situation of the interpreter are also rendered transparent in their emergence from tradition, and thus absorbed into reflection.

III

Historical accounts that have the form of narrative statements can appear to be in principle incomplete and arbitrary only if they are measured against a mistaken ideal of description. The statements of empirical science do not themselves meet this standard of contemplative comprehension and corresponding representation. Their accuracy depends on criteria that determine the validity of technically utilizable knowledge. Correspondingly, if we examine the validity of hermeneutic statements in the framework proper to them, the framework of knowledge that has consequences for practice, then what Danto has to regard as a defect proves to be a transcendental condition of possible knowledge. Only because we project the provisional end-state of a system of reference out of the horizon of life-practice can the interpretation of events (which can be organized into a story from the point of view of the projected end) as well as the interpretation of parts (which can be described as fragments from the point of view of the anticipated totality) have any information content at all for that life-practice. I find Gadamer's real achievement in the demonstration that hermeneutic understanding is linked with transcendental necessity to the articulation of an action-orienting self-understanding.

The immanent connection of understanding and application can be seen in the examples of theology and jurisprudence. Both the interpretation of the Bible in preaching and the interpretation of positive law in adjudication serve simultaneously as guideposts of how to apply the evidence in a given situation. The practical life-relation to the self-understanding of the clients—the church congregation or the legal community—is not simply a subsequent corollary to the interpretation. Rather, the interpretation is realized in the application itself. Gadamer does not want to restrict the scope of this constitutive connection between understanding and practical transposition into life only to certain traditions that (like the sacred texts of a canonical tradition or the valid norms of positive law) are already institutionally binding. Nor does he want to extend it merely to the interpretation of works of art or the explication of philosophical texts. He persuades us that the applicative understanding of distinguished traditions endowed with a claim to authority provides the model for hermeneutic understanding in general.

> The close relationship that originally linked philological hermeneutics with legal and theological hermeneutics was based on a recognition of application as an integrating moment of all understanding. Constitutive for both legal and theological hermeneutics is the tension between the fixed text—of the law or of revelation—on the one hand and, on the other hand, the meaning acquired through its application in the concrete instant of interpretation, whether in preaching or in the legal judgment. A law is not to be understood historically but is supposed to be concretized in its legal validity through interpretation. Similarly, a religious revelation is not to be interpreted merely as a historical document but is supposed to be understood in such a way that it exercises its redemptive influence. In both cases, this involves that the text (the law or the message of salvation), if it is to be understood properly, i.e., corresponding to the claim that the text puts forward, must be understood anew and otherwise at each moment, i.e., in each concrete situation. Understanding is here always application. We took as our point of departure the knowledge that the understanding exercised in the cultural sciences is also essentially historical, that is, that there too a text is understood only if it is understood each time in another way. The task of a historical hermeneutics was characterized precisely by the fact that it reflects on the tension between the sameness of the shared reality [*Sache*] and the changing situation in which it is supposed to be understood.[18]

Gadamer explains the applicative knowledge engendered by hermeneutic understanding through the Aristotelian determinations of practical knowledge.[19] Hermeneutic knowledge has three features in common with that political-ethical knowledge that Aristotle distinguished from both science and technical knowledge.[20] *In the first place*, practical knowledge has a *reflective* form; it is simultaneously "knowing oneself." For this reason we experience mistakes in the areas of practical knowledge in ourselves. False opinions have the habitual form of false consciousness. Deficient insight has the objective power of delusion. The *second* aspect is connected with this—practical knowledge is *internalized*. It has the power to fix drives and to shape passions. In contrast, technical knowledge remains external. We forget technical rules as soon as we fall out of practice. Practical rules, once mastered, become by contrast components of our personality structure. For this reason practical knowledge can also not be gained in the same presuppositionless way as theoretical knowledge; it must fasten on to a structure of prejudgments or prejudices [*Vorurteilsstruktur*]. Only the hearer who has already acquired a foreknowledge [*Vorwissen*] on the basis of appropriated traditions and experienced situations can be enlightened by lectures in practical philosophy. Practical knowledge fastens on to a socialization process and develops it further. The *third* aspect becomes comprehensible at this point—practical knowledge is *global*. It refers not to particular aims that can be specified independently of the means for their realization. The action-orienting goals, as well as the ways in which they can be realized, are components of the same form of life [*bios*]. This is always a social form of life that is developed through communicative action. Practical knowledge orients by way of rules of interaction. These transmitted [*tradierten*] rules are acquired by training; but the historically changing conditions of their use call for an application that, for its part, further develops the rules through interpretation.

If the hermeneutic sciences occupy the same position with respect to tradition as a practical philosophy that, enlightened by historical consciousness, has abandoned an ontologically grounded natural law, then the Aristotelian determinations can be claimed for hermeneutics as well.

> The interpreter who is occupied with a tradition seeks to apply the latter to himself. But here too this does not mean that the traditional text is for him given and understood in its general nature and only afterwards put to particular uses. Rather, the interpreter wants nothing other than to understand this general sense—the text, i.e., to understand what the tradition says, in what the meaning and significance of the text consist. In order to understand this, however, he cannot disregard himself and his concrete hermeneutic situation. He must relate the text to this situation if he wants to understand at all.[21]

Hermeneutic understanding is structurally oriented toward eliciting from tradition a possible action-orienting self-understanding of social groups. It makes possible a form of consensus on which communicative action depends. It eliminates the dangers of a communication breakdown in two directions: vertically, in one's own tradition, and horizontally, in the mediation between traditions of different cultures and groups. If these communication flows come to an end and the intersubjectivity of understanding either hardens or falls apart, an elementary condition of survival is disrupted—the possibility of agreement without constraint and recognition without force.

The dialectic of the general and the particular, which also obtains in the appropriation of traditions and the corresponding application of practical rules, shows once again the brokenness of intersubjectivity. That something like tradition exists at all involves an aspect of nonobligation—the tradition must also be revisable; otherwise what is nonidentical in the sustained group identity would be destroyed. Ego-identities can be formed and maintained in linguistic communication only if the related group-identity can constitute itself, vis-à-vis the collective other of its own past, as simultaneously identical with and different from it. For this reason the global generality of practical rules requires a concretizing interpretation through which, in the given situation, it is molded into a concrete generality that is intersubjectively valid.

A technical rule is abstractly general. It can be compared to a theoretical sentence whose conditions of application are formulated in general terms. Intersubjectivity is established at the theoretical level by a prior definition of fundamental predicates and at the operational level by invariant rules of application. The identification of states of affairs to which the sentence can be applied does not affect its semantic content. We can thus subsume cases under something abstractly general. It is otherwise with practical rules. We compare them with traditional meaning-contents, which are only understood when we have arrived at a consensus about their significance; only then do they have intersubjective validity in a social group. Understanding becomes a problem in this case because both the binding definition of fundamental predicates and the invariant rules of application are lacking. A prior understanding guides us in the search for states of affairs in which the meaning can be made precise; but this identification of the range of application qualifies in turn the semantic content. The global generality, which we must already have understood diffusely, determines the subsumed particular only to the degree to which it is itself first concretized by this particular. Only through this does it gain intersubjective recognition in a given situation; the recognition is tied to this situation. A new situation demands a renewal of intersubjectivity through repeated understanding. And intersubjectivity does not come to pass arbitrarily; it is, rather, the result of thoughtful mediation of the past with present life.

To be sure, Hegel could speak of thought in this connection with greater legitimacy than Gadamer. It is difficult to fix the moment of knowledge in hermeneutic understanding independently of the absolute movement of reflection. If the framework of tradition as a whole is no longer regarded as a production of reason apprehending itself, then the further development of tradition fostered by hermeneutic understanding cannot eo ipso count as rational. It would, however, be precipitous to take the logical dependence of interpretation on application and the interlacing of normative anticipation with cognitive experiences as sufficient cause for banishing hermeneutic understanding from the realm of substantial research and possible knowledge. At the level of hermeneutic understanding, the mobile relation that makes cognitive processes at all possible is not yet shut down—the relation between the formation of standards and description according to standards. The methodology of the empirical sciences pulls the two apart—theoretical constructions from the observations on which they can founder. But both aspects are previously coordinated in a transcendental framework. Protophysics makes an interpretation of reality binding, a reality that has been previously constituted under the conception of possible objects of technical control. With this constitution, the rules according to which theoretical sentences can be applied to facts are predecided; thus they are unproblematic within the sciences. Application is problematic and inseparable from interpretation wherever a transcendental framework that coordinates sentences and facts is not yet established once and for all but is undergoing transformation and must be determined ad hoc.[22]

The appropriation of traditional meaning-contents proceeds on a level at which schemata of possible world-conceptions are decided. This decision is not made independently of whether such a schema proves itself in a given and preinterpreted situation. It is therefore senseless to assign hermeneutic understanding either to theory or to experience; it is both and neither. What we have called communicative experience will normally take place within a language whose grammar fixes a connection of such schemata. But the brokenness of intersubjectivity renders the continuous coordination of views in a common schema a permanent task. Only in extreme cases does this inconspicuously ever-present transformation and development of transcendental schemata of world-interpretation become a problem that has to be explicitly mastered through hermeneutic understanding. Such cases appear when traditions are disrupted or foreign cultures are encountered—or when we analyze familiar traditions and cultures as if they were foreign. A controlled distanciation [*Verfremdung*] can raise understanding from a prescientific experience to the rank of a reflected procedure. In this way hermeneutic procedures enter into the social sciences. They are unavoidable as soon as data is gathered at the level of communicative experience. They are equally important for the selection of a categorial framework if we do not want to behave naively in the face of the unavoidably historical content of even the most general categories.

Gadamer unwittingly obliges the positivistic devaluation of hermeneutics. He joins his opponents in the view that hermeneutic experience "transcends the range of control of scientific method."[23] In the preface to the second edition of his work he sums up his investigations in the thesis

> that the moment of historical influence is and remains effective in all understanding of tradition, even where the method of the modern historical sciences has gained ground and makes what has become historically into an "object" that has to be "ascertained" like an experimental finding—as if tradition were foreign and, humanly regarded, incomprehensible in the same sense as the object of physics.[24]

This correct critique of a false objectivistic self-understanding cannot, however, lead to a suspension of the methodological distanciation of the object, which distinguishes a self-reflective understanding from everyday communicative experience. The confrontation of "truth" and "method" should not have misled Gadamer to oppose hermeneutic experience abstractly to methodic knowledge as a whole. As it is, hermeneutic experience is the ground of the hermeneutic sciences. And even if it were feasible to remove the humanities entirely from the sphere of science, the sciences of action could not avoid linking empirical-analytic with hermeneutic procedures. The claim which hermeneutics legitimately makes good against the practically influential absolutism of a general methodology of the empirical sciences, brings no dispensation from the business of methodology in general. This claim will, I fear, be effective *in* the sciences or not at all. The ontological—in Heidegger's sense—self-understanding of hermeneutics that Gadamer expresses in the preface mentioned above does not, it seems to me, suit his intentions.

> I did not want to develop a system of rules of skill that would be able to describe or even to guide the methodological procedure of the cultural sciences. It was also not my intention to investigate the theoretical foundations of work in the humanities in order to turn the knowledge gained to practical ends. If there is a practical implication of the investigations presented here, it is not an implication for unscientific "engagement" but for the "scientific" honesty to admit to oneself the engagement operative in every understanding. But my real claim was and is a philosophical one. Not what we are doing, not what we ought to be doing but what happens with us beyond our wanting and doing, is in question.[25]

This thesis is grounded with the statement:

> Understanding itself should be thought of not so much as an action of subjectivity but as entering into the happening of tradition [*Überlieferungsgeschehen*] in which past and present are constantly mediated. It is this that must be acknowledged in hermeneutic theory, which is much too strongly dominated by the idea of a procedure, a method.[26]

In Gadamer's view, on-going tradition and hermeneutic inquiry merge to a single point. Opposed to this is the insight that the reflected appropriation of tradition breaks up the nature-like [*naturwüchsige*] substance of tradition and alters the position of the subject in it.[27] Gadamer knows that the hermeneutic sciences first developed in reaction to a decline in the binding character of traditions. When he emphasizes, nevertheless, that traditions are not rendered powerless by historical consciousness (p. xv), then he overlays the justified critique of the false self-understanding of historicism with the unjustified expectation that historicism is without consequences. Certainly, Scheler's grounding of the thesis that historical traditions lose their nature-like efficacy through scientific objectivation is methodologically false. And compared with this, the hermeneutic insight is certainly correct, viz., the insight that understanding—no matter how controlled it may be—cannot simply leap over the interpreter's relationships to tradition. But from the fact that understanding is structurally a part of the traditions that it further develops through appropriation, it does not follow that the medium of tradition is not profoundly altered by scientific reflection. Even in traditions whose efficacy is unbroken, what is at work is not simply an authority detached from insight and blindly asserting itself. Every tradition must be woven with a sufficiently wide mesh to allow for application, i.e., for prudent transposition with regard to changed situations. But the methodic cultivation of prudence in the hermeneutic sciences shifts the balance between authority and reason. Gadamer fails to appreciate the power of reflection that is developed in understanding. This type of reflection is no longer blinded by the illusion of an absolute, self-grounded autonomy and does not detach itself from the soil of contingency on which it finds itself. But in grasping the genesis of the tradition from which it proceeds and on which it turns back, reflection shakes the dogmatism of life-practices.

Gadamer turns the insight into the structure of prejudgments [*Vorurteilsstruktur*] involved in understanding into a rehabilitation of prejudice as such. But does it follow from the unavoidability of hermeneutic anticipation eo ipso that there are legitimate prejudices? Gadamer is motivated by the conservatism of that first generation, by the impulse of a Burke that has not yet been turned against the rationalism of the eighteenth century; he is convinced that true authority need not be authoritarian. It distinguishes itself from false authority through recognition [*Anerkennung*]: "indeed, authority has immediately nothing to do with obedience but with cognition [*Erkenntnis*]."[28] This strikingly harsh statement expresses a basic philosophical conviction that is not covered by hermeneutics itself but at most by its absolutization.

Gadamer has in mind the type of educational process through which tradition is transferred into individual learning processes and appropriated as tradition. Here the person of the educator legitimates prejudices that are inculcated in the learner with authority—and this means, however we turn it around, under the potential threat of sanctions and with the prospect of gratifications. Identification with the model creates the authority that alone makes possible the internalization of norms, the sedimentation of prejudices. The prejudices are in turn the conditions of possible knowledge. This knowledge is raised to reflection when it makes the normative framework itself transparent while moving around in it. In this way hermeneutics also makes us conscious of that which is already historically prestructured by inculcated tradition in the very act of understanding. At one point Gadamer characterizes the task of hermeneutics as follows: it has to return along the path of Hegel's phenomenology of spirit in such a way that it demonstrates the substantiality that underlies and shapes all subjectivity.[29] However, the substantiality of what is historically pregiven does not remain unaffected when it is taken up in reflection. A structure of preunderstanding or prejudgment that has been rendered transparent can no longer function as a prejudice. But this is precisely what Gadamer seems to imply. That authority converges with knowledge means that the tradition that is effectively behind the educator legitimates the prejudices inculcated in the rising generation; they could then only be confirmed in this generation's reflection. In assuring himself of the structure of prejudgment, the mature individual would transfer the formerly unfree recognition of the personal authority of the guardian to the objective authority of a traditional framework. But then it would remain a matter of authority, for reflection could only move within the limits of the facticity of tradition. The act of recognition that is mediated through reflection would not at all have altered the fact that tradition as such remains the only ground of the validity of prejudices.

Gadamer's prejudice for the rights of prejudices certified by tradition denies the power of reflection. The latter proves itself, however, in being able to reject the claim of tradition. Reflection dissolves substantiality because it not only confirms, but also breaks up, dogmatic forces. Authority and knowledge do not converge. To be sure, knowledge is rooted in actual tradition; it remains bound to contingent conditions. But reflection does not wrestle with the facticity of transmitted norms without leaving a trace. It is condemned to be after the fact; but in glancing back it develops retroactive power. We can turn back upon internalized norms only after we have first learned, under externally imposed force, to follow them blindly. Reflection recalls that path of authority along which the grammars of language games were dogmatically inculcated as rules for interpreting the world and for action. In this process the element of authority that was simply domination can be stripped away and dissolved into the less coercive constraint of insight and rational decision.

This experience of reflection is the unforgettable legacy bequeathed to us by German Idealism from the spirit of the eighteenth century. One is tempted to lead Gadamer into battle against himself, to demonstrate to him hermeneutically that he ignores that legacy because he has taken over an undialectical concept of enlightenment from the limited perspective of the German nineteenth century and that with it he has adopted an attitude which vindicated for us (Germans) a dangerous pretension to superiority separating us from Western tradition. But the matter is not this simple; Gadamer has a systematic argument at hand. The right of reflection demands that the hermeneutic approach restrict itself. It calls for a reference system that goes beyond the framework of tradition as such; only then can tradition also be criticized. But how could such a reference system be legitimated except, in turn, out of the appropriation of tradition?

IV

Wittgenstein subjected linguistic analysis first to a transcendental and then to a socio-linguistic self-reflection. Gadamer's hermeneutics marks a third stage of reflection, the historical. At this stage the interpreter and his object are conceived as elements of the same complex. This objective complex presents itself as tradition or historical influence. Through it, as a medium of linguistic symbols, communications are historically propagated. We call this process "historical" because the continuity of tradition is preserved only through translation, through a large-scale philology proceeding in a nature-like manner. The intersubjectivity of ordinary language communication is broken and must be restored again and again. This productive achievement of hermeneutic understanding, whether implicitly or explicitly carried through, is for its part motivated by the tradition that it further develops in this way. Tradition is not a process that we learn to master but a transmitted language in which we live.

> The mode of being of tradition is not, of course, one of sensuous immediacy. It is language; and the hearing that understands it in interpreting texts draws its truth into its own linguistic behavior-in-the-world [*Weltverhalten*]. Linguistic communication between the present and tradition is, as we have shown, the happening that extends its trajectory in all understanding. Hermeneutic experience must, as genuine experience, take on everything that is present to it. It does not have the freedom to select and disallow before the fact. But it also cannot claim an absolute freedom in that tolerant neutrality that appears to be specific to understanding. It cannot undo the happening that it is.[30]

The hermeneutic self-reflection of language analysis overcomes the transcendental conception that Wittgenstein clung to even in the face of the plurality of grammars of language games. As tradition, language encompasses all specific language games and promotes unity in the empirical multiplicity of transcendental rules. At the level of objective spirit, language becomes a contingent absolute. It can no longer comprehend itself as absolute spirit; it only impresses itself on subjective spirit as absolute power. This power becomes objective in the historical transformation of horizons of possible experience. Hegel's experience of reflection shrinks to the awareness that we are delivered up to a happening in which the conditions of rationality change irrationally according to time and place, epoch and culture. Hermeneutic self-reflection embroils itself in this irrationalism, however, only when it absolutizes hermeneutic experience and fails to recognize the transcending power of reflection that is also operative in it. Reflection can, to be sure, no longer reach beyond itself to an absolute consciousness, which it then pretends to be. The way to absolute idealism is barred to a transcendental consciousness that is hermeneutically broken and plunged back into the contingent complex of traditions. But must it for that reason remain stuck on the path of a relative idealism?

The objectivity of a "happening of tradition" that is made up of symbolic meaning is not objective enough. Hermeneutics comes up against walls of the traditional framework from the inside, as it were. As soon as these boundaries have been experienced and recognized, cultural traditions can no longer be posed as absolute. It makes good sense to conceive of language as a kind of metainstitution on which all social institutions are dependent; for social action is constituted only in ordinary language communication.[31] But this metainstitution of language as tradition is evidently dependent in turn on social processes that are not reducible to normative relationships. Language is *also* a medium of domination and social power; it serves to legitimate relations of organized force. Insofar as the legitimations do not articulate the power relations whose institutionalization they make possible, insofar as these relations merely manifest themselves in the legitimations, language is *also* ideological. Here it is a question not of deceptions within a language but of deception with language as such. Hermeneutic experience that encounters this dependency of the symbolic framework on actual conditions changes into critique of ideology.

The nonnormative forces that infiltrate language as a metainstitution originate not only from systems of domination but also from social labor. In this instrumental sphere of action monitored by success, experiences are organized that evidently motivate linguistic interpretations and can change traditional interpretations through operational constraints. A change in the mode of production entails a restructuring of the linguistic world view. This can be studied, for instance, in the expansion of the realm of the profane in primitive societies. Of course, revolutions in the reproductive conditions of material life are for their part linguistically mediated. But a new practice is not only set in motion by a new interpretation; old patterns of interpretation are also weakened and overturned "from below" by a new practice.[32] Today the institutionalized research practice of the empirical sciences secures a flow of information that was formerly accumulated prescientifically in systems of social labor. This information digests natural or contrived experiences that are constituted in the behavioral system of instrumental action. I suspect that the institutional changes brought about by scientific-technical progress indirectly exert an influence on the linguistic schemata of world-comprehension not unlike that formerly exerted by changes in the mode of production. For science has become first among the productive forces. The empirical sciences simply do not represent an arbitrary language game. Their language interprets reality from the anthropologically deep-seated vantage point of technical mastery. Through them the factual constraints of the natural conditions of life impinge on society. To be sure, even the statements of the theories of empirical science refer in turn to ordinary language as final metalanguage; but the system of activities that they make possible, the techniques of mastering nature, also react back on the institutional framework of society as a whole and alter the language.

An interpretive [*verstehende*] sociology that hypostasizes language to the subject of forms of life and of tradition ties itself to the idealist presupposition that linguistically articulated consciousness determines the material practice of life. But the objective framework of social action is not exhausted by the dimension of intersubjectively intended and symbolically transmitted meaning. The linguistic infrastructure of a society is part of a complex that, however symbolically mediated, is also constituted by the constraint of reality—by the constraint of outer nature that enters into procedures for technical mastery and by the constraint of inner nature reflected in the repressive character of social power relations. These two categories of constraint are not only the object of interpretations; behind the back of language, they also affect the very grammatical rules according to which we interpret the world. *Social actions can only be comprehended in an objective framework that is constituted conjointly by language, labor, and domination.* The happening of tradition appears as an absolute power only to a self-sufficient hermeneutics; in fact it is relative to systems of labor and domination. Sociology cannot, therefore, be reduced to interpretive sociology. It requires a reference system that, on the one hand, does not suppress the symbolic mediation of social action in favor of a naturalistic view of behavior that is merely controlled by signals and excited by stimuli but that, on the other hand, also does not succumb to an idealism of linguisticality [*Sprachlichkeit*] and sublimate social processes entirely to cultural tradition. Such a reference system can no longer leave tradition undetermined as the all-encompassing; instead, it comprehends tradition as such and in its relation to other aspects of the complex of social life, thereby enabling us to designate the conditions outside of tradition under which transcendental rules of world-comprehension and of action empirically change.

A descendent of Marburg neo-Kantianism, Gadamer is prevented by the residues of Kantianism still present in Heidegger's existential ontology from drawing the consequences that his own analyses suggest. He avoids the transition from the transcendental conditions of historicity to the universal history in which these conditions are constituted. He does not see that in the dimension of the "happening of tradition" he must always conceive as mediated what, according to the ontological difference, cannot be mediated—linguistic structures and the empirical conditions under which they change historically. Only on that account can Gadamer conceal from himself that the practical [*lebenspraktische*] connection of understanding with the hermeneutic vantage point of the interpreter makes necessary the hypothetical anticipation of a philosophy of history with a practical intent.[33]

NOTES

1. H. G. Gadamer, *Wahrheit und Methode*, 2nd. ed. (Tübingen, 1965), p. 380.
2. Ibid., p. 362 f.
3. Ibid., p. 364.
4. (*Editors' Note*) *Überlieferung* is the nominal form of *überliefern*: deliver up, hand down, pass on, transmit. Because the German term retains the aspect of activity or process, of something that is done or happens, while the English "tradition" has largely lost the connotation of delivery or transmission present in its Latin roots, there are some difficulties in translation. In this sentence, for example, to speak of tradition as taking place or being carried out is odd; whereas a (literal) passing-on, handing-down or transmission might, perhaps, be spoken of in this way. When similar problems arise below, the German term will be noted in the text. As will become evident, Habermas uses *Überlieferung* and *Tradition* interchangeably.
5. K. Heinrich, *Versuch über die Schwierigkeit nein zu sagen* (Frankfurt, 1964).
6. Cf. my review of Heinrich reprinted in *Zur Logik der Sozialwissenschaften* (Frankfurt, 1970), pp. 322 ff. This examination shows that hermeneutic self-reflection passes over freely into a dialectical theory of language. Bruno Liebrucks's planned six-volume work, *Sprache und Bewusstsein*, promises to provide such a theory. To date there have appeared volume 1, *Einleitung und Spannweite des Problems* (Frankfurt, 1964), and volume 2, *Sprache* (Frankfurt, 1965). Liebrucks's critique of Gehlen's anthropology is important for the methodology of the sciences of action. Because Liebrucks accepts a restricted concept of practice—which he foreshortens to instrumental action—he ends up with an abstract opposition between language and action. The peculiar connection of language and practice, which Wittgenstein and Mead worked out in the symbolically mediated interaction of language games and of communicative action, has not yet been given its due in those volumes which have appeared.
7. Gadamer, *Wahrheit und Methode*, p. 288 f. (*Editors' Note*) The German word translated here as "prejudices" is *Vorurteile*. This is somewhat misleading, since the English term now has an almost exclusively pejorative connotation, whereas Gadamer—while allowing for the similar connotation of the German term—attempts to elaborate a positive sense of the concept. A *Vor + urteil* is literally a prejudgment; as Gadamer uses the term, its meaning corresponds more closely to the etymological meaning of prejudice (Latin: *prae + judicium*) than to current usage. The accent here, as in the case of the other key hermeneutical concepts compounded from *vor*, is on this prefix (e.g., *Vorverständnis*—"prior understanding"; *Vorgriff*—"anticipation"; *Vorbegriffe*—"preconceptions"). This is meant to bring out the fact that the interpreter's own language, practice, form of life, etc., are *pre*conditions for understanding. They belong to the initial situation (*Ausgangssituation*) from which interpretation proceeds. Cf. *Wahrheit und Methode*, p. 255, for Gadamer's elucidation of the concept of a *Vorurteil*.
8. Gadamer, *Wahrheit und Methode*, p. 277.
9. Ibid., p. 280.
10. Cf. ibid., p. 355.
11. A. C. Danto, *Analytical Philosophy of History* (Cambridge, 1965), p. 142.
12. Gadamer, *Wahrheit und Methode*, p. 211.
13. Danto, *Analytical Philosophy of History*, p. 169.
14. Ibid., p. 115.
15. Ibid., p. 17 f.

16. Ibid., p. 142.

17. W. Dilthey, *Der Aufbau der geschichtlichen Welt in den Geisteswissenschaften*, in *Gesammelte Schriften*, vol. 3, p. 233.

18. Gadamer, *Wahrheit und Methode*, p. 292.

19. Cf. especially the *Nichomachean Ethics*, VI, 3–10.

20. The comparison *phrónesis* and *téchne* is particularly timely, since science —which was once reserved for contemplation—has become methodologically obligated to the attitude of the technician.

21. Gadamer, *Wahrheit und Methode*, p. 292.

22. (*Editors' Note*) Habermas's conception of the different "transcendental frameworks" guiding different types of inquiry is developed in his theory of cognitive interests. Cf. especially *Knowledge and Human Interests* (Boston, 1971). He argues there that "empirical-analytic" inquiry is ultimately grounded in the structure of human labor whereas "historico-hermeneutic" inquiry is rooted in the structure of human interaction. Both "anthropologically deep-seated structures of human action" give rise to "cognitive strategies" that determine the different logics of inquiry. In the one case there is an "orientation toward technical control," and in the other, an "orientation toward mutual understanding in the conduct of life".

23. Gadamer, *Wahrheit und Methode*, Introduction.

24. Ibid., p. xix.

25. Ibid., p. xiv.

26. Ibid., p. 274 f.

27. (*Editors' Note*) There is no precise English equivalent for the term *naturwüchsig*. The suffix *-wüchsig* (from *wachsen*: to grow) means literally "growing." The term is used by neo-Marxists to refer to processes that develop without reflection or plan. It is employed by way of contrast to consciously directed processes or structures that are the result of human will and consciousness.

28. Gadamer, *Wahrheit und Methode*, p. 264.

29. Ibid., p. 286.

30. Ibid., p. 439.

31. This is the point of view adopted by K. O. Apel in his critique of Gehlen's institutionalism. Cf. Apel "Arnold Gehlen's Philosophie der Institution," in *Philosophische Rundschau*, vol. 10 (1962), pp. 1ff.

32. Cf. J. O. Hertzler, *A Sociology of Language* (New York, 1965), especially chapter 7: "Sociocultural Change and Changing Language."

33. W. Pannenberg has seen this: "It is an odd spectacle to witness how a clear-sighted and profound author has his hands full keeping his thoughts from taking the direction in which they themselves point. This spectacle is presented by Gadamer's book in its efforts to avoid Hegel's total mediation of present truth through history. These efforts are indeed grounded by the reference to the finitude of human experience, which can never be transcended in absolute knowledge. But strangely enough, the phenomena described by Gadamer push again and again in the direction of a universal conception of history which he—with Hegel's system before his eyes—would precisely like to avoid." (W. Pannenberg, "Hermeneutik und Universalgeschichte," in *Zeitschrift für Theologie und Kirche*, vol. 60 (1963), pp. 90 ff.) In recent Protestant theology the reception of Ernst Bloch's work has, as far as I can see, given an impetus to overcoming the ontology of historicity (Bultmann, Heidegger) through a reflection on the dependence of the transcendental conditions of understanding on the objective complex of universal history. In addition to the works of Pannenberg, cf. also J. Moltmann, *Theologie der Hoffnung* (1964).

Suggested Readings

APEL, Karl-Otto. "Das Verstehen." In *Archiv für Begriffsgeschichte*. Vol. 1, pp. 142–99, Bonn: Bouvier, 1955.

_____. *Transformation der Philosophie*. 2 vols. Frankfurt: Suhrkamp, 1973.

APEL, Karl-Otto, et al. *Hermeneutik und Ideologiekritik*. Frankfurt: Suhrkamp, 1971.

BETTI, Emilio. *Allgemeine Auslegungslehre als Methodik der Geisteswissenschaften*. Tübingen: Mohr, 1967.

BOURGEOIS, Patrick. "Paul Ricoeur's Hermeneutical Phenomenology." *Philosophy Today* 16 (1972):20–27.

BUBNER, Rüdiger, Cramer, K., and Wiehl, R., eds. *Hermeneutik und Dialektik*. 2 vols. Tübingen: Mohr, 1970.

CORETH, Emerich. *Grundfragen der Hermeneutik*. Freiburg: Herder, 1969.

DALLMAYR, Fred R. "Critical Theory Criticized: *Knowledge and Human Interests* and its Aftermath." *Philosophy of the Social Sciences* 2 (1972):211–29.

_____. "Reason and Emancipation: Notes on Habermas." *Man and World* 5 (1972):79–109.

DALLMAYR, Fred R., ed. *Materialien zu Habermas' Erkenntnis und Interesse*. Frankfurt: Suhrkamp, 1974.

DANTO, Arthur C., Donagan, Alan, and Meiland, J. W. "Symposium: Historical Understanding." *Journal of Philosophy* 63 (1966):566–82.

FLÖISTAD, Guttorm. "Social Concepts of Action: Notes on Habermas's Proposal for a Social Theory of Knowledge." *Inquiry* 13 (1970):175–98.

FUCHS, Ernst. *Hermeneutik*. 4th ed. Tübingen: Mohr, 1970.

GADAMER, Hans-Georg. *Hegel's Dialectic*. New Haven, Conn.: Yale University Press, 1976.

_____. *Kleine Schriften*. Tübingen: Mohr, vol. 1–2, 1967, vol. 3, 1972.

_____. *Philosophical Hermeneutics*. Berkeley: University of California Press, 1976.

_____. "Rhetorik, Hermeneutik, und Ideologiekritik" and "Replik." In *Hermeneutik und Ideologiekritik*, edited by Karl-Otto Apel, pp. 57–82 and 283–317. Frankfurt: Suhrkamp, 1971.

_____. *Truth and Method*. New York: Seabury, 1975.

GEERTZ, Clifford. *The Interpretation of Cultures.* New York: Basic Books, 1973.

HABERMAS, Jürgen. *Knowledge and Human Interests.* Boston: Beacon Press, 1971.

—————. *Theory and Practice.* Boston: Beacon Press, 1973.

—————. "Der Universalitätsanspruch der Hermeneutik." In *Hermeneutik und Ideologiekritik,* edited by Karl-Otto Apel, pp. 120–59. Frankfurt: Suhrkamp, 1971.

HIRSCH, Eric D. *Validity in Interpretation.* New Haven, Conn.: Yale University Press, 1967.

IHDE, Don. *Hermeneutical Phenomenology: The Philosophy of Paul Ricoeur.* Evanston, Ill.: Northwestern University Press, 1971.

KISIEL, Theodore. "Ideology Critique and Phenomenology." *Philosophy Today* 14 (1970):151–60.

McCARTHY, Thomas A. "The Operation Called *Verstehen*: Towards a Redefinition of the Problem." In *PSA 1972,* edited by Kenneth F. Schaffner and Robert S. Cohen, pp. 167–93. Dordrecht, Holland: Reidel, 1974.

PALMER, Richard E. *Hermeneutics: Interpretation Theory in Schleiermacher, Dilthey, Heidegger, and Gadamer.* Evanston, Ill.: Northwestern University Press, 1969.

RADNITZKY, Gerard. *Continental Schools of Metascience.* Contemporary Schools of Metascience, vol. 2. Göteborg, Sweden: Akademiförlaget, 1968.

RICOEUR, Paul. *The Conflict of Interpretations: Essays in Hermeneutics.* Evanston, Ill.: Northwestern University Press, 1974.

—————. "Ethics and Culture: Habermas and Gadamer in Dialogue." *Philosophy Today* 17 (1973):153–65.

—————. *Freud and Philosophy: An Essay on Interpretation.* New Haven, Conn.: Yale University Press, 1970.

SEEBOHM, Thomas M. *Zur Kritik der hermeneutischen Vernunft.* Bonn: Bouvier, 1972.

SYMPOSIUM. "The Frankfurt School." *Continuum* 8 (1970):3–133.

SYMPOSIUM. "Hermeneutics and Critical Theory." *Cultural Hermeneutics* 2, no. 4, special issue (February, 1975):307–90.

WARNACH, Viktor, ed. *Hermeneutik als Weg heutiger Wissenschaft.* Salzburg, Austria: Anton Pustet, 1971.

WELLMER, Albrecht. *Critical Theory of Society.* New York: Herder and Herder, 1971.